STUDIES ON ETHNIC GROUPS IN CHINA

Stevan Harrell, Editor

Cultural Encounters on China's Ethnic Frontiers

Edited by

STEVAN HARRELL

University of Washington Press

Seattle and London

GN
635
.C5
C85
1995

Studies on Ethnic Groups in China is supported in part by a grant from the Henry
Luce Foundation to the Henry M. Jackson School of International Studies of the
University of Washington.

Library of Congress Cataloging-in-Publication Data

Cultural encounters on China's ethnic frontiers / edited by Stevan Harrell.
     p. cm.—(Studies on ethnic groups in China)
   Includes bibliographical references (p.   ) and index.
   ISBN 0–295–97380–3 (acid-free paper)
     1. Ethnicity—China—Social life and customs.   I. Harrell, Stevan.
II. Series.
GN635.C5C85   1994   94–15697
305.8'00951—dc20   CIP

Contents

v

CONTENTS

CONTENTS

Maps

viii

Cultural Encounters

on China's Ethnic Frontiers

Introduction

Civilizing Projects and the Reaction to Them

Stevan Harrell

Around the geographic periphery of the Chinese empire, later the Republic of China, and now the People's Republic of China, as well as in some of the less accessible parts of China's interior, and sometimes even in its cities, live a variety of peoples of different origins, languages, ecological adaptations, and cultures.[1] These peripheral peoples or, as they are now customarily tagged, "minorities," have been subjected over the last few centuries to a series of attempts by dominant powers to transform them, to make them more like the transformers or, in the parlance of the transformers themselves, to "civilize" them.[2] There have been at least four such civilizing projects in recent history, carried out by the three successive Chinese governments and by Western missionaries who operated in China between the Treaty of Nanjing in 1842 and the establishment of the People's Republic in 1949. This book is concerned with the ideology of three of these projects and with the similarities and differences among them, as well as their effect on the peripheral peoples (particularly in the development of ethnic consciousness) and on the central, civilizing powers.

---

1. In writing and revising this introduction, I have benefitted greatly from written comments, discussions, and suggestions about sources provided by Ann Anagnost, Peggy Swain, Simon Cheung, Norma Diamond, Ralph Litzinger, Hehralin Park, Tsianina Lomawaima, Nancy Pollock, Jack Dull, and Kent Guy. The odd turns of phrase, both intentional and unintentional, are entirely my own.

2. I use the term "peripheral peoples" for both negative and positive reasons. On the negative side, I want to avoid "minorities," a term that refers to a subset of peripheral peoples—those found in a modern nation-state with boundaries and citizenship papers; "national minorities," which is even more restrictive, and also implies complicity in the Leninist project; and the currently popular "indigenous peoples," which implies that the Han are not indigenous, which they of course are in at least some of the regions they share with non-Han peoples. On the positive side, the term "peripheral peoples" reinforces the important fact that the reason they are in this kind of a mess is that they are far from the centers of institutional and economic power and of dense population concentrations.

THE NATURE OF CIVILIZING PROJECTS

A civilizing project, as described in this book, is a kind of interaction between peoples, in which one group, the civilizing center, interacts with other groups (the peripheral peoples) in terms of a particular kind of inequality. In this interaction, the inequality between the civilizing center and the peripheral peoples has its ideological basis in the center's claim to a superior degree of civilization, along with a commitment to raise the peripheral peoples' civilization to the level of the center, or at least closer to that level. Simple relationships of military conquest and subsequent domination, such as that exercised by the Mexica (Aztecs) over conquered peoples elsewhere in Mesoamerica, or by the Romans over some of the provincial peoples in the Near East or northern Europe, are not at issue here, even though those relationships involve an ideological as well as a political and economic basis of domination. Rather, the civilizing center draws its ideological rationale from the belief that the process of domination is one of helping the dominated to attain or at least approach the superior cultural, religious, and moral qualities characteristic of the center itself.

As an interaction between peoples, a civilizing project requires two sets of actors, the center and the peripheral peoples; in no case can we understand the entire project by looking from the perspective of only one side. And as with any interaction between peoples, participation in the civilizing project affects the society, culture, morals, and religion of both the civilizers and the civilizees.

The effect of the civilizing project on the peripheral peoples varies not only with the success of the project (the degree to which they become "civilized"), but also with the degree and nature of their complicity in the project. As one possibility, we have the cases of conquered peoples resisting any attempt whatever to civilize them, so that government agents have had to resort to virtual kidnapping of Native American children to educate them in boarding schools (Sekaquaptewa and Udall 1969:90–93; Pratt 1964:202), or Ferdinand and Isabella deciding they had to forcibly prohibit all aspects of Islamic culture, from veiling to couscous, in the newly conquered territories of Granada after 1499. In the Chinese context, this may be most characteristic of the situation in Tibet, where Tibetan nationalists (who knows what percentage of the Tibetan population) reject all claims of the Chinese state to be raising the level of Tibetan anything, from philosophy to mortuary practices to land tenure systems.

MAP 1. China. Provinces and autonomous regions with large minority populations shown in CAPS.

At the other extreme, peripheral peoples become partly or wholly complicit in the civilizing project, often when their relationship of asserted cultural inferiority is balanced by superiority or equality on another plane, as when the Yaqui, recent victors over Spanish armies in the early seventeenth century, requested Catholic missionaries to instruct them in the true religion (Spicer 1988:4), or, in this book, the case of the Manchus, conquerors of China and emperors of the Qing dynasty (1644–1911), selectively absorbing parts of Chinese culture while maintaining their position as rulers.

In between these extremes lie the majority of cases, in which peripheral peoples are concerned with maintaining their own identity, and thus resisting any implication that all aspects of their culture, religion, or morals are unequivocally inferior to those of the civilizing center, but nevertheless participate to some degree in the project of importing some elements from the center into their own culture and society. Most of the cases in this book, in which peripheral peoples acknowledge at least some aspects of central civilization to be desirable, fit into this intermediate category. In some such intermediate cases, however, the peripheral peoples, while resenting the attempts to civilize them, nevertheless accept the general premise that they are less civilized or morally less worthy. They thus develop a "stigmatized identity" (Eidheim 1969; Hsieh 1987), a sense of themselves as backward, uncivilized, dirty, stupid, and so forth.

In all these cases, the effect of a civilizing project seems to be to engender, develop, sharpen, or heighten the consciousness of the peripheral people as an ethnic group. In this sense, ethnogenesis can be seen primarily as the reaction (reaction, of course, is not so simple as just opposition or resistance) to a civilizing project.

At the same time, participation in a civilizing project also has an effect on the center. In the first place, certain dominant civilizations seem to have a greater propensity to engage in civilizing projects than do others; as a rough approximation Hindu and Buddhist civilizations, for example, seem to be less inclined toward such projects than their Christian, Muslim, or Confucian counterparts.[3] But even

3. This is not to imply that Hindu and Buddhist civilizations have never promoted civilizing projects. Certainly Sanskritization in modern India has characteristics of a civilizing project, with participation from both an ideological center and an ambivalent set of culturally peripheral groups. And modern Thailand uses many of the same mechanisms of cultural integration that Chinese civilizing centers have used over the

6

those civilizations with an innate propensity toward undertaking civilizing missions are transformed by the nature of the actual missions they carry out.

For example, the civilizing center, in its formulation of its project, needs to develop formal knowledge of the other and of itself. The development of social evolutionary theory in the West in the nineteenth century by such authors as Morgan (1985 [1877]), Tylor (1871), and Spencer (1860) coincided rather neatly with the expansion of Western colonies into new parts of the world, inhabited by peoples with social and cultural structures that differed considerably from those of the center, and the adoption of a modified version of such theories by Marxist governments in the Soviet Union (Connor 1984) and China coincided with the attempt to turn what had previously been rather pluralistic empires into more unified nation-states. The Orientalism described by Edward Said (1979) is after all a scholarly component of a larger project by which the West aimed to civilize the Muslim world.

In addition, the civilizing center, through its project, almost always develops a more conscious and sharper image of itself, in contrast to its images of the periphery. The true religion is contrasted with the mistaken beliefs of the heathens, as Arthur Smith did over and over in comparing Confucianism to Christianity (1970 [1899]), or the European stage is seen as a higher stage, a culmination of a series of inferior steps, as in the social evolutionary formulations, or Confucianism defines itself as having culture (*wenhua,* lit. "literary transformation") in contrast to the cultureless peoples of the periphery.

Looking at civilizing projects in this way, as asymmetrical dialogues between the center and the periphery, allows us to analyze the projects into two components: the ideological discourse of the center (to which the members of the peripheral peoples may subscribe or contribute in varying degree), and the ethnic discourse of the periphery. The center's discourse is ideological in the narrow sense of justifying or legitimizing a particular power-holding institution (which, in this book, is either the Chinese state or the missionary wing of Western imperialism). The peripheral discourse is ethnic in the sense outlined below—the development of the consciousness that a people exists as an entity that differs from surrounding peoples.

ages. But it seems to me that the Confucian, Muslim, and Christian civilizations have all had a driving sense of a civilizing mission, while the Hindu and Buddhist civilizations have pursued civilizing projects only under certain circumstances.

THE IDEOLOGY OF THE CIVILIZERS

As with any ideology, the ideology of a civilizing center tailors itself to its goals, in this case the facilitation of the civilizing project through the creation of hegemony, a relationship of superiority and inferiority that maintains the hierarchy by justifying it through ideology and institutions, making it seem both proper and natural to both the rulers and the ruled (in this case the center and the periphery) and enlisting both rulers and the ruled in service of the institutions that maintain the order (Gramsci 1971 [1930s]:12–13; 55–56[4]). Civilizers—at least those who have worked with the peripheral peoples of China—have based their attempts to establish hegemony on a particular formulation of the nature of ethnicity, many of whose characteristics recur from one project to the next.

The Hegemony of Definition

The first requirement for those who would civilize is to define, to objectify, the objects of their civilizing project (Said 1979:44–45). The definitions produced must consist of two parts: a demonstration that the peoples in question are indeed inferior, and thus in need of civiliza-tion, and a certification that they can in fact be improved, civilized, if they are subjected to the project. Such a definition process serves several functions: it establishes the assumptions and rules according to which the project is to be carried out; it notifies the peripheral peoples of their status in the system, and of why and how this requires that they be civilized; and, perhaps most importantly, it gives the imprima-tur of science to what is essentially a political project.

All the civilizing projects described in this book have had the pro-cess of definition and objectification at their base. The Confucians, beginning with an assumption of hierarchy based on the moral values

---

4. The application of Gramsci's notions of hegemony to the Chinese case requires something of a reformulation. Gramsci's own writings, concerned primarily with Italy and almost entirely with Europe, discuss two forms of social control—direct domina-tion, exercised by the state, and hegemony, exercised by the civil society. Since the existence of "civil society" is questionable in Communist China (it is less questionable in the Qing dynasty), it follows that this neat heuristic conception of the political division of labor is not applicable to China today. But we can see the equivalent mechanisms of hegemonic control going on in China, albeit they, like the mechanisms of direct domination, are controlled by the state. See also Gates and Weller (1987).

of "literary transformation," set out to classify peoples as closer to or farther from the center on the basis of just how much *wenhua* they had. This both legitimized the superior status of the center (thus giving it a mandate to carry out the process) and determined the methods to be used in ruling over peoples, according to how close to civilization, and thus how civilizable, they were. In Southwest China most of the Miao, for example, as treated in Norma Diamond's chapter, were seen as so distant from civilization as to be barely susceptible to rule, let alone transformation, while various peoples known as *yi* 夷 (a category not coextensive with the Yi 彝 treated in Stevan Harrell's paper) were more civilized already, and thus susceptible to being brought yet closer to the ethics and culture of the center. The Manchus, who themselves as rulers controlled the process, were of course fully capable of absorbing, even improving upon, the literary, moral, and cultural accomplishments of Han civilization, even while they preserved and refined for themselves a separate, distinct identity (Crossley 1990a; Rigger, this volume).

In the missionary project, definition placed peripheral peoples along a series of axes, some of them technical-cultural (many peoples were beloved by missionaries for being simple, guileless, direct, and so forth, as indicated in Swain's contribution here) and others religious, which at one level consisted simply of contrasting the heathen delusions of native religions with the revealed truth of Christianity, but at another attempted to certify the potential for Christianization (a version of civilization) by tracing links between the superficially superstitious beliefs of the natives and the traditions of monotheism.

The Communist project has been the most explicit and systematic in its process of definition. It has classified the population within China's political borders into fifty-six *minzu,* or "nationalities," so that every citizen of the People's Republic is defined as belonging to a group that is more civilized or less so. This scaling of groups, in turn, is based on an avowedly scientific scale of material stages of social process (derived from Morgan and Engels, refined by Lenin and Stalin), that tells each group exactly how far it needs to go to catch up with the civilizers.

In every case, then, the process of definition is one of both objectification and scaling. And while the scales used by the various civilizers seem on the surface to be quite different from each other, they all have in common certain metaphors that lend force and coherence to the scale created. In particular, the metaphors of sex (peripheral peoples as women), of education (peripheral peoples as children), and of history (peripheral peoples as ancient) stand out as recurring themes in the definitional process.

The Sexual Metaphor: Peripheral Peoples as Women

Sexual relations, seen as a man doing something to a woman, are a pervasive metaphor for a variety of relations of domination in many cultures,[5] but they are particularly noteworthy in the imagery of civilizing projects. This eroticization and feminization of the peripheral occurs at a series of levels and in a series of differing contexts.

At the simplest and most direct level, civilizers of all sorts have seen peripheral peoples as both erotic and promiscuous in their behavior, as being at a lower level of culture where they have not yet learned the proper civilized morals of sexual repression and/or hypocrisy. Since Chinese culture has strict rules of sexual propriety (as well as a long and honored tradition of sexual hypocrisy), both the Confucian and the Communist versions of the civilizing project have defined peripheral peoples as erotic and seen the imposition of proper sexual morals as an essential part of the process of civilizing. For example, as Diamond mentions here, "Miao albums," which portrayed and classified the upland peoples of the Southwest in Ming (1368–1644) and Qing times, commented extensively on their loose sexual customs, and in addition often portrayed these people acting provocatively, immodestly, or as if they were about to engage in sexual relations. At the other end of our time scale, any researcher who has spent time in China has heard from Chinese colleagues of the sexual customs of certain peripheral peoples—the current favorite seems to be the "walking marriage" of the Mosuo people mentioned in Charles F. McKhann's contribution here. I remember vividly my conversation in 1988 with a schoolmaster at a middle school that enrolled minority students in special classes. He was proud of his *minzu ban,* but confided that there were certain problems. For example, a boy and girl in one of the classes had fallen in love, and started going everywhere and doing everything

5. This is illustrated beautifully in a related context by the richly symbolic play *M. Butterfly* by David Henry Hwang, in which a European diplomat has a decades-long sexual affair with a Chinese opera singer, who turns out in the end to be a man. The subordinate people (in this case, clearly the Chinese, or even the Orient, in Said's broader sense) are unconsciously feminized; even the Chinese man becomes the sex object of a heterosexual male Westerner.

together. Fortunately, teachers and counselors were able to educate them, to persuade them that this kind of behavior was no longer appropriate in a modern, socialist society, and the couple broke up.

Also at a rather direct level, civilizers have seen the peripheral peoples as objects of sexual desire. The long tradition of this in the colonizing Orientalist writers and artists such as Gauguin and Flaubert is well analyzed in Said's now-canonical work (1979:190), and we all know of the tradition of Western sailors and native girls throughout the era of imperialist maritime expansion. But it also occurs specifically in China.

Most obviously, there is the portrayal of women of peripheral peoples in Han art and literature. Already mentioned are the scantily clad Miao women of the Ming-Qing pictorial albums, but there is also the "Yunnan school" of painting (McKhann n.d.), which consists primarily of portraits (some innocent enough, some verging on the sexually exploitative) of *minority*, never Han, women.[6] Even in Sichuan, where the tradition is less well developed, some of the first paintings on nonrevolutionary themes that were exhibited in Chengdu in the late 1970s were portraits of pretty Tibetan women.[7] They were in no sense erotic pictures, let alone pornographic, but it is significant that when the artist wanted to paint a young, desirable female, he portrayed a Tibetan, not a Han Chinese. And finally, there is the curious practice among Han tourists, reported here by McKhann, of using telephoto lenses to take surreptitious pictures of Dai women bathing in the Lancang (Mekong) River in the southern Yunnan prefecture of Xishuangbanna.

One might suggest that this erotic portrayal of women of the periphery is simply a response to the strict sexual morals of the Han, which have probably become less widely hypocritical since the overlay of Communist puritanism. It would simply be too scandalous to portray a Han woman in this way, but minority women, being less civilized (perhaps slightly less human?) are fairer game.[8] This analysis

6. That many of the artists in the Yunnan school are themselves minority males (such as Su Jianghua) or even minority females (such as Yang Huangli of the Buyi) is simply an indication that the civilizing project works, draws its hegemonic force, from co-opting the peripheral peoples themselves into active participation.

7. I am indebted to Jerome Silbergeld for showing me slides of these paintings.

8. As Esther Yao puts it with regard to modern films, "The non-Han women on screen provided an erotic and convenient site for the representation of sexuality not assigned to the Han women's bodies" (1989:122).

is correct as far as it goes, but what it neglects are the consequences of this portrayal. These include the eroticization and feminization of minorities in general and denial, in a male-dominant society, of full male status to those whose cultures are of the periphery.

This point is reinforced by another and less directly erotic aspect of the metaphor of peripheral peoples as women: in fact the great majority of portrayals of non-Han peoples, whether in traditional albums or modern tourist guides, are pictures of women. For example, two sets of fifty-six collector's cards each, one for each *minzu* in each set, include seventy-six that show only women or feature women, twenty-five that show only men or feature men, and eleven in which the sexes are relatively balanced. In each case, the women shown are invariably young and pretty; the only exception in the two sets of cards is a curious picture of a fat babushka in a dirty dress representing the Eluosi (Russian) *minzu* of Xinjiang. The men, where they are shown, are about equally divided between young and old.

Once again, an objection might be raised—it is the women, after all, who wear the fancy clothes, the "traditional ethnic costumes," which may or may not have much past history (see Trevor-Roper 1983), so they are more interesting to show in pictures. Although this is undoubtedly true, it raises the further question of why the women have distinctive costumes while the men do not. It appears, at least tentatively, that the women are carriers of this tradition (both in the hegemonic ideology of the civilizers and in their own practice) precisely because women are thought to epitomize peripheral peoples, since peripheral peoples are in some sense feminine. It is perhaps also true that because women are less likely to participate in such concrete institutional aspects of the civilizing project as schools and local government, they are thought of as "more ethnic," and thus more appropriately dressed in ethnic costumes.

There may be a parallel here between the construction of *funü* (women) as a category in the Communist ideology of women's liberation and sexual equality (Barlow 1990) and the construction of *shaoshu minzu* (minorities) in the Communist ideology of nation-building and ethnic equality. In both cases, there is an objectification of a category that is peripheral (or, perhaps, in the linguistic sense, simply marked) with respect to the normal category of the civilizers, who are, in the first instance, male, and in the second, Han. As pointed out above, to stand up for the rights of a category, one must first define it. And because both minorities and women are subordinate categories under the tutelage of the state's civilizing project, they are conflated at some level of the imagination. Minorities are like women, so women represent minorities.

Finally, we might mention that peripheral peoples, like women, are seen as polluting—both dirty and dangerous—at least in the ideologies of the China-centered projects. Women, of course, are seen as polluting in Chinese folk ideologies generally (Ahern 1975); menstruating women or those who have recently given birth are offensive to the gods of popular religion, and their presence or that of others who have recently had contact with them chases the gods away. This idea of pollution—dirt and danger—is also extended to minorities. Lack of sanitation is one of the points Han ethnologists almost always bring up when they are swapping stories about field-work in peripheral regions; I once heard an informal exposition on this point that began with "Each *minzu* has its own *zangfa* [way of being dirty] . . ." And Diamond has pointed out graphically that Miao people, particularly Miao women, have been thought by their Han neighbors to be especially adept in the art of poisoning by magical means (1988). In all these cases, the peripheral peoples are dangerous in the same ways women are dangerous: by their power to pollute.

At all these levels, then, the sexual metaphor is one of domination, in which the literal or figurative femaleness of the peripheral peoples is one aspect of the act of defining them as subordinate.

The Educational Metaphor: Peripheral Peoples as Children

As mentioned above, the definitional process has two elements: it not only demonstrates the inferiority of peripheral peoples, but also certifies their civilizability, and thus legitimates not just domination but the particular kind of domination we call a civilizing project. The sexual metaphor, powerful as it is, addresses only the first half of the definitional task; it demonstrates inferiority, but inferiority of the sort that cannot readily be corrected. If peripheral peoples were visu-alized according to the sexual metaphor only, this would present difficulties for the civilizing project. Seeing peripheral peoples as children, on the other hand, is potentially even more useful: since children are by definition both inferior and educable, the peripheral peoples represented as childlike are both inferior and civilizable, and it becomes the task of the center to civilize them.

Like the sexual metaphor, the educational metaphor operates on different levels. The first of these is a quite literal one: civilizers see their peripheral subjects as childlike. This is often the case with missionaries in various parts of the world. The comments of Catholic priests working among the Yanomamö (Chagnon 1983:196–98) and the Sani (Swain, this volume), as well as those of Protestants working among the Miao in Yunnan (Cheung, this volume), all attest to the simple nature, the lack of guile, and ingenuousness of peripheral peoples. As Margaret Byrne Swain points out here, Vial often referred to his Sani flock as "mes enfants." And, like children, the objects of missionizing can be trained, educated out of their childlike state.[9]

But missionaries, who often refer to their subjects as children, are not the only ones who have viewed peripheral peoples in this way. Popular images of minority peoples in today's People's Republic also include childlike elements. Educators I have known who work with minority education often comment that minority students, while every bit as intelligent as the Han, nevertheless require a different approach; they are unacquainted with abstract or metaphorical thought, and need to have everything explained to them in literal detail. The toning-down of educational rigor reported by Wurlig Borchigud (this volume) also seems to stem from an idea of peripheral peoples as childlike.

On another level, the juvenile image of the peripheral is presented in official discourse in which the Han and minorities are described as *xiongdi minzu,* or big-brother/little-brother *minzu,* with the Han (the socially and economically more advanced group) representing the big brother. It is by following the previous example of the big brother that the little brothers can advance to the more developed state represented by the Han. When brothers grow up, of course, they are all adults, but then, in Chinese at least, an older brother is still an older brother. Here again, the idea is that the peripheral peoples are like children—inferior but potentially educable.

Finally, there is the rather more concrete level at which children represent to the civilizers the best hope for accomplishing the civilizing project. Missions almost everywhere have established schools, and China is no exception, for it is by educating the young minds—

9. An extreme instance of this occurs in the title of W. Fielding Hall's book about the Burmese under colonial tutelage, *A People at School* (Hall 1913).

those not yet fully enculturated into the less civilized ways of the periphery—that the project can most effectively proceed. And as Borchigud so effectively shows in her contribution to this volume, *minzu jiaoyu* (ethnic education) serves the identical purpose for the Chinese government. Not only are peripheral peoples childlike, but actual children, like actual women, are in a way most representative of peripheral peoples.

The Historical Metaphor: Peripheral Peoples as Ancient

A third metaphor that is common to all the civilizing projects examined here stems from a potential contradiction in the civilizing ideology. If peripheral peoples are, as the project requires, both primitive and civilizable—that is, if the scalar differences between them and the civilizers are not permanent—then there must be some explanation for why the difference exists. Racial explanations, though often employed, heighten the paradox: if the scalar differences are really inborn, then there is a question of whether they can be overcome. The paradox is partially resolved, however, when the historical metaphor is employed. Peripheral peoples are ancient, unchanged, not so far along on the same scale as the people of the civilizing center. But if the ancestors of the center were once as primitive as the periphery is now, then the project of trying to civilize them has some chance of success.

We find in the particular civilizing projects studied here a recourse to historical formulations of the primitive that derive from a variety of historiographic traditions. For example, there is the matter of tying knots and notching sticks. As early as the *Yi jing* (Book of changes), Chinese historiographers have seen tying knots in strings as a sort of protowriting; the usual formulation is that a big knot stood for a big event, while a small knot recorded a lesser event. This seems to have been accepted as a common practice everywhere among preliterate peoples. It crops up in the descriptions of small, remote *minzu* even in reports from the 1950s. People who are in a "primitive" state, since they do not have writing, must have cord-knotting and stick-notching; this makes their primitiveness equivalent to that of ancient peoples, and makes them a survival of ancient times.

Western attempts to trace world historical migrations, from the seventeenth-century Jesuit Athanasius Kircher, who traced all learning, including ancient Chinese philosophy, back to Egyptian roots

(Mungello 1985:134–73), through the *Kulturkreislehrhe* (Culture Area Theory) of Father Schmidt and his early twentieth-century Vienna School (Schmidt 1939), also served to place peripheral peoples somewhere way back in history. Perhaps the clearest example in this volume occurs in the attempts by French and German missionaries and explorers in the early twentieth century to sort out the origin and history of the various "races" of Southwest China. The autochthonous strain, the most primitive, was related to peoples of the Pacific, while the ancestors of the Liangshan Yi were seen as of Eurasian origin, and indeed as preserving many of the admirable qualities of the early nomadic peoples of biblical times (see Harrell, this volume). Contemporary peripheral peoples were seen as survivals of forms that had existed everywhere much earlier in history.

It remained, however, for the Communists to develop the historical metaphor to its fullest. Because they have adopted and developed the notion, systematized by Lewis Henry Morgan, that the development of human history proceeds everywhere in distinct stages, and that each of those stages consists of a complex of related culture traits, it follows that peoples who display certain sorts of culture traits *must be* representative of the particular stage in which those traits occur. Matriliny occurs, for example, as the second substage of the primitive stage, while certain kinds of metallurgy are characteristic of slave society. In this way, almost any difference between the center and the periphery can be readily translated into a historical gap between the way things are done now and the way they were done at the evolutionary stage represented by the peripheral people. Many examples could be cited, but perhaps the most telling is the famous statement, widely repeated not only in Chinese ethnology but in such unexpected places as English-language coffee-table books (Wong 1989:48) that the Mosuo people of Ninglang County, Yunnan, are "living fossils" because of their matrilineal household organization and their lack of formal marriage bonds (see McKhann, this volume).

Through pervasive metaphors of this sort, civilizing projects explain and legitimize themselves. By portraying peoples of the periphery as female, juvenile, and historical, the Han or European center, which is by implicit or explicit contrast male, adult, and modern, legitimately assumes the task of civilizing, and with it the superior political and moral position from which the civilizing project can be carried out.

In line with their various claims on moral and cultural superiority, the civilizing centers of all three projects discussed in this volume have seen their approach to China's peripheral peoples as but part of a larger project that has also aimed to civilize that portion of the Chinese population that is less cultured than the center: the black-headed masses for the Confucians; all heathen Chinese (that is, all Chinese) for the Christians; and the uneducated or politically unaware masses for the Communists. From the reading of the Kangxi emperor's sacred edict in the Qing dynasty marketplaces on market days (Hsiao 1960:185–205) to the Civilized Village Campaign of the 1980s (Anagnost n.d., ch. 3), Chinese governments have seen their own role as a civilizing one, and missionaries of course were interested in converting—civilizing—the Chinese in general. But the approach to the peripheral peoples is a more extreme form of the civilizing project, and for two reasons. First, the cultural distance between the civilizing center and the peripheral peoples is greater than that between the center and the Chinese masses. Second, the civilizing project engenders in the peripheral peoples a particular kind of reaction: the formation of ethnic consciousness. This is a paradoxical result; it tends to emphasize or re-emphasize the very difference between center and peripheral peoples that the civilizing project was ostensibly trying to reduce or eliminate. It is when directed at peripheral peoples that the civilizing project takes on its full and paradoxical character.

A SUCCESSION OF CIVILIZING PROJECTS

The successive civilizing projects that have approached the peripheral peoples of China have had much in common, as indicated in the above section, but they have also had their differences, and these differences have of course affected the ways in which the peripheral peoples have reacted. We can form a first impression of the most important individual characteristics of the Confucian, Christian, and Communist projects from the simple chart in table 1. Each project is conceived of as emanating from a particular center, as defining civilization (or the desired state) according to a certain set of philosophical principles, as separating groups according to some sort of criterion of "ethnic identification," and then giving these groups equal or unequal legal status, while scaling them according to one or another variable.

TABLE I

Comparison of Civilizing Projects

	Confucian	*Christian*	*Communist*
Location of civilizing center	China	West	China (and Moscow)
Defining features of civilization	Humanist/moral	Divine/moral	Humanist/scientific
Differentiator of groups	Culture (*wenhua*)	Race	Political economy (Stalin's four criteria)
Legal status of groups	Unequal	Unequal	Equal
Variable for scaling groups	Culture, technology	Religion, technology	Mode of production

The Theory of the Confucian Project

To date, the Confucian project is the least well studied and thus least understood of the three. But that the attitude of the late Imperial (Ming and Qing) Chinese state toward its peripheral peoples can be characterized as a civilizing project, we have no doubt. From the standpoint of Confucian worldview, civilization was characterized by *wenhua*, which refers to the molding of the person (and by extension the community to which the person belongs) by training in the philosophical, moral, and ritual principles considered to constitute virtue (Schwartz 1959:52). It follows that there was a scale of civilizedness, with the most civilized being those who had the greatest acquaintance with the relevant literary works, namely the scholar-officials who served the imperial state and who served as theoreticians of the moral order. Other Chinese were somewhat cultured; their family life, religion, language, and other attributes were similar to those of the literati, even if they had no refinement or direct knowledge of the important literature. Non-Chinese were a step down, being not even indirectly acquainted with the moral principles laid out in the classics.

But what seems important here is that who was cultured and who was not depended not so much on race but on moral education, so that the process of acculturation was eminently possible. Peoples who had been beyond the pale of civilization could enter if they acquired the requisite knowledge and the proper modes of life. Hence Ming "ethnologists" were concerned not with race or language as determining characteristics of peoples, but with modes of livelihood; agriculturalists were more civilized than herders of the steppes (Crossley 1990b). Similarly, people whom we today might consider members of minority nationalities or ethnic groups—on the basis of their language, for example—were not excluded from participation in the bureaucracy or even in the examination system if they had acquired the requisite literary (that is, moral) knowledge.

This moral scale of peoples fits in nicely with the continuing historical process of absorption of once-peripheral peoples into the broader category of *Zhongguo ren* (people of the central country), or Chinese. We know that ever since the southward expansion of the Han dynasty (206 B.C.E.–220 C.E.), regions had been sinified by a combination of Chinese migration, intermarriage, and cultural assimilation of the former natives. And that process was legitimized by the ideology that it was behavior, rather than race, that determined civilization.

This does not mean, however, that at any particular time all peoples within sight of the Confucian center were considered equally capable of being civilized. As Diamond shows in this volume, peoples in the Southwest, for example, were readily divided into raw (*sheng*) and cooked (*shu*), according to whether they were cultured enough to accept moral edification and eventual civilization (in the case of the cooked peoples) or whether at present they were so wild and so far from the standards of civilization that they were fit for nothing but being controlled and perhaps painted in one of the famous "Miao albums."[10] A similar raw/cooked distinction was made until very recently when talking about the aborigines in Taiwan, and

10. Lest the reader feel we are getting too Lévi-Straussian here without sufficient cause, it should be pointed out that the *sheng/shu* opposition is used to classify many domains other than peripheral peoples. For example, acquaintances are classified this way: *shengren* are strangers, *shuren* are those with whom one has enough experience to make them familiar and at least partially trustworthy. See Mayfair Yang (1989:40–41) for a discussion of this broader use of *sheng* and *shu*.

indeed the distinction has been borne out in practice: most lowland (*shu*) aborigines have lost records of their aboriginal status and have simply become Han Chinese. Upland (*sheng*) aborigines, on the other hand, maintain a separate ethnic identity even as the government attempts to assimilate them into the great Chinese nation (Hsieh Shih-chung 1994).

The most important thing to remember about the Confucian attitude toward peoples of the periphery, then, is that the center saw its relationship with the rest of the world as a process of making it more cultured, as a transformation from raw and untutored to fully civilized. The center believed so strongly in the moral rightness of this project that it tended to phrase all its accounts of its dealings with the outside in these terms. When the Qianlong emperor sent his famous letter to George III, expressing his gratitude that George had expressed "humble desire to partake of the benefits of our civilization" (Cameron 1970:313), he may or may not have believed that the British monarch was inspired by such a desire, but he was speaking the conventional language that stemmed from the presumed relation between the Chinese center and everyone else. In the case of the peripheral peoples, in many cases the emperor must have believed it; certainly the common people did and still do.

The Theory of the Christian Project

This project involved more than just the Christian conversion of China's peoples. Particularly in the nineteenth and twentieth centuries, with which the essays in this book are primarily concerned, the mission enterprise sought to bring not only the Gospel, but the modern life of Christian nations—with all its advantages in health, technology, and science—to the peoples of China (Smith 1970 [1899]; Hunter 1984 is a particularly revealing instance of this attitude on the part of American female Protestant missionaries). It is also important to remember that the Christian project, at least in its nineteenth- and twentieth-century versions, was closely connected to the project of Western imperial expansion generally. At the same time, the missionaries stand out from most traders and warriors, and many colonial administrators, in that the missionaries' *primary* motivation lay in the civilizing project itself, whereas the primary motivations of their compatriots were often profits, markets, resources, and military strongholds. It would be inaccurate to call the whole colonial enterprise simply a civilizing project (though it did contain elements of one), but the missionary portion of the West's nineteenth-century expansion can stand as one of the prototypes of a civilizing project.[11]

The Christian civilizing project was, of course, directed at various times and places toward the whole non-Christian world, and this included the Han as well as China's peripheral peoples. But in many ways, the peripheral peoples provided more fertile ground than the Han on which to sow the seeds of the Gospel and modern life. This may well have been because many peripheral people saw the missionaries as a useful counterweight to the Han (see below), but for whatever reason, it meant that missionaries paid the peripheral peoples attention disproportionate to their numbers.

It is also, at times, difficult to separate the efforts of missionaries from those of other agents of Western imperialism in China, such as traders, explorers, and government representatives. This is particularly true for the definitional aspect of the civilizing project: Catholic missionaries such as Paul Vial (Swain, this volume) and his colleague Alfred Lietard, along with their Protestant counterparts such as Samuel Pollard (Diamond, Cheung, this volume) provided information that was used by explorers such as A.-F. Legendre (Harrell, this volume) and by stay-at-home scholars in Europe itself. Insofar as the missionaries provided accounts of the life of the peripheral peoples, they participated in the great scholarly enterprise that Said (1979) has characterized as Orientalism,[12] as Swain points out in her contribution here. This involved defining and scaling groups, in this case identified primarily by race and presumed racial origins, along a scale that was both moral (Christianity providing the only true morality, but others possibly approaching the ideal more or less closely in the absence of revealed truth) and technological, with the advanced peoples of the Christian West demonstrating the overall superiority of Christian

11. John Comaroff points out that British missionaries in the Cape of Good Hope region in the early nineteenth century saw their own version of colonialism as a "civilizing colonialism," in contrast to British administrators' "state colonialism" and the Boers' "settler colonialism" (1989:672).

12. The similarities between Orientalism and the classifying aspects of the respective Chinese projects were pointed out to me by Hehrahn Park.

civilization. In a large number of cases, Vial's included, the peripheral peoples fared rather better in the rankings than did the Han, especially in the moral ranking, where peripheral people's honesty, simplicity, and hard work (or even their brave, martial nature, in the case of Egon von Eickstedt's racial characterization of the Lolo [1944]), along with their failure to practice certain Chinese customs that the missionaries considered abhorrent (such as footbinding, infanticide, and arranged marriage), contrasted with the clever but sly, sneaky, and untrustworthy trading mentality of the Han.[13]

But missionaries themselves, of course, were interested not only in classifying and scaling the peripheral peoples; they also, more importantly, wanted to convert them. In converting their charges, the missionaries took their first step toward bringing them up to equality with the missionaries' own civilizational standard. But in most cases, missionaries did not then feel that their work was done, or that the new Christians were really at the level of the old. People were still in need of tutelage before they could be independent in their new faith and whatever cultural and technological innovations it brought with it. Although by the time the missionaries were expelled from China between 1949 and 1951 many congregations had been turned over to peripheral peoples, they remained under the supervision of missionaries. Perhaps the reckoning was still to come; eventually, we may expect, the Christian congregations would have been given autonomy or would have demanded it for themselves. But by the time the Christian project was brought to an abrupt and involuntary end, its promise of fully civilized status for the peripheral peoples was yet to be realized.

The Theory of the Communist Project

The Communist project is at least superficially quite different from both its predecessors. This difference is rooted in aspects of both the definition and the goal. The definition in this case is undertaken against the background of China's existence as a modern state with fixed borders and an enumerable citizenry; in this context the pe-

---

13. Comparisons to anti-Semitic stereotypes in the West are tentative but suggestive here; it was not too long ago that the Cantonese were known in English as "the Jews of Asia."

ripheral peoples become "minorities," since the Han are over 91 percent of the population. And in this definitional process, the criteria for group differentiation are clearly separated from those for scaling. Definition of a *minzu* depends on Stalin's four characteristics of a nationality (common territory, language, economy, and psychological nature), while scaling depends on the particular stage in the universal progression of history (the primitive, slave, feudal, capitalist, and socialist modes of production) that people have reached at the time of classification. Thus there is no a priori assumption that any one group—such as the Han in the Confucian project or the European Christians in the Christian project—is innately superior. In fact, there is no a priori assumption that the center consists of a particular group; Han have an overwhelming majority of positions in the Chinese state, but they do not have a monopoly, in the way that civilized Chinese constituted the center for Confucians, or Europeans for the Christian project. From this stems the further difference that the Communist project, unlike the other two, immediately grants full legal equality to the peripheral peoples.

The goal of the Communist project, on the surface, also differs from the goals of the other two. In the Communist project, the goal is not ostensibly to make the peripheral peoples more like those of the center, but rather to bring them to a universal standard of progress or modernity that exists independent of where the center might be on the historical scale at any given moment. The achievement of historical progress is thus fully independent of any approach to Chinese norms; the Russians in the pre-1991 Soviet Union, for example, were just as far along the road to socialism as the Han (maybe, depending on the stage of the current propaganda war, even farther along).

To accomplish this project, then, the Chinese Communist center implemented the most thoroughgoing definition program in China's history: the ethnic identification (*minzu shibie*) project of the 1950s (Fei 1981a; Lin 1987; Jiang 1985). This project, which occupied its participants for several years and still is not complete, involved sending teams of researchers to all areas of the country where local people had claimed status as a separate *minzu,* and evaluating their claims ostensibly according to Stalin's criteria, but in many cases also considering traditional Han folk categories, and sometimes giving weight to the people's own ethnic consciousness. This resulted initially in recognition of fifty-four *minzu,* including the Han; two have been added since to bring the total to fifty-six.

In addition, an important part of the identification process was determining where each *minzu* fit on the scale of history; this was important in order to plan the political struggles and developmental campaigns that would raise the civilizational levels of the various *minzu* (Chen Yongling n.d.). For example, people judged to be at the late-feudal stage of the landlord economy (which is where most of the Han peasantry was judged to be also) were to undergo the violent class struggles of the Land Reform program, while those who were still at the slave stage, or even showed vestiges of the primitive commune, were subjected to a much milder process, involving co-optation of leaders to the state project, and known as Democratic Reform.

Once this definitional stage was completed, it fell to the center to do the actual civilizing—the *minzu gongzuo* (work) of creating autonomous regions, implementing educational and developmental plans, bringing leaders of the peripheral peoples into the Party-state apparatus that carries out the center's project—in general, fulfilling the promise that all *minzu,* equal legally and morally, would march together on the road to historical progress, that is, to socialism. If some had farther to march than others, this was because of unequal historical progression up to the time of Communist takeover. But from here on out, China was to be a "unified, multinational state" (*tongyi duominzu guojia*) with all *minzu* working together toward common goals.

Contradictions between Theory and Practice

Despite these rather clear theoretical differences among the three projects, however, the actual situations of their implementation have been more complicated, due chiefly to the fact that only the Confucian project has ever been implemented by itself. Both the Christian and the Communist projects have faced competition from the Confucian project, and this has affected the outcome of the projects in various ways.

Competition between the Confucian and Christian Projects. Since the Confucian project was there first, when the Christians arrived among China's peripheral peoples, they were always in competition with the Confucians. There were two aspects to this competition. First, the

Christian project, as mentioned above, was directed not only at transforming the peripheral peoples, but also at transforming the Han; it thus not only created competing centers but defined the Chinese center as being inferior to its own, and thus in need of civilization. In many cases, as mentioned above, the peripheral peoples came out ahead of the Han on the Christian scale of civilization (at least the moral part if not the technical); this often was a result of the greater susceptibility of the peripheral peoples to conversion (see below), and it often resulted in the missionaries' taking the side of peripheral peoples in disputes with Chinese officials, as is related in Swain's and Cheung's contributions to this volume.

More importantly, competition between the Confucian and Christian civilizing projects often gave the peripheral peoples an opportunity to choose. And since the definitional aspect of the Confucian project assumed the moral rightness of certain exploitative economic arrangements (prominently working for Han landlords or Han-appointed native leaders—*tusi* and *tumu*), while the Christian economic approach was more benign or sometimes even helpful, peripheral peoples were prone to choose the missionaries as protectors against their Han oppressors or exploiters. This, of course, meant ready converts, as well as the missionaries' more positive evaluation of peripheral peoples.

Confucian Co-optation of the Communist Project. As was mentioned above, in the Communist project, everything was supposed to be different: the center was progressive but not explicitly Han, and all *minzu* were equal now. But in fact the Communist project has run into two kinds of obstacles, both of which render it in practice less like its own theory and more like the Confucian project, with culture as the measure of centrality and Han as the actual center.

The first obstacle is simply ingrained prejudice and local negative evaluation of minorities. This manifests itself at practically every level of Chinese society today. I have spoken to Han scholars who are experts on the Yi but speak nothing of the Yi language, and who can tell one in great detail the particulars of the dirtiness, backwardness, and stupidity of the Yi and other minorities. The first time I visited a Sani village in Yunnan, I was told by one of my Han companions that "what these people need is culture," and he didn't mean traditional folktales or minority dances. He meant culture in the classical sense of *wenhua*, the literary transformation that brings forth civilization. One Han official who had worked on a government forestry project in the middle of a Yi area had lived there twenty years and never tried Yi food; he was sure it would be dirty and make him sick.[14]

Such attitudes are extremely common at the local level, but they manifest themselves among the highly educated as well. A minority graduate student of my acquaintance, for example, used to dread revealing her identity in a crowd of students; as soon as they found out she was a minority, she said, they would begin simplifying their vocabulary. A schoolmaster in a successful minority education program in the Southwest complained about how difficult it was to educate these people, not only in conventional academic senses but in the social sense of persuading them to give up such primitive practices as dating in high school.

As long as such an innate, almost visceral Han sense of superiority remains, the actual program of the Communist project will be based on the unconscious assumption that Han ways are better, more modern ways. Peripheral peoples who act like Han—who are educated, Hanophone, *cultured*—will be treated equally with their Han compatriots. But it is Han culture that sets the standard.

This lingering social prejudice is reinforced by a second obstacle, which stems from the heart of the Communist project itself: the theory of the five stages of history. With this theory, which Chinese schoolchildren learn as objective fact on the level of the periodic table of the elements or the order of planets around the sun, the scaling of *minzu* can claim a scientific validity, one that is objective in the sense that the standpoint of the viewer does not change the picture. But it just happens that the Han (along with the Manchus and perhaps the Koreans) are higher on this objective scale than any of the other groups. This fits in handily with the aforementioned continuing Han prejudice against peripheral peoples. If the Dai actually *are* feudal, then of course they need to be brought up to the socialist stage, and the example for doing that are the Han, who moved from the semifeudal, semicolonial to the socialist level in the 1950s. The end

---

14. As with other aspects of the Communist civilizing project as directed at minorities, this abhorrence of the less civilized has its counterpart in many Han intellectuals' disdain for Han village life as well, a disdain graphically illustrated in the attitude of urban cadres who came to a Fujian village to promote "civilization," accepted the villagers' hospitality, and then criticized them for their backward ways (Huang 1989:168–69). This parallel, and many other helpful observations, were provided to me by Ann Anagnost.

result is that there is in fact very little challenge to the assumption of the Confucian project—the assumption that Han ways represent true culture and are therefore a model for other *minzu* to follow.

Some authorities have seen this Communist project as one that will ultimately lead to assimilation (Dreyer 1976:261–62; Heberer 1989:130), and in a sense it may amount to that in the long run. But we must remember two things. First, the long run is very long—it is the run all the way to communism, which is inconceivably far in the future (unless it was in the summer of 1958). Until then, according to Leninist theory, *minzu* will remain (Connor 1984:28–30; Dreyer 1976:262). And because *minzu* are destined to remain for a very long time, it is important that their differences are preserved. But, according to the theory of the Communist project, some *minzu* differences get in the way of progress along the stages of history, so these must be eliminated. The things that remain are those that foster ethnic pride, but do not impede progress. This is why the Communist state has placed so much emphasis on festivals, costumes, and the inevitable dancing in a circle, which is close to universal among China's minority *minzu*.

PERIPHERAL PEOPLES' REACTIONS TO CIVILIZING PROJECTS

The Development of Ethnicity

If the civilizing center initiates and organizes a project by developing an ideology of definition and scaling, the peripheral peoples, those worked on as objects of the civilizing project, respond at least partially by developing an ideology of ethnicity or ethnic consciousness. (I say "developing" because that word has a shaded scale of meanings: something can be developed de novo where it has not existed previously, or something that already exists can experience development in the sense of growth or change.) And so it is with the ethnic consciousness of peripheral peoples as the projects work on them. Such consciousness may already exist, but it will be sharpened, focused, perhaps intensified by the interaction with the center. Or in some cases, a peripheral people that has no ethnic consciousness may develop one in response to the pressures of the civilizing project.

Exactly what constitutes ethnicity or ethnic consciousness is a subject of much debate in anthropological circles (see Keyes 1981, Bentley 1987, and Williams 1989 for useful summaries at various stages in the evolution of the controversy), but it is probably inoffensive, at least, to define ethnic consciousness as the awareness of belonging to an ethnic group, and to define an ethnic group as a group that has two characteristics to its consciousness. First, it sees itself as solidary, by virtue of sharing at least common descent and some kind of common custom or habit that can serve as an ethnic marker (Nagata 1981). Second, an ethnic group sees itself in opposition to other such groups, groups whose ancestors were different and whose customs and habits are foreign, strange, sometimes even noxious to the members of the subject group.

There is further controversy as to when—under what circumstances or in what sorts of societies—ethnic groups and ethnic consciousness arise. For Abner Cohen (1981), ethnicity arises out of new kinds of interaction between peoples, where they have to confront each other in novel situations. For Soviet and Chinese Marxist scholars, ethnic groups arise only in situations in which there are social classes, so that different groups of people, taking different parts in the social division of labor, form perceptions of group interest and of opposition to other groups, leading to the commonalities of territory, language, economy, and culture that are the defining characteristics of a "nationality" (Li Shaoming 1986, Gladney 1987, Shanin 1989). In a recent article, Brackette Williams sees ethnic consciousness as arising out of the confrontation between a modern nation-state (or a governing group that is attempting to constitute itself as such a state) and minority peoples living within that state's territory (1989). Despite superficial differences (and a sometimes regrettable accusatory tone), it seems to me these authors are all pointing toward the same thing: the development (invention or change) of ethnic consciousness in situations where a group is confronted in some way by an outside power with whom it is in competition for resources of some kind, whether they be material (as in the Marxist formulation of class struggle and the division of labor) or symbolic (as in the conferral of not-quite-us status to minority groups even in states that attempt to insure the legal equality of majority and minority).

The situation of the civilizing project clearly fits right into this paradigm. When peripheral peoples are confronted with a center that not only attempts to rule them and the territory they inhabit, but also to define and educate them, they are forced to come to terms with who they are and with how they are different from those who are attempting to civilize them. So quite naturally they rethink their own position and their own nature, and in most cases, they seem to come up with a self-definition that is ethnic in the terms outlined above.

If developing an ethnic consciousness is an almost inevitable result of becoming the object of a civilizing project, then this development has two aspects: the development of consciousness of belonging to a group, and the development of consciousness of being different from other groups. The form that these developments take can vary greatly according to the pre-existing nature of the peripheral group and its preproject consciousness (if any), the definition imposed by the project, the perceived harm or benefit the project promises to confer, and the relative power of the center and the periphery in the individual situation. Some examples, drawn mainly from the case studies in this volume, may help to clarify the range of possibilities.

Miao as a designation for certain upland peoples of the Southwest is at least as old as the pre-Imperial *Shu jing* (Classic of history), in which the San Miao are referred to as the aboriginal inhabitants of the Yangtze River region. But the modern consciousness of a Miao ethnic group is still tenuous, and may never completely gel. We see in two different articles in this volume, however, ways in which first the Christian, and then the Communist civilizing projects have contributed to the development of this consciousness. Siu-woo Cheung's treatment of the role of Christian missionaries in the Miao social movements of the late nineteenth and early twentieth centuries shows how the image of Jesus as savior was fused with an earlier messianic idea of the Miao King to form a focus of identity for Miao groups all over northeastern Yunnan. And Diamond shows how the imposition by the Communists of the category Miaozu for a wide range of peoples in several provinces has prompted at least some of those people to think of themselves in some contexts as part of this larger group—an ethnic consciousness probably helped along today by frequent visits of Hmong (one group included in the category Miao) from Southeast Asia and North America. Here is a case of a category of linguistically related peoples, which did not previously constitute in any sense a group, developing the idea that they are members of a kind of collectivity that transcends local differences and includes them all. These people have always had the second component of ethnic consciousness—the realization that they are different from the Han. What they lacked previously, but have gained partially as a result of these projects, is the idea that they are related to each other, that they are all members of a community.

The Sani, described here by Swain in their interactions with Catholic missionaries, present a rather different picture. In certain ways, the Sani before Fr. Vial's mission were something like one of the local Miao groups before the early-modern ethnic movements. The Sani were one of those local groups classified by the Han as Luoluo (usually spelled Lolo in European sources), a congeries of peoples, speaking related languages, stretching from northern Vietnam to western Sichuan. They had no name in their own language for the Lolo as a whole (this was a Han category), but they did refer to themselves as Ni or Sani. Vial took a liking to them, seeing them as his children, his charges, as morally superior to the cunning and wily Han, even if they were technically more primitive and politically much less powerful. But he engaged in no action that fostered any kind of union of different "Lolo" groups, as Pollard and his colleagues had brought together different subgroups of the Hmong. The reaction to Vial's project seems to have been a heightening of the Sani consciousness (they still are loath to recognize their official status as Yi, the polite successor term for the category formerly called Luoluo) without creating a new consciousness of a wider identity.

In a slightly larger arena, the Yi in general (described by Harrell here, though this chapter deals only peripherally with ethnic consciousness; see Harrell 1990 for a fuller treatment) have experienced a process quite similar to that undergone by the Miao since 1949. A conglomeration of linguistically related groups has been incorporated as a *minzu,* and educated elite members of this category, at least, have at various times seen their Yi identity as being equal to or greater in importance than their local identity as Nuosu, Lipuo, Axi, Luoloupo, Nasu, and so forth. But the process here, as with the Miao, is far from complete.

The Manchus present a still different case. As outlined in this volume by Shelley Rigger (see also Crossley 1990a), Manchu identity went through a series of stages as the position of Manchus in the Chinese state went from challengers to conquerors to overlords to defeated remnants. Manchu was originally a political category, consisting of followers of Nurgaci and his descendants; it was not ethnic in the sense of including notions of descent or of common ethnic markers. As the military banner organization changed with the stabilizing of Manchu rule in the mid-Qing dynasty, however, the Qianlong emperor, worried that the basis for Manchu consciousness was eroding, consciously attempted to "ethnicize" their identity, drawing especially on notions of equestrian martial traditions and shamanistic rituals. In a sense, he was reacting to his own civilizing project, in which his people had become successful and stable rulers of China, and thus inevitably had begun to identify with China, to speak and write the Chinese language, to participate in many aspects of Chinese life. When the Manchu rulers were overthrown, there was no longer a context for ethnic consciousness, and in most Chinese cities Manchuness quickly dissolved except as a tale of ancestry. It was to be revived, however, by the Communist project, which for unclear and perhaps purely scientific reasons reconstituted the Manchus into a *minzu*, which they remain today. Some of them are taking language lessons.

Qianlong's attempt to revive Manchu identity accomplished the opposite of what happened to the Miao in the nineteenth century. The Manchus already had a sense of themselves as a solidary group; they were the conquerors and rulers. What they did not have was a clear sense of their ethnic markers, of how they were different from the Han. This the Manchu cultural revival of the mid-eighteenth century attempted to give to them. The second (or Communist) revival, which continues as I write, is more ambitious, for after the fall of the Qing most people with Manchu ancestry had neither a clear group consciousness nor a sense of how they were different from the Han; in fact, most of them were not different in any linguistic, territorial, or cultural sense, and retained only a vague sense of identity without clear markers or borders.[15]

A somewhat similar process has occurred among the Bai of Yunnan, as described by David Y. H. Wu (1989, 1990). These people, known formerly as Minjia (civilian households) live around Er Lake in western Yunnan; their ancestors may have been the rulers of the Nanzhao and Dali kingdoms of the ninth through thirteenth centuries. Though they have their own language, which has so far eluded the classificatory efforts of linguists because of its extensive borrowings, they were well on their way, in the decades before 1949, to complete assimilation as Han Chinese. Francis Hsü's famous monograph, *Under the Ancestors' Shadow* (1948), for example, makes little mention of the Bai origin

---

15. For the insight that Manchu identity, though submerged, was not really obliterated in the early twentieth century, I am indebted to recent unpublished research by Lisa Hoffman.

of its subjects, whom Hsü takes as an example of Chinese peasant culture and personality. But in the process of ethnic identification, the Bai idea was revived, and since then *minzu* policy has encouraged the development of ethnic markers, such as costume, music, and festivals, and the Bai have been given a *minzu* identity on the same level as other peripheral peoples. Here is a case like the second Manchu revival, where there was little consciousness of group solidarity or opposition to others, but these were revived and in some cases re-created by the Communist project.

The Yao, treated here by Ralph Litzinger, underwent a process formally similar to that experienced by the Manchus, but in a fundamentally different context, since they have always been the ruled rather than the rulers. Yao appears originally to have been a political category of upland peoples who could range across the South China mountains without paying taxes or corvée. Even in the Da Yao Shan (Great Yao Mountains) area, they speak three unrelated or distantly related languages, and their other customs and beliefs are quite different; one group, the Tai-speaking Lakkia or Tea Mountain Yao, were lords of the other groups before the Communist takeover. But with the Communist project, which includes the idea that *minzu* share cultural markers (see below), they have been led to develop a consciousness not only of being a we-group, opposed to the Han, but of having a large number of cultural continuities, including origin myths and the practice of ritual Daoism. The Yao have developed this consciousness in response to pressure of a civilizing project imposed from outside, unlike the eighteenth-century Manchus' response to their own voluntary but disturbing co-optation by the culture of which they themselves were the overlords.

The Dai of Sipsong Panna, described in this volume by Shih-chung Hsieh, present a still different case, one of a people originally independent on the farthest periphery of the Sinocentric world, who were forced to move from a consciousness of themselves as a nation, a people who ran their own state, to an idea of themselves as an ethnic group within a larger political system. Previous to their partial incorporation into the Nationalist state, and their fuller absorption under the Communists, they certainly had a fully formed ethnic identity; they were a solidary group organized around their lords (*chao*) and they were distinct from the subordinate upland peoples of their own kingdom (they knew little about the Han except as a political power to be reckoned with). When they were included within the borders of China, the most important other to which their ethnic identity was contrasted shifted from their upland vassals to their Han overlords. But the boundaries of the group and its internal markers have remained basically the same.

Then we have the Mongols, treated here by Almaz Khan and Wurlig Borchigud. There have always been political confederations on the northern marches of China; several of them ruled China at various times. But it seems that, prior to the late nineteenth and twentieth centuries, the important identifying marks for people in this area were their allegiance to particular lords or confederations, and their membership in descent groups that held claims to certain political titles. As Pamela Kyle Crossley has recently demonstrated (1990b), there was in the late Ming dynasty no classification by language or culture in the modern sense, but rather a classification by ecological adaptation, into herders, agriculturalists, and people who did a bit of both. It is with the decline of such obvious distinguishing characteristics that the ethnic markers and the notion of common descent have become important definers of the category Mongol. Almaz demonstrates this process with regard to descent from Chinggis Khan, which has changed from a political privilege to an ethnic marker; Borchigud shows how, with the further erosion among urban Mongols of cultural markers such as language (both Borchigud and Almaz speak Chinese as their native language), common descent and endogamy have come to be the markers that separate Mongols from Han. The Mongols, in a sense, did not think much about group identity until recently; their difference from the Han was obvious and ecological until the late nineteenth century, and since then has become an aspect of group identity.

As a final example, we ought to examine the Hui, the strangest ethnic category recognized by the Communist project. There is no real definition of Hui in terms of Stalin's four criteria: they have no common territory, being scattered throughout China; no common language, since they almost all speak Chinese; and no common economy or culture either (Gladney 1987, 1991). There are about eight million Hui scattered around most of China; concentrations lie in the Gansu-Ningxia-Qinghai border region, in cities of North China, and along the southeast coast. The only thing they may have in common is a tradition of descent from Muslims, although not all of them practiced Islam, even before the ascension of godless Communism. In the areas of the country where there are great concentrations of Hui Muslims, such as the Gansu-Ningxia-Qinghai area, Hui have long had an ethnic consciousness that has opposed them to the Han, Tibetans, Turkic Muslims, and Mongolians who also inhabit that area (Lipman 1990; Gladney 1988). But in the Southeast, no such consciousness existed until certain groups remembered their Islamic ancestors and applied for Hui minority status on that basis. When the status was conferred, they had to become Muslims, so they began giving up pork, Chinese temple worship, and other non-Islamic customs (Gladney 1991). Here is a case where a local ethnic consciousness was created virtually ex nihilo by the Communist project; an ethnic consciousness for the whole *minzu*, like that for the Yi and Miao, probably now includes only members of the elite, but will certainly spread, perhaps faster among the Hui, since the peasants of the Northwest, as well as most city dwellers (Gladney 1991) already have a local ethnic consciousness, and those in the Southeast have gone through the conscious process of acquiring one.

Meshing Project and Reaction: The Provisional Granting of Voice

The reactions of peripheral peoples to civilizing projects are not, however, limited to the development of ethnic identity. Insofar as civilizing projects are wholly or partly successful, they include the participation of the peripheral peoples. And in fact, as long as peripheral peoples agree, at least on the surface, to the terms of definition and scaling imposed by the civilizers, the civilizees will be granted a voice to speak to themselves and the world about the success of the project. In this sense, the answer to whether the subaltern can speak is that the subaltern can speak on the sufferance of the civilizer. Voice is granted on the provision that it will speak in favor of the project, or at least in the project's terms.

From the standpoint of the civilizers, the ideal form of the taking up of voices by the subaltern is the creation of "compradore elites." The term *compradore* (Portuguese: "buyer") originally referred to a Chinese who was an agent for a foreign company operating in China. But in the broader sense, it refers to members of peripheral or colonized peoples who participate in a colonizing or civilizing project. We can see examples in this volume in Litzinger's discussion of Yao cadres, who rule not only on behalf of the state, but on behalf of the state's "minority regional autonomy" policy. These people are often among the real leaders of the Yao communities, and it is they more than any Han bosses who determine the success or failure of the developmental aspects of the civilizing project. At the same time, the definitional aspects of the project, the classification and standardization of language and other cultural traits, depend heavily on the participation of Yao scholars.

We find another example of peripheral elites taking up a permitted voice in the Christian church leaders who emerged among the Miao (Cheung, this volume) and Sani (Swain, this volume) in quite divergent circumstances early in the twentieth century. In the Miao case, Christianity was taken up by leaders and participants in ethnic social movements, but it remained, in some places, as an outright ethnic marker of the Miao long after the movements had been suppressed or run out of steam. In the Sani case, there was no massive movement, but Fr. Vial, for all his Orientalist assumptions and writings about his childlike flock, did provide the Sani a counterweight to Chinese officialdom. Similar experiences are reported by Shepherd (1988) and Hsieh Shih-chung (1987) for missionized aboriginal peoples in Taiwan.

More than this, the simple adoption of state-imposed *minzu* identities is a weak form of peripheral peoples' speaking in the idiom of the civilizing project. This, however, is not as satisfactory a result from the viewpoint of the civilizers. The ethnic identity, originally weak, unformed, or nonexistent, once imposed can serve to unify resistance or even rebellion against the center that created the category that unifies. Thus the Pan-Mongol sentiment that became so much stronger and so much more overtly anti-Han during the Cultural Revolution of 1966–76 (Borchigud this volume; see also Jankowiak 1988). And in a sense, even the successful anticolonial rebellions that ended up dismembering the European empires in the mid-twentieth century were perpetrated in the name of nations that were originally the creations of the colonizers.

The paradox of civilizing projects is that they can, in some circumstances, turn back on themselves. With their avowed (and often sincere) intention to raise the cultural or civilizational level of the peripheral peoples, civilizers also make an implicit promise to grant equality, to share power, to give up ultimate control over how and when the subalterns speak. When the first happens without the second, when the peoples of the periphery gain advancement without equal empowerment, revolts can be the result. This has clearly been the case in almost every overtly colonial situation in this century; it may turn out to happen in Tibet, Inner Mongolia, and parts of Xinjiang as well. On the other hand, in some cases, as demonstrated above, the process has not gone that far yet, and the definition of peripheral peoples as less civilized, and thus legitimately subordinate in the political and economic order, still holds.

A civilizing project is thus not a unified thing, either in its purposes and methods or in the reaction of the people civilized. Only one thing remains constant: the assumption of cultural superiority by the politically and economically powerful center and the use of that superiority, and the supposed benefits it can confer on the peripheral peoples, as an aspect of hegemonic rule.

As indicated in the beginning of this introduction, civilizing projects have not been peculiar to China. In fact, much recent scholarly attention has been devoted to colonial discourse, almost always analyzing the ideological side of European colonial domination of Asian and African peoples in the eighteenth through twentieth centuries, as well as its neocolonial descendants in the postwar policies of the United States in particular. Much of this work is insightful and useful; it gives us some insight into the nature of the colonial enterprise. In addition, recent work, such as the articles collected in the November 1989 issue of *American Ethnologist,* is beginning to look beyond the simple dichotomy of colonizer and colonized to try to define varieties of colonial discourse as they changed over time and as they were different from one colonizer to another—bureaucrat and missionary, aristocratic administrator and peasant soldier, Frenchman and Englishman, man and woman. But this introduction, despite its admirable objective of putting the European empires of the late nineteenth and early twentieth centuries into perspective, does not even mention the Japanese colonial empire, which was contemporaneous with those European empires, let alone the Confucian project, which was going on even as China itself was the object of Western imperialism (Cooper and Stoler 1989).

This is not to maintain, of course, that every book has to be about everything; this one is only about China and its periphery, for example. But it is still necessary to point out that those of us who study the civilizing centers of the East have it incumbent upon ourselves to begin making our voices heard in the growing scholarly community discussing civilizing projects generally; it would be ironic if a community dedicated to deconstructing the ethnocentric formulations behind its own colonialism ended up excluding colonialisms of other centers. It is in this spirit that we offer *Cultural Encounters on China's Ethnic Frontiers* to the wider community.

PART I
The Historiography of Ethnic Identity
Scholarly and Official Discourses

The Naxi and the Nationalities Question
Charles F. McKhann

The fact of such a variety of families all existing at the same time is most spectacular both in Chinese and foreign society, contemporary or historical. [The Yongning Naxi] are like a colorful historical museum of the evolution of families in which one finds living fossils of ancient marriage formations and family structures.—Yan Ruxian, "A Living Fossil of the Family"

[Lewis Henry] Morgan used contemporary primitive tribal systems as a basis for inferences about the nature of ancient tribal systems. . . . This method is tantamount to making contemporary primitives into "living fossils."—Tong Enzheng, "Morgan's Model and the Study of Ancient Chinese Society"

Time was when ethnologists in the People's Republic of China had only two and a half theories of society and culture to work with: Stalin's theory of national identity, Morgan's theory of social evolution, and Engels' reworking of Morgan in *The Origin of the Family, Private Property, and the State*. Since the mid-1980s, however, Chinese ethnologists have shown signs of increasing dissatisfaction with the limits imposed on their work by this narrow theoretical framework. Two of the sharpest critiques have appeared in the English and Chinese versions of the journal *Social Sciences in China* early in 1989. In "Ethnic Identification and Its Theoretical Significance," Huang Shupin (1989), a member of one of China's two fledgling anthropology departments, offers a critical reassessment of Stalin's criteria for determining national identity. Tong Enzheng's (1989) criticisms of Morgan-Engelsian evolutionist theory may seem old hat to Western readers, but although

The present version of this essay has benefitted from the advice of my cohorts in the dissertation reading group at the University of Chicago. I would also like to offer my special thanks to Shih Chuan-kang, whose direct knowledge of Mosuo society and the post-Liberation Chinese ethnological project has helped shape this work. Most of the views expressed and all of the mistakes are mine.

39

he does not directly address the issue of so-called "contemporary primitives" in China, the publication of his forthright critique reflects a significant shift away from state-sponsored dogmatism in Chinese social science theory. It is in the Hundred Flowers spirit present in the writings of these and other contemporary Chinese critical theorists that I make the following observations on the general theory and practice of ethnology in post-Liberation China, and on the particular case of the Naxi nationality of northwestern Yunnan Province.[1]

THE NATIONALITIES QUESTION
AND THE CONSTITUTION OF ETHNOLOGY
IN THE PEOPLE'S REPUBLIC OF CHINA

Ethnology in contemporary China is generally regarded as an applied science, and its products to a large degree reflect the government's interest in resolving what it calls the "nationalities question" (*minzu wenti*). With a population that is 92 percent Han, the "nationalities question" in essence concerns problems with the economic, political, and social integration of the several dozen ethnic minorities that make up the remaining 8 percent of China's people. The government has correctly identified relative poverty as one of the principal features distinguishing the members of most minority ethnic groups from the average Han farmer. In an effort to redress this imbalance, laws and policies—especially in the area of education—have been designed to afford selective advantage to the members of China's fifty-five officially recognized "minority nationalities" (*shaoshu minzu*). At the same time, the government promotes a model of national culture that derives largely from the (Confucian) traditions of the Han majority, and in this respect minorities policy has been broadly assimilationist (see Borchigud, this volume).[2]

1. The term "post-Liberation" (*Jiefang hou*), referring to the period since the 1949 revolution, is borrowed from the Chinese vernacular in the People's Republic of China. Of the other readily available terms, "post-revolution" is ambiguous, and "post-1949" is not sufficiently imbued with political value.

2. An example of the government's desire to break down ethnic boundaries is the attention given in the late 1950s and the 1960s to determining the class structures of China's minority nationalities. In an attempt to simultaneously promote class struggle and de-emphasize ethnic differences, it was argued that in various nationalities the traditional elites (sometimes represented in aristocratic lineages) had more in common with each other than they did with the lower classes of their own societies. While crudely conceived power relations became the significant comparative dimension, culture was often treated almost incidentally.

Although the "nationalities question" in principle concerns the mutual integration of all nationalities, the discipline of "ethnology" (*minzuxue*)—translated alternatively as "nationalities studies"—has been charged exclusively with the study of China's *minority* nationalities. Before Mao Zedong's death in 1976, the study of contemporary Han society and culture was largely under the purview of political studies, economics, history, philosophy, and demography. In 1979, after nearly three decades in exile as "bourgeois sciences," sociology (*shehuixue*) and anthropology (*renleixue*) were rehabilitated—the former to extend the research being done on Han society, and the latter, in its sociocultural aspect, again focusing primarily on China's minority nationalities.[3]

The separation of majority and minority nationality studies into different academic disciplines is rooted in Marxist theory. Following Marx and Engels, Chinese Communist theorists consider different societies to be characterized by one of several broad types of "social formations," each representing a different stage in a more or less universal history of social evolution. In the study of China's nationalities the number of these stages has often been effectively reduced to two: modern or modernizing societies (as typically represented by the Han majority) and culturally and economically "backward" (*luohou*) or premodern societies (including almost all of China's minority nationalities).[4] While the work of Marx and Engels centers on a critique of capitalism and includes analyses of societies characterized by slavery and feudalism (the stages thought to be the immediate predecessors of capitalism on the evolutionary scale), on the relatively rare occasions that they turned their attention to more "primitive" societies Marx and Engels drew heavily on the work of Lewis Henry Morgan.

Morgan's (1985 [1877]) theory of social evolution, outlining three main stages—savagery, barbarism, and civilization—has been the

3. The relationship between ethnology, anthropology, and sociology continues to be widely debated in China, and in the past several years the amount of cross-fertilization between these disciplines with regard to theory and methodology has been increasing. For a mid-1980s view of the revival of sociology and anthropology, see Rossi 1985.

4. I am overgeneralizing here, but only a little. The Hui—who, with the exception of their belief in Islam, are culturally quite similar to the Han—and the Koreans in China's northwest are the only significant examples of minority nationalities that are reckoned as advanced as the Han (see Gladney 1987).

cornerstone of Chinese ethnology for forty years. Apart from the study of contemporary minority nationalities, the chief application of Morgan's theory in China has been in the archaeology of the Chinese neolithic period. This dual usage serves to identify living peoples with cultures that existed four millennia ago and to distinguish them categorically from some of their more "advanced" contemporary neighbors (particularly the Han). As Stevan Harrell notes in his introduction to this volume, the hierarchy implicit in this constructed order is spatial as well as temporal: the Han represent the advanced core, whereas the backward minority nationalities exist at the geographical, social, and cultural periphery.

The view of non-Han peoples as "barbarians" (*man, yi,* or *fan*) which we usually associate with the bygone Imperial Chinese world system—what is today officially called "great Han chauvinism"—is not dead in China. Like Confucian moralism, Morganian evolutionism primitivizes and exoticizes peoples who would be reckoned at the "backward" end of the cultural evolutionary scale, and simultaneously absolves its proponents of moral culpability by proposing a natural order of culture.[5] In some of its historical forms the Confucian view has even dehumanized peoples belonging to other cultural traditions. Dating to the Han dynasty, policies for governing barbarians—such as the "loose rein" and the "bone and stick"—called forth images of domestic animals in reference to peoples whose Chinese names were often rendered in characters using the dog or insect radical (Lien-sheng Yang 1968). In 1743, the first Han magistrate to govern the Naxi territory explained the Naxi request for naturalization by supposing that "they [were] attracted by the Imperial Benevolence as animals are attracted by sweet grass" (in Rock 1947:46).[6] Contemporary statements exhorting minority peo-

5. While pointing out the similarity between these two theories, I would hasten to add that they are not so different from two other theories that enjoy great currency in the Western social sciences today, namely, "modernization" and "world system" theories. Confucian moralism, Morganian evolutionism, and modernization theory all hinge on what Nisbet (1969) calls the "metaphor of progress." While Wallerstein (1974) and other "world system" theorists have challenged the natural agency implied by this metaphor, for the most part their work affirms the social-typological categories established by evolutionist and neo-evolutionist theory.

6. This formulaic assessment ignores the obvious reason for the Naxi request. For the entire first quarter of the eighteenth century the Naxi were piggies-in-the-middle in a prolonged war between China and Tibet.

ples to follow directives from the center often appear to be under-lain by similar presuppositions regarding the self-evident value of such programs as the Four Modernizations.

The contemporary Chinese ethnological literature contains numer-ous examples illustrating researchers' confidence in their ability to assess the general level of sociocultural development of the different minority nationalities and to identify factors that may be inhibiting evolutionary progress. In a 1987 article in *Minzu yanjiu* (Nationalities research), for example, Long Yuanwei suggests that "an inability to administer production," "closed-mindedness," and "objectionable customs" have retarded the development of a commodity economy in minority areas (1987:20–21).[7] The institutionalized sexual relationship called *zouhun* (walking marriage) practiced by the so-called Yongning Naxi (whom I will call Mosuo, following self-identification practices) is an example of a custom that was for many years judged "objection-able."[8] Residence in *zouhun* relationships is duolocal: the man visits the woman and may spend the night, but they maintain separate residences in their natal households, and any children born of the relationship are raised in their mother's house. In the post-Liberation ethnographic literature on the Mosuo, *zouhun* relationships are held to represent an evolutionary stage only slightly more advanced than that characterized by Morgan's hypothesized "consanguine family"— what Chinese authors call "group marriage." According to Cai Junsheng (1983) group marriage involves the collective marriage of the men belonging to one "gens" to the women of another. Because indi-vidual marriages are not recognized, the argument goes, paternity is always in question and descent is necessarily reckoned in the matriline. The model implies widespread, continuous, and nearly indiscriminate sexual promiscuity, and assumes that women are unaware of the

7. I discovered Long's article through a reference in Meng Xianfan's (1989) article on the development of Chinese ethnology in the 1980s. While Meng praises Long's work, I suspect others might regard some of Long's statements as racist. While "closed-mindedness" and "objectionable customs" might be viewed as surmountable psychological and cultural problems, "inability to administer" would seem to imply a basic mental deficiency. Such examples echo Stevan Harrell's point (Introduction, this volume) that China's minority nationalities are regarded as at once redeemably and irredeemably "backward."

8. Following the Oxford *Concise English-Chinese Chinese-English Dictionary,* I have translated the Chinese term *louxi* as "objectionable customs." The component *lou* also carries the meanings "ugly," "mean," "vulgar," "corrupt," and "undesirable."

significance of their menstrual cycles and that exclusive sexual relations between couples do not exist even for short periods of time.

During the 1960s and 1970s Mosuo couples maintaining *zouhun* relationships were pressed to enter into "formal marriage" relations and to establish joint households.[9] While the ethnologists studying the Mosuo were not responsible for this unfortunate situation, clearly their work was used to validate a policy that derived primarily from an incensed Confucian moral sensibility.[10]

It is this same moral sensibility that lies behind the feminization of peripheral peoples and the sexual exoticization of non-Han women in Chinese popular culture. Stevan Harrell (this volume) and Norma Diamond (1988) discuss these issues at some length, so I will confine myself to two examples, each with its own implications. In the early 1980s I attended a performance of the Yunnan Province Nationalities Dance Troupe as a guest of the provincial governor. As anyone with knowledge of nationality dance forms who has attended one of these events will attest, the so-called "ethnic dances" performed by such groups usually bear little resemblance to the genuine dance traditions on which they are based: clothes become "costumes," and steps become slick "moves." This and countless similar examples illustrate two points. First, the government is highly selective in what aspects of nationality culture it chooses to promote. Clothes, dance, song, and "festivals" (i.e., annual rituals with the religious content largely extracted) are the principal subjects of government presentations of minority cultures. Second, even these relatively superficial markers of cultural difference are transformed (read: civilized) to appeal to Han aesthetic standards, including standards of barbarianness. What made this particular performance even more interesting, however, was the inclusion of an "Afro-Caribbean" dance, in which the solitary female dancer wore a lurid polka-dot dress, a rag kerchief, and

9. In recent years, this policy has been discontinued, with the result that many of the marriages formed during that period are being dissolved and fewer new ones created.

10. Even armed with Morganian theory, the government had a difficult time convincing the Yongning Naxi that their *zouhun* relationships represented uncivilized sexual promiscuity. The policy of encouraging relationships defined as "formal marriage" was therefore justified as a means to reduce the incidence of venereal disease among the Mosuo population. One cannot help but feel that if this really were the issue, antibiotics, condoms, and health education might have been more effective than attempting to fiddle with social organization.

blackface. Perhaps because the signs were so much closer to home, I found it particularly appalling. And indeed, while the erotic gyrations of this stylized Aunt Jemima were loudly applauded by most of the audience, they had the only person of African descent present, an American sitting next to me, in tears.

Among China's minorities, Dai women especially are often depicted as sexual exotics. One example is the printed curtain fabric, very popular in Kunming, that bears images of particularly large-breasted Dai women traipsing through the lush jungles of southern Yunnan. In recent years the popular image of Dai women's sexuality has even led some Han men to make a sport of covertly photographing the women as they bathe in the Lancang River outside the popular Dai tourist town of Jinghong in southern Yunnan. Even this obnoxious behavior sometimes has its funnier moments. Several years ago, an American anthropologist doing fieldwork in Xishuangbanna spotted a man with a telephoto lens photographing a Dai woman bather from the bushes by the river's edge. At first she simply watched the scene from a distance, but when the man kept creeping closer, she finally rushed over and yelled at him to go away. Looks of surprise were exchanged all around, and after some initial embarassment, both he and the woman bather began to laugh. Ultimately it emerged that they were a married Bai couple visiting from another part of the province. Wanting some sexy pictures, they had purchased a set of Dai women's clothes and staged the whole thing.[11] The story illustrates both the pervasiveness of the image, and its power of appeal—as part of the culture of the modern multinational state—even to those whom it deprecates.

In an odd reversal of the evolutionist paradigm, customs deemed "primitive" are sometimes touted as having positive value. The idea expressed in certain sectors of contemporary American society that some non-Western peoples—otherwise reckoned as "primitives"— are more spiritually in tune with the "natural" world than are Westerners is a familiar example. Two similar examples from post-Liberation Chinese ethnology concern the Wa, whose relatively egalitarian social structure has earned them the bittersweet label of "primitive communists," and the Naxi, whose traditional custom of burning the dead (which is rarely practiced nowadays due to increasing sinicization) has been opportunistically raised as a positive example in the national

11. I am indebted to Heather Peters for this story.

push to maximize the land available for cultivation by promoting cremation in place of traditional Han burial practices.

By virtue of their structural position as advisors to government policymakers, Chinese ethnologists can play a central role in framing the discourse on the "nationalities question." For most of the post-Liberation period, however, their freedom to do so has been sharply circumscribed by the theoretical framework within which they are required to work. Especially as it reverberates with traditional Han concepts of ethnicity, the use of Morganian theory largely precludes the development of an appreciation of minority nationalities' history, culture, society, and politics in their own terms. The diverse ethnographic features of minority nationalities' cultures have generally been shoehorned into the Morgan-Engelsian framework, with facts at odds with preconceived images of particular social formations either ignored completely or explained away as the aberrant "survivals" of a hypothetical earlier stage. In a recent critique of post-Liberation ethnology, Meng Xianfan writes: ". . . people mistakenly thought that the aim of their research work was to prove the correctness of Morgan's theory . . ." (1989:206). But Meng misses the point. Insofar as that aim was largely defined for them by the state, it was precisely to prove the correctness of Morgan's theory.

ETHNIC IDENTIFICATION: THE NAXI CASE

After the founding of the People's Republic in 1949, the first task set to Chinese ethnologists was to help the government identify China's minority nationalities. Large-scale but somewhat superficial "investigations" (involving hundreds of ethnologists) extended through the 1950s, and the findings were published—first as "internal" (*neibu*) reports, and later publicly in revised editions—in more than three hundred volumes, divided into five main categories (ibid.:213).[12] A notable feature of books belonging to the "brief histories" (*jianshi*) category is that one rarely finds reference in them to either the dates when particular ethnic groups were granted nationality status, or the procedures followed and the per-

---

12. These are: (1) a general one-volume encyclopedia on minority nationalities; (2) brief histories (*jianshi*); (3) language summaries (*yuyan jianzhi*); (4) descriptions of minority nationalities' autonomous areas (*zizhiqu gaikuang*); and (5) field reports on society and history (*shehui lishi diaocha baogao*).

sons involved in the decision-making process (but see Lin Yaohua 1987). Insofar as other significant dates and players in a nationality's past are generally noted and incorporated into these official histories, the omission of this material serves to mystify the concrete process of ethnic identification, giving the impression that the established ethnic categories are timeless, scientifically unimpeachable, and agreed upon by all (see Litzinger, this volume).

The official criteria used to classify nationalities in China are those outlined in Stalin's definition of a nation.[13] To wit:

> A nation is a historically evolved, stable community of people, based upon the common possession of four principal attributes, namely: a common *language*, a common *territory*, a common *economic life*, and a common *psychological make-up* manifesting itself in common special features of *national culture*. (Stalin 1950:8, my emphases)

In his essay on Yi history (this volume), Stevan Harrell argues that in fact Stalin's four criteria have "not [been] employed in any strict manner, but rather to confirm or legitimate distinctions for the most part already there in Chinese folk categories and in the work of scholars who wrote before Liberation." Harrell goes on to suggest that the ultimate basis for distinguishing nationalities in China has been the creation of nationality histories within which these criteria can be credibly situated. I believe that the category Naxi is, as Harrell suggests, a thing of the (Han) Chinese past, and that post-Liberation Chinese ethnologists have necessarily relied on Morgan's historicism to validate a formulation of Naxi identity allegedly based in Stalin's essentialist criteria. In actuality, Stalin's criteria alone are inadequate. Without the support of a Morganian reading of Naxi history, their use to define the category Naxi appears highly problematic.

One of the few nationalities in whom "traces" of several of Morgan's major stages are held to exist concurrently, the Naxi are the example par excellence of the application of Morganian theory in Chinese ethnology today. The Chinese government considers the

---

13. There is considerable slippage between Stalin's concept of a nation and the modern Chinese concept of a nationality. I will not address the issue here, but interested readers may consult Cai Fuyou (1987).

people referred to here as Naxi and Mosuo as comprising a single nationality—the Naxi. However, not all so-labelled Naxi agree with the label or with the idea that they are members of the same group. Specifically, the peoples centered in the Yongning basin and Lugu Lake regions of Yunnan Province's Ninglang County call themselves Mosuo, Hli-khin, or Nari, and distinguish themselves from the much larger group—living mostly west and south of the Jinsha River (in Lijiang, Zhongdian, and Weixi counties)[14]—whom they call Naxi.[15] Members of the larger western group, on the other hand, call themselves Naxi and refer to the people of Yongning as Luxi or Mosuo.[16] (See map 6, p. 302.)

In the pre-Liberation Chinese literature and in contemporary Taiwanese publications (e.g., Li Lin-ts'an 1984) these groups are collectively called Mosuo or Moxie. Perhaps the earliest mention of the Mosuo is in the T'ang dynasty *Man shu* (Book of the southern barbarians 1961:39), and the name appears to have been in common use by the Han and possibly other neighboring ethnic groups since at least the thirteenth century (Rock 1947). In working among the peoples of the Lijiang plain, the Austrian-American botanist-turned-ethnographer Joseph Rock used the locally self-ascribed term Na-khi (Naxi) in his publications dating from the 1920s. Whether he was the first to make this transition is not clear. What *is* clear is that the name Mosuo has disappeared completely from the official post-Liberation vocabulary. Thought to originate with the Han people, it was considered pejorative by some Naxi, although the people of the Yongning region prefer it, and are called by that name by most of their neighbors. Hence, whereas the name Naxi in reference to the current Naxi nationality is a recent addition to the Chinese vocabulary, it encompasses the same semantic field as the earlier term Mosuo.

Post-Liberation Chinese ethnologists distinguish between eastern and western branches of the Naxi nationality, corresponding to the

14. This division by county is intended as a rough generalization only. While perhaps 95 percent of the Naxi live in the four counties mentioned, there are sizeable populations in neighboring counties as well (see PAC 1987).

15. According to Shih Chuan-Kang (personal communication, 1990), while the people of Yongning ordinarily refer to themselves as Nari or Hli-khin (=Luxi?) when speaking in their own language (Naru), they use the term Mosuo when speaking Mandarin and prefer to be called by that term by other peoples.

16. The name Luxi means "people of Lu" and refers to the area of Lugu Lake.

groups living in the two regions outlined above.[17] Whereas the people of the Yongning–Lugu Lake (eastern) region are called by the geographically descriptive term Yongning Naxi (cf. Zhan et al. 1980; Yan and Song 1983), the larger western group is usually referred to simply as Naxi, rather than Lijiang Naxi or some other term using a geographical locator.[18] Since the groups presumably are equal in the eyes of the scientist, we may wonder on what basis one branch has come to represent, in linguistic terms, a marked category. To avoid confusion, I refer to the two groups by their self-ascribed names, Mosuo and Naxi, and to both groups together (as in the official category Naxi) by the term Naxizu (the Naxi nationality).

Stalin's Criteria Applied to the Naxizu

This section provides a brief overview of the Naxizu in light of Stalin's criteria. The assessment is my own, and in making it I have tried to preserve the meanings present in Stalin's original discussion of the "National Question" (1935 [1913]), the source most often cited by contemporary Chinese ethnologists.

A Common Territory. The Naxi and the Mosuo inhabit contiguous regions along the western border between Yunnan and Sichuan. Within the area occupied by both groups, they are the numerically dominant populations, and so may be said to meet the requirement of possessing a common territory.[19]

17. The term "branch" (*fenzhi*) has no official standing in the classification of China's minority nationalities. Its use appears to represent ethnologists' attempts to unofficially denote perceived subcategories of particular nationalities. The Mosuo ethnologist He Xuewen (1991) takes a bolder stand when he publishes using the term Mosuo *ren* (Mosuo people), in place of the accepted Yongning Naxi. My thanks to Stevan Harrell for pointing me to He's essay. Whether it signifies the beginning of a terminology shift in Chinese writings on the Mosuo remains to be seen.

18. The use of geographical locators to distinguish subclasses of general barbarian types dates to the earliest Chinese periods. In the Han dynasty, all barbarians were lumped into four categories associated with the cardinal directions. Later, these were refined as the Han created names for the distant places into which they expanded. In the literature of the Republican period, for example, one finds the term Liangshan Lolo used to designate a branch of Lolo (now called Yi) centered in the Liang Mountains of southern Sichuan. Insofar as the place names used derive from Han geography, this traditional practice is especially problematic where nationality self-identification is concerned.

19. For a county-by-county breakdown of the Naxi population, see PAC (1987).

A Common Language. Contemporary Chinese linguists divide the Naxizu language into two "dialects" (*fangyan*): an "eastern dialect" (*dongbu fangyan*), spoken by the Yongning Naxi (i.e., the Mosuo), and a "western dialect" (*xibu fangyan*) spoken by the Naxi. According to He and Jiang (1985), grammatical differences are not great, but the phonological and lexical differences between the two dialects are quite marked.

Indeed, most Naxi and Mosuo with whom I have discussed the question agree that although the two dialects are more similar to each other than either is to any of the other Tibeto-Burman languages spoken in the region, they are mutually unintelligible. As Norma Diamond argues regarding the Miao in her chapter in this volume, these "dialects" could by some standards pass as separate languages. While I have little experience with the eastern dialect, I can attest to considerable variation within the western dialect alone. Naxi living on the Lijiang plain, the type locale for the western dialect as defined by contemporary Chinese linguists, find the language spoken in northern Lijiang County (which is within the western dialect area) almost as unintelligible as the eastern dialect. Moreover, the language spoken in the town of Lijiang itself differs somewhat from that spoken in the villages on the surrounding plain. The differences in the latter case, however, are principally lexical and not grammatical or phonemic. In particular, urban Naxi vocabulary includes a greater proportion of what are at root Chinese loan words, although marked differences in pronunciation often make recognition difficult for the inexperienced listener.[20]

A Common Economy. In "Marxism and the National and Colonial Question" (1935 [1913]:7), it is clear that by a "common economy" Stalin means an integrated economic community defined on the basis of trade under a unified administration. He makes no reference to the central Marxist concepts of the means and relations of production.[21] Both the Naxi and the Mosuo have been under nominal Chi-

20. The use of Chinese loan words in Lijiang Naxi speech derives in large part from the presence of significant numbers of Han people in the town of Lijiang dating back to the Ming dynasty. Han artisans and scholars were welcomed by the royal Mu lineage, whose position in Naxi society at that time was a product of their close relations with the Chinese authorities.

21. See Lin (1987) for a discussion of problems encountered in applying the criterion of "common economy" to the minority nationalities of southwest China during the identification project of the 1950s.

nese rule since the Yuan dynasty (1280–1368), when the Mongols established hereditary "native chiefs" (*tusi*) to govern in each area. The Naxi *tusi* (the head of the Mu lineage) was replaced by a regular Chinese magistrate in 1723, while the Mosuo *tusi*ship lasted until 1956. Trade between the two regions certainly existed throughout this period, but it was not limited to direct exchange. Occupying a middle-altitude zone between the Chinese lowlands and the Tibetan plateau, both the Naxi and the Mosuo participated actively in long-distance trade that extended from Lhasa to Chengdu to Dali and involved several ethnic groups.

If we expand Stalin's explicit notion of "economy" to include the principal productive activities in which people engage, then the economies of the Naxi and the Mosuo are broadly similar. In both areas we find some combination of agriculture and pastoralism, supplemented by specialized work in trades such as mule-skinning, carpentry, basket-making, and coppersmithing. The kind of agriculture practiced, as well as the relative proportion of agricultural and pastoral production in a given location, varies greatly with altitude and the availability of surface water. In general, the warmer lowlands, especially along the Jinsha River, are devoted to high-yield summer paddy, winter wheat, and semitropical fruit crops; middle altitude areas (ca. 2,600–3,100m) produce wheat, barley, maize (all mostly unirrigated), and temperate fruits; while the highlands yield only potatoes, turnips, and fairly meager grain crops. In general, the place of herding activities within local economies varies inversely with agricultural productivity: people in the highlands raise more horses, cattle, sheep, and goats than the lowlanders do.

Because the relative weight of agricultural and pastoral activities varies tremendously with village location, it is impossible to say with precision what "the" Naxizu economy is. More difficult yet is the question of how we might use an image of the Naxizu economy—however we conceptualize it—as a distinguishing feature of the Naxi nationality. There are members of the Han, Bai, Lisu, Pumi, Tibetan, Hui, and Yi nationalities, all living in and adjacent to the Naxi-Mosuo homeland, whose "economies," measured in these terms, are virtually identical to those of their Naxi and Mosuo neighbors.

A still broader Marxian sense of economy emphasizes the relations (or social organization) of production. In this respect the Naxi and Mosuo economies are radically different—so different, in fact, that the Naxi appear much more similar to the local Bai, Han, and Lisu peoples than they do to the Mosuo. The explanation for this falls more properly under the heading of "a common national culture."

A Common National Culture. This is clearly the area of sharpest distinction between the Naxi and the Mosuo. Since Rock's and Li Lin-ts'an's pioneering studies on Naxi society and religion, researchers have recognized marked differences between the social organization, descent systems, marriage and residence patterns, and religious practices of the Naxi and the Mosuo. Traditional Naxi society is organized on the basis of exogamous patrilineal descent groups called "bones" (*coq-o*), within which major property—land, livestock and houses—is controlled and inherited by men. Patrilateral cross-cousin marriage, resulting in a pattern of delayed exchange between local "bones" whose members are related as "flesh" (*nal*) kin, represents the ideal form of marriage in Naxi society.[22] With rare exception, residence after marriage is virilocal.

By our present understanding—based partly on Rock, but mostly on the post-Liberation Chinese ethnographies—Mosuo social organization is more complicated.[23] Among the aristocracy (*sipi, sipei*), including the *tusi* family and its collateral relatives, descent and inheritance have traditionally been reckoned in the patriline, and marriage is generally virilocal. Among the commoner (*dzeka, zeka*) and slave (*wer, e*) classes, descent and inheritance are generally reckoned in the matriline, and residence is duolocal. The most common form of institutionalized sexual relationship between men and women of the two lower classes is the *zouhun* described above. Patrilateral cross-cousin marriage is neither idealized nor practiced by any sector of Mosuo society (Shih Chuan-kang, personal communication, 1990).[24]

22. Naxi refer to the practice of patrilateral cross-cousin marriage by the phrase *eqgv zzeimei ggaiq* (the mother's brother [also *eqjiu*] possesses/holds the sister's daughter). The phrase implies that a girl's mother's brother has the right to bring her into his household to marry his son. In actuality, he isn't always allowed to exercise that "right." That is to say, while a girl's mother's brother may look upon his right as "prescribed," her father can sometimes "prefer" to ignore it and arrange her marriage elsewhere. Despite the fact that such marriages are illegal in post-Liberation China, they remain common among the Naxi in the more remote districts of Lijiang and Zhongdian counties.

23. Rock was the last non-Chinese to work in Yongning. Since Liberation the area has been closed to foreign researchers, although Stevan Harrell informs me that the Lugu Lake district has recently been opened to tourism.

24. According to Shih Chuan-kang (personal communication, 1990), the Mosuo have no indigenous term for the institution of "walking marriage," although they

The differences between the residence patterns, descent systems, and hierarchical structures of Naxi and Mosuo societies have obvious economic implications. The Naxi have no "slave" class (although some historians have suggested that they did have at some time prior to the seventeenth century [Guo Dalie, personal communication, 1986]) and they organize everyday productive activities on the basis of the patrilocal household. The Mosuo economy, by contrast, involves relations of production that run generally along matrilineal lines and which (prior to 1956, when the last *tusi* was deposed) sometimes included slave labor.[25]

This is not the place to begin an involved discussion on Mosuo social organization. Several Chinese ethnologists have been studying the problems of Mosuo household structure, matrilineal descent, and "matriarchal" power (Zhan et al. 1980; Zhan 1982; Yan 1982; Yan and Song 1983; Cheng 1986), but the overwhelming influence of Morganian theory in their accounts limits our ability to generate alternative interpretations of the rich ethnographic data they contain. In the present context we are concerned more with the question of how Chinese ethnologists have reconciled the obvious cultural differences between the Naxi and the Mosuo to validate the overarching category Naxizu now recognized by the state.

CONSTRUCTING NAXI HISTORY

In the 1940s both Joseph Rock (1947 and 1948) and the prominent Naxi historian Fang Guoyu (1944) developed the thesis that the Naxi are descended from the proto-Qiang people of the Sichuan-Gansu-

---

have a phrase that expresses its meaning and use the term *zouhun* when speaking Mandarin. In the post-Liberation ethnographic literature this practice is usually called *azhu hunyin* (friend marriage), but Shih notes that the Mosuo term *arju* (transliterated in Mandarin as *azhu*) is used to denote "friend" in numerous other contexts as well, and he argues against regarding the institution as a kind of "marriage."

25. The terms "class," "slave," "commoner," and "aristocrat" are part of the vocabulary of post-Liberation ethnographies of the Mosuo. I use them here uncritically and without precise definition, for that is the way they appear in the ethnographies in question. For the most part, the ethnologists responsible for these writings appear to assume that everybody knows what these things are. In fact, in post-Liberation social science literature as a whole, the meanings of these elastic categories are anything but self-evident.

Qinghai border region.[26] They based this thesis on the similarity between Naxi and Qiang ritual forms, as well as on the Naxi written and oral traditions claiming migration from the mountain grasslands in the north.[27] After Liberation, Fang continued to promote this view of ancient Naxi history, and it is now widely accepted within the Chinese ethnological community.

According to Chinese historical sources (in Rock 1947), the Mosuo (i.e., the Naxizu) arrived in northwestern Yunnan around 24 C.E., settling first in the Yongning area. Later, during the T'ang dynasty (618–907), they are said to have extended their influence to the Lijiang plain, after displacing a people recorded as the Pu. This history accords well with the Naxi's own records of their past, which consist primarily of genealogies contained in pictographic ritual texts. The genealogies claim that four brothers, each the apical ancestor of one of the four recognized Naxi patriclans, arrived in the broader Lijiang area after crossing the Jinsha River from the north, in the general direction of Yongning and Muli.

In asserting the common identity of the Naxi and Mosuo, contemporary Chinese ethnologists point to these recorded myths and argue that the Naxi in Lijiang are a derivative branch of the Yongning Naxi (i.e., the Mosuo). This claim is supported by an interpretation of Naxizu social history that, following Morgan, regards the patrilineal descent system of the Naxi as a natural evolution of the system of matrilineal descent found among the Mosuo lower classes.[28] The transformation is thought to have begun with establishment of the *tusi* system in both regions. However, due to their relative isolation from the more advanced Han, the argument goes, the process of

26. The authorship of this thesis seems to have been centered between Rock and Fang. Although Fang's article appeared earlier (1944), Rock (1948:8–9) claims that in reading the Reverend Thomas Torrence's essay on Qiang religion (1920) he had suspected a connection between the Qiang and the Naxi, wrote Torrence, and received confirming information in a letter from Torrence dated March 20, 1933. Although Rock makes no mention of Fang's article, his insistence on detailing his correspondence with Torrence suggests that he was on the defensive. I want to thank Shih Chuan-kang for pointing Fang's article out to me.

27. Rock (1963a:xxxviii) says that the Tibetan name for the Naxi, lJang, is identical to that for the modern Qiang in Sichuan. Lawrence Epstein, a Tibetologist familiar with the Khams dialect of Tibetan, has expressed doubts to me on this claim.

28. Given this interpretation of Naxizu history, the semantic marking evident in the category Yongning Naxi (see above) makes even less sense. One would expect the group held to represent the primordial state to be labeled with the unmarked term.

evolution has been slower among the Mosuo, affecting mainly the aristocratic lineage, whose ties to the Chinese government have been strongest. In the Lijiang area, on the other hand, the origin of socio-economic conditions favorable to the rapid development of a patrilineal system is located in the early replacement of the *tusi* by a Han magistrate and the direct integration of the Naxi into the Chinese state. Note that in both cases it is the Chinese government, the civilizing center, that is cast as the agent of change.

Following a different logic, Anthony Jackson's study of Naxi religion (1979) arrives at this same conclusion. Where Chinese ethnologists see the transformation from matrilineal to patrilineal descent as a natural process of social evolution, Jackson sees it as resulting from a policy of forced sinicization. Writing at a time when fieldwork in China was not possible and post-Liberation Chinese ethnographic literature was unavailable in the West, Jackson had to rely almost exclusively on the earlier work of Joseph Rock and a Soviet ethnologist, A. M. Reshetov, whose work on the Mosuo appears to have consisted of translations from Chinese investigation reports of the 1950s.[29] In his early days in Lijiang, where he lived off and on between 1924 and 1949, Rock subscribed to the prevailing Han notion that the Na-khi (Naxizu) were a unified people. Rock specialized in Naxi religion, and it was in reference to their differing religious practices that he later came to distinguish between the Na-khi of Lijiang and the people he called the Mo-so (or Hli-khin) "tribe" of Yongning (Rock 1947). In his visits to Yongning, Rock noted that the indigenous Mosuo ritual specialists did not possess the pictographic texts used by the Naxi, nor did they perform the Naxi Sacrifice to Heaven (Mee Biuq) ritual.

Banned by the government since 1949, the Sacrifice to Heaven was traditionally performed collectively by the members of local patrilineal "bones" at the time of the lunar new year. Focussing on the opposition between "bone" and "flesh" relations, the ritual's charter is located in the Naxi myth of anthropogenesis, which relates the first

---

29. Reshetov studied in China between 1958 and 1961, but according to his Chinese advisor, Chen Yongling, did not travel to the Yongning area (Shih Chuan-kang, personal communication, 1990). I have never seen a copy of Reshetov's book, cited in Jackson (1979) as *Matrilineal Organization Among the Na-khi [Mo-so]* (Moscow, 1964). From the phrasing of the quotations translated into English in Jackson (1979), Shih believes the material to have come directly from the Chinese investigation reports.

instance of marriage, including a dispute over the mother's brother's right to arrange his sister's daughter's marriage. Naxi *dobbaqs* (ritual specialists) regard the Sacrifice to Heaven as among the most ancient of Naxi rituals, but more importantly for our purposes, it serves as an important element in Naxi self-identification.[30] According to the myth, it is the performance of the Sacrifice to Heaven that distinguishes the Naxi from other ethnic groups in the region. The Naxi are quite conscious of this, and so every performance of the ritual serves to re-establish ethnic boundaries.[31]

Apparently influenced by his reading of Reshetov, Jackson (1975 and 1979) argues to the contrary that the Sacrifice to Heaven is a recent creation. In his view, it (and indeed the whole complex of *dobbaq* rituals and ritual texts) originated among the Naxi at a time when their historical transition from matriliny to patriliny required ideological support. He interprets the high status of the mother's brother in Naxi mythology and society as a trace of the matrilineal period.[32]

30. Some empirical evidence supports claims for the antiquity of the Sacrifice to Heaven. First, as the botanist in Rock initially noted, many of the plant and animal species recorded in the Sacrifice to Heaven ritual texts are not local to the present Naxi homeland, but are found further north, in the area from which the Naxi claim to have emigrated two thousand years ago. Second, the Sacrifice to Heaven belongs to a general class of Naxi periodic rituals called "Rituals to obtain *neeq* and *oq,* the male and female elements of reproduction" (*neeq xiu oq xiu bbei*), which is distinguished from the other two major classes—funerary and demon-eviction rituals—by a relative absence of introduced Buddhist symbolism.

31. While the Mosuo are not among the several groups distinguished in the Naxi myth of anthropogenesis, neither do they perform the Sacrifice to Heaven. The idea held by some Naxi that the performance of this ritual is a determining factor in Naxi identity is reflected in the historical relations between local groups in the Mingyin-Baoshan region of northern Lijiang County. While the vast majority of the lineages in that area do perform the ritual, a few do not, and for this reason members of the other lineages have traditionally refused to intermarry with them. While all of these people are now included in the category Naxi, the nonperforming lineages were considered something less than Naxi in the recent past.

32. While I agree that patrilateral cross-cousin marriage and the high status of the mother's brother are important features of Naxi kinship organization, I disagree with Jackson's conclusions. Based on discussions with *dobbaqs,* my own analyses of Naxi kinship, ritual, and cosmology (McKhann 1988, 1989, and 1992) suggest that these features can be adequately explained within the patrilineal framework as it is currently constituted and without recourse to a theory of matrilineal-patrilineal transformation.

Jackson points to the relatively high Naxi suicide rate as another indication of the transition from matrilineal to patrilineal organization. He suggests that with the

In his preliminary study of Mosuo society, Shih Chuan-kang (1985) pays scant attention to the history of patrilinearity among the Mosuo aristocracy. Ignoring Jackson's (1975 and 1979) "forced sinicization" theory and studiously avoiding comment on the evolutionist cast of post-Liberation Chinese interpretation (Zhan et al 1980, Yan and Song 1983), he nevertheless regards patrilocal marriage and patrilineal kinship as adopted practices, linked first to the establishment of the *tusi* system and later emulated by wealthier households from the lower social classes as a kind of "noble fashion" (1985:23).[33]

In yet another interpretation, G. Prunner (1969), following Rock, considers the Na-khi (Naxi) and Hli-khin (Mosuo) as separate yet closely related peoples. On the basis of kinship terminology found in the Naxi ritual texts, Prunner argues that the Naxi have always been patrilineal and, in light of the fact that none of the other Tibeto-Burman groups in the region possess similar traits, treats skeptically the claim that the Mosuo are matrilineal. As regards Naxizu religion, Prunner asserts the exact opposite of Jackson, suggesting that the Hli-khin (Mosuo) "have lost the knowledge of pictographic writing" (1969:102). Thus, the impression conveyed is that the Naxi have better preserved some of the characteristic features of a primordial Naxi-Mosuo culture, while it is the Mosuo who have changed.

We are left, then, with the none-too-clear picture that the Naxi and the Mosuo are either distinct peoples, or that they are the same people, but that one or the other of them has gained or lost something over time. Never having done ethnographic research in the Yongning–Lugu Lake region, I am hesitant to comment on the "scientific" validity of the category Naxizu. Nevertheless, I would

establishment of a Han magistrate in the county seat of Lijiang in 1723, the Naxi were forced to follow the Han practice of arranged marriages and give up the system of "free love" reflected in contemporary Mosuo *zouhun* relationships. The transition from "free love" to arranged marriage is argued to have had a negative psychological impact on the Naxi, many of whom have chosen to commit suicide with their lovers rather than accept their parents' choice of a spouse. Considering the lack of historical evidence that Han practices were imposed in this way, and that patrilateral cross-cousin marriage did not exist in Naxi society prior to their incorporation into the Chinese state, this position is untenable. There is certainly nothing "free" about patrilateral cross-cousin marriages, some of which are arranged even before the candidates are born.

33. Shih's doctoral dissertation (1993) contains a more complete treatment of this issue.

like in conclusion to offer some observations on the differing social histories of the Naxi and the Mosuo as possible subjects for future research.

First, although a generic relationship clearly exists between them, I think there is a danger in relying on the Naxi and Mosuo migration legends as a means to reconstructing history.[34] The problem with using these genealogical road maps is in deciding which exit to take. In both Naxi and Mosuo culture, unilineal descent is the dominant metaphor of history, a metaphor which at its limits can and does subsume the universe. In the Naxi myth of anthropogenesis, for example, not only are all Naxi related as the descendants of four brothers, but the Tibetans, Naxi, and Bai (or in some versions, the Han) as separate peoples are also regarded as elder, middle, and younger brothers, and even Earth and Heaven sleep together as husband and wife. The Mosuo myth of anthropogenesis is a little different. Today the Mosuo recognize four matriclans, but claim that there were originally six. In some versions the four apical ancestors of these clans are also regarded as brothers: Mosuo, Tibetan, Naxi, and Han (Shih Chuan-kang, personal communication, 1990). While a comparison of these myths and the rituals in which they occur may improve our understanding of Naxi and Mosuo conceptions of self-identity, I do not think they will get us very far toward writing an "objective" history of the Naxizu.

The relatively recent history of the Naxi and Mosuo is better documented and presents another set of problems. One subject re-quiring further attention is the question of Tibetan influence in the Mosuo area. Just when the Naxi were coming under direct Chinese rule, the Mosuo converted in large numbers to the dGelugs-pa sect of Tibetan Buddhism. The dGelugs-pa monastery in Yongning is to this day populated largely by Mosuo monks, and Shih Chuan-kang (personal communication, 1988) estimates that prior to 1949 as

34. Both sets of legends emphasize migration from the north, recorded as lengthy series of place names leading to present locations. Ethnologists who have attempted to trace these routes have positively identified a few locations in southern Sichuan, but none farther north (He Fayuan, personal communication, 1988). As in the use of genealogical reckoning in contemporary Naxi and Mosuo societies, historical realities quickly give way to mythical ideals. In Naxi society, for example, the disjuncture between the realpolitik of relations between existing patrilineal "bones" and the ideal-ized relations between the four primordial patriclans is nearly absolute: all Naxi can name their clans, but no one can tell you how they know, what it means, or why.

much as one-quarter of the male Mosuo population may have been living the religious life.[35] Conceivably, the large-scale movement of Mosuo men into Tibetan monastic institutions may have produced changes in Mosuo household structure, inheritance, and descent. In the fragment quoted at the beginning of this chapter, Yan Ruxian marvels at the structural diversity of Yongning Naxi (i.e., Mosuo) households, calling it "spectacular both in Chinese and foreign society" (1982:61). But as studies by M. C. Goldstein (1971), B. N. Aziz (1978), and N. E. Levine (1988) indicate, diversity in household structure is hardly uncommon in Tibetan society. Moreover, such variation appears to be especially true for the Kham region, which abuts Naxizu territory. Li An-che notes in one of the few descriptions we have of Kham society:

> Being bilateral in descent (either matrilineal or patrilineal), the Tibetans are not particular whether the male or the female inherits the family line. When girls pass a certain age, say 17, they are free either to marry formally or to accept informally a lover without entering into matrimonial ties. In the latter case, when babies are born they belong to the mother and are taken as such by the society. (Li An-che 1947:291)

Here and elsewhere, Li's discussion of Kham Tibetan society bears a strong resemblance to current accounts of the Mosuo, perhaps even more so if we consider the possibility that the Mosuo "class" system described by contemporary Chinese ethnologists may in some way be related to the system of manors and hereditary land and tax relations in Tibet.

The Mosuo bear other similarities to the Nuosu and Pumi who live alongside them in Yunnan's Ninglang Yizu Autonomous County, where Yongning is located. Before Liberation, the Nuosu (formerly Lolo, now officially Yi) had a similar tripartite class system of aristocrats, commoners, and slaves. The Nuosu prohibited sexual relations (and marriage) between aristocrats and the two lower classes—leading some to dub it a "caste" system (Pollard 1921)—and while the

---

35. There are several Karma-pa lamaseries in the Lijiang area, but they never attracted the local population to nearly the degree that the dGelugs-pa lamaseries did in the Yongning–Lugu Lake region, and were continuously forced to recruit new members from Tibet.

Mosuo did not enforce so strict a separation, the division was nonetheless marked by different rules for reckoning the lineage affiliation of children born of aristocrat–lower class sexual relations, depending on the sex and class affiliations of the parents and on the sex of the child (Shih 1985).

Recent fieldwork by Stevan Harrell suggests an even stronger cultural affinity between the Mosuo and neighboring Pumi (Prmi) groups, with whom they regularly intermarry. In the Yongning area, Pumi religious practices, dress and architectural styles, and patterns of institutionalized sexual relations—including *zouhun*—are virtually identical to those of the Mosuo. Said one self-identified Pumi woman to Harrell (who had taken her as Mosuo): "Pumi, Mosuo . . . it's all the same" (Harrell 1993a:30).

By pointing out these similarities I emphatically do not mean to imply a need to run out and reclassify the Mosuo as Tibetans, Nuosu, Yi, or Pumi. I am simply suggesting that a variety of plausible alternatives to the Morganian theory of Mosuo-Naxi history can be constructed on the basis of the limited historical and ethnographic evidence that we now possess.[36] Although the complexity of Tibeto-Burman kinship systems and their implications for social and political organization has long been recognized (e.g., Lévi-Strauss 1969 [1949] and Leach 1954), our models for understanding them remain inadequate. Roughly equal cases can be made for the positions that Mosuo and Naxi forms of social organization are: (1) essentially unrelated; (2) related as contemporary structural variants (in the manner of Leach 1954); or (3) stand with respect to each other as successive historical transformations. Most of all, we need to look more closely at indigenous Mosuo and Naxi models of cosmos and society, and at the same time divorce our questions

36. Superficially at least, *zouhun* relationships among the Mosuo appear similar to some patterns of sexual-residential relationships found in the West, namely, "visiting" relations in the Caribbean and "matrifocal" households among urban African Americans in the United States. Usually these Western institutions are associated with what are considered "modern" socioeconomic conditions, a well-developed system of class relations in particular. Similarly, the Nayar of Kerala, who had in the seventeenth and eighteenth centuries a family and marriage system very similar to that reported for the Mosuo, were also part of a society with complex class relations (Gough 1961). Because Naxi relationships are also linked to class distinctions (see below), perhaps a better explanation might be found by pursuing this tack and abandoning the evolutionary paradigm.

about structure and history from the antiquated propositions of Morganian evolutionism.

Finally, to return to the politics of the "nationalities question," there is an important point to be made about the way the Mosuo regard their own history and identity. Members of the former Mosuo *tusi* lineage claim direct patrilineal descent from a Mongol officer said to have remained behind after Qubilai's armies swept the area at the founding of the Yuan dynasty. Accordingly, some Chinese ethnologists believe the reckoning of patrilineal descent within the Mosuo aristocratic class to be a Mongol invention. The Naxi have similar legends relating their chiefly Mu lineage to the Mongols, but it is the Mosuo villages just north of Yongning in southern Sichuan that have capitalized on their alleged Mongol ancestry. Virtually indistinguishable in terms of language, custom, and so forth from the Mosuo in Yunnan, these people made a successful bid for Mongol identity. The fact that this group has been officially recognized as Mongols raises a number of issues concerning the identification of minority nationalities in post-Liberation China. First, provincial politics is clearly a factor: groups that "objectively" appear identical may be differently classified on either side of a provincial border. Second, although unrecognized in the Stalinist formula, the case suggests that people's subjective views of identity may be effectively expressed in certain circumstances. Most Mosuo with whom I have spoken strongly object to being classified as Naxi. In Yunnan, this objection has not made any difference. In Sichuan, which also has people classified as Naxi, it has.[37] Perhaps the Mosuo of Yunnan should exploit their "living fossil" status and try to get themselves reclassified with their ancient brethren, the Qiang.

In a well-worn passage, Marx reminds us that "Men make their own history, but . . . they do not make it it under circumstances chosen by themselves" (in McLellan 1977:300). The "circumstances" under which Chinese ethnologists labored during the busy period of nationalities identification in the late 1950s included two countervailing influences. The first was political pressure from a young

37. Whether these Mosuo first attempted to get themselves classified as a separate nationality, I am not sure. One suspects they were fortunate to have plausible (if tenuous) arguments linking them to one of the established minority nationality categories (i.e., Mongol).

government whose ideological program called for the immediate emphasis of class relations and the ultimate de-emphasis of ethnic distinctions. Equally important was the received weight of ethnic categories long ascribed to, validated, and revalidated in the Chinese dynastic histories and local gazetteers. The Mosuo, now Naxizu, constitute one such category.

The History of the History of the Yi

Stevan Harrell

YI AS AN ETHNIC CATEGORY

The question "Who are the Yi?" was much more puzzling to me, a neophyte in Yi studies, than it seemed to have been to most Chinese writing on the subject either before or after 1949. The Chinese, in fact, be they scholars or ordinary southwestern peasants, seem to have always known who the Yi were or, before 1949, who the Lolo were.[1] But to me the answer was not an entirely obvious one. There was, to begin with, considerable diversity within that group of approximately six and a half million people defined as Yi by the Chinese People's Government.[2] For example, I knew that they spoke languages that, while fairly closely related to each other, were by no stretch of the aural imagination mutually comprehensible. *Yiyu jianzhi* (A short account of Yi languages) gives figures of anywhere from 20 to 42 percent shared vocabulary between the Northern Dialect standard (Xide accent) and examples of the other five regional dialects of Yi (Chen Shilin et al. 1984:178). The fact that, after studying the Nuosu language of Liangshan (Northern Dialect, in the official classification), I could in fact converse in that tongue, but could understand nothing of the Lipuo (Central Yi) language of north-central Yunnan, confirmed in practice what I had learned in theory. And when the Lipuo people told me they could understand Lisu (the language of a non-Yi ethnic group) pretty well, but could make no sense of Nuosu,[3] I began to wonder how the Chinese government structured its ethnic categories.

1. There have been a number of names for these people in the Chinese language. Before 1949, the most common were Luoluo (usually spelled Lolo in Western languages), Manzi 蛮子 , Yiren 夷人 , and Yijia 夷家 . Western and Chinese authors alike tell us that the people themselves much preferred the latter two names, considering the former two to be insulting (Lietard 1913:1; Lin 1961:2; Mueller 1913:39).

2. For a general account of the official position, see Guojia Minwei (1984:296–318).

3. This is confirmed by Bradley (1979) who places Lipuo (he spells it Lipo) and Lisu in the Central Loloish subgroup, but Nuosu in the Northern Loloish subgroup. See also my article "Linguistics and Hegemony in China" (1993).

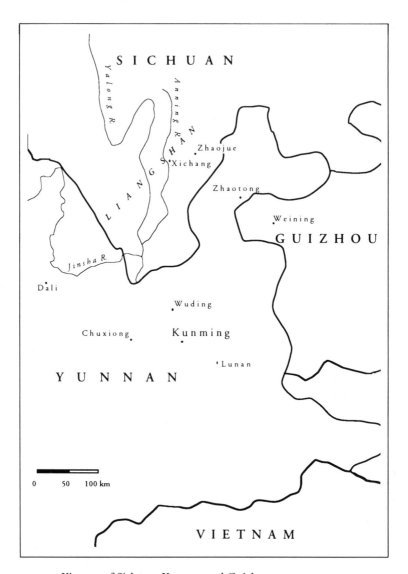

MAP 2. Yi areas of Sichuan, Yunnan, and Guizhou

Cultural diversity was similarly puzzling. The Yi of Yunnan (outside the northwestern corner of the province, anyway), while showing considerable diversity among themselves, still seem to possess some traits in common, such as lowland agriculture, Han-style housing, and patrilocal marriage. But their society is structured on very different principles from that of the Nuosu, or Liangshan Yi, who have neolocal marriage, a highly developed patriclan system, and a structure of social levels (called castes, classes, or strata by various authorities), and who are strictly ranked and stratum-endogamous. And the Yi of Guizhou and northeastern Yunnan seem to have a still different structure. Some Yi have writing and some do not; those who do use similar scripts, but why are those who lack writing classed with Yi and not with Lisu or Hani, other *minzu* that are closely related in certain ways but have no writing system?

And then there are the disputed cases. The Sani of Lunan and Luliang counties, the folks who sell "beautiful bags" around the stone forest and in downtown Kunming, embroider their needlework with the designation Sani *Zu*, or Sani *minzu*, not Yi *zu*. Some of them now claim that they are not in fact Yi (see Swain, this volume). I had the opportunity myself to stay briefly with a group of people in Panzhihua City, southern Sichuan, who call themselves Shuitian *zu* (Rice-field people), though the government classifies them as a branch of Yi. They have no desire to be associated with the people they themselves consider Yi, that is the Nuosu of the surrounding hills, whom the Shuitian consider to be wild and uncouth barbarians (Harrell 1990).

Other foreign observers also have wondered about the boundaries of the Yi category, or drawn them differently from the way they have been officially drawn by the authorities. Lietard, for example, the most meticulous and unbaised of the early observers of the Yi, includes in his list of "Lolo tribes" the Lisu (1913:43–44). Herbert Mueller, in an authoritative summary published about the same time, includes the Woni of Puer and Simao, a group now officially classified as Hani (Mueller 1913:44). He, perhaps with foresight, expresses the Westerner's exasperation with the problem: "Still, it remains difficult to decide which tribes should still be seen as Lolo and which as more separate relatives of this people" (ibid:40). And A.-F. Legendre, a doctor who spent years traveling here and there across Yi territory in Sichuan and Yunnan, is sure that the peoples in this category ought not be classed together: "This time I became convinced that there are numerous tribes in Yunnan attributed as 'Loloish,' even calling themselves such, that have virtually nothing in common, physically or morally, with those [tribes] of Liangshan" (Legendre 1913:392).

Finally, there is the widely attested fact that the Yi themselves have never had a common name that encompasses all the people the Chinese have referred to as Yi or Lolo (Hsieh 1982:1; Vial 1898:24; Mueller 1913:39). Yi and Lolo are thus names applied by others, rather than names originally applied by the group itself; the category of Yi is one that has been constituted by outside observers.

So the problem presents itself clearly not as "Who are the Yi?" which is easily answerable by "Whoever the Nationalities Commission says they are," but rather "How did the Yi get an identity?" The quick answer to the question when phrased this way is "Through the process of ethnic identification conducted in the 1950s, which employed Stalin's criteria of a nationality as having a common territory, language, economy, and psychological makeup expressed in a common culture" (Lin Yaohua 1987; Jiang Yongxing 1985). Again, the Yi were who the Nationalities Commission said they were, according to Stalin's four criteria. But it is clear from reading these retrospective accounts of the ethnic identification process that Stalin's criteria were not employed in any strict manner, but rather to confirm or legitimate distinctions for the most part already there in Chinese folk categories and in the work of scholars who wrote before Liberation. So the question is unanswered: If the Yi already had an identity in 1956, how did they get it?

My reply is that they have acquired an identity, in scholarly circles at least, by having a history. It is generally accepted that groups of people consider themselves, or are considered by others to be, ethnic groups, if they see themselves or are seen as having common descent, and as acquiring certain common characteristics (ethnic markers) by virtue of common inheritance (Keyes 1976; Nagata 1981). Since the category Yi (along with its preceding category, Lolo) was created not by the Yi people themselves but by the Chinese who administered, fought, and interacted with them, and by the Chinese and Western scholars who studied them, it is in the minds of the outsiders that all the Yi have always been assumed to be descended from a common ancestor. And in order to demonstrate this descent, the outsiders, Chinese and Western, have found it necessary to create the History of the Yi. Those who would create or defend the category (including scholars as well as the Nationalities Commission) must first write the History.

But of course the category Yi or Lolo has meant different things to participants in different civilizing projects. To the majority of Western authors, most of whom wrote about the Yi in the early decades of this century, the category was first and foremost a racial one, its history to be found in the migrations of peoples. To most Chinese scholars writing before the establishment of the People's Republic, when the Confucian civilizing project was still implicit even in the modernization and development schemes of various Republican and warlord governments, the category acquired meaning in the context of traditional historiography, of matching names of non-Chinese peoples found in standard histories to the non-Chinese existing in our own time. And to the scholars of the Chinese People's Republic, the category was important in the present as a nationality that met Stalin's four criteria, and in the past as a group that was passing through the five universal stages of human history as defined by official Marxism. For them, the history was one of the development of productive forces and relations, and the Yi were thus defined and scaled as the first step of the Communist project. In each case, the History of the Yi served to show that the Yi category was a valid one, that it consisted of people with common descent, but because of the different ways people thought common descent ought to be manifested, the content of the history was different in each case. Let us examine the history of the History of the Yi as it was practiced by Westerners, by Chinese before the revolution, and by Chinese after the revolution.

WESTERN WRITERS AND THE HISTORY OF THE YI

Westerners were not the first to mention Yi history. There are the written accounts of the Yi themselves, in the forms of genealogies and legendary history (e.g., Zheng 1947; Ma 1985),[4] and there are

4. Many Chinese scholars, such as those mentioned here, have made studies of Yi myths and genealogies. Those who go beyond simple redaction and translation seem always to use these original sources as one sort of evidence demonstrating the historiographic thesis of their own work. Thus the original account of the past, written by the Yi themselves, becomes but a building block in someone else's Yi history. I find this process somewhat suspect, since the myths and genealogies are not really historiographic in nature; they either explain the world (myths) or justify social position in terms of ancestry (genealogies); as such they are concerned either with humanity in general, with the ethnic distinctions between Yi and other peoples, or with the ancestors of specific groups. Unlike the Western and Chinese histories, they do not tell the history of the Yi as a group. In speaking to themselves, then, the Yi have not effectively spoken for themselves; this chapter is in a sense the history of those who have presumed to speak for the Yi.

There is clearly a need for further study of these Yi materials from a less preformed perspective; unfortunately my ability in the written Yi languages is not yet at that level.

mentions of people thought to be the ancestors of the Yi in much of the traditional Chinese historiography, perhaps even from the pre-Imperial *Shu jing* (Book of history)[5] on; certainly from the *Shi ji* (Historical records) of Sima Qian (2nd and 1st cent. B.C.E.) and the two Han dynasty histories. In addition, there are several geographical works dating from various historical periods, such as the *Huayang guo zhi* (Account of Chinese and foreign countries) and the *Man shu* (Book of the southern barbarians), that treat non-Chinese peoples in a somewhat systematic way. But none of these books concerns itself with the project of Yi history: defining a people by delineating its origin and development. The first to address themselves specifically to the project of Yi history were foreign scholars and travelers.

Foreigners had been coming into contact with Yi or Yi-type peoples for centuries; the Yi may even be mentioned in Marco Polo's book. But it was toward the end of the nineteenth century that two events stimulated foreign interest in a project on Yi history. First and more generally, foreign travelers began crisscrossing China, and some of them took particular interest in the borderlands between China and Tibet, roughly the area where the Yi live. The English diplomat and explorer Edward Colbourne Baber traveled along the Anning and Jinsha river valleys in 1877, ringing but not crossing Liangshan (Baber 1882), and several expeditions followed. These included, most noteworthily, those of the French physician A.-F. Legendre, who made and wrote about several trips around Sichuan and Yunnan in the first decade of the twentieth century (Legendre 1905, 1913).[6]

The second development involved the colonization of Indochina by the French; they acquired Annam and Laos as protectorates in 1874 and outright in 1885, and became interested in expanding their presence in China through the "back door" of Yunnan. The railroad from Kunming to Hanoi was begun in 1895 and completed a few years later and, more importantly, French Catholic missionaries, mostly from the Société des Missions Étrangèrs de Paris, took Yunnan as their province, evangelizing both Han and minority peoples (see Swain, this volume). Certain of these missionaries compiled

5. Both Lu Simian, writing in 1933 (237–39), and Chen Tianjun, writing in 1985 (109), equate peoples mentioned in the *Shu jing* with the Yi or their ancestors. See below.

6. An account of the early travelers' and missionaries' writings on the Yi and related peoples is given in Dessaint (1980:27–28); a fairly comprehensive bibliography comprises the bulk of Dessaint's book.

and/or published more-or-less full and detailed accounts of Yi customs, culture, language, and religion. Of the published accounts, by far the most complete and scientific is that of Alfred Lietard (1913) concerning the Lolopo, a Central-Yi speaking group living between Dali and the Jinsha River; the account by Vial (1898) of the Sani (or Nyi or Gni) of Lunan and Luliang is also fairly complete. From Liangshan we have no formal missionary accounts, but several authors, including Lietard and Legendre (1906) derive much information from a certain Fr. Martin, resident for at least eighteen years in Fulin (Hanyuan), outside Liangshan proper but definitely in Nuosu territory, who, according to Lietard, "seems to be horrified by publicity" (1913:18), and thus did not author any published works. Finally, an English missionary, Samuel R. Clarke, lived in Guizhou for several decades and published an account of the local Yi, among other peoples (Clarke 1911).

Western accounts of the history of the Yi continued into the 1930s and 1940s; notable from that period are the synthetic treatment by Feng Han-yi and John K. Shryock (1938)[7] and the chapter on the Lolo in Egon von Eickstedt's massive *Rassendynamik von Ostasien* (1944: 162–78).[8] After the 1949 communist takeover of China, Western scholarship on the Yi seems to have disappeared, with the exception of Bradley's linguistic studies and a brief summary account by Alain Y. Dessaint, until the 1980s, when minorities in China once again become reachable by Western researchers. Some of these, at least, have accepted without much question the now orthodox Chinese History of the Yi (see, for example Heberber 1984:209–10). Things may change in the next few years; some (e.g., Harrell 1989, 1990) intent on calling the whole enterprise into question with critical metahistorical speculations. But at present, the Western chapter of the history of the History of the Yi extends from the 1880s to the 1940s.

What then of the content of the History of the Yi as written by Westerners? The earliest missionary accounts, by those who in fact

7. Despite its Sino-Western joint authorship, this account seems to follow Western rather than Chinese modes of explanation. I thus include it in the tradition of Western studies.

8. Any book published in Berlin in 1944 with *Rassen* in the title is and ought to be suspect. But in fact von Eickstedt's racial theories seem to have less in common with those of Hitler and more with those of Legendre, Feng and Shryock, V. K. Ting (Ding Wenjiang), and other earlier authroities on the Yi.

knew Yi peoples best, tend to rely on native legends and cultural traits in tracing the origins of the people. Vial, for example, deduces from linguistic affinities and Sani legends that the Yi probably came from "the region between Tibet and Burma" (1898:2), led by chiefs of families or clans, of which there must have been two, because of the nature of division of eastern Yunnan and northwestern Guizhou Yi society into Black (landlord) and White (subject) dialect and culture groups (*tribus*). There in eastern Yunnan, he says, the Lolo had a kingdom, which endured until it was conquered in the third century B.C.E. by the First Emperor of the Qin dynasty. He says little of the later history. Lietard's account follows a similar course: he sees the Lolo as originating in northwest Yunnan—as attested to by the similarity in language, culture, and customs with Tibeto-Burman peoples (1913:58)—and as having formed the population of the state of Dian in the second and first centuries B.C.E., a state whose king was, in all probability, "a Loloized Chinese" (ibid.:55). The Cuan lords of Yunnan in the sixth and seventh centuries were likely also Lolo kings of Chinese origin. When the Nanzhao polity was formed, most of its subjects were Yi, but the king was from the Minjia (today called Bai).

In the accounts of these missionaries, very little about race or physical characteristics is used to explain Yi history. But in the accounts of scientists, natural and social, we find an explicitly racialist paradigm, one that derives more from the scientific impulse of generalization and systematization than from the intimate knowledge and desire to describe accurately that seem to have motivated the missionaries. For these scientists, beginning with Legendre and in rudimentary form even with Baber,[9] the History of the Yi is the history of a

9. Baber did not feel himself qualified to engage in the History of the Yi. He says:
> What the Lolos are, whence they have come, and what is their character, are questions to which I can only make a very incompetent reply; and it must be premised that it would be very unfair to draw a definite general conclusion from a small number of scattered and embarrassed inquiries at points round their frontier. (1882:66)

Nevertheless, he expresses little doubt that they are a distinct race:
> They are a far taller race than the Chinese; taller probably than any European people. . . . They are almost without exception remarkably straight-built, with slim, but muscular limbs. . . . Their handsome oval faces, of a reddish brown among those most exposed to the weather, are furnished with large level eyes. (1882:60)

For more on Baber's place in the history of Orientalist scholarship, see Swain (this volume).

race, built on a series of unexamined assumptions, probably part of the "habitus" of Western culture, about the nature of ethnic or social groups. The first of these assumptions is that there are, inherent and inherited in groups of people, certain traits of personality, culture, and even economy that persist over generations. The second is that these inherent and inherited *cultural* characteristics correlate more or less exactly with inherited *physical* characteristics. The third assumption is that there is such a thing as a pure race, a physical-cultural combination that originated who knows when (but far enough back in the past that we don't need to worry about it) and has persisted through the ages, at least in those places where the race has remained genetically pure. Corollary to this third unexamined assumption is a fourth: that mixed races are different from pure races, and that when members of these pure races intermarry, not only physical features, but cultural ones as well become blurred, mixed, undistinguishable. Hence there are no cultural characteristics that "belong" to these mixed races; in order to trace these people's origins, one must sort out the original, pure elements that went into the mixture.[10]

Examining the accounts of Legendre, Mueller, von Eickstedt, and Feng and Shryock will give us a feel for how these racialist assumptions shaped the history of the Yi as seen by foreign scientists. Legendre was the first to do "physical anthropological" studies on the Yi; when he traveled to Hanyuan he took cephalic indexes of some people introduced to him by the modest Fr. Martin. From these and from measurements in Yunnan, he determined that the current Lolo population in fact came from three strains. There was an autochthonous strain, represented by Tai and Mon-khmer peoples, that was short, dark, brachycephalic, "a Polynesian race very low on the human scale" (1906:399): the Negrito. Mixed with this was the Chinese, the Mongoloid type, which had entered Sichuan and Yunnan early in the historical era. And then later, there came the Lolo. The original Lolo strain, which was related to Caucasoid peoples of central Asia, was "un

10. Without knowing much about it, this seems to me to resemble the assumptions that lie behind the "scientific" reasoning justifying the apartheid system in South Africa, as well as the current general discourse about South Africa in the Western press. "Colored" is defined as "mixed-race" in articles in the Western press, implying that there is, once again, a "pure" African type and a "pure" white type. The same kind of assumptions also seem to be inherent in the American idea that one can be "half Italian" or "three-sixteenths Cherokee," statements that, I know from experience, are nonsensical to Chinese, who are either one thing or another.

type supérieur" (1906:477): tall, high-nosed, dolicocephalic, with broad shoulders, erect carriage and perfect proportions.

In Legendre's account, the Lolo of his day in Sichuan and Yunnan were in fact very different because they represented mixtures of these races. In Liangshan, where the Lolo remained unconquered and unmixed with the other races, they retained not only their racial purity but their original cultural characteristics; they were warriors, bold and sometimes treacherous, ready to counter their invaders to the point where the Chinese, to whom Legendre concedes superior intelligence, had to overcome the Lolo slowly and peacefully (ibid.: 478–79). In Yunnan, however, the people the Chinese call Lolo are hardly worthy of the same designation. These people were mostly Mongoloid with some apparent mixture of Negrito or autochthonous blood, with none of the fierceness or love of vendetta found among the Lolo in Liangshan. They were peaceable, resigned, capable of submitting to all yokes (1913:391). From this Legendre derives the conclusion that there is in fact no unity to the Lolo, that the latter is a category imposed by the Chinese, one with no justification in the scientific facts (1913:392). As a Westerner, he doubts the category; as a man of the early twentieth century, he does so on the grounds of racialist assumptions about the relationship between what he calls "physical and moral" characteristics.

Mueller, in a synthetic article written around the same time, is willing to give more credence to Chinese sources, at least of the traditional historical kind, and is less extreme than Legendre in rejecting the connection between northern and southern Yi. Even he admits that physically and culturally, the Lolo of Liangshan and those of Yunnan have little in common, though linguistically, he says, there is more justification for placing them all in a single category (1913:48). Since he is unwilling to give up the category Lolo altogether, he reconciles the physical and cultural differences by attributing to the Yi of Yunnan great mixtures with other peoples, both in (Thai) blood and in culture, and keeping those of Liangshan as a relatively pure type (ibid.:50–51). These, he says, must have come from the north or northwest; by the Former Han (206 B.C.E.–9 C.E.) the historical sources mention people in Yunnan who bind up the hair on their forehead into a kind of horn; because of the similarity to today's Yi in Liangshan, one can suppose that these were Yi, as were the later commoners of the "Thai-Reich" of Nanzhao from the ninth to the eleventh centuries (ibid.:48–49). Mueller thus manages to retain both the unity of the Yi category and the assumption that race and culture are united, even if this is hard to see when mixing of one sort or the other has occurred.

Von Eickstedt, whose data for his comprehensive work include visits to Liangshan and other areas of China, presents a similar picture, but with the further wrinkle that the difference between Black and White (aristocrat and commoner) castes in Liangshan is also attributable to racial differences. His historical scheme goes like this: The Lolo and the Miao-Yao peoples were originally part of the same group, Europid (sic.) peoples of Central Asia who were driven from their homelands by droughts in the first millennium B.C.E., and who then settled in the high plateaus of northeastern Tibet. From there, however, they were compelled by population pressure to move again into the still largely empty lands to the south (1944:174–75). This meant, of course, that they first settled Liangshan, and it is in Liangshan that the aristocratic Black Lolo preserve the true nature of that race:

> They doubtless make up the true core of Lolodom, counting as bold, rapacious, hospitable and open, accustomed to war and ready to fight, and are full of hate and distrust toward the Chinese, while they in no way bow before Europeans.

> Bloody feuds, killing, thievery, and unmitigated greed rule here, but also love for their noble beasts and consideration for women. (ibid., 168)

Among the White Lolo, who are ordinarily the descendants of captured Han slaves, as well as among the Lolo of Yunnan, however, little of that lawless martial tradition remains; they are basically a Mongoloid type, or at best a mixture of these with true Lolo, and retain little or nothing of the Black Lolo system of social classes or their former pastoral economy.

Such attention to racial factors may not seem surprising in a German writing during the Nazi period, or even in a Frenchman or German writing before World War I. But Feng and Shryock's account of 1938, written by an American and a Chinese in the time of Franz Boas and Melville Herskovits, seems more surprising: although it, like Mueller's account, relies on culture as well as race, it seems to assume that the two naturally go together. In the first place, they use data from Legendre and V. K. Ting to argue that Black and White Lolo were racially different: the Blacks were a conquering group of a single racial stock, while the Whites were subjugated peoples from a mixture of different stocks. Due to pressure from the Han, Blacks in Yunnan in recent centuries have been decimated or driven northward, and remain only in a few areas (presumably, but not explicitly, the northwest of the province) (Feng and Shryock 1938:107–108). Exactly how this happened is hard to know, since it is difficult or impossible to match the names of former peoples found in Chinese historical sources with the ethnic groups that must have existed at the time: "Because of the presence of other tribes, it is often hard to tell whether a mentioned tribe was Lolo or not" (ibid.:108). In other words, there *were* Lolo all through history, but we can't tell whether particular sources were talking about them or somebody else. The Cuan peoples of the Northern and Southern Dynasties (311–589) and early Tang (618–c.740) period were, according to Feng and Shryock, of mixed ethnic stock: while the Eastern Cuan were definitely Lolo, the Western Cuan were probably composed of several different ethnic groups. The authors can conclude only that Cuan was a political, rather than ethnic, category; the conclusion I draw is that for the authors, an ethnic group is a racial and/or cultural, but not political, group (ibid.:117). At the very moment Feng and Shryock were working out this analysis (and not far from Yi territory), Edmund Leach was studying the Kachin.

If the later History of the Yi, as presented by Feng and Shryock, is clear in its outlines if not in its details, the Yi's origin and early history are still matters for speculation. Feng and Shryock dismiss theories based on language, because of insufficient knowledge, and concentrate on the two characteristics they think most salient: race and culture. They discuss at length racial theories propounded by Legendre, V. K. Ting, and others, all of which connect the Lolo to Iranian or other Central Asian, Caucasoid types. In the end, though, they find these theories inconclusive (ibid.:126). They then go on to consider cultural hypotheses, noting that there are affinities to Mongols and other north*eastern* Asian peoples in the use of felt, the lack of pottery, and the possible division into Black nobles and White commoners. But contrary evidence comes from the fact that the Lolo, while they keep herds, do not use milk; thus they must not have originally been a pastoral people, and the origins in northern Asia thus seem questionable (ibid.:126–27). In the end, Feng and

Shryock, unlike many analysts, do not put forward a pet theory of their own. But they do hold to the assumptions about the importance of race, and about the enduring nature of a group, with its own racial and cultural characteristics that persist across the ages.

CHINESE HISTORY OF THE YI BEFORE 1949[11]

As mentioned above, traditional Chinese scholars did not engage in the History of the Yi project in any systematic way. When they began to take up the project, many did so as part of an international ethnological or ethnohistorical community, so that their scholarship did not evolve entirely independently of that of their Western colleagues. But there are definite differences of emphasis that reflect the fact that whatever methodological influence the Chinese scholars may have received from the West, they were still engaging in a project derived from a purely Chinese assumption: that Lolo or Yi was a real category. For the Chinese scholars, such an assumption is not explicit; rather it is part of their conception of the world from the beginning, something that is not examined and does not have to be. Thus we do not find, as among the Westerners, any speculation that the Lolo might not be a single people after all; rather, the assumption is that the category is real and the task is to find out how the people got where they are today.

In addition to this paramount assumption of a real category, there are other characteristics that distinguish the Chinese approach from the Western. Closely connected to the first assumption is the premise that the categories with which we deal are very old; certainly by the time historical records appear, the Lolo were already in existence. Another important assumption is that names hold the most important key to unlocking the secret of the Lolo's origins and history. If one can correlate the names of peoples living at different epochs, as described in traditional historiographic works, with the peoples known to exist in our time, one has solved the puzzle: in a sense one has traced the Yi through their history, which is a branch of History with a capital H, which stands for Han. A final important assump-

---

11. My analysis in this section must be considered more tentative than that in the two other chapters of the Yi History's history; this is because it has been very difficult to find representative Chinese sources, and I have thus relied somewhat on the summaries of various people's work found in Hsieh Shih-chung (1982).

tion, not nearly so prominent in Western works, is that cultural differences among various Yi groups are due to differential exposure to a higher, more advanced Han culture. In the service of this eminently Chinese project, scholars of the Republican period (1911–1949) used many of the tools used by their Western counterparts: they paid attention to race, to character traits, and to cultural practices. But the fundamental assumption remains that of the real category, which can be traced through history. Let us examine briefly some of the tracery.

One of the earliest accounts is Lu Simian's *Zhongguo minzu shi* (History of the peoples of China), in which each chapter covers a category of people named in the early histories, whose descendants could presumably be traced until the 1930s, when the book was written. For example, describing the history of the peoples in West and Southwest China, there are chapters on the Miao and the Qiang. The Yi are treated in the chapter on the Pu, which begins: "The Pu are also called the Pu, and in addition called the Pu, and today are known as Lolo. They are also one of the large races of the Southwest" (Lu Simian 1933:237). The Pu, a name that goes as far back as the *Shu jing* and the *Zuo zhuan*, in the first millennium B.C.E., were a group found in Yunnan by the time of the Han dynasty, but who had earlier been spread out over Henan, Hubei, Hunan, Guizhou, Yunnan, and Sichuan. They were forced out of their eastern territory, but later formed the Yelang kingdom in Yunnan. After that, they appear again as the rulers of the Eastern and Western Cuan, whose black *man* (barbarian) and white *man* inhabitants correspond to the Black Lolo and White Lolo of today (ibid.:241).

This account is in some ways the most purely Chinese of the sources I examine here: it begins with a name from ancient historical sources, assumes that the group named existed even earlier, and traces the group through to the present. It says little about cultural traits; its main interest is in the history of the assumed category.

Another explanation, by Jiang Yingliang, also relies on historical documents, but comes to completely different conclusions. According to Jiang, who visited Liangshan in 1941, but did not publish his results until seven years later, the Yi夷of Liangshan have an even longer history. The earliest mention of these people is in historical accounts of the Zhou dynasty (1048–250 B.C.E.), which, even before it conquered the Shang, was having trouble with peoples, variously referred to as Rong and Man, who belonged to the Qiang groups. From the time of the earliest Zhou rulers to that of You Wang, the last king of the Western Zhou, there were frequent attacks from the Qiang, which eventually forced the Zhou to move their capital eastward from Changan to Luoyang. During the Spring and Autumn period (771–481 B.C.E.), the Chinese kingdoms of Qin, Han, and Zhao all attacked and defeated various groups of Qiang, who were forced to move westward. After this, they dispersed into areas in the Sichuan-Gansu border region. The Baima people, for example, as described in the *History of the Later Han,* showed such traits as manufacture of felt and legal protection of women, traits they hold in common with the Yi of Liangshan today. From here the Qiang/Yi people moved farther south, until by the end of the Northern and Southern Dynasties they occupied most of the territory east of the Tibetan massif, south of the Chengdu plain, and north of modern Kunming.

The continuity of these peoples, according to Jiang, was broken up in the Sui (581–618) and Tang dynasties, when they were dispersed, some of them becoming the various peoples of the Tibeto-Burman family found today, some assimilating to Han language and culture. Only those remaining in Liangshan, because of their lack of contact with the outside and their independence from government rule, have preserved their primitive social conditions (Jiang Yingliang 1948b:20–22).

Jiang's account, unlike Lu's, is interested in cultural traits and linguistic relatedness, but it basically follows the same Chinese strategy of assuming that the cultural unit in question is very old (in this case, at least three thousand years), equating its identity with that of non-Han peoples described in traditional Chinese historiography, and tracing cultural differences at least partly to differential contact with advanced Han civilization.

Another account from about the same time, by Zeng Chaolun (1945), follows this basic pattern but includes more factors in its explanation and gives an even clearer picture of the distinctive Chinese approach to the History of the Yi. The Southern Yi 夷, as mentioned by the poet Sima Xiangru of the Han dynasty, are the base group for Zeng. Unlike the Miao, originally a lowland people forced out by the Han, the Yi have always occupied the entire Liangshan region (ibid.:94). Where they came from is not certain, but racial and linguistic factors seem to point to affinity with the Tibetans, since the Yi language, like those of Tibet and Japan, has an "inverted word order."[12]

The differences among various groups of Yi are also explicable by history, according to Zeng. The majority of the Yi in Yunnan, for example, are so sinified that their original customs and habits have almost completely disappeared (ibid.:95). It is only in Liangshan, where the Yi have lived undisturbed and unacculturated for thousands of years, that one can find the pure, unadulterated Yi culture.[13] There the Yi are divided into tribes, by which Zeng seems to mean something like clans, each of which has its own character traits: some friendly, some hostile, some strong and some weak, some treacherous, ruthless, or fierce, some more gentle (ibid.:96–97). It is also in Liangshan that the "social class" division into Black aristocrats and White commoners is found; although we cannot prove that this existed among the other branches of the Yi, Zeng thinks that it did, and was abandoned under Han influence (ibid.:95). The system, as it is found in Liangshan, seems to be a relic of the "outmoded feudal system," and is something that ought to be abolished. At the same time, Zeng sees the slave system as providing more security for the *wazi* (captured Han slaves) than the tenancy system provides for tenants in the Han areas (ibid.:112).

Zeng's account, like Lu's and Jiang's, traces the Yi from a known historical people, and although he does not correlate the Yi at every step of their history with some people mentioned in the books (his main purpose, after all, is ethnographic rather than historical), we can still see the basic assumptions of descent from an ancient people with a name and an essence, and of influence by "superior" Han culture as the explanation for any internal contradictions or differences among Yi groups. Zeng's criticism of the "outmoded feudal system" is also characteristic of Chinese accounts. Scholarship on

---

12. Zeng does not suggest, however, that the Yi might therefore be related to the Japanese. Perhaps this is because the Japanese, unlike the Tibetans and Yi, are not presumed to be part of China. I did find that thinking of or in Japanese helped me a lot when I was trying to internalize syntactic structures of the Nuosu language. I also heard a rumor from Chinese friends in 1988 that there had been a Japanese anthropologist trucking around the Southwest doing blood groups and other tests looking for the origin of the Japanese people among the Yi.

13. Lin Yaohua's 1943 account, which is almost entirely ethnographic, nevertheless stresses the same point: the Yunnan Lolo are acculturated, and only in Liangshan can one find the true culture (1961:2).

Chinese minorities in this period is often rather applied in nature; it assumes not only Han superiority, but superiority of modern institutions over traditional ones.

Such a vision of Yi history as a branch of History seems to have been all pervasive in pre-1949 Chinese ethnology and other scholarship. For example, Wei Huilin (1947), in an article concerned with reform and community development in Yi areas, prefaces his remarks by reciting the historical names of the Yi people, starting with the Lu and Luo of the Spring and Autumn period, and running through the Xi, Kunming, and Qiongdu of the Han, the Nanman (Southern Barbarians) attacked by Zhuge Liang in the Three Kingdoms period (222–265 C.E.), the two Cuan of the Southern Dynasties, the Nanzhao and Wuman of the Tang and Song (960–1279), the Wuyi and Luolouman of the Yuan and Ming, and the Luoluo of the Qing. Many other examples, each deriving the modern Yi from a slightly different succession of ancient groups, are mentioned by Hsieh Shih-Chung in his 1982 study. And while the particulars of these hypotheses differ, as does the evidence they use, they all hold to the position that an ethnic group has existed over the long haul from the times of earliest historiography to the present.

THE REVOLUTION IN THE HISTORY OF THE YI AFTER 1949

The history of the History of the Yi since 1949 is much longer than either of the earlier two episodes. There are two reasons for this. First, there has been much more official and scholarly attention paid to minorities generally in the People's Republic than was paid to them earlier; the national policies of jural equality as well as integration into a "united, multinational state" certainly have a lot to do with this. The result is the second reason, that simply a lot more is known about the Yi and their history than was ever known before. In particular, more Yi-language manuscripts and stone inscriptions have been found, and scholars have begun to take seriously accounts that were previously dismissed as unreliable legends. Also, there have been many archaeological studies, and, as with the trends in Chinese history, archaeology and legends have been correlated into a much more detailed and coherent picture of the past. If a neophyte (even more neo than I) asked me for a recommendation on what to read about Yi history, I would certainly recommend a PRC account over either an older Chinese one or one from a Western pen.

But PRC history is, of course, no more "objective" than is earlier history from China or history written by Westerners. It too has its purposes and assumptions. One of the purposes of this modern History of the Yi is carried over from its Republican predecessor: to document the integrity of the category and show how it has persisted through time in spite of the changes that the Yi have gone through. But added to this is another element, which is at the same time a purpose and an assumption. This is the construction of the History of the Yi, like the history of everything else, according to the five stages of history laid out by Soviet historiography: the stages corresponding to the primitive, slave, feudal, capitalist, and socialist modes of production. Added to this is the breakdown of the primitive stage into matrilineal and patrilineal phases, following the plan laid out by Lewis Henry Morgan (1985[1877]) and distilled by Friedrich Engels (1883).[14] Adopting the five-stage model of history and Morgan's model of the primitive stage makes possible a much more complete and detailed History of the Yi. This is primarily because the five stages of history are defined in terms of their forces and relations of production, and the substages of the primitive stage are defined in terms of the particular social structures. So source materials that were formerly ambiguous or difficult to interpret can be made clear; details can be filled in. Most importantly, cultural traits, only hinted and guessed at in previous kinds of history, can now be supplied by inference from what we know must have existed when the Yi were at a particular stage. The result is a History of the Yi that for the first time contains fairly detailed reconstructions of the culture and social structure of the Yi in premodern times.

14. These universal formulations of the laws of historical development are taught in Chinese schools and colleges as fact, not as theorizing or speculation or anything that is the opinion or particular intellectual property of any single school of thought. Perhaps the best analogy from the West is the teaching that the solar system consists of nine planets, extending outward from the sun in the order of Mercury, Venus, etc. One might at some time discover another planet, which would have to be inserted in the order somewhere, but this would not disturb the basic fact that planets go around the sun in roughly concentric orbits. Similarly, one might argue, for example, that there was an Asiatic mode of production, or even that some societies under some conditions could skip stages of history. But this would not invalidate the basic, "objective" laws of historical development that say the development of productive forces leads societies through a series of universal and uniform stages.

Morgan's model (if not the five-stage model of history) has recently been challenged as the work of a bourgeois idealist that bears no relation to Marxist dialectical reasoning. See Tong (1988).

Other assumptions in the modern History of the Yi carry over from the Chinese model of the prerevolutionary period. The existence of the category, basically unchanged from very early times, is of course still assumed, and the formulation of the history acts to justify the boundaries of the category, just as the boundaries of the category define the scope of the history. This is reminiscent of the dialogue between history and legitimately traced by P. Steven Sangren (1988) in his analysis of temples in Taiwan: as with the Yi as an ethnic category, the present defines the scope of the history, and the content of the history legitimates claims made in the present.

Another carryover assumption is that internal cultural, linguistic, or even mode-of-production differences between different branches of the category are to be explained not by any kind of original differences, but by the effects of different kinds of environmental and acculturational influences. Those branches of the Yi that had more contact with Han culture (now defined not as inherently superior, but rather as farther along in the five-stage developmental scale) are likely themselves to be more developed. Those whose natural environments were more favorable are likely to have developed further on their own. And any branches with characteristics more like Han society than the corresponding characteristics of other branches are assumed to have undergone acculturation toward Han culture. In other words, what is Yi is assumed to be whatever is most different from Han; other variations are assumed to be the result of Han influence.

Finally, race is out; language and culture are in as the primordial characteristics that originally define a group and constitute its basic essence.

The interaction between the definition of the category in the present and the formulation of the history is a constant and seamless one, but for the purposes of this analysis it is easier to look at it from one side at a time. I will thus first describe briefly how the category Yi was formulated in the process of ethnic identification, which used history as an important guide to identification. I will then describe at somewhat more length how, given the category that was now official and buttressed by historical evidence, the more complete History of the Yi has been written by different authors.

Long shrouded in silence, the process by which the ethnic identification process was actually done has now become the subject of a few articles (Lin 1987; Jiang Yongxing 1985). The announced method was first to ask social groups that thought themselves to be *minzu* to make application to the authorities; in Yunnan 260 groups submitted their names. After this, teams of specialists in culture (led by Lin Yaohua) and in language (led by Fu Maoji) would investigate the validity of the claims according to the standard of Stalin's four criteria (Lin 1987:1). But in fact the investigators ended up using the criteria very flexibly. In particular, they found that the third criterion, a common economic base, was not a characteristic of very many *minzu* in China. We can see this with the Yi; according to official histories, Liangshan was still in the slave stage of society in 1950, while Yi areas in Yunnan and Guizhou had passed into feudalism hundreds of years ago. But, argued the identification teams, the criteria delineated by Stalin were based on what happens in capitalist society; "the common economy of areas where many *minzu* lived together linked together different *minzu,* but it did not eliminate their respective ethnic characteristics; the result was that the existence of a common economy was not obvious in any *minzu* area" (Lin 1987:2). What this says, it seems to me, is that the identification teams already had their categories in mind; when Stalin's criteria went against the pre-existing categories, the pre-existing categories took precedence.

There were, of course, problematic cases, small groups that claimed independent *minzu* status, and whose claims had to be investigated. Several of these were people who spoke Yi languages; Lin gives the example of two groups that reported themselves as Tujia (no relation to the officially recognized Tujia *minzu* of Guizhou, Hunan, and Hubei) and as Menghua. About 170,000 people reported that they were Tujia; another 40,000 claimed to be Menghua. Investigation teams first determined that the Menghua and Tujia were the same; the Menghua were Tujia who had migrated south from Menghua County, and 76 percent of a sample of one thousand vocabulary items were the same. Then, ethnographic investigations disclosed that this Tujia group (including the former Menghua) had

> retained many common Yi [cultural] features, such as clan-elder systems, surname exogamy, levirate, remnants of cremation, ancestral spirit platforms, polytheism, and magical arts. In addition, they could intermarry with Yi. For this reason, the Tujia and Menghua were determined to be a branch [*zhixi*] of the Yi. (Lin 1987:3–4)

This description of the actual process reveals the presence of several of the abovementioned assumptions about ethnic groups. The Chinese investigators already knew what Yi meant; not fitting Stalin's criteria was no serious impediment to declaring them a *minzu*. In addition, when there were problematical cases, language and culture traits were examined in order to determine where these people fit. Common vocabulary items indicate a genetic relationship between languages, that is, a common linguistic history. And common cultural traits are always spoken of as "retained" (*baoliu*). That is, there is the presumption that all Yi had common traits in a primordial past, and that any group with any of these traits has retained them in the face of acculturative pressure (rather than borrowing them, for example), as well as the converse proposition that progress comes from contact with the outside rather than from the people's own internal development.

All along, there has been a stated principle that the process of ethnic identification should not be carried out by fiat, but that the wishes of the people themselves ought to be taken into account. But, as admitted in Jiang Yongxing's 1985 retrospective on thirty years of identification work, this principle was not followed. Jiang states, in fact, that one of the reasons why there are so many unsolved ethnic identification problems in the Southwest is that identification work has consistently overemphasized historical kinship (*lishi shang de xueyuan lianxi*) and underemphasized the wishes of the ethnic peoples (*minzu yiyuan*) (Jiang Yongxing 1985:309–15). This critique, I think, strikes at the heart of the matter; the wishes of the ethnic peoples cannot always be made to coincide with the pre-existent Chinese category, while history can usually be formulated in such a way that the category remains intact (see McKhann and Diamond, this volume). This seems to be the reason why most remaining problems of ethnic identification involve groups that want to break away from the larger (Han or minority) *minzu* in which they have been classified, rather than independent groups who want to be amalgamated with a larger *minzu* (ibid.:304).

The process of ethnic identification was thus little threat to the category Yi (which, by common consent of representatives of many branches, was the name adopted for the whole group); history had been used in the formulation of the category, as had linguistic and cultural commonalities, both inferred as demonstrating a common history. This did not mean, however, that the definitive History of the Yi had been written. Of course there was and still is a lot more to find out, in the sense of strictly empirical facts. What the completion of ethnic identification did mean for history was that any serious historical treatment would have to contribute to the demonstration that history was something common to the whole category. In addition, history would have to show how the category or branches thereof passed through the five universal stages.

All this has resulted in a richer, more complete, more detailed history, and one in which differences among branches of the category must be explained in terms of differential experience rather than any kind of primordial or essential separateness. This does not mean that there is a single, official, orthodox history, without any disputes. There is, on the contrary, still no agreement about where the Yi originated. What is agreed on is that wherever they originated, they *all* originated there and diverged afterwards.

To illustrate how the History of the Yi looks under modern conditions, that is, assumed unity of the category, progress through the five stages, and explanation of differences in terms of differential environmental conditions and varying degrees of Han influence, I will recount in some detail the story as told by one historian. Since I have read only one full-scale history, Ma Changshou's *Yizu gudai shi* (Ancient history of the Yi), I will use it as the example, keeping in mind that some of Ma's positions, particularly regarding the origin of the Yi, are still quite controversial.[15]

Ma Changshou's Account of Yi History

The first topic treated in Ma's history is the nature of primitive society among the Yi. The only sources available for investigating this question are Yi traditions, which are available in two forms: books of stories about the creation of the world, and recitations of genealogies at festivals, war councils, and so forth. From these sources, we can tell that the first, or matrilineal, stage of Yi primitive society was longer than the patrilineal stage; this is because many Yi genealogies recite twelve "dynasties" at the beginning of the world; of these, only the last two show the characteristic Yi pattern of

---

15. This is the same Ma Changshou who, in a work written in 1930, advocated the theory of descent of Yi from the ancient Lao. His methodology is considerably changed here under the influence of the new way of writing history.

"father-son linked names" (*fu zi lian ming*), in which a man's second name becomes his son's first name. That the Yi were matrilineal in late prehistoric times is also confirmed by the legend of Asu Awo (a Chinese transcription of a Yi name) looking for his father. Briefly, this is the tale of a man who was born in the old days, when people "after birth knew their mother but not their father." Asu Awo went looking for his father, but was not successful until a spirit told him to perform ancestor worship. After this, paternal grandfathers and grandsons, as well as fathers and sons, knew each other. This is a story of the transition from matrilineal to patrilineal descent in the later stages of primitive society (Ma Changshou 1985:1–2).

The next question is where and when this happened. The key figure in all this is a man called Zhongmuyu in Chinese, or Zzemuvyvy in Yi, who is acknowledged by all Yi and some Hani to be their common ancestor. If we figure the numbers of generations in genealogies, we come up with about eighty, which at twenty-five years per generation comes to the Former Han dynasty (ibid.: 10). With regard to the place, Zzemuvyvy is referred to in Yi manuscripts from as far afield as Liangshan and parts of Yunnan as living in places that can tentatively be located near Kunming; in Guizhou manuscripts, his abode can be located in northeastern Yunnan, near present-day Zhaotong. Therefore we can posit an early migration of the Yi from central Yunnan toward the northeast (ibid.:5–7).

After Zzemuvyvy in many Yi manuscripts come the six ancestors (*liu zu*). Since their names do not link with Zzemuvyvy, the chances are that they were more than one generation after him; anyway, legend has it that the eldest pair were the founders of clans who settled in the south (near Kunming again), the next pair founded clans that settled in the north (near Zhaotong), and the youngest two established clans that settled in the east (in northwestern Guizhou) (ibid.:9). At the time of the formation of the clans, the Yi had not yet divided into classes; that is, they were still in the stage of primitive society. But interclan fighting, especially involving the eldest two clans, which had settled in the south, resulted in the enslavement of war captives, which, according to Engels, was the origin of the slave system, the second stage of history and the first to involve class divisions (ibid.:12–13).

By the Later Han period, then, the Yi had populated most of eastern and northeastern Yunnan, as well as northwestern Guizhou. It remained for them to enter Liangshan. Those who did so were members of one of the middle pair of clans, called Heng (Yi, He) in Guizhou and called Guhou in Liangshan. These clans, it will be recalled, were originally settled in northeastern Yunnan; some of them remained there and became the historical Pu. Others either stayed in the area, moved to Yongning in the extreme south of Sichuan, or combined with the other of this pair of clans to form what would become most of the aristocratic Black Yi clans of Liangshan today (ibid.:14–15). If it sounds complicated, it is. The point is, it all fits together: Yi traditions, Chinese history, the five stages, and, most importantly, all the branches of the Yi come into one coherent account.

When the clans moved from the east into Liangshan, they subjugated the natives; this probably happened between the end of the Han dynasty and the first few decades of the Tang. The subjugated natives, referred to as Puren, Tulao, and other names that may correspond to modern Xifan and Naxi, as well as another group which is now extinct, all became the commoner subjects of the Black Yi clans; they are thus ancestral to the White Yi of present-day Liangshan society (ibid.:19–22). Not only the Yi category, but also the Naxi and Xifan,[16] can be traced through history in this way.

The next question Ma takes up is the formation of the slave mode of production. This probably happened first in Yunnan: we can see from the Dian bronzes of the early Han period that there was a slave polity existing in central Yunnan at that time. Many of the scenes show masters or mistresses and slaves, the latter sewing, spinning, working in the fields, or, in one very striking casting, about ready to be the victim of a human sacrifice. That this was slave labor is beyond doubt, since lots of people are working together, and we know that labor is more individualized under the later feudal system. These slaves all appear from their costumes to be of different *minzu;* from the specific nature of their clothes or hairstyles at least four of the eight identifiable *minzu* are probably Yi. The slave system was thus established in all the Yi areas at least by the Three Kingdoms period (ibid.:39–49).

Generally characterized, the period of the Later Han and Three

16. Xifan (most of whom seem to be speakers of languages related to Qiang) are one (or several) of those problematic groups that have never acquired official status as a *minzu;* theirs is probably the only case where scholarly circles openly and consistently disagree with the official classification, which locates almost all the Xifan as a branch of the Tibetans.

Kingdoms was characterized by competition between the slave system of the Yi and the feudal system of the Han; from the end of the Three Kindoms to the beginning of the Tang, a time in which the Chinese polity was weak in the Southwest and had very little influence on Yi society, was the period of consolidation of the slave system, culminating in the establishment of the Nanzhao kingdom, itself a polity based on the slave mode of production (ibid.:54–55).

This stage of the development of slave society was the period of dominance of the Cuan. Cuan was originally the surname of one of the biggest slaveowning families in Yunnan; later it came to be applied to the people under this and other families' rule. Most historical sources speak of the Wuman (Black Barbarians) of the Eastern Cuan and the Baiman (White Barbarians) of the Western Cuan; the question debated by historians is the connection between these and the later Black and White social strata in Yi society. According to Ma (this is still a disputed issue), there is no direct correspondence. The Baiman, living in the Western Cuan area (roughly between Kunming and Dali) were influenced early on by Han society, especially after the opening up of the trade route from Chengdu through the Anning River valley after Zhuge Liang's southern expedition in the third century C.E. In the fertile plains of this area, they developed irrigated agriculture and a flourishing economy, and also adopted many features of Han culture and society. In the Eastern Cuan area, by contrast (in eastern and northeastern Yunnan), development proceeded more slowly because of a less favorable natural endowment and less contact with progressive (feudal) forces; here the slave system became consolidated. It is clear that the Eastern Cuan were the Yi; the Western Cuan seem to have been of several sorts, of which at least one was the ancestors of the modern Bai people (ibid.:69–73).

The Nanzhao kingdom, established in Yunnan in the eighth century, was the inevitable result of the development of the Yi slave polity to a certain degree. Nanzhao was a multi-ethnic polity; it is still under dispute who the rulers of the first, or Meng, dynasty were; the subsequent Qi, Yang, and Duan ruling lineages were definitely Bai. The social system, although possessed of some feudal influences already, was basically a slave polity, in which the ruler gave land to lords of different ranks. According to the *Man shu*, "After the harvest is over, the barbarian official [*manguan*] divides the grain according to the population of the tenant households; what is left over is transported to the official" (quoted in ibid.:80).

87

Ma points out that this demonstrates that there was no fixed amount that was due to each household, but rather the slavelord gave the slaves just enough so they wouldn't starve. This was reminiscent of Liangshan before the Democratic Reforms, when the slaves were in an equally oppressed position.[17]

During the Nanzhao period (740–973) and the time of the subsequent Dali kingdom (973–1283) there were a lot of migrations of peoples, many of them part of royal schemes to settle or defend various areas, others the result of people fleeing the control of the central authorities. In general, in the Dali kingdom there was more and more development of the productive forces, more and more influence of feudalism (ibid.:91–94). But the transformation was not complete until the conquest by the Mongols in 1283, when Qubilai issued an order prohibiting the capture of slaves in northeastern Yunnan, and when the Central Asian general Sai Dianchi distributed land and tools to conquered Yi peoples, showing that the tenants, who had no land or tools previously, were still working under the slave mode of production.

The Yuan period represented the real watershed for the Yi in Yunnan. The area was once again, for the first time since the Later Han, a fully integrated province of China, and Han migration into the area, as well as economic development in terms of trade, mining, and intensified agriculture, brought about the complete triumph of the feudal system there (ibid.:96–97). In Liangshan, on the other hand, the slave system persisted until 1956, though it, too, was not devoid of feudal influences, especially in the Qing dynasty around the peripheries of the area. Here the slave system persisted under the rule of *tusi* (native officials) during the last three dynasties. In Liangshan, unlike Yunnan, land was poor and trade routes inconvenient, so the productive forces were unable to develop. The result was that the Ming and Qing governments retained big slave-owning clans as *tusi,* and did not try to alter the social system in the area (ibid.:106–108).

17. All post-1949 sources on the Yi stress the cruelty of the slave system and the constant but doomed revolts of the slaves against it. This contrasts with pre-1949 statements by Lin (1961 [1947]) and Zeng (1945) in which the situation of slaves in Liangshan is compared favorably to that of Han tenants. There seems to be an implicit moral scale in the Chinese Marxist conception of the five stages of history, in which things are worst right at the beginning of class society, with the establishment of the slave system, and then get progressively better with feudalism, capitalism, and socialism.

But even in Liangshan there was influence from Han society. During the Ming and Qing periods, there was a gradual encroachment of Han peasants and feudal land relations, especially in the peripheral areas around the Anning Valley. The result was that the big *tusi* became more and more agents of the central feudal regime, and less and less representatives of the slaveowning class. This in turn led to revolts in the late Ming, and the replacement of *tusi* in the core areas of Liangshan with independent rule by local slaveowners (ibid.:110–12). In more peripheral areas, however, the feudalization of society continued, so that prominent Black Yi often had two kinds of dependents at the same time: Yi slaves and Han tenants (ibid.:116–18).

Other Accounts

As was mentioned above, Ma Changshou's account, written in 1959 but not published until 1985, is not without its controversial points: in particular, the ethnic identity of the Nanzhao rulers is still a matter for lively discussion (see Qi 1987), and the Yunnan origin of the Yi is disputed by those who think they came from the Northwest. With regard to the latter issue, a recent article by Chen Tianjun (1985) demonstrates even more clearly than Ma Changshou's book the power of the five-stage and Morganian historical schemes. According to Chen, the origin of the Yi goes back further, to the San Miao of classical History, who were always fighting against the Xia dynasty (c.2200–1600 B.C.E.). These San Miao most likely lived in the middle reaches of the Yangtze River, whence some of them were driven westward into modern Qinghai, where they amalgamated with local peoples to become the Qiang. The San Miao were already patrilineal when they fought the Xia, which means that the matrilineal-patrilineal transition recorded in the Yi genealogies and in the story of Asu Awo looking for his father probably happened between four and five thousand years ago in that area (Chen Tianjun 1985:109).

The Qiang, in turn, according to Chen, were driven out of their homeland in the Northwest by pressure from the Qin in the fourth and third centuries B.C.E. (see Jiang Yingliang's account, above [1948b]); they fled south along the Tibetan marches to the later homeland of the Yi in Yunnan. Their patrilineal clan society lasted until this time, and the Yi show up again as the Kunming, a tribal people harassed and eventually enslaved by the Dian kingdom, which was dominated by the Pu. Under the influence of the Han dynasty, with its opening up of salt and mining industries in Yunnan, the Yi passed from the primitive to the slave stage (ibid.:112–13).

In this account, we can see the slave-feudal transition occurring at three different times in the three different areas of Yi settlement. In Yunnan, it came earliest, at the time Nanzhao was taken over by Dali, while it persisted in Guizhou and northeastern Yunnan until the Ming period, and in Liangshan, in modified form at least, until the 1950s (ibid.:114–17).

Both in Ma Changshou's account and in Chen Tianjun's, the five stages of history are a unifying force. They not only make sense of what would otherwise be ambiguous statements in old historical records; they also explain why, in modern times, people as diverse as the Lipuo, Sani, Menghua, and Nuosu can be shown to be nothing but varieties of a single category Yi, distinguished from each other by nothing but unequal rates of development through those stages ordained by the objective laws of historical development. We even find the Yi following the basic patterns of development *within* the feudal stage: a recent article by You Zhong shows how, in areas of heavy Han influence, the overthrow of *tusi* in the late Ming and the replacement by officials appointed from the center represent the transition between the earlier substage of manorial feudalism and the later stage of the landlord economy, which was the status of most of Chinese society in the late centuries of the Imperial era (You 1987:190–92).

DISCUSSION

The History of the Yi thus has its own history; in the hands of different kinds of writers the Yi have acquired very different kinds of histories. I am not here to judge the varieties against one another. I think that in each case, the historians have known what they were going to write before they even did the research for their history. Westerners were interested in races; Chinese before 1949 in correlating the Yi History with the Capital H–History; and Chinese after 1949 in using objective and universal historical laws to lend legitimacy to an ethnic classification (see Litzinger, this volume, for a comparable case among the Yao). And in each case, they did a fairly good job, that is, they produced internally consistent histories that explain what they set out to explain: in each case, who the Yi are and how they got to be that way.

Again, though, the outsider finds himself a bit disturbed by this. Is a relatively ideologically neutral History of the Yi possible? Could one write such a history with an agenda that was neither racialist nor nominalist nor orthodox Marxian? What would an observer who studied Yi society anew from an ethnographic perspective, visiting communities and interviewing local people in Liangshan, Guizhou, and many parts of Yunnan, and then reading the classical sources and the Yi traditional manuscripts, come up with? Would such an observer find a unified group, a Yi category that was internally consistent? A series of related peoples with different, though perhaps related, histories and only remotely similar societies? A native history and a history created by outsiders, or several histories created by outsiders? It is difficult to predict, since it is difficult if not impossible to write the History of the Yi over again from scratch. Since 1956 the category Yi has come to exist not only in the minds of Han scholars and administrators, where it has always been, but also in the administrative and budgetary plans of the Nationalities Commission and the provincial governments, and increasingly in the minds of the various kinds of Yi, who learn their own history and culture not only through native ceremonies and recitations of genealogies (which, as we see, can easily be shown to support the orthodox, unified interpretations), but also through the curriculum of the schools. They too have come to be Chinese, and as such their history has become part of Chinese history. And Chinese history, now as in the Imperial era, belongs to and is defined by the ruling orthodoxy. Under this orthodoxy, though there may be disagreements about specific points, *minzu* have already been defined, and the Yi are a single *minzu*. Any future historian of the Yi must take this into account.

Defining the Miao
Ming, Qing, and Contemporary Views
Norma Diamond

Although the Miao are one of the "nationalities" currently recognized within China's borders, whether the close to seven and a half million people currently categorized as Miao constitute a nationality (a single ethnic group) is somewhat problematic, as are earlier usages of the term Miao (lit., "sprouts," "seedlings," and in some usages, "weeds") to indicate a number of disparate indigenous peoples distributed across Southwest China. Populations referred to as Miao are located in Guangxi, Guizhou, Yunnan, Sichuan, and, according to some current writings, in Guangdong and Hainan as well. Linguistically and culturally some of these groups are related to the Hmong (Meo) of Thailand and Laos.

What constitutes a *minzu* is still a matter of debate. Indeed, many pages have been devoted to that question over the past decade. In 1986, three issues of *Minzu yanjiu* gave space to the various papers presented at a symposium on nationality theory (see nos. 4, 5, and 6). Much of the discussion concerns what Stalin said or meant to say by his criteria of common language, territory, economy, and psychological characteristics or sentiments—criteria that have not been consistently applied in granting official recognition, but that continue to be a part of official discourse on ethnicity. In the case of the Miao, it is difficult to see how any of them apply.

SPATIAL DISTRIBUTION

The Miao are scattered over several provinces, their communities interspersed with those of other minorities and Han Chinese settlements. As a result, there are a number of autonomous prefectures (*zhou*) and

I would like to thank the Luce Foundation, the Wang Foundation, and the Center for Chinese Studies, University of Michigan, for financial assistance that made this research possible. For their cooperation and assistance, I am indebted to the Yunnan Academy of Social Sciences, the Central Nationalities Institute in Beijing, and the Oriental Manuscripts Department of the British Museum Oriental Library.

MAP 3. Major Miao groups, showing some concentrations of Hmong (or Hua Miao, Qing Miao), Hmu (or Hei Miao), and Xioob (or Hong Miao)

counties (*xian*) in which Miao constitute one of several minority groups. In most of these, the term Miao does not even appear in the name of the territorial unit. In a few the Miao are named in conjunction with one or two others, as in Qiandongnan Miaozu-Dongzu Autonomous Prefecture in eastern Guizhou or Weining Yizu-Huizu-Miaozu Autonomous County in western Guizhou. The exceptions are Songtao Miao Autonomous County at the northeastern tip of Guizhou, Pingbian Miao Autonomous County on the southernmost border of Yunnan (which, despite its name, is shared with Yi, Yao, and Zhuang), and Chengbu Miao Autonomous County in southwestern Hunan, shared with Yao, Zhuang, Dong, and Hui. Large numbers live outside these regions, some within recently recognized *minzu xiang* (nationality townships), which are usually multi-ethnic and in which Han Chinese form the majority population. In some instances the Han numerical dominance is of fairly recent origin.

MIAO LANGUAGES

Just as there is no territorial unity among the Miao, there is no linguistic unity either. Though some publications continue to refer to the Miao "language," regarding all variants as "dialect," more informed and recent linguistic scholarship suggests that there are at least three major Miao languages (*fangyan*) within the Miao branch of the Miao-Yao language family. These divide into a number of distinct sublanguages or dialects of varying degrees of closeness (Wang Fushi 1985:103–106). The Xiangxi languages of Hunan, with some eight hundred thousand speakers, have two divisions, which Wang terms "dialects" (*tuhua*), the larger of which has been provided with pinyin romanization for school texts and other publications. The Qiandong languages found in central and eastern Guizhou break into three subdivisions: the largest, with over a million speakers, has its own pinyin system, while the other two, with over half a million speakers, do not. Most problematic are the Chuan-Qian-Dian languages, a category that seems to be a repository for everything that does not fit into the other two. It has over two million speakers living in Sichuan, Yunnan, and Guizhou. The seven subdivisions are themselves refered to by Wang as *fangyan,* suggesting that the distance between them is more than that of "dialect." These in turn are, for the most part, divided into *tuhua,* in several cases as many as four. Until recently, pinyin texts and publications were available for only one of the Chuan-Qian-Dian languages. In the early 1980s, persistent lobbying by speakers of the Diandongbei *fangyan* (formerly known as Hua Miao [Flowery Miao]) in the Yunnan-Guizhou border area led to the recognition of a second romanization system and the creation of a set of school primers. It replaced an outlaw phonetic writing system known as the Pollard script that the Hua Miao had devised early in this century with the assistance of Christian missionaries (see Cheung, this volume). The language, which has some 250,000 speakers, is said to be surprisingly uniform across western Guizhou and eastern Yunnan, perhaps due to the continued use of the writing system in churches and schools over a period of fifty years and in house churches (private Christian worship groups) and private use for another thirty years.

Beyond these, Wang Fushi lists another eight dialects spoken in Guizhou, which have several thousand speakers each and which may be related to Chuan-Qian-Dian. In brief, there is great diversity within that category, and the various "dialects" are not mutually intelligible since they are in some cases heavily influenced by other languages. Miao speakers in Sichuan, Yunnan, or western Guizhou may have as much or more difficulty understanding each other as in understanding Miao speakers from eastern Guizhou or Hunan. He Guojian (1982) suggests that the Xiangxi and Qiandong languages have about a 42 percent correspondence in vocabulary, but between them and the third division the correspondence is no more than 28 percent, some of that due to fairly recent borrowings from Chinese.

ECONOMIC DIVERSITY

Given the geographical spread, it is also difficult to speak of the Miao as having a common economic system. Climate, altitude, and access to markets and transport vary. The usual generalization is that the Miao are mountain dwellers formerly engaged in a self-sufficient economy based on slash-and-burn farming of hardy dryland crops, varying from upland rice to cold-weather crops such as buckwheat, oats, corn, and potatoes and supplemented or even overshadowed by hunting and forest gathering. While there is a grain of truth here, that description cannot stand as a general statement describing all local Miao economies throughout the Southwest over the past several hundred years.

The reliance on oats, buckwheat, and the New World crops of corn and white potatoes seems to be a recent adaptation as groups were pushed higher into the mountains by the pressures of state military actions and settlement by Han colonists. If this description were applied to the mountain-dwelling Hua Miao during the nineteenth and twentieth centuries, we would have to add that raising sheep and goats for market sale was also a core part of the economy. Moreover, most Hua Miao were tenants of powerful Yi nobles who had been enfiefed by the Chinese state, and less often the tenants of Han and Hui settlers. Few Hua Miao communities existed outside the wider feudal system. Their rental obligations involved crop payments; labor service in agriculture, forestry, and transport; and the forced growing of opium. Furthermore, they were tied to local market systems, dependent on selling furs, wool, hides, livestock, and a variety of forest products to local Hui and Han merchants. In this exchange, they purchased items they were unable to produce themselves, most particularly salt, sugar, metal tools, rice, pottery, and cotton cloth.

In contrast, the Miao near Guiyang (the Cowrie Shell [Haipa] Miao) were valley dwellers whose main crop was rice grown in flooded fields. Spring wheat and subsidiary crops of tobacco, beans, maize, millet, and vegetables rounded out the agricultural cycle (Mickey 1947:11, 29–40). Relative ease of transport and travel, and population density allowed for the proliferation of periodic markets, at which the local Miao were active in the sale of their agricultural produce and livestock (mainly pigs and poultry) along with specialty handicrafts, firewood, and expensive delicacies such as bamboo shoots and water chestnuts. Some Miao in the area were artisans, merchants, and shopkeepers (ibid.:41–45). In short, their economy was very similar to that of their Han and Chung-chia (Bouyei) neighbors, and aside from their crafts specialities of woven hemp cloth and grass raincoats and sandals, there was nothing to distinguish their economic activities from those of other peasants in the area. Mickey says nothing directly about land tenure but gives the impression that these Miao peasants were mainly small landholders rather than tenants.

The economy of the Miao of Congjiang County in the mountain regions of southeast Guizhou will serve as our final example. De Beauclair (1960) insists on calling this group Sheng Miao and referring to them as born hunters, but her own data paint a different picture. Though *sheng* here is meant to suggest that they are "raw" (i.e., uncivilized), they grew rice in terraced irrigated fields wherever possible, and dryland crops where it was not, supplemented by hunting and exploitation of forest resources. Most in the community she investigated in the 1940s were tenants to local Han or Bouyei landlords or served as hired laborers for the landholding Buddhist monasteries in the area. A later research report under the auspices of the State Nationalities Commision (Guizhou-Hunan Shaoshuminzu Shehui Lishi Diaochazu 1958) focuses on a cluster of mountain villages in the same county and similarly describes them as wet-rice farmers, with dry rice, corn, potatoes, and millet grown on higher fields. Markets were widely separated so that most households attended only bimonthly and relied on peddlers and merchants (mostly Han) who traveled in circuit throughout the area purchasing pigs and poultry and selling a variety of daily necessities. The Miao economy differed from that of the Han in lineage and hamlet ownership of large tracts of mountain and hillside lands that could not be sold to individuals or used by outsiders. Some land was household property and could be inherited by daughters as well as sons, but the report suggests that much of the land in use was in fact communal property, with members of the community having use rights. Labor exchange between households was very common, and households with a labor shortage relied on this and on hiring day labor rather than renting out land. The report notes that even those who were classified as landlords during Land Reform in the early 1950s rented out only 7 to 20 percent of their holdings. Moreover, landlords customarily worked in the fields themselves, often putting in more work than did the day laborers they had hired (ibid.:49–53).

These cases are cited to suggest some of the regional variations and to underscore the point that the Miao, like others, were participants in localized multi-ethnic economic systems whose members shared some features in common and who were at the same time distinguished from each other by specialized production and activity. Sometimes there was a ranked ethnic hierarchy of wealth and power, with the Miao usually towards the bottom. There was no pan-Miao economy: the Miao, depending on location, were interdependent with neighboring groups, not with Miao hundreds of miles distant.

CULTURAL DIVERSITY

Establishing evidence of common psychology or sentiments is even more problematic, since even recent work by Chinese researchers has tended to focus on economic organization, social organization, history, local customs, and traditions, but has not addressed such issues as socialization, worldview, values, symbolic systems, personhood, or similar topics that might lead to valid generalizations about shared cultural behavior and meanings that distinguish the Miao from other groups. One runs across generalizations to the effect that the Miao are "brave" or "hardworking" or "conservative," but such statements tend to be made about all ethnic groups in China today.

During the recent debate on nationality theory the concept of "culture" has been introduced into the Stalinist framework, though it is usually phrased as "customs and traditions" (*fengsu xiguan*) since "culture" (*wenhua*) carries overtones of "civilization." Thus, each nationality is identified by the presence of various customs that differ from those of the Han and/or from those of neighboring ethnic groups. The key markers are those most easily observed and described: house styles, costumes and jewelry, hairstyles, handicrafts, unusual foods, and some of the exotic activities and rules surrounding marriages, funerals, and festivals. These fill many pages of recent ethnographic writing on the Miao, yet if the various accounts and glossy photographs are compared, the issue becomes muddled rather than clarified. A recent prohibitively expensive volume on Miao women's clothing and ornaments (Zhao Yuchi et al. 1985) arranges the materials into five major models, which are further broken down into twenty-three distinctive regional styles. There is some overlap, of course. A number of groups favor short pleated batik skirts, as do some non-Miao peoples. Others wear long skirts or trousers and would not recognize the pleated short skirt as proper Miao attire. Some groups (the ones most frequently shown on television) wear elaborate silver headdresses for festivals or marriage ceremonies, but most do not. The variations in dress and adornment are at least as great as those in language. There is also considerable variation reported for house design, preferred foods, and the observable content of marriage ceremonies, funerals, and festivals. Other aspects of cultural and social life are less well documented for specific local populations. Discussion in the literature generalizes from one to all in regard to kinship terminology; norms and permitted variations of household organization, courtship, and marriage; inheritance patterns; religion; ethnomedicine; and the performing arts. Selective cultural features that are by no means universal are taken as the "special characteristics" (*tedian*) that mark the Miao as a group. There is great reluctance to address the considerable variation among the dispersed Miao populations or to admit that some of the chosen markers are shared with non-Miao peoples, as for example the playing of the *lusheng* (reed-organ pipes) or cattle sacrifices.

Summarizing the work done on identification of the nationalities, Fei Xiaotong notes that the Miao populations, dispersed over a wide area, show considerable differences as well as similarities. But he accepts the assumption of a common origin and argues that they have been referred to as Miao for a long time by others, and therefore consider themselves to be one people (Fei 1980:62–63). Even so, after 1950 some local populations that were called Miao by their Han neighbors and had accepted that designation as a way of identifying themselves to outsiders, took on new minority identities as Shui, Dong, or Tujia. This could be justified on linguistic grounds: Tujia is related to Yi, and Shui and Dong are related to Zhuang. Others were told by the scholar-experts that they were the descendants of Han military or civilian households settled on the frontiers during the Ming or Qing period, and therefore were disqualified from minority status despite some *tedian* shared with the Miao and some striking

differences from their Han neighbors. Whether, after this houseclean-
ing, the remaining Miao groups really regarded themselves as the
same nationality or ethnic group is unclear.

Most current scholarly writings on the Miao state that they all
originated from a common center of settlement around Dongting
Lake in Hunan and are the *miao* and even the *man* referred to over
the centuries, forced westward by the advance of the Chinese empire.
The offered proofs rest heavily on variant origin myths and on the
generalizations of Chinese dynastic histories and local gazetteers,
which used the term Miao loosely. For those now included in the
category, linguistic and cultural diversities are explained as the end
results of migration and scattering of the population, new ecological
adaptations, borrowings from new neighbors, and cultural drift, particularly in the past few hundred years. In an argument used to deny
claims of separate identity by any of the component groups, or claims
to being the original inhabitants in an area, these are seen as devia-
tions from the "real" Miao culture.

Variations in present-day cultural practice are regarded as having
resulted from relatively recent changes from some imagined model of
Miao culture. As a 1987 volume on Guizhou costumes explains:
"They vary even among people of the same ethnic group owing to
their differences in locality, custom, and habit. Those who live on
plains and valley areas prefer long skirts and loose jackets with broad
sleeves, whereas those high on the mountains wear tight clothes with
narrow sleeves and short skirts or trousers. The 2.6 million Miao
people in the province are scattered in the various mountainous areas
in all parts of the province and their differences in location can easily
be distinguished through their garments and hair styles, as well as the
designs, colors, and composition of the decorative patterns on their
kerchiefs and clothes" (Huang Shubao and Liu Zhonghe 1987:7–8).

MIAO AS A CHINESE CATEGORY

The general term *miao*, referring to a culturally and linguistically
diverse category of non-Han peoples, dates back to early writings,
such as the Han period *Shi ji* and *Zhanguo ce*, in which it referred to
peoples of the wild southern regions, inhabitants of a San Miao
kingdom said to have existed around the third century B.C.E, and
other pre–Han and Han dynasty states or tribal confederations. In
the Ming period the term was applied to many indigenous peoples of

the new southwestern frontier, and used interchangeably with *man* or *yi*. All three terms meant "barbarians," and did not refer to any self-defined ethnic group. Through the Ming and Qing dynasties, *miao* came to be modified by more specific terms to distinguish between local populations. Late Ming and Qing gazetteers from the Yunnan-Guizhou area and other writings (see below) attempted to classify the different "barbarians" in the region. The *Yanjiao ji wen* (Notes on the southern frontiers) of 1558 favored a simple division that distinguished between the Raw (Sheng) and the Cooked (Shu) Miao, meaning the unassimilated barbarians as opposed to those who were sinicized and therefore more civilized. The latter lived nearer to Han centers of settlement or military outposts, came under the control of the state or the appointed local *tusi*, and had taken on some Han customs or at least relinquished some of their own customs that were offensive to Han sensibilities. The Raw Miao resisted assimilation, pacification, and state control (You 1985:289). In later decades, the classification would become far more complex, but it still retained Raw Miao as a particular category.

The 1741 *Guizhou tongzhi* (Guizhou provincial gazetter) names and describes thirteen different kinds of Miao, citing materials from a Kangxi period (1661–1721) gazetteer and other sources, while adding new information. The text lists the counties or districts in which each group can be found (there is some overlap) and then goes on to describe dress, features of economic and material life, and some of the unique or exotic customs that characterize them and justify putting them in separate groups (You 1985:690–96). Miao subgroups are distinguished from subgroups of Yao, Kelao, Mulao, Songjia, Longjia, Zhongjia, and others in the region. In general usage the term Miao continued to designate the indigenous non-Han peoples. In other Qing texts, it refers less to shared ethnicity than to the shared "barbarianness" of all of these indigenous peoples. However, the gazetteers and the "Miao albums" that derive from them recognize that not all barbarians are Miao, and continue to refine the distinctions within the larger Miao category.

Locality is a defining feature, but it is cultural traits that distinguish the various Miao from the Han, and along some dimensions differentiate between Miao and other ethnic groups. The texts record perceived differences between Bai Miao (White Miao), Hei Miao (Black Miao), Qing Miao (Green Miao), Hong Miao (Red Miao) and Hua Miao who are distinguished by the dominant color of some part of the women's costume, but dress is not the sole consideration. Certain cultural features are highlighted, particularly those that stand in contrast to the Han culture of the times. It is noted that some groups lack a system of surnames that parallels Chinese practice or have only a few "surnames" among them. Some do not bury their dead in coffins, and those who do celebrate the funeral with drumming and singing rather than with the order and content of prescribed Han ritual. They fail to keep ancestral tablets, and their offerings to the ancestors involve animal sacrifices and rituals led by shamans. It is often mentioned that women industriously weave and spin, but they do not bind their feet; they participate in agriculture and even in hunting, and they wear improper and immodest dress. Among some groups, marriage is said to be by parental arrangement and the use of go-betweens, but this is rare. Many of the entries highlight the sexual freedom of young men and women, which takes the form of dances by moonlight, assignations and premarital sex, and marriages arranged by the young people themselves. A few groups are praised for having learned to speak and even read Chinese and for adopting some proper Chinese customs. And, not unexpectedly, such peoples are usually described as tractable and obedient to the law, while the less assimilated are seen as fierce by nature, quarrelsome, and in flight from the authorities.

The odd ways of the peoples of Guizhou and Yunnan became a focus of a genre of books that Western scholars refer to as "Miao albums" since the term Miao appears in most of the titles. These began to appear in the early eighteenth century and continued on into the mid-twentieth century. The format is a collection of paintings or block prints, each with a descriptive text that derives primarily from the Guizhou gazetteer materials, sometimes shortened and sometimes elaborated. The artist may have added a short poem. Each depicts a different group, as defined by the gazetteer classification. It is questionable whether most of the artists had ever traveled extensively through the Yunnan and Guizhou frontier areas, let alone spent any time in the Miao communities. At best they may have seen some of these peoples in towns, markets, or along the roads and then, relying on available texts and/or access to other "Miao albums," let their imaginations take over to highlight a special marker discussed in the text.

What is missing, at least in the dozen or so albums I have examined, is any indication that these peoples live in organized communities.

The scenes usually are set in the wilderness or outside an isolated homestead, and only occasionally inside a dwelling. All lack the villages and towns that are a mark of civilization. Wilderness scenes give not even a hint of a village nearby, and homestead scenes give no indication that there are neighbors. The sylvan wilderness here is not to be confused with the landscapes of Arcadia in Western art—the wilderness of nymphs and shepherds, saints and Madonnas, and members of the aristocracy playing at the rustic life. Nor are these the landscape paintings of the Chinese literati, with scenes of scholar-poets sipping tea at a country retreat or journeying through the mountains. The inhabitants and wayfarers in this wilderness are barbarians, following strange customs in remote places. The occasional Chinese traveler seems to be undertaking a lonely and perilous journey.

These albums usually include some eighty-two different groups, but some cover half that number or less. Though the term Miao appears in the title, some of the plates are identified as Kelao, Lolo, Longjia, Songjia, or Yiren. The majority are presented as Miao subgroups. The pictures tend to be stereotypical. There is variation in artistic style and in the arrangement of figures and elements of scenery; they are not direct copies from a model volume. But the basic content and message of the illustration rarely varies. For example, the recurrent theme for the Hua Miao is a scene showing several young men and women dancing to the pipes out in the wilderness. The number of dancers may vary, but rarely is there an audience. The standard picture for the Yao Miao (not to be confused with Yao) shows one or two young couples meeting for sexual dalliance at a crude hut out in the countryside. In some versions, one couple is already inside engaged in lovemaking, while a second young woman entices a passing man to join her. The Sheng Miao are represented by one or two couples on a hunting trip. The Hong Miao are said, in the text, to have a fierce nature, and the usual picture shows two women trying to restrain their armed male companions from getting into a physical fight. Each painting thus highlights a special characteristic of the group in question, as suggested by the accompanying text and elaborated on in other albums. In the volumes that present all eighty-two groups, at least ten emphasize the quarrelsome and dangerous nature of these peoples (be they Miao or one of the other ethnic groups), with scenes of armed men embarked on hunting or banditry, or engaged in fights among themselves. Another ten focus on sexual license, with variants on the theme of young men and women meeting in the wilderness to dance, sing, drink, or repair to the nearest shelter for further intimacies. Several depict the nuclear family journeying through the wilderness.

A large number show economic activities: farming, hunting, and fishing scenes that usually include both men and women, or homestead scenes focused on women weaving and spinning. Whether afield or at home, the family is small in number, and even scenes showing religious rituals involve few people. The impression given is that not only is village community absent, but even the lineage or extended family is a rarity. There are no scenes of local markets.

In virtually all the albums, the women appear far more attractive than the men. Their faces are rounded and smiling, their complexions lighter despite their exposure to the elements; they are uniformly beautiful unless they are wrinkled old women. The men, however, usually have coarse, even cruel, faces, and their skin is dark, no matter what their age. If there is resemblance to the Han, it is to Han of the lowest classes. However, the encoded messages are ambiguous in regard to the women. Despite their lovely faces, they fall short of the ideal. The pictures emphasize their large natural feet and the shamelessness of their dress. The Duan Qun (Short-Skirt) Miao women are the worst, as the name suggests: they wear mini skirts that barely cover the buttocks when standing, and that in some albums show a hint of genitalia when sitting. Blouses expose part of the midriff. The present-day descendants of this group, the Miao of the Leigongshan region of eastern Guizhou, do have short skirts, worn with a long apron or as a topskirt over a series of longer ones of varying length, according to photographs from the 1930s and the more recent compendium on clothing and ornaments of the Miao (see Zhao Yuchi et al. 1985:70ff.). But all but the longest skirts were probably shocking to the Han observers of the time, as were the tunics with open necks and short sleeves worn by women in different localities.

In addition to showing the oddness or impropriety of dress and looseness of morals, the Miao album pictures and gazetteer texts highlight wherever possible the occurrence of reversal of proper gender roles: among the Nong Miao men are expected to care for infants, among the Bafan Miao women do most of the agricultural work, and in several groups men and women join together in farming, raiding the fields of others (presumably Han settlers), or hunting. Of course some groups have a more proper division of labor, just as some wear longer skirts or go abroad unarmed. But that is less interesting and so the marked differences are highlighted in the illustrations.

As suggested earlier, there are groups in the Miao albums who do not appear in the 1741 *Guizhou tongzhi*, on which many of the album texts are based. I have not been able to locate additional text sources for these. The groups concerned tend to be described as unpacified, dispersed, or declining. For example, the Hei Sheng Miao are described as having been a treacherous and aggressive people. But one Miao album assures us that in 1725 about half of them were killed and the rest surrendered, while another album, clearly of later vintage, reassures the reader that in 1736 they were conquered once and for all (see Clark 1883:387; Bridgeman 1859:265).

It is necessary to bear in mind that the spread of Chinese rule into these areas was hardly a peaceful one. The Miao and other groups put up considerable resistance, and as government control became more firmly established in the early eighteenth century the state pursued an active policy of conquest and pacification (see Jenks 1985:94–99). Many local groups put aside whatever quarrels they had and made common cause against government authorities, sometimes joined by disaffected Han of the lower classes and even some disillusioned members of the higher strata of local society. Identifying the non-Han peoples by categorizing them in terms of their degree of assimilation and willingness to cooperate with the state or submit to state rule was at least as important as underlining the features that marked them as barbarians and justified expropriation of their lands and dispersion of the population or even its annihilation.

The so-called "Miao rebellions" continued well into the nineteenth century, as did concern with accurately identifying the various groups. The *Qiannan zhifang jilüe* (An official description of Guizhou) (see Lin Yaohua translation [1940–41]), which dates from the 1840s, was compiled by Luo Raodian, a scholar-official who served as governor of Guizhou and Yunnan in the early 1850s. Some of his earlier assignments were of a military nature, including direct involvement in defense work and supression of several uprisings. His section on the Miao-Man is not completely original. As Lin points out, it draws heavily on the work of Luo's immediate predecessors in the government offices and on a number of eighteenth-century texts, as well as on his own observations (Lin 1940–41:266–70). Despite potential access to first-hand data, he relied heavily on earlier texts and made no attempt at a wider or deeper description of the various

groups. Like the gazetteer and album compilers, Luo is more concerned with the exotic features of each group. However, he attempts
to reclassify the earlier material, noting that some of the groups are
not unique but only localized populations of some larger entity. For
example, he identifies the La Pa Miao as a part of the Hua Miao
group, and the Shan Miao as an upland version of the Hei Miao,
thus reducing the Miao categories down to some seventeen or eighteen subgroups from the ballooning numbers. The Hei Sheng Miao
disappear completely in his classification, though they linger on in
the Miao albums. In his view there are five main groups (Bai, Hei,
Hong, Qing, and Hua) who internally distinguish themselves by the
major color of their clothing. He says little about language, focusing
instead on some of the cultural features that separate these groups, as
well as on those seemingly shared in common which justify classing
them as Miao. Another five groups are then identified as mere subgroups of one or another of these larger units, and four more are
described as so sinicized that it is hard to place them. This still leaves
him with some leftovers: the Caijia Miao, who he feels are people
transported to the frontier during the Spring and Autumn period
who have "become Miao," the very primitive Eastern Miao, and the
Western Miao, who are more sinicized but still show signs of their
original culture. What is interesting in this work is the view that
adoption of Han language, clothing, surnames, and a number of
customs is not sufficient to change Miao into Han, though taking on
Miao characteristics can change Han into Miao. Perhaps this was a
reaction to finding assimilated Miao and disloyal Han within the
rebel forces.

During the Qing period, it was only the more "advanced" groups,
such as Mongols, Tibetans, Hui, and the Turkic peoples of the Northwest, who came under the Court of Colonial Affairs (Lifan Yuan)
and whose hereditary elites were granted court titles and received
confirmation to rule in their areas. For the nationalities of the Southwest, some were more equal than others. That is to say, the elites of
some groups were absorbed at the lower levels of the government
hierarchy and given an official title, with power to collect taxes and
keep the peace (*tu guan* system), or were designated as *tusi* with
hereditary succession of office. In the Miao areas of northeastern
Yunnan and northwestern Guizhou, these posts went to leading
members of the Yi nobility, and the system continued up until the
Republican period or even beyond. For the Miao areas over the rest

of Guizhou, western Hunan, and Guangxi, where there was increased Han immigration and settlement, the minorities were, by the late Qing, under the rule of the regular bureaucracy, following the policy of *gai tu gui liu* (replacing local with posted [officials]) (Dreyer 1976:10ff.).

THE MIAO DURING THE REPUBLICAN PERIOD

During the Republican period, the ethnic identifications made during late Qing continued in use, as did the general attitudes of the Han toward minority groups. There were strong pressures for assimilation during most of the period even though the Nationalists spoke initially of self-determination and self-government for minority peoples. Sun Yat-sen recognized that China was a multinational country, as symbolized by the new flag, but the official nationalities other than the Han were the Mongols, Manchus, Tibetans, and Tatars (Turkic Muslims). The point was not lost on the minorities of the Southwest, particularly in Yunnan, where the provincial government under Tang Jiyao was connected only tenuously to the central government between 1911 and 1928, and was only slightly better integrated under the subsequent governership of Long Yun, himself of Yi nationality. The Miao, among others, might well have feared that their lifestyle and identity were endangered by government policies. The fears intensified in the late 1930s with the retreat of the Nationalist government, armies, and large numbers of refugees to the Southwest in the face of Japanese invasion. As Moseley points out, the formally proclaimed policies of assimilation were not effectively implemented (Moseley 1973:30–32). However, rising (Han) Chinese nationalism and claims to modernity were reinforced by invoking traditional views that pointed to the economic backwardness and presumed moral weakness of minorities.

Ethnology had by then become a recognized social science, and scholars were engaged in field research, but much of the writing was a "colonialist anthropology," its ultimate purpose being control and assimilation. The studies focused on particular localized and named groups within the Nationalist-controlled areas, dwelling on those features that the Han would find odd or exotic, and occasionally pointing to aspects of belief or practice that could be presented as amusing or ridiculous. Much of the writing is descriptive rather than explanatory and does not attempt to present the native viewpoint.

Though some published material of this period is based on field-work, there is also a heavy reliance on older texts and on the comments and explanations offered by local Han settlers or sinicized members of other groups, or even, by extrapolation, readings in the ethnography of unrelated "primitive" peoples in other parts of the world. There are some exceptions, most notably the work of Yang Hanxian, one of the first generation of college-educated Hua Miao and one of the few scholars on the Miao whose work involved a knowledge of at least one of the Miao languages.

The materials on the Miao from this period are difficult to work with. The cultural biases are particularly notable in a series of articles written by various scholars during the early 1940s on the subject of *gu* (magical poisoning), which was widely believed to be a common practice among all Miao groups (see Diamond 1988). It is evident also in writings dealing with courtship, marriage, dietary practices, funeral rites, religious beliefs and ceremonies, and other aspects of culture that differ significantly from Han ways. The term "superstition" (*mixin*) is too often used to describe beliefs and practices, and the authors are quick to point out that despite the colorful diversity and some examples of social complexity, the Miao have a low cultural level that can best be understood by reference to the ancient beginnings of Chinese civilization and comparison with primitive peoples elsewhere (see Zhang Yongguo et al. 1983).

The writings of the 1930s and 1940s sometimes generalized about "the Miao" but were more likely to follow the divisions that had become customary in the Qing period (Qing Miao, Hei Miao, etc.) or to define groups by locality (Qian Miao, Fenghuang Miao). Sometimes these categories coincided with linguistic boundaries. But the names were Chinese names and not even translations of the internal ethnonym of the group under study. There seemed to be little interest in what the people called themselves, how far that term extended, and how they referred to other groups. The ethnic boundaries were left unclear. Yet the Chinese names took on a social reality: they were used by group members to identify themselves to outsiders and in some cases came to be regarded as alternate names. They were seen by government administrators and by ethnologists as meaningful divisions. As for the divisions themselves, they continued to be based on dress, location, the presence of a few particular customs deemed significant by Han investigators, and degree of sinicization, as adjudged by Han observers. Relatively little work was done on language, and though some authors wrote descriptions of funerals, marriages, or festivals, the use of Chinese terms tended to blur cultural meanings and mask differences or similarities between groups. Still, there was a growing sense that visible markers such as costume or hairstyle were not in themselves the key differences between the various kinds of Miao but were indicators of much deeper differences in social organization, cultural beliefs, and practice.

BEING MIAO IN THE PEOPLE'S REPUBLIC

After 1949 the official terminology changed. Under the new government minority policies, the differences between linguistically varied and geographically separated Miao populations were seen as superficial. Miao was defined as a single entity. Visible differences were attributed to historical drift within small populations, to separation and dispersion of the original core population, to influence from neighboring peoples, and to the characteristics of particular localities (e.g., altitude and climate), but it was assumed that there was great unity underlying superficial differences.

This shift in attitude had much to do with the difficulties facing the state in its identification of non-Han peoples within the larger population, not the least of which was a shortage of trained linguists, sociologists, and anthropologists. During the first stage of identification of China's minorities, some four hundred groups nationwide asked to be recognized as distinct, separate cultures. Most petitions were denied: initially only eleven minority nationalities were given official recognition. The Miao were one of these, and the category consolidated most of the groups that had previously been referred to as Miao, making no distinctions among them. There was no attempt to follow self-definitions or linguistic guidelines. To subdivide them by language would have opened a Pandora's box—Chinese, after all, is not a single language either. They were also classified as preliterate, despite widespread use of the missionary-introduced writing system among the Hua Miao, its adoption by some of the Chuan Miao, and attendance at Chinese schools by individuals from virtually all groups. It was said of most minority nationalities that prior to Liberation they "recorded events with knots on a string, and numbers with notches on a piece of wood," a set phrase indicating the absence of civilization (Minzu Gongzuo Editorial Board 1985:72).

That the Miao were initially identified as an example of primitive communal society is somewhat surprising, since the bulk of the survey work on the Miao was carried out in Guizhou. It was the absence of clear-cut class stratification within many Miao communities; the absence of "big landlords," full-time artisans, and merchants; and the existence of communal lands that were a basis for viewing Miao populations as representative of an early stage of society. The investigators underplayed Miao involvement in local marketing systems and their use of currency, stressing instead the self-sufficiency of the household economy. Much the same evaluation could have been made of many Han peasant villages. There is an irony, not lost on the Miao, that under a socialist system prior existence of communal lands held by descent groups or village communities was taken as evidence of economic backwardness. But then, courtship, free choice in marriage, and egalitarian division of labor were also seen as survivals of promiscuity. And as late as 1985, Hua Miao women were being urged by cadre to exchange their skirts for trousers, in the name of modernization.

Writings about the Miao have proliferated since 1949. Various studies were done between 1956 and 1963 under the auspices of the Nationalities Commission, with research teams from the Academy of Sciences and various universities and research units. These are localized, focused on the economic conditions, cultural practices, and history of the Miao of particular counties or townships. Some still attempt to distinguish between groups. More recent work is constrained by the pressure to present the Miao as a single entity. The 1985 *Handbook for Minority Work* (Minzu gongzuo shouce) issued by Yunnan Province is a case in point. The Miao section (ibid.:66–72) starts with the assurance that the Miao are linguistically unified, with only two *fangyan* to be found within the province, and widespread proficiency in speaking Chinese. These statements are questionable but initially comforting to cadres drawn from other nationality groups, who are primarily Han. The expectation pressures the various Miao speakers to learn Chinese in order to deal with representatives of the state.

The *Handbook* identifies the Miao as one of the peoples referred to as Man from the Qin dynasty on (221–206 B.C.E.). During the Han period, they migrated from their original homeland (somewhere between the Yellow River and the Yangtze) into parts of Guizhou and Hunan. In the Ming and Qing they lost further territory to the invading and settling armies of the empire. Dispersed in all directions, they did not enter Yunnan until the Qing (ibid.:69). In short, the *Handbook* makes a point of defining the Miao as newcomers to Yunnan, preceded by Han settlement in some areas and certainly preceded by other ethnic minorities. Presumably the equivalent handbooks for minority work in Hunan and Guizhou grant the Miao a longer historical claim to being among the original settlers, but I have not been able to consult those texts. The Yunnan *Handbook* quotes a couplet that appears in many of the Republican period writings as well, and that rhymes nicely in Chinese: "The old crow has no nest / and the Miao have no homeland" (Lao ya wu shu zhuang / Miao jia wu difang) (ibid.:69). Possibly this is an old and widespread Miao adage, but what I heard during my fieldwork among the Christianized Hua Miao was a conscious paraphrase of a biblical verse (Luke 9:58): "The birds of the air have their nests, and foxes their holes, but the Miao have nowhere to rest their heads."

The pre-Liberation Miao economy is presented in the *Handbook* as a "natural economy" based on farming and hunting (there is no discussion of pastoralism, despite its importance in northeastern Yunnan), with household production of handicrafts for use, and little involvement with the market. However, it is noted that this was not an "independent economy" since in many areas the Miao were exploited as tenants by landlords of other nationalities. It is noted that the Miao in Guizhou and Hunan rebelled frequently against Manchu and Han landlords and against the Qing armies, and that the Yunnan Miao participated in the rebellion of 1885. Greater attention is given to their alleged opposition and resistance to French and British imperialist activities in Yunnan, particularly opposition to the railroads and to missionary organization of schools and churches. This is debatable. The railroad controversies of the early twentieth century were sparked primarily by the Han, while the schools and churches introduced by the China Inland Mission and the Methodist Missionary Society were, to the contrary, welcomed by the Hua Miao and continued to be seen as an important development in their recent history (see Cheung, this volume).

The *Handbook* encourages a selective continuation of the colorful aspects of Miao culture. This excludes overtly religious events; traditional religion is summed up as the worship of spirits of nature, ancestors, and ghosts, involving the waste of great sums of money on superstition. Yet some of the music, dance, and costume formerly associated with religious festivals are acceptable, provided that they are presented in a secular framework and packaged for tourism.

Some eighty pages of the *Handbook* are devoted to state-sanctioned minority festivals, with two noted for the Miao (ibid.:312–90, esp. 323–27). One of these is the Han-influenced Dragon Boat Festival, which is celebrated by Qiandong speakers in southeastern Yunnan and in parts of Guizhou and Guangxi. This is by no means an ancient pan-Miao festival retained over the centuries. Schein's account of the festival as held in Qiandongnan makes clear that it has become a commoditized, state-sponsored media event drawing large numbers of outsiders as well as local Miao populations (Schein 1989:206–10).

The other approved festival is glossed in Chinese as the Huashan Jie (Flower-Mountain Festival), a term used since the early Qing to indicate a range of events, from courtship assemblages and song competitions of small groups of youth at mountain retreats to larger intervillage ceremonies at mountain locales of sacred significance. The *Handbook* model is the festival as held in the 1980s in Pingbian. The purpose and content of the original festivals held there, or of parallel festivals elsewhere, are not explained. The description reflects confusion and raises doubts that even the Miao in Pingbian would recognize the festival as their own. Cadres are advised that it may be held in the first lunar month or in the fifth. It may occur every year, or once every three years, or perhaps once every seven or twelve years. It should involve not only the playing of *lusheng* pipes in solo and group competitions but also performance on the Chinese *suona* and bronze drums, and presentations by costumed choral and dance groups. In addition, the *Handbook* recommends Lion Dances, martial arts exhibitions, bullfights, horse races, pole climbing contests, and athletic events. And of course, there should be song competitions between young men and women. The festival described is a conglomerate of a number of festivals held by localized and culturally distinct Miao groups in the past, with state-advised additions and deletions. Finally, it is secularized and politicized: the minority workers are informed that the festival commemorates Miao resistance against a feudal ruler. Such events tend to draw a large audience (including many Han), and are reported in the press and on television as proof that the culture of the minorities is respected and encouraged. But to many Miao these state-sanctioned events seem like new creations by outsiders. They receive some support because they allow the Miao to present their songs, dances, and music and because they bring people together from small villages scattered across the area. On the other hand, many are unwilling to participate because the religious aspects are absent or because so many of those attending are outsiders drawn by curiousity or search for novelty. Among Hua Miao in Xuanwei Prefecture, the so-called Flower Mountain Festival arranged by state organs (which coincides with the Chinese New Year) is spoken of as a terrible time when crowds of drunken young Han men descend upon their community, trampling fields, frightening newborn lambs and kids, and making insulting remarks to young women.

Though the *Handbook* reiterates the need to respect and preserve the cultures of the minority peoples, it provides the minority-work cadres with very little information about those cultures. The bibliography lists relevant materials by Marx, Engels, Lenin, Stalin, and Mao. There are no references to works by historians, anthropologists, linguists, or others whose research touches in any way on social organization and cultural beliefs. Suggested references include the Tang dynasty *Man shu,* with a guide to its contents. The contemporary Miao are identified as the descendants of the Miao or *man* discussed in the writings of a thousand years ago, with little change save in their geographical location. Implicit in the text is the idea that most aspects of their lives that differ from the current Han model will and must change so they can advance historically and become full participants in a modernizing state.

The *Handbook* and similar texts are easily available in bookstores for the curious general reader, not just for the target audience of cadres at the prefectural, county, or township level. They emphasize that the Miao are one people, with odd and colorful customs, who are casting off their superstitions and advancing under socialism. Despite the realities of underdevelopment in the Miao areas of settlement in Yunnan's northeast and reportedly in parts of Guizhou as well, they speak glowingly of post-1950s development models, which include urban growth; electrification; irrigation; the development of tea, coffee, sugar, and other commercial crops; and the spread of modern education. These models bear little resemblance to Miao life in Yunnan's Zhaotong Prefecture or the mountain areas of Xuanwei and Anning where I have done fieldwork. Nor do these areas match the image of Miao presented on state television, which concentrates on elaborate costumed festivals and lavish silver jewelry (from eastern Guizhou) and presents these as the norm of everyday life for Miao everywhere. The television image suggests that the Miao are now a wealthy people, and the *Handbook* pretends the same.

Many Miao areas do not have educational resources for effecting economic development. According to the 1982 census, only 1,436 Miao were enrolled in post-secondary schooling, a figure well below national percentage figures for college and technical school training. As of 1985, in all of Zhaotong Prefecture, with its heavy concentration of Hua Miao, there had been only one Hua Miao college graduate since 1949. In Anning one of the local cadres voiced hopes that a particular young woman might be the first Hua Miao from that county to attend college. According to the 1982 census figures, no more than 30 percent of those over age six had attended primary school, again placing the Miao below national levels for literacy. That figure presumably included a large number of Miao educated before 1949 in Yunnan and western Guizhou in schools organized through the Christian churches, and a large number of children educated since in three-year lower primary schools that may be an hour's walk from their home hamlet. Higher primary schools and secondary schools are few and require a boarding arrangement for most students. Access to schooling beyond third grade may be more easily come by in the Miao areas of western Hunan and eastern Guizhou, but even so, the 1982 census reports that only 2 percent of the Miao population as a whole had ever attended a senior high school, compared to a figure of 7 percent for the Han.

In 1986 in the areas of Miao settlement in northeastern Yunnan there was little evidence of economic development that involved the Miao communities. State plans for improving pasturage and livestock breeding, a provincial project aided by Australian advisors, targeted the Han population as the work force. New mining and timber enterprises were recruiting urban workers from Yunnan's cities. Most Miao villages lacked electricity, schools, and access to off-farm employment. In 1985, when the provincial average per capita income for all peasants was 338 yuan, the average in the Miao villages ranged from around 60 yuan in a better-than-average village in Anning to a high of 200 yuan in parts of Zhaotong where tobacco had been introduced as a cash crop. Presumably Miao incomes were higher in western Hunan and in Qiandongnan or in Pingbian and other parts of southeastern Yunnan.

In official discourse, the absence of economic development in the minority areas is blamed on a number of things: the distance from road and river transportation, the Cultural Revolution, the Gang of Four, the shortage of trained cadres from minority backgrounds, and often on the cultural backwardness and conservatism of the minorities themselves. In general discussion the more sinicized Miao populations of western Hunan are seen as the most advanced, and the Miao of most of Yunnan as the most backward and resistant to change.

CONCLUDING REMARKS

It is not possible for me to guess at how the various Miao populations regard their present circumstances. I can comment only on the feelings that I found in northeastern Yunnan. Among the Hua Miao themselves there is the expressed opinion that their continuing or increased economic difficulties stem from the various government policies that have been attempted since 1949. For them, being Miao means living in areas where schooling is often unavailable, being excluded from jobs in the modern sector (even when these do not require even basic literacy), and being controlled by state policies into which they have had little or no input. Most particularly, it now means restricted access to pasturage, woodlands, and farmland at the same time that they are experiencing population growth, and very firm restrictions on moving into unsettled mountain areas to open up new lands as they have done in the past. However, they are aware that other minorities in this mixed area suffer from the same problems. In unintended ways, the state has fostered unity among the nationalities in that they share many of the same problems. On the plus side, the Miao value the fact that they have been able to retain their ethnic identity, much of their traditional culture, and, since the post-Mao reforms, their participation in some religious activities (which for a large number of Hua Miao means Christian church attendance).

At the level of common discourse, as opposed to official writings, there is some disagreement about whether the Miao are a single unified nationality, but it is not an issue expressed in demands for reclassification. Rather, it is voiced in requests for school primers and writing systems that meet the needs of the diverse languages and dialects, for more village schools, and for an increase in the number of minority autonomous units at the level of the township or county. Otherwise, the Miao seem willing at present to go along with the classification provided by the state. Among themselves, they know what their real name is and how they differ from or are similar to other segments of the Miao category. The older Chinese terminology of Hua Miao, Qing Miao, Hei Miao, and Bai Miao is still in use along with terms in the local language. Given the size of the dominant Han population, there is a perceived strength in numbers that comes from being one of the five largest minority groups. The small number of Miao intellectuals writing today, for example the novelist Wu Lüe, seek to emphasize the underlying unity rather than the diversity within the ethnic category.

For most Miao, the geographical boundaries of their day-to-day world are those of the hamlet, township, local market, and perhaps the county. Within those boundaries neighboring Miao hamlets are homogeneous, speaking the same language and following the same cultural patterns. Most have little or no contact with Miao speaking other languages and following other cultural norms. If they travel farther afield it is to areas where members of the same subgroup are settled. Hua Miao in northeastern Yunnan maintain contact with Hua Miao in Weining in western Guizhou, and continue to establish marriage ties across the provincial boundary. Their recently issued school primers were jointly developed by Miao cadres from Zhaotong (Yunnan) and Weining (Guizhou). Those who do come into contact with other varieties of Miao usually are higher level cadres drawn from the minority ranks, students being trained at provincial or national minorities institutes, or, less frequently, scholars. Mandarin serves as the common language in such contacts. There is no national Miao representative body as such and it is doubtful that the state would welcome attempts to organize one.

At the local level of townships and counties, competition for political office or economic advantages is usually not between subgroups of Miao. It is more likely to be a contest between local Miao, Han, and whatever other ethnic groups are in the area. There is a reasonable chance that all groups will be represented in provincial people's congresses, since delegates are chosen by area as well as ethnicity. Only at the level of the National People's Congress are some groups slighted.

Lack of contact and absence of competition for local resources may explain, in part, the willingness to accept the Miao classification as a valid one. Thus, in a sense, Fei Xiaotong is correct: these peoples are Miao because that is what they have always been called by others. State encouragement of festivals, with music, dance, and bright costumes, has strengthened ethnic identity. State discouragement or banning of various features of local culture over the past decades has also strengthened ethnic identity: with the recent liberalization there seems to have been a reemergence of male national dress as well as an elaboration of women's national dress. And finally, in the absence of widespread and well-thought-out programs for economic development and education in minority areas, the Miao, like other minorities, have tended to turn inward and seek their own local solutions.

Some Han say that the minorities resist assimilation or cling to minority status because of the benefits that come with it. The perks are negligible: permission to have more than one or two children (which wealthier Han peasants and free-market entrepreneurs can do easily if they are willing to pay the cost), relief grain, and the supposed ease with which minority youth enter university with lower examination scores, assuming they have been able to attend high school. The popular image of the Miao, on television or in pictorial magazines, shows them as a wealthy people who spend most of their time singing, feasting, drinking, and dancing, dressed in embroidered gowns and decked with silver ornaments. Their source of wealth remains mysterious: they are not shown engaged in hard work like good Chinese peasants. The media do not document daily life or write about the poorer mountain hamlets. They do not attempt to explain the Miao ways of life or mention that there have been and still are strong pressures from the state to change or abandon highly valued aspects of culture.

Life in most Miao communities is of course quite different from what the media presents. In some areas, the Miao are the poorest of any of the ethnic groups, for reasons beyond their control. Forty years of socialist reconstruction have done little for them. They continue to be regarded as backward and ignorant by Han villagers and cadres, and their response is to hold on even more tightly to their traditions and to a glorified, romanticized image of their past.

Making Histories

Contending Conceptions of the Yao Past

Ralph A. Litzinger

Publications on the Yao minority nationality (*minzu*) in the post-Mao period reveal a vast range of representational strategies, but one of the more dominant concerns the place of the Yao in the history of the People's Republic of China. The Yao people are portrayed as hardy and culturally resilient mountain dwellers, having for centuries lived far removed from the administrative reach of successive imperial regimes. The Yao are known for their persistent rejection of civilizing logics claiming that participation in a tax and corvée labor system signify a kind of cultural enlightenment. As stubborn mountain recluses, the Yao are represented at once as outside the history of China's imperial past and, by virtue of their will to resist, central to social and political processes that culminated in the revolutionary victory of 1949. A remarkable transformation has thus occurred since the early 1940s, as the Yao peoples have been incorporated, both administratively and discursively, into China's modern multi-ethnic nation-state. Once viewed by Imperial and Republican officials as dangerously inaccessible, prone to banditry, and possessing strange and distasteful customs, the Yao today, under the leadership of the Communist Party, are portrayed through a wide range of media as embracing their membership in the larger national community of the People's Republic of China.

My concern here is with the writing of official histories of local Yao communities and of the Yao minority nationality. Constructing histories of China's officially recognized minority nationalities constitutes one important practice in which identification with the "imagined community" of the People's Republic of China is both produced and contested. My interest in the writing and dissemination of these histories is prompted by several interrelated questions: What is the relationship between official and popular histories? How do subordinated ethnic and social groups develop and maintain a sense of their own history? For what political purposes are such histories

MAP 4. Guangxi Zhuang Autonomous Region and adjacent provinces

mobilized? How much autonomy is there for those involved in the production of these histories to contest the theoretical contours and dominant narratives informing the practice of research and writing? How are standard versions of the past produced, privileged, and maintained as part of national discourses on the intersections between history, culture, and politics?

Stretching back at least to the "self-strengthening" movement in the mid-nineteenth century, there has been a lively history of debate and contention about how China should culturally define itself as a nation in the modern age.[1] This nationalist and culturalist project was later fused, albeit not unproblematically, with a Marxist historiography highly informed by social evolutionary conceptions of the "movement" of history. A theoretical practice serving broader revolutionary goals, this historiography attempted to instill meaning in the great sweep of Chinese history. By focusing on urban commer-

1. The "He shang" (River elegy) television documentary is one recent example of the modern Chinese concern for culture and its relationship to a modern, national identity. See Paul A. Cohen (1988) and Watson's (1991) study on the construction of Chinese cultural identity.

cial development, popular literature, and minority-nationality resistance to dynastic regimes, it also attempted to promulgate a new
history, a history of and for the masses.[2] With the emergence of the
socialist-modernization project in the post-Mao period, these historiographical practices have moved away from the strict class-based
interpretations that dominated the first three decades of post-1949
China. These writing practices have gained a renewed intellectual
momentum, as histories that bring together both evolutionary and
culturalist conceptions of the past are once again being written and
published. For the Yao, the dominant post-Mao historical narrative
delimits the stages of history the Yao *minzu* has developed through
and emphasizes the modes of Yao resistance to imperial regimes.
The Yao are represented as important historical agents, as integral
members of a multi-ethnic Chinese state. Although the events and
contours of Yao history differ from the histories of other minority
nationalities and from the Han majority, the history of the Yao, as a
history of an exploited and oppressed *minzu,* is also the history of
the national past of the People's Republic.

While the Chinese term Yao as a referent to non-Han peoples in
the south of China has been floating around official Chinese historical records since the Tang dynasty, the Yao *minzu* was officially constituted only in the mid-1950s.[3] This linguistically and culturally diverse
category is comprised of peoples living predominantly in the mountainous regions extending across the south of China. These peoples
are dispersed across six different provinces in China, but are also said
to be found in Burma, Thailand, Vietnam, and a host of Western
countries, where Yao peoples live without claiming membership in
China's *minzu* category. The category includes three mutually unintelligible languages, each of which is comprised of a variety of dialects
(Xu Jiewu and Deng Wentong 1985). There are over thirty different
ethnonyms for groups subsumed under the category, but these
groups are viewed, in China, as mere subgroups (*zhixi*) of the *minzu.*

2. A penetrating analysis of the origins of Marxist historiography in China is to be
found in Dirlik (1978).

3. This Yao category is comprised of some 1,400,000 people living in six Chinese
provinces: Guangxi, Guangdong, Yunnan, Hunan, Jiangxi, and Guizhou. Population
figures for Yao in other parts of the world are as follows: Vietnam, 165,000; Thailand,
40,000 (half of whom are refugees from Laos); Burma, 15,000; Laos, 10,000; the
United States, 9,000. There are also Yao living in France, Australia, Canada, and no
doubt in other countries as well.

To further lend to this profusion of names, there are over three hundred different terms for the Yao in the Chinese language (usually descriptive of clothing or styles of ornamentation), which many of the Yao find degrading. Finally, many of the Yao groups worship deities, celebrate religious festivities, recognize historical events, and proclaim mythological origins that, at least before 1949, were not known to some of the other groups to be distinctly Yao.

Despite this cultural and linguistic diversity, none of the Yao subgroups has ever openly contested its official designation as a member of the Yao *minzu*. One of the reasons for the seemingly unproblematical nature of the category concerns the popularization of the term Yao during the Ming and Qing periods. Yet the popularization of the name must be understood in the context of political and social processes underway in the south of China since the mid-nineteenth century, if not before. Many of the Yao groups practiced swidden horticulture in the pre-1949 period, which led to competition and conflict over land and other resources; this, in turn, necessitated the adoption of a common political identity in order to successfully negotiate with powerful outsiders demanding tax, labor, and allegiance.[4]

More importantly, the uncontested nature of the category in the contemporary period must be placed in the context of the proliferation of minority nationality and ethnological studies in the post-Mao period. The 1980s witnessed a remarkable growth in this theoretical and applied enterprise, as evidenced in the promotion of conferences, workshops, and publications exploring the relationship between traditional ethnic cultural practices and modernization. Local Yao support for the projects of socialist modernization is thus furthered through an official discourse set forth in the growing body of Yao studies. While the immediacy of this discourse to the social world of local Yao communities is questionable, its power to remake social realities lies in the fact that many of the scholars and administrators who work on the "problems" of the Yao *minzu* are Yao themselves, with social ties throughout Yao communities. They have been trained in the post-1949 educational system, usually in institutes far from their home villages. Many have subsequently returned to hold government positions, working as county magistrates, promoting the national birth control project, or instructing villagers in the te-

4. See Hu and Fan (1983) on settlement patterns in the Da Yao Shan area of east-central Guangxi.

nets of the Civilized Village Campaign.[5] Some have become scholars and hold positions at one of the minority nationality institutes across the country; they too continue to play an active role in the formation of policy, the implementation of campaigns, and the study of the many "problems" said to hinder the modernization drive. Their involvement at the local level serves as a reminder that local affairs continue to be informed by the administrative practices and discursive injunctions of the official center.

And yet, noting that the Yao have not disputed their membership in the Yao *minzu* category does not mean that contest has not informed the Yao relationship with the shifting goals, projects, and ideologies of the state in China. The Yao *minzu* is one whose members—especially those connected in various ways to the state apparatus—see themselves as important national subjects and as worthy ethnic peoples. Because the Yao are constituted by the state as an ethnic other, defined by cultural traditions said to lag behind those of the dominant Han majority, Yao ethnicity emerges as a negotiated and at times contested terrain. The history of the Yao, and its place in the historical processes that resulted in the founding of the People's Republic, is central to processes in which Yao ethnicity is being interpreted, negotiated, and reformulated in the midst of the changing political, economic, and discursive processes of post-Mao China.

Due to the existence of numerous historical references to peoples referred to as Yao, Western and Chinese scholars in pre-1949 China produced an extensive literature on the history of the group. Who were these people? Where did they reside? What peoples were subsumed under the category and why? What did the Chinese term Yao mean? Did its meaning change through time and, if so, why? This essay addresses these questions and examines how post-1949 research by scholars in the People's Republic on Yao origins and resistance has been informed by earlier historiography. In both periods the defining assumption is that the Yao have an ancient history, and that

5. The Civilized Village Campaign (*wenmingcun yundong*) is one means by which the post-Mao state attempts to institute moral and legal codes at the local level. Local government officials and villagers are together responsible for monitoring behaviors that violate the tenets of the code: excessive drinking, gambling, disorderly conduct, prostitution, and domestic disputes. See Anagnost (1992) for a discussion of how such practices reconstitute the power of the Communist Party even while the party claims to be promoting democratic self-government.

this history, the social evolution of the group, can be traced to the present moment.

The crucial difference, however, rests in what this historical "fact" has meant for those constructing the history of the Yao in the post-1949 period. One of the most important strategic moves in the ethnic-history writing project in the People's Republic has been the inclusion of ethnic subjects in the research and writing process. The history of the Yao *minzu* is not in any way a false construct without historical referents or significance in everyday lived reality; nor is it one merely constructed in order to legitimate Yao claims for officially recognized *minzu* status. There are local histories of Yao communities, of important families and Yao leaders, of the many different groups that make up the *minzu*. Though they may not have been articulated locally as histories of the Yao *minzu*, they nevertheless have been constituted as part of the history of the *minzu* and thus of the People's Republic of China. Many of those who have been involved in the writing of the official history of the Yao are aware of the ideological underpinnings of this project; however, as one scholar put it to me, there has been little opportunity to popularize different conceptions and understandings of the history of the Yao. China's post–Cultural Revolution economic reforms, coupled with the state's promotion of things ethnic, have allowed the Yao to begin to recover and reconstruct many cultural practices previously silenced under the dictates of the Maoist regime.

The most visible, and perhaps most highly contested, of these is the popular practice of Yao Taoism, which is seen by the state as potentially undermining modernist and evolutionary discourses which imagine a socialist-modern landscape cleansed of popular ritual and religious practice. Yet there are other practical effects as well, such as the hardening of ethnic boundaries along subgroup lines. The proliferation of these identities puts the discursive nature of the *minzu* category into sharp relief and speaks against ideological claims of an uncontested minority nationality unification (*minzu tuanjie*). It is in the recovery of such practices that the different Yao groups are negotiating the defining characteristics of their people, struggling to give voice to the heterogeneous histories and identities that proliferate amidst the homogenizing *minzu* history, and contesting the dominant historiography which defines traditional ethnic practices as paralyzing to the project of socialist modernization.

THE SEARCH FOR THE YAO IN HISTORY

Two major themes structure the pre-1949 ethnohistorical research on the Yao. Both are then taken up in the post-1949 period, though they are interpreted and utilized differently. The first is the question of the origins and social evolution of a Yao ethnic or tribal people; the second is the representation of the Yao as possessing a tradition of sustained resistance to the imperial regimes ruling China until the fall of the Qing dynasty. This becomes the flip side of the dominant representation of the Yao in the Chinese historical record as barbarians, mountain recluses, and worshipers of a mottled dog-king. As barbarians on the borders of empire, the Yao persistently resisted incorporation into the administrative structures of successive dynastic regimes. Yao resistance to imperial control has been incorporated into the *minzu* historiography of the People's Republic. Before we turn to this history, it will prove helpful to examine how these two issues were set forth in the pre-1949 conceptions of the history of the Yao.

Richard Cushman's doctoral dissertation provides the most comprehensive examination of Western, Japanese, and pre- and post-1949 publications (up until early 1966) on the Yao.[6] Cushman explicated the dominant theoretical problems in Yao ethnohistory and charted the changing Chinese perceptions of the Yao through successive dynastic and modern political regimes. Many of the concerns in this early anthropological and linguistic literature have remained central to the contemporary field of Yao studies: how to account for the extraordinary linguistic diversity of the Yao; how to explain their wide geographical dispersal; and the problem of how the Yao, given these two conditions, have resisted absorption by neighboring peo-

---

6. See Cushman (1970). Cushman's study deals to a limited extent with the ethnographic research that was carried out on Mien-speaking Yao in Thailand in the 1970s. I have not presented it here because little if any of it provides a historical perspective on the Yao or discusses in any detail the Yao discourse on their own history, save for references to recent migration routes and to certain Chinese regions in traditional songs and folklore. As for Cushman's treatment of post-1949 work on the Yao in China, he refers only tangentially to the increase in linguistic research in the late 1950s and early 1960s. I have come across only nine sources on the Yao published in China between 1949 and 1979. In contrast, for the period between 1979 and 1986, I know of over 120 articles or books. Research and writing on the Yao in the People's Republic has continued to proliferate since 1986.

ples and maintained group integrity. Cushman showed how scholars of the Yao, confounded by the seemingly inexplicable diversity of the group, retreated to the historical record, seeking to trace the origins of the Yao by reference to the earliest citations in the imperial record. The Yao have been traced back to around 220 C.E. as one of the ethnolinguistic groups subsumed under the category Nanman (southern barbarian). The origins of this term are found in the first of the official histories of China, the *Shi ji*, in a chapter entitled "The Aborigines of the Southwest" (Xinan Yi). This chapter is devoted solely to describing events and peoples of the South. Utilizing the classification system set forth in the *Shi ji*, subsequent dynastic scholars divided the peoples of the South into two broad categories: the Xinan Yi, the indigenous populations of present-day Yunnan, southern Sichuan, and western Guizhou; and the Nanman, those who lived in present-day Guangxi, Guangdong, Fujian, Zhejiang, Jiangxi, Hunan, and eastern Guizhou. From Han to Tang times these broad categories were refined into smaller units, usually by designating a group of people by their geographical location. The term *man* (barbarian) was not discarded, but was attached as a suffix to a place name. By the end of the Southern Song (1127–1279), new and more detailed information was being recorded about the southern peoples. This deluge of information was made possible by the transfer of the capital to Hangzhou and by the policies initiated by the first emperor of the Song, Zhao Kuangyin (known posthumously as Song Taizu). This period marks the subjugation and incorporation of the independent kingdoms south of the Yangtze (excluding the state of Nanzhao in the far Southwest) into the Song's administrative system. Most of the terms in modern usage were in widespread use among imperial scholars by the late Southern Song.[7]

The term Yao as a mode of classification for a group or groups of non-Han peoples does not appear in the Chinese historical record until the Tang dynasty, when it appears in the expression *moyao*, usually translated as "not subject to corvée labor" (Lemoine 1982:11). Many scholars, both Chinese and Western, have attempted to link the origins of the Yao to this administrative category. The writings of

7. In the eleventh century we find for the first time references to Yao *ren* (Yao people), in which the character *yao* is written with the insect radical and is not prefixed by the word *man*. See Cushman (1970:50, 53) for a discussion of eleventh-century sources.

Tang Cui, an observer of events in the South during the Qing, are often cited as evidence of this link:

> [The aborigines] who have diffused throughout Hunan, Kwang-si and Kwangtung are called Yao [written with the "insect" radical]. In earlier times those who had merit were released from their corvée duties [*yao*, written with the *chi* or "step" radical] and were called *moyao* ["not subject to corvée"]. Later the name was changed to Yao [a similar character written with the "insect" radical]. (Tang Cui quoted in Cushman 1970:56)

Cushman dismissed the entire enterprise of linking the present-day Yao to the category *moyao*. He argued that there are only six uses of the term *moyao* in five sources, the earliest occurring in the *Liang shu* (History of the Liang dynasty; c. early 6th cent. C.E.). In each of these sources there is no indication that the term refers to a particular ethnic group; in fact, there is evidence to suggest that it referred to both *man* and Han Chinese, the criteria being avoidance of tax and corvée obligations.[8] And finally, Cushman pointed out that no one has been able to offer a reasonable explanation for shortening *moyao* to Yao; neither has anyone produced documentary evidence for why such a change may have occurred. In other words, the then extant historical reconstructions of the Yao failed to convincingly show that the peoples referred to in the Tang dynasty as enjoying the privileges of *moyao* status are the direct ancestors of those people who, in the Southern Song, were referred to as the Man Yao. In his critique of this now infamous "*moyao* argument," Cushman revealed the inconclusiveness of historical reconstructions of present-day ethnic groups based solely on philological grounds.

Most importantly, Cushman argued that conceptions of the Yao history and identity owe much to the definitions set forth by imperial scholars and administrative officials. Contemporary historical reconstructions of the shifts and transmutations of Yao identity are severely constrained by the Sinocentric perspective that permeates the historical record on the non-Han peoples of the South. At best, Cushman reasoned, it is possible to arrive at certain objective criteria—language, dialects, mythology, religious practices, and cus-

8. See Cushman (1970:55–59) for an overview of research on the *moyao* category. See also Wiens (1967).

toms—that indicate the existence of a historic ethnic group. But the question of subjectivity remained an elusive problem. Reflecting upon his own invocation of objective markers as the defining features of the ethnic group, Cushman saw clearly the futility of talking about Yao identity when the Yao themselves have never had a voice with which to speak. He thus stumbled upon the problem of voice, which is today so central to post-structuralist approaches to writing the history of subaltern groups: as the creation of the imperial imagination, the Yao existed only as a noncultured other, situated on the borders of empire and civilization.

The second theme recurring throughout writings on the ethnohistory of the Yao concerns the question of Yao resistance to an everexpanding imperial state. This theme also emerges from the historical materials of Imperial China: when the Yao were not being mentioned as descendants of the dog-king Pan Hu (who seldom ventured into cities and markets and who ate the strangest of foods), they were represented as ferocious and mountain-wise, stubborn rebels who refused to be seduced by the lure of the superior, lowland Han culture, which meant paying taxes and providing corvée labor to local imperial administrators. Take, for example, the following description written by a nineteenth-century Chinese historian:

> The Yao are stupid and violent by nature and they do not have any intercourse with the Chinese. The Chinese take advantage of their stupidity by wresting things from them by force, by stealing from them, and by raiding and insulting them. The officials are prompt to assist wicked people to bind them fast [in this condition]. The Yao accumulate malice and hatred and then rebel, and events [tribal rebellions] have ever followed this course. (Wei Yuan 1842, quoted in Cushman 1970:36)

The recurrence of Yao rebellions has been an important element in the construction of a historic Yao ethnic or tribal group. Major Yao "tribal uprisings," as Wiens characterized these historic events, were first mentioned during the rule of the Song emperor Renzong (1023–1064); one occurred in Guangdong in 1035, another in Hunan in 1043. There is mention of a rebellion in the Guangzhou region in 1281. By the mid-Ming, the incidence of Yao uprisings had increased dramatically. And then there was the famous 1832 Yao rebellion in Hunan, in which the Yao, reacting to theft of cattle and grain by members of the

Triad Society, organized an uprising that took several months and armies from three provinces to squelch (Cushman 1970:225–31).[9] The reports on these uprisings usually pointed to Yao refusal to pay taxes, or attempts to reclaim land confiscated by the Han. In all of these accounts, regardless of the period in which they were written, there is a persistent tension between the desire to incorporate the Yao into the administrative domain and a sense of utter hopelessness in the face of the task. The reasons provided for this feeling of desperation had little to do with the inadequacies of the civilizing regime and everything to do with the stupidity of the Yao. The Yao are depicted as a people who both resisted sinification (*hanhua*) and refused incorporation into the Chinese political order. As local officials in the Ming responded to increasing imperial pressure to bring the recalcitrant "barbarians" under administrative control, it may well be, as Cushman argues, that this process of interaction and conflict gave rise to a Yao ethnic identity and increased the importance of its maintenance and reproduction (Cushman 1970:233).[10]

Whatever the relationship between Yao rebellions (or participation in major uprisings such as the Taiping) and the emergence of a Yao sense of ethnic identity, Yao resistance to imperial control is central to the construction of a contemporary Yao identity.[11] For those writing on Yao ethnohistory in the pre-1949 period, resistance was seen s an inevitable consequence of the southward expansion of northern-

9. Kuhn (1980:106–107)) discusses an entirely different series of rebellions, the so-called Xinning rebellions, the first of which occurred in 1836. Xinning is in a valley just to the west of the Xiang River valley, which was a major route by which the opium trade had spread to the North. The Yao in this region were involved in this trade as well as in a number of secret societies, such as the Black Lotus Society (Qinglian Jiao) and the Cudgel Society (Bangbang Hui). Due to yamen extortion of local peasants, several Yao leaders with connections to these societies began to secretly organize themselves, drawing support from large segments of the local Han peasantry. By 1847, another revolt occurred in Xinning lead by a Yao named Li Caihao. The Yao were brutally defeated by a locally organized militia after several months. Kuhn finds these rebellions instructive in two senses: they point to interethnic alliances that arose in the face of local imperial oppression, and they demonstrate that powerful and successful local militias, typically the instruments of lineage elites, even in the face of growing provincial-level distrust were able to put down such revolts.

10. Many scholars of ethnicity have noted the links between competition and conflict over resources and the crystalization of ethnic identity. See Keyes (1981) and Francis (1976).

11. See Cheung (this volume).

ers, be they Mongols or simple Han peasants in search of new rice land. Some saw conflict and loss of life as an invariable component of expansion into the southern frontier. For others, perhaps empathetic with the Yao, violent resistance was viewed as the only course of action available to defend one's land and clanspeople.

Both pre- and post-1949 historiography views Yao resistance as the result of conflict and struggle between opposed groups: the former emphasizes ethnic interaction and conflict, while the latter stresses feudal exploitation and oppression and the imperial quest to assimilate the noncultured other. The crucial distinction, however, is the way in which the history itself is constructed. The pre-1949 literature is remarkably devoid of the teleological conceptions of historical progress that imbue the PRC historiography of the Yao: that the Yao, through their social intercourse with the expanding imperial regime and by virtue of the conflicts this interaction engendered, socially matured as they moved through successive evolutionary stages. To be sure, this narrative strives to grant the Yao with a certain agency in this movement through history, but it is an agency subsumed to the unfolding of History itself. An essential part of being a *minzu* is being an active agent, however imaginatively constituted, in the historical process culminating in the people's victory over China's feudal past. It is this narrative of Yao history, to which we now turn, that works to firmly situate the *minzu* in the larger community of the People's Republic of China.

THE MAKING OF THE YAO IN HISTORY

The history of the Yao *minzu* has been structured in the People's Republic by a Marxist and evolutionary historiography. This discourse has delineated the successive stages of Yao *minzu* social development and specified the social forces causing the transition from one stage to another. The Yao are also represented as important historical agents in their encounter with an opposition to successive "feudal" dynastic regimes. China's so-called "feudal" past is mobilized as the very cause of Yao social and economic "backwardness" (*luohou*) and, at the same time, as the source of the Yao revolutionary spirit.

As I stressed earlier, the Yao themselves have been instrumental in the writing of a Yao-*minzu* history. When the research for this history-writing project was begun in the mid-1950s, and then, after the turmoil of the Cultural Revolution, renewed in the early 1980s, members of the Yao community were called upon to collect the information that eventually gave shape to the production of the history. They brought to the project experiences and perspectives derived from their home communities, and their own knowledge of traditional Yao cultural practices and of the assortment of Yao oral histories, expressed in traditional songs and long ritual incantations. This local perspective was then reworked into the narrative structure of the dominant historiography, as it was determined what had import within this framework and what was epiphenomenal and thus of little significance.

While the writing in China of a Marxist-informed history has not been without its moments of struggle, debate, and controversy,[12] certain fundamental premises have remained constant: that the writing of history, like any intellectual pursuit, must "serve the people"; that popular history, the history about and for the masses, is more valuable for understanding the present than are histories about feudal emperors, scholar-officials, and imperial intrigue; that history is not a document of lifeless events and facts but an explanation for the conditions of the present and a vehicle for action and change in the world; and that statements and representations of history invariably have social and political roots and consequences (Weller 1987:731). This historiography has struggled to sever itself from the Confucian literati tradition. An assessment of the success of this purported amputation is beyond the scope of this essay. What is important for now is that this "new tradition" has represented itself as promulgating a more "real" history.

Since the early 1980s minority nationality publishing houses in China have issued works on the various Yao autonomous counties. These short and informative publications provide brief histories of the (Communist) liberation of the area, as well as information on

---

12. One of the recurrent struggles in the post-1949 historiography has been the debate between "historicism" (*lishi zhuyi*) and the "class viewpoint" (*jieji guandian*). The former, perhaps best represented by Liu Jie's arguments in the early 1960s that class analysis is an inappropriate analytical tool when applied to ancient historical events, has attempted to delineate those features of China's cultural legacy that should be preserved and embraced. For example, Liu argued that the Confucian concept of *ren* (roughly, "benevolence") was devoid of class content, a position for which he was severely attacked. See Feuerwerker (1968a) for a discussion of these struggles over historiographical method.

economic development projects initiated in the reform period and an examination of forces retarding socialist modernization. In addition to these local histories, there is a general history of the Yao, *Yaozu jianshi* (A concise history of the Yao), hereafter referred to as the *Jianshi*.[13] This book represents the work of over thirty scholars of the Yao in China, the majority of whom are Yao themselves (*Yaozu jianshi* 1983:132). No one pretends that the *Jianshi* exhausts every possible historical source or that it is in any way devoid of points of controversy. This history is a simplified, encapsulated version of how the Yao have progressed through history; it charts the obstacles they have encountered in their long and arduous path to realize full social and economic potential, to become a socialist, modern *minzu*.

The *Jianshi* takes the reader on a tour through the long historical stretch of Chinese history, as moments in the history of the Yao are situated in different dynastic regimes and related to social evolutionary stages. The book begins with an analysis of the theories, some already reviewed above, on the origins of the Yao. There is reference to the many *man* terms rampant in the first millennium C.E. The original homeland of the Yao is situated in the valleys and mountains south of Dongting Lake in northern Hunan. In pre-Han times, the people living in this area were referred to as Jing Man. By the Han dynasty they had come to be known as the Changsha Man or Wuling Man. In the histories of the Liang (502–557), Sui, and Song dynasties, these peoples are referred to as Wuxi Man (*Man* of the Five Streams, referring to the river system extending southward from Dongting Lake) (ibid.:12–13). As we saw in our examination of Cushman's work on the ethnohistory of the Yao above, this style of reasoning is an example of the historical reconstruction of present-day groups based on philological grounds.[14]

---

13. A concise history has been written for nearly every minority nationality in China. Much of the material for these histories was collected during the *minzu* identification process in the 1950s, though the funds to compile and publish the histories were not made available until the early 1980s.

14. Philology is not the only means of attack. Reconstructions of the historic Yao are based on the relationship between present-day Yao traditional customs and apparently similar practices mentioned for this region in such sources as the *Hou Han shu* (History of the Later Han dynasty) (*Yaozu jianshi* 1983b:20). Unfortunately, perhaps due to the survey nature of the *Jianshi,* there is no mention of what these traditional customs might be (see Harrell, this volume).

The *Jianshi* situates the original Yao dwelling place just south of Dongting Lake. The history of the Yao therefore emanates from this geographical location (ibid.:20). We are informed that when Qin Shi Huang unified China in the third century B.C.E. and implemented the "system of prefectures and counties" (*junxian zhidu*), the Yao in this region, for perhaps the first time in their history, were brought into close contact with a centralized government. The argument of interethnic or tribal contact and borrowing is an important strategical move in this historical narrative. It constitutes the Yao in a kind of dependent relationship for all technological and social advancement. For example, Qin Shi Huang's policy of *zheshumin*, in which low-ranking officials were sent to remote areas to establish garrison command posts, enabled the Yao to adopt more advanced agricultural tools and begin to engage in trade activities with other tribal peoples. It was also in the reign of Qin Shi Huang that the Yao were first incorporated into the tribute system. This interaction with the Qin state, although marking the beginning of feudal exploitation, is presented in an almost positive light, as a necessary moment in Yao social and economic advancement.

In the Later Han dynasty the Yao began what was to become a long history of revolt against "feudal" China's tribute and tax systems. The *Hou Han shu* records uprising after uprising among the recalcitrant Yiren, the category thought to have subsumed the Yao (ibid.:21). By around 300 C.E., due to the increased migrations of people from the North, the Yiren (the Yao) established closer ties with the northerners and began to adopt surnames and other elements of Chinese culture. Some of the Yiren became "aristocrats" (*guizu*) themselves, owning large tracts of land and bringing other Yi peoples under their control. This represents the beginning of processes of assimilation for some Yao peoples (ibid.:23). Yet, more importantly, it divided the historic Yao community. By the middle of the sixth century the Yao had begun to migrate into the region that would later come to be known as Nanling Shan, the mountain range that forms the borders of present-day Hunan, Guangdong, and Guangxi.

The *Jianshi* also notes the controversial Tang dynasty *moyao* institution (ibid.:24–25). Yet, unlike the Western and pre-Liberation Chinese research that concerned itself almost solely with the origins of the Yao, the *moyao* category gets only scant attention in this regard. This is because the origins of the Yao have already been traced back to the pre-Han period. The term is presented as just one more way in which feudal rulers classified the Yao; in no way is it used to search for the origins of the Yao *minzu.* Yet *moyao,* as a political category, marks an important historical development. It represents a negotiation between isolated tribal peoples and an imperial state extremely wary of the "barbarian" other—an other who, in the official imagination, was more often equated with monkeys, wild dogs, and quick and elusive deer than with the civilized center.[15] The granting of exemption from taxes and other obligations was a way for the Tang court to maintain cultural distance; it was also a way to induce the "southern barbarians" to open up the mountains for agricultural purposes. Thus, through the widespread adoption of iron tools and other advanced agricultural implements, these Tang dynasty institutions contributed to the further development of the Yao economy.

These social developments, not unlike those in Qin-Han times, brought with them a certain cost: inter- and intra-ethnic conflict. Due to the introduction of the so-called "loose reign policy" (*jimi zhengce*) of "using barbarians to rule barbarians" (*yi yi zhi yi*), the Yao, especially those in the area known in the Tang as Lingnan Dao (comprising the eastern, Guilin section of present-day Guangxi and all of Guangdong) were increasingly pitted against each other. This system, the precursor to the Ming and Qing *tusi,* was constructed so that local tribal leaders were induced, usually by the granting of official rank, to govern Chinese-style administrative districts. These tribal chiefs (*qiuzhang*) were required to collect taxes and goods— such as the high-quality silk knit goods (*sizhipin*) produced by Yao women—for tribute (ibid.:28). Yao farmers, presumably skeptical of the practical use of symbolic titles, refused the tax system and were subsequently pushed deeper and deeper into the mountains. The political divisions and class contradictions (*jieji maodun*) that Communist Party cadres found rampant in the Yao mountains in the 1940s are said to have their social roots in the expansion of the imperial state into the south of China in the Tang and the Song. Although the Yao economy saw further advances in its productive base, society was increasingly divided. Tribal chiefs were increasingly

---

15. See Schafer (1967) for the standard English-language source on the representations of the non-Chinese peoples of the south of China during the Tang.

incorporated into the imperial system, while farmers and peasants were driven into isolation.[16] In the *Jianshi*, this constitutes the "feudalization" (*fengjianhua*) of Yao society.

The Song empire succeeded in incorporating large tracts of "untamed" land into its administrative domain. As the *Jianshi* points out, this was accomplished by the further exploitation and elaboration of the Tang "loose reign policy." In the Song we begin to see the use of the term *tuguan*. These were "local officials," usually Zhuang peoples in the areas of present-day Guangxi and Guangdong, who were given the responsibility of distributing land to the Yao and other tribal groups. To receive land, however, one had to register with the *tuguan* through either the *jikou jitian* (distributing land by population) or *jihu shoutian* (allocating land by household), which determined the amount of land per household (ibid.:31). In return, taxes would be collected in the form of crops and other locally produced goods. Those who failed to pay their required tax or refused to offer corvée labor in its place were harassed and sometimes severely punished. In social evolutionary terms, the *Jianshi* (ibid.:32–33) argues that these Song and Yuan dynasty methods of feudal control represent the shift from the stages of primitive society (*yuanshi shehui*) and agricultural communes (*nongcun gongshe*) to that of feudal society (*fengjian shehui*), bypassing, unlike other minority nationalities in the South and Southwest, the stage of slave society (*nuli shehui*). The reasons provided for this are consistent with the evolutionary paradigm. Driven to isolated regions in the mountains, the Yao were forced to practice swidden horticulture and, having never established permanent, stable residences, they were unable to support political, economic, and cultural centers that would allow the emergence of a slave society. The imperial practice of "using barbarians to rule barbarians" and the *tuguan* institution kept the Yao competing against each other. While some maneuvered to open up land for wet-rice cultivation (which could be acquired only through the household registration system), most remained tied to a migratory existence in

16. This argument can be contrasted to one set forth in Cushman (1970:168). He states that according to the *Guangxi tongzhi* (Provincial gazetteer) eleven of the twelve tribal officers recognized by the Song court whose ethnic origins were recorded were Han from the province of Shandong. It is not certain, however, whether this reflects the ethnic distribution of hereditary tribal positions or whether local tribal officers fabricated Han descent in order to pursue political interests.

the mountains. The Yao were forced, due to historical processes beyond their control, to "eat up one mountain and move to the next" (*chi yi shan, guo yi shan*).

Although the *tusi* system came into full bloom under the Ming and the Qing dynasties,[17] the patterns of development and forced migration remained the same. In both periods the Yao continued to encounter the ever-expansionary imperial state. By the mid-Qing, it is said, the present-day Yao regions in China were all established. However, certain regions—such as the Da Yao Shan (Great Yao Mountains), Shiwan Yao Shan (Hundred Thousand Yao Mountains) in Guangxi, and areas in southern Hunan—were never brought under effective control. This returns us to the other foundational theme circulating through the *Jianshi:* the Yao as historical agents, fomenters of uprisings and rebellions.

In the Song, Yuan, Ming, and Qing periods the Yao were caught up in the stormy "feudalization" of the South. While Yao encounters with Han society and with imperial administrators facilitated the development of the Yao economy, feudal exploitation and oppression drove the Yao deeper into the mountains and thus undermined any gain in social development. As this process unfolded—as more and more Yao refused administrative incorporation—the local officials attempted to cut off trade between various regions, blocking the importation of salt and other foodstuffs that could be had only from markets at lower elevations. These actions left the Yao with no alternative but to attack the garrison command posts, which in turn led to imperial retaliation. In the year 975, for example, one third of the Yao in the Mei Shan area in Hunan were murdered by imperial troops (ibid.:34–35). This led to a series of skirmishes, which finally culminated in a large-scale Yao uprising. The Yao of southern Hunan organized themselves and on fifteen occasions attacked the command posts at Lianshan and Lianyang in the northwest corner of present-day Guangdong. The pacification officer (*anfushi*) in the area was thus forced to resort to the then extant *zhaofu* or *zhaoan* policy, whereby amnesty was offered to the rebels if they agreed to halt their attacks. These offers were considered by five leaders of the rebellion, but the struggle was sustained for another five years, until it eventually died out (ibid.:36).

17. For an important work on the *tusi* system, see She I-tse (1947). See also Wiens (1967).

CONTESTING THE HISTORY OF THE YAO

Circulating throughout the history of the Yao *minzu* is the assumption of historical continuity: the Yao, bounded by distinct and essential cultural traits and ethnic practices, have been around since the beginnings of recorded history in China. In contrast to the pre-1949 ethnohistorical work, the writing of ethnic history within a nationalist framework precludes the search for the Yao in history. The project is rather one that traces the Yao movement, the Yao progression through History. History here is constructed as a body of knowledge that reveals the making of a modern Yao identity, and becomes the very foundation by which to interpret what it means to be Yao. Throughout the *Jianshi,* we see an unfolding of a governing structure of Yao self-realization, a narrative resolutely Hegelian, even though the *Jianshi* always portrays Yao social development in materialist terms.[18] Of course, as many scholars in China have pointed out, the historical sources are continuously being debated and reinterpreted, but what remains constant is the unfolding of History. The category *minzu* is taken not as a cultural construct but rather as an unproblematic embodiment of objective reality. For those who write and contemplate the history of the Yao *minzu,* it is a fact of everyday lived reality that the Yao have a long history, that they are a people who have been exploited by successive feudal regimes, a people driven to the mountains, who have for centuries carved out a meager existence on unforgiving terrain, struggling against the elements and encroaching, arrogant, feudal masters. The claim that the Yao *minzu* has evolved through clearly defined stages of social development remains unchallenged—how else, as one scholar answered my stubborn queries, could Yao *minzu* history be understood? What seems to matter is that the discourse offers a consistent explanation of the current "backward" economic and social state of Yao communities and, at the same time, justifies their involvement in the struggle to liberate the country and their current participation in the nationally defined projects of modernization and nation-building.

The interpretation and construction of Yao histories through this

18. See Young (1990) for a discussion of the concept of History in the modern West, the Hegelian roots of many materialist conceptions of history, and the problems involved in poststructuralist attempts to reconceptualize and indeed politicize the writing of history.

conceptual framework work to situate the Yao *minzu* within the larger community of the People's Republic of China. The historiographic framework that informs the *Jianshi* also demonstrates how the structure of the Yao past closely corresponds to that of other minority nationalities in the People's Republic of China. This is not simply an enterprise whereby a past of exploitation and oppression at the hands of feudal rulers is made visible, so that a once-subordinated ethnic group can now reclaim its history. It is rather a means by which local Yao histories are expropriated and incorporated into larger discursive constructs. These constructs infuse meaning into the sorted jumble of local Yao specificities and provide the very voice whereby the history of the Yao past is articulated within the contours of a larger political arena, the multi-ethnic community of the People's Republic.

Have the Yao finally acquired the capacity to represent themselves in history within China? Through the "making of histories," Yao scholars and others instrumental in this practice have seemingly embraced their participation in the state apparatus and their apparent incorporation into the Chinese multi-ethnic nation. Those Yao who are in positions of power and able to do research and write know perfectly well what they are doing when they "make" these histories. They are not only rediscovering and bringing to the written page a past that has been silenced by the previously dominant Confucian-literati tradition of historiography. They are also constructing conceptions of Yao history, society, and culture that become the official representation of what demarcates the Yao as a bounded *minzu* community. These histories are on the lips of many a Yao scholar, local teacher, and Communist Party member. They are lived and experienced and have become an important part of these people's sense of what it means to be Yao.

Because it takes social backwardness and the revolutionary spirit as its foundational themes, Yao history, as with other nation-oriented histories, homogenizes that which remains heterogeneous to it (see Prakash 1992). For this reason the expropriation and incorporation of local Yao histories into nationalist and modernist frameworks of conceptualizing the past call up points of contestation and negotiation. The *Jianshi* touches only tangentially upon many of the cultural features that Yao, in other contexts, assert mark the boundaries that define their *minzu*. It is at the juncture between a narrative that tells a story about historical self-realization and the cultural traditions and local histories that don't easily conform to this governing structure that debate, negotiation, and contest become possible and apparent.

What, then, are the other modes of reckoning social reality that potentially disrupt these dominant conceptual frameworks? At the present time the most important of these seems to be Yao Taoism, a practice that the Maoist regime effectively silenced but is now being rediscovered as an important element of Yao identity. The *Jianshi* provides a brief concluding section on the religious beliefs of the Yao, yet the approach to religion and popular ritual is marked by ambivalence: ritual and religion are apprehended as lingering survivals of the primitive and feudal stages of Yao social development, although the connection to Taoist practices and traditions is noted as somehow central to a Yao identity. The spread of Taoism into Yao regions in the Song and the Yuan periods is treated, for example, as being paralyzing (*mabi*) to the historic Yao revolutionary spirit, just one more example of the many innovative methods of feudal control (ibid.:122–27). And yet as a symbol of traditional Yao identity, the *Jianshi* opens up the possibility that Yao Taoism may have a place in a modernizing China.

The ambivalent treatment of religion and popular ritual is thus further played out in the increasing expression of, discussion about, and action upon Taoism as an integral element of what it means to be Yao. This raises important questions about the interaction between the traditional practice of Yao ethnicity and the official conception of what constitutes a Yao *minzu* identity, of how this official discourse has influenced popular practice, and how, in turn, the popular has shaped and is reshaping the official. Kandre's (1976) work on the relationships between supernaturalism, language, and ethnicity among Mien-speaking Yao in Thailand provides an interesting contrast to the discourse on matters of identity among the Yao as set forth in official publications in China. Kandre begins by pointing out that for the Mien (known in China as the Pan Yao and by other Han appellations) with whom he worked, linguistic competence in the Mien dialect is not coextensive with a specific identity. Rather, Mien identity is "ascribed as a combination of name and rank, to which graded doses of supernatural power, blessing, and purity are usually attached" (ibid.:13). In other words, ethnic identity is indirectly ascribed as a result of the individual's ritual incorporation into a patrilineal unit of a clan defined in terms of descent from the mythological dog-king Pan Hu. "One is Mien by virtue of his belonging to certain temporal or supernatural masters who in turn belong to other masters" (ibid.:14). My own fieldwork among Yao in China suggests that this ritual basis of Mien identity, created and reproduced by the ritual intervention of Taoist priests, is today a significant aspect of native practice among Mien and other Yao subgroups. Taoist practice among the Yao is being rediscovered by scholars working on the Yao in China. Yao Taoist practice is increasingly becoming a mode of *minzu* identification for those scholars who are Yao themselves. Yao Taoist funerals and other rituals that call for the intervention of trained priests in everyday human affairs are once again becoming popular. The resurgence of Taoist practice among the Yao therefore poses interesting questions concerning the relationships between state discourse on religion, local religious beliefs and practices, and the ways in which the state attempts to interpret, manipulate, and control these practices, and how locals, in turn, respond to the everyday state penetration into local religious and social affairs.

That religion and other features of traditional culture are increasingly becoming the focus of scholarly attention also raises the question of whether the Chinese Marxist conception of the influence of traditional culture on the revolutionary—and now modernizing—potential of the peasantry is currently being reevaluated. The Yao *minzu*, as an oppressed minority that throughout history has undertaken rebellions aimed at overthrowing China's feudal system, is represented in the *Jianshi*, by virtue of this oppressive past, as invariably revolutionary. The contemporary discourse on the relationship between traditional culture (*chuantong wenhua*) and modernization (*xiandaihua*), with the assumption that the two invariably confront and oppose each other, suggests that the Yao have not been able to overcome the cultural and social influences of the old feudal system. And yet many Yao scholars have suggested to me that traditional culture should not be viewed as inherently contradictory to projects of development and social transformation. The official practice is still to approach traditional practices with caution; the state still closely monitors local events, and local administrators continue to discuss and haggle over which features are appropriate to the times and which are dangerous and counterproductive to the socialist modernization agenda. The historic and contemporary practice of Yao Taoism is increasingly at the center of this discourse.

We have seen here that the creation and reproduction of an identification with the People's Republic among members of the Yao *minzu* is realized in part through the practice of writing and disseminating state-sponsored official histories. Yet we need to distinguish between writing and dissemination. For many Yao peasants these official histories make little immediate sense; they are probably rarely read and they certainly have not yet replaced the oral historical traditions that remain widespread in the majority of Yao villages. Rather, they are significant for those who are connected with the state apparatus— such as scholars, local administrators, and teachers. And they are increasingly becoming relevant for those local Yao who make their way through the educational system, who acquire training in the official discourses of the past and the present. These official histories, then, are part of a larger state modernization project that aims to create "nontraditional" persons, agents of the state who will return to local regions and organize and facilitate projects of economic development and social change. Such histories are important not only because they interact with and possess the potential to supplant popular oral histories, but also because they provide continued reminders that the dispersed communities that comprise the larger community of the Yao *minzu* are, in fact, an important part of the larger community of the People's Republic of China. As a member of the state apparatus, one becomes involved in the creation of new histories, often at odds with the older, more traditional ones. The potential power of official conceptions of the Yao past to reinscribe the meanings of Yao history and culture rests in the return of these people to their home villages, whether for extended visits or as newly appointed local administrators. New worlds are then opened up for those who have remained behind, as the images of the Chinese nation, the Party, and the state find their way into the imaginative contours of everyday social life.

Père Vial and the Gni-p'a
Orientalist Scholarship and the Christian Project
Margaret Byrne Swain

Civilizing projects of various ruling centers have formed a complex pattern of interactions with distinct linguistic/ethnic groups settled in Southwest China's peripheries. During the late nineteenth century, European and American missionaries introduced variations of the Christian civilizing project into the region (see Harrell, Introduction; and Cheung, this volume). Some of these missionaries were practitioners of Orientalist scholarship, which shaped their responses to indigenous groups they targeted for conversion. Missionary Orientalism can be understood as a type of Christian civilizing project that provoked ethnogenic reactions among its "flocks." It is possible that such missionizing brought about consciousness of membership in an ethnic group opposed and perhaps superior to the Han Chinese.[1]

This type of civilizing project came to my attention as I searched for historical information on the Sani Yi, previously labeled Gni-p'a Lolo, a small ethnic group in Yunnan that has persisted despite its homeland's proximity to Kunming, the provincial capital.[2] Research

1. The potential effects of missionizing among peripheral peoples are addressed by Siguret (1937:2), who quotes the head of the Yunnan Bureau of Popular Education as saying that the Chinese government has not seen to the needs of the peripheral peoples, while Western religious orders have "won the hearts of the inhabitants," who, in the case of conflict, will support the French and the British along the borders, not the Chinese. Moseley also notes that "Christianity was very attractive to the animistic hill peoples, . . . for it made possible feelings of equality and self-respect which had been denied them by the arrogant [Han] plainsmen. These sentiments were reinforced by the loss of prestige, in the eyes of the the hill peoples, of Chinese . . . by comparison with the modern civilization of the West. . . . Christian influence among the uplanders of Yunnan and Kwangsi persisted into the Communist period" (1973:29–30). If Moseley's generalization is accurate, then colonial missionizing efforts to incorporate peoples into a world religious network could be seen as a vehicle for ethnic resistance to state assimilation.

2. My work with the Sani began in 1987 with a brief field study of Sani women's commoditization of ethnicity (Swain 1989; 1990). I wish to thank Stevan Harrell for his encouragement and editorial nurturing of this chapter. I use the current indige-

led me to the writings of missionary Père Paul Vial. Attempting to isolate ethnography, history, and opinion, I began an exhilarating, French-mangling *affaire du texte*. Toward an ultimate aim of understanding the effects of Vial's Orientalist missionizing on Sani ethnicity, I gathered his published writings and photographs (dating from 1888 to 1917), as well as contemporary writings of other missionaries, engineers, and travelers. By today's standards, what they have to say sounds romantic and humane at best, ethnocentric and racist at worst. Vial was part of a French and British network of individuals who followed their countries' colonial expansions from India and Indochina into Yunnan. A number of these colonists indulged in an ethnological hobby of romancing the indigenous, of collecting and classifying while they explored, exploited, and converted in Southwest China. Their writings form an ironic Orientalist commentary by external imperialists on the internal colonizing by China of indigenous peoples.

A typology of Orientalist approaches—based on individuals' occupational motivations, research agendas, and their results in terms of scholarly contributions and impacts on the "host" society—is proposed here.[3] Vial was a missionary type of Orientalist scholar who had sustained contact with the objects of his study. He emerges from his writings and from comments of contemporaries as a flamboyant character with a mission to convert and a fascination with "archaic" societies. Vial's mission was to convert Sani to Christianity and European modernity while maintaining their distinction from Han society. His fascination with Lolo writing and literature fits into this mission as a key to continued Sani Yi ethnic identity as a separate group with a history. Reading his materials as colonial discourse raises a number of questions about their meaning. What was the context in which he wrote? What were Vial's self-image and motivation? What was his understanding of Chinese society, Sani life, and the future of his civilizing project for the Sani?

nous term Sani, rather than Vial's Gnip'a, to refer to these people. However, I follow Vial's use of the term Lolo rather than the current Chinese *minzu* classification of Yi when discussing Orientalist writings about this linguistic group.

3. I am indebted to G. W. Skinner, who, in discussing a draft of this chapter, raised possible distinctions between an "old school" understanding of Orientalists (as students of the Orient who fell in love with a particular language and became fluent in it) and Said's (1979) politically charged understanding, and suggested developing a typology of Orientalists.

These questions are addressed by exploring factors that shaped Vial's discourse on the Sani. His classification of the Sani as a dialect group, and his understanding of their relationship to the Han are analyzed in the context of European imperialism and Orientalism, Vial's personal experience with the Sani, and the objectives of his missionary organization, the Société des Missions Étrangères de Paris. From his perspective as a Roman Catholic Orientalist mission-ary, Vial saw his conversion efforts and scholarly study of Sani cul-ture as a civilizing project constructing a new Sani identity. Evaluat-ing Vial's efforts in terms of Sani thoughts about the effects of Vial's mission on their ethnic identity is a goal of my current research among the descendants of Vial's congregations.

By "ethnic identity" I mean the sociocultural construction of a unique group identity, based on shared descent expressed in cultural traits or markers, and perceived in opposition to other such groups (Spicer 1971; Keyes 1981; Bentley 1987; Harrell, Introduction, this volume). When the Sani were missionized, a new factor or "other" was added into their equation of Sani/not-Sani ethnicity. Vial offered Sani people a new identity of conversion, linked with powerful Euro-pean colonial imperialists who contested the Chinese state's author-ity. Sani response to this missionary civilizing project has functioned within the history of colonialism and revolution in China, while contributing to a transforming sentiment of ethnic difference or ethnogenesis.[4]

ORIENTALISM AND EUROPEAN IMPERIALISM IN SOUTHWEST CHINA

The political and intellectual milieu in which Vial wrote is well de-fined by one word—Orientalism. Edward Said's seminal work (1979) on the subject is so widely cited that a brief introduction should suffice here. Orientalism is a Western European (male) representa-tion of the East or Orient, an us-them dichotomy on a global scale

---

4. I have argued (Swain 1989, 1990) that with the growth of ethnic tourism, the Sani developed a position of some power in relation to the state. This feeds back into sentiments of uniqueness and global perception in the Sani's process of ethnic identifi-cation. This chapter begins to explore the effects of conversion to Christianity and development of a Euro/global consciousness in this process as well. The issue of individual actor vs. group ethnic identity is beyond the scope of this chapter.

and a justification for colonial domination. It became an academic tradition based on a style of thought, as well as a corporate institution for dealing with the Orient. Orientalism can be examined as a discourse for understanding "the enormously systematic discipline by which European culture was able to manage—and even produced—the Orient politically, sociologically, militarily, ideologically, scientifically, and imaginatively. . . . From the beginning of the nineteenth century until the end of World War II France and Britain dominated the Orient and Orientalism" (ibid.:3–4). Orientalism can thus be seen as a "dynamic exchange between individual authors" (ibid.:15) produced in the framework of colonial political concerns of overlapping empires.

Although Said focuses on their shared pursuit, a typology of Orientalists can be constructed by grouping occupational motivations which then correlate with distinct research agendas and results.[5] The Orientalists discussed here have a common interest in indigenous peoples, but there is variation in insights and arguments in their writings that often can be explained by motivation. There is some gradation of commitment to the colonial enterprise—from colonial agent to missionary to traveler to academic—although individuals ranged widely over these hypothetical boundaries.

Colonial agents, whether diplomats or engineers, were motivated by a political mandate (in this case European expansion into Southwest China for economic gain). Their research agendas may have included in-depth study of the "high" culture (Han) Chinese, with incidental study of minority ethnic groups they came across illustrating racial/cultural theories of the day. Research results were usually in the form of information reports to government or scholarly institutions in the agents' own countries supporting colonial activity in the host country.

Missionaries, motivated by a conversion goal, sought to change radically the religious beliefs and self-identity of the mission community. Their research agendas were determined by their gender, religious affiliation (Protestant or Catholic) and theology, and by their sustained contact with specific groups. Research results were in the form of letters for fund raising, language-study materials prepared

5. These characteristics are typical of scholarship by members of colonizing nations about colonized peoples. What makes this specifically Orientalist is the subject's geographic/cultural dimension (e.g., this could also be Africanist or Latin Americanist).

143

for local instruction, and scholarly reports. Said notes missionaries as agents of colonialism but does not specifically examine their role in the Orientalist project. T. O. Beidelman in *Colonial Evangelism* calls for study of the missionary role in colonialism by investigating missionaries' perceptions of themselves and their stereotypes about those they sought to dominate and change (1982:27). Such an approach would enable us to gain insight into what made missionaries act within imperialistic colonialism, and the impact of their missionizing on host indigenous societies.

Orientalist travelers and explorers were motivated by adventure in parts of the world made marginally safe by colonialism. Their research agendas were carried out in brief encounters with distinct cultures, the more remote and exotic the better. Research results (including photographs) were published for popular consumption on postcards and in magazines and travel books, which impacted Westerners' images of host cultures.

Academic Orientalists were theoretically motivated by scholastic curiosity, either within or beyond the armchair. Their research agenda was to compile and analyze materials on specific ethnological or linguistic topics collected in the field by other types of Orientalists, by colleagues, or by themselves. Their research results were presented at academic conferences and published in journals and books. The impact of their study in the host culture continues as new generations of scholars reassess their work. As we shall see in this study of Père Vial, characteristics of these four basic types were combined in many individual Orientalists, and all shared an interest as Westerners in the other, the Orient. This typology shows that within the Orientalist pursuit there was variation in focus and results, as well as in degree of engagement in the colonialist enterprise.

During the late nineteenth and early twentieth centuries, French from Indochina and British from India and Burma competed to build a transportation network connecting their colonial possessions to Chinese materials and markets. British and French arms had supplied both sides of an Islamic rebellion (1855–1873) in Yunnan, which the Chinese state suppressed, while unable to curb Anglo-French incursions. China's defeat in the Sino-French war of 1884–1885, and the British annexation of upper Burma in 1886 set the stage for further European exploitation.

In a pattern found in other parts of the colonialized world (Beidelman 1982:12), British Protestant and French Catholic missionaries in China claimed their exclusive turfs in the contest for souls. Some missions targeted the Han majority, while others aimed at distinct peripheral groups. Although there were a number of Christian missions in China, two organizations specifically devoted to work in Southwest China dominated missionizing in Yunnan for a number of years. The first Protestant missionary activity was established in Yunnan in 1877 by the interdenominational, British-run, China Inland Mission, which grew from 52 missionaries in 1876 to an all-China total of 1,063 in 1915 (Latourette 1929:389, 584). French Catholic missionaries of the Société des Missions Étrangères de Paris had a significant presence in Sichuan since 1756, and were well established in Indochina before they became active in Yunnan. In 1870 there were approximately 80,000 Catholic converts in Sichuan, and 8,000 in Yunnan (ibid.:327). After the Islamic revolt, the Society fully incorporated Yunnan into its field of influence, with the regional French bishop housed in Kunming. In 1872 the society had 78 European missionaries in China and 71 native priests, and by 1918 there were 319 European and 207 native priests (ibid.:323, 326).

Père Paul Vial became a member of this organization just as it flourished in Southwest China. In 1894 the Australian traveler G. E. Morrison (1895:171) reported that there were 22 French priests, 8 ordained Chinese priests, and 15,000 converts under the guidance of Mgr. Fenouil in Yunnan, while at the same time the China Inland Mission had 23 missionaries in the field, with a possible convert total of 11 (ibid.:178). Observing this apparent difference in conversion success, a contemporary British engineer, Major H. R. Davies, concluded that French Catholic defense of their flock against official actions had been a more effective means of proselytizing than British Protestant nonintervention with the local system (1909:217–20). This interpretation is echoed by Morrison (1895), who found the British and American Protestants naive, dogmatic, and inept, and the French Catholic missionaries realistic and relatively successful, though disenchanted with the sincerity of most Chinese converts. In the early 1900s, however, some Protestant missionaries in Guizhou and northeastern Yunnan did take an interventionist stance while ministering to large groups of non-Han converts (see Cheung, this volume).

British and French colonial agents often found themselves dependent on the hospitality of each other's missionaries stationed in remote areas. Major Davies, who was an explorer for the British

India–Yangtze Railroad route in 1894, wrote in reference to a French priest that "it is only necessary to meet in a country like China, to realize how very much alike are the ways of thought of all Europeans," and notes the help and companionship of a number of missionaries (1909:218). Despite nationalistic and religious sniping and hasty claims of "we discovered it first" in their writings, these British and French scholars found reinforcement and comfort in each other as co-Orientalists. Said notes that what these colonialists shared "was not only land, or profit or rule; it was a kind of intellectual power. . . . [A] family of ideas and a unifying set of values proven in various ways to be effective. These ideas explain the behavior of Orientals; they supplied Orientals with a mentality, a genealogy, an atmosphere; most important they allowed Europeans to deal with and even see Orientals as a phenomenon possessing regular characteristics" (1979:41–42).

In Southwest China when Orientalists ran into a number of aboriginal groups decidedly not Han, their classification systems went into overdrive, providing explanations with Orientalist logic. In their desire to classify and explain the origin of the language and physical appearance of diverse peoples, this Anglo-French network of colonial agents, missionaries, travelers, and academics constructed explanatory histories (albeit often confused about who was who) tracing peoples' supposed migrations. Their conclusions, especially about the physically distinct, indigenously literate Yi, were often that these non-Han peoples were more Occidental than Oriental—more like us (though of course inferior) than like the Han.

Harrell (this volume) sees two modes in the Western construction of Yi ethnic history, depending on the writer's religious or scientific orientation. He argues that missionaries, with their intimate knowledge of particular groups and motivation to accurately describe language, myths, and cultural traits for their own purposes, devised a history from native legends. Natural and social scientists, on the other hand, developed their history from a racialist paradigm. The scientific impulse to generalize and systematize produces a racial ethnic-group history based on unexamined assumptions about the correlation of "pure" cultural traits with physical characteristics that persist over generations, but become blurred when "pure" races are mixed. Although there are extremes, both modes of analysis are present and inform each other in many Orientalist texts on peripheral peoples.

Orientalist intellectuals were also heavily influenced by the uni-lineal evolutionary theory of Social Darwinism, which ranks cultures by developmental stages.[6] Missionaries, whose motivation was to change the societies they studied, often viewed these societies as developmentally inferior to those in the industrialized West. Oriental-ists with different motivations formed an audience for each other, networking to produce reams of texts. Among the materials related to the Sani (and to the Yi linguistic group in which they are usually classified by outsiders) there is a similarity in interpretation and cross-referencing. As authors wrote about each other as well as their professional work and ethnological hobby in Yunnan, they provided a window in on the process of Orientalist discourse.

E. Colbourne Baber, a career diplomat, was the self-proclaimed first Orientalist to write about Yi people, then glossed by the Chinese derogatory term Lolo. Baber's paper describing his 1877–1878 explora-tion of Sichuan and Yunnan was read at an 1881 meeting of the Royal Geographical Society in London and subsequently was published. A member of the audience lauded Baber's "discovery of what appears to be a new language, and of a new people never before visited by any European, not even Marco Polo. [It] was a feat that could be reserved for very few in the present age of the world" (1882:142–44). M. Terrien de LaCouperie (a scholar, according to Morrison "who had a happy faculty of drawing upon his imagination for his facts" [1895:257]), noted that Baber "has the right to the recognition of the Orientalists" and proffered his own opinion from examination of Lolo writings that it is a phonetic language with remarkable affinities to Sumatran.

Baber wrote on meeting Lolo in the isolated Da Liangshan interior:

> They are a far taller race than the Chinese. . . . Many of them are robust, but without anything approaching the pork-fed obesity of an affluent sedentary Chinese. . . . Of their women I have unhappily seen few but the younger folk; joyous, timid, natural, open-aired, neatly dressed, barefooted, honest girls, devoid of all the prurient mock-modesty of the club-footed Chinese

6. The five stages of development used in orthodox Marxism to classify sociocul-tural groups and used in the Chinese government's *minzu* classification process is a classic case of unilineal evolutionary thinking. Orientalists and Chinese Communists ironically share an ideology.

women; damsels with whom one would like to be on brotherly terms. . . . tall, graceful creatures with faces much whiter than their brothers'. (1882:60–61)

. . . an oval faced, Aryan-like race. (ibid.:72)

Baber included a description of the Da Liangshan Lolo caste system of Black Bone elite and White Bone subjugated and slave peoples, written about by many later observers and a key in the Chinese Marxist classification of Nuosu Yi at the slave stage of development.[7] He commented that "what the Lolos are, whence they have come, and what is their character, are questions to which I can only make a very incomplete reply. . . . No description of them exists in any extant work, with the exception of a passage to be quoted [Mgr. Fenouil's description of his own capture by Lolo published in the French mission journal *Annales de la propagation de la foi* in 1862]" (ibid.:66, 118–24). Baber wrote that this language group is often mislabeled with various names "devoid of ethnological significance," and that the term Lolo is an insult of Han origin. He also notes that these people have localized native names in their own language marking dialect differences (ibid.:66–67).

Refering to Lolo astronomical practices, Baber commented that "there is no prima-facie reason for denying that this isolated people may possess the rudiments or, perhaps, the relics of certain sciences in the rough, since there is no doubt they have books" (ibid.). A French missionary had told Baber of an indigenous writing system, and remarked of seeing bushels of texts that he was not allowed to examine. After collecting a few examples of writing in "Lolodom," Baber, however, was fortunate to secure "through the kind offices of the French Missionaries" an original Lolo manuscript of eight pages, which he copied for scholars to study in the West (ibid.:128). It is intriguing that although Baber's exploits were claimed by the British to be the first information on the Lolo, he repeatedly noted help from various French missionaries in his quest, and even quoted Mgr. Fenouil's letter on his experiences with the Lolo published some twenty years before.

---

7. This distinguishes them from other Yi groups and the majority of *minzu*, who are classified at the feudal stage.

PÈRE PAUL VIAL

The earliest reference I have found to Père Vial's presence in Yunnan is in British engineer Archibald Colquhoun's 1883 account of explorations for a Burma–China route during 1882. This survey was conducted for the British government from their colony in India and the Royal Geographic Society in order to open up Indochinese commerce. Here again the British explorer was aided by French as well as China Inland Mission missionaries. Colquhoun had bad luck with interpreters, funds, and weather, and was basically stuck on the road to Burma until Vial offered to act as his guide. Vial had been in Yunnan for more than a year, was fluent in Chinese, and welcomed the opportunity to travel from his mission station for Han at Chutung, southwest of Dali. He seemed to be a combination missionary-explorer/guide-scholar. Colquhoun described Vial's skill in negotiating troublesome matters with Chinese servants and officials, his amiable sharing of his last bottle of wine with his European fellow travelers, his fascination with the indigenous Lolo living near his mission, and his willingness to take the more interesting dangerous route. Indeed, Colquhoun reported that "Père Vial was strongly in favour of risking the Ta-ping route [site of Kachin tribal warfare], but at such time I thought the truest courage was . . . 'to be prudent and discreet in everything' " (ibid.:14–15).

On the safer route Vial demonstrated his cultural sensibility by stopping an Englishman from drinking out of a sacred container, which would have disturbed Kachin Nat spirits and perhaps started a fight. Colquhoun and Vial shared numerous adventures, then parted company in Mandalay, where Vial stayed to confer with the regional bishop. Vial's expenses to and from Burma were paid by Colquhoun. When the British explorer subsequently published a monograph in French describing indigenous peoples in Yunnan, the French missionary praised it as the most sincere and exact of European accounts to date (Vial 1893:160). Morrison is not so congratulatory about their exploits. He remarks that the "famous missionary traveller, Père Vial, . . . led Colquhoun out of his difficulty in that journey 'Across Chryse' which Colquhoun describes as a 'Journey of Exploration' (though it was through country that had been explored and accurately mapped a century and a half before by Jesuit missionaries) and conducted him safely to Bhamo in Burma. . . ." (1895:151).

The next chronological record of Vial is in his own words, the first in a series of letters published in *Les Missions Catholiques*. This tabloid was started by L'Oeuvre de la Propagation de la Foi to promote funding for Catholic missions worldwide. From 1888 on Vial wrote "back home" about his living experience with the Sani. As a missionary of the Société des Missions Étrangères de Paris, Vial attended seminary in France (Avignon), then pledged a commitment to missionary work. Although many missionaries went out with the expectation of dying isolated in the field, this society made an effort to keep its missionaries in touch with world events and allowed some furloughs back to France (Latourette 1929:343). Vial, as we have seen, traveled about. Once he made the Sani his primary focus, his mission spanned years of turmoil in China, marked by the Boxer Uprising in 1900 and the Republican Revolution in 1911, while Europe metamorphosed into modern industrial states fighting the First World War. The last of Vial's extant records are his final letters to *Les Missions Catholiques* in 1917.

Vial published letters and photographs for his popular audience in the mission journal, and scholarly works on Lolo language and culture for his fellow ethnologists, and perhaps the Sani themselves. In all of his writing there are constant reminders of his mission to convert the Sani and consistent ethnographic themes: that Sani are part of the Lolo (a larger linguistic/racial/cultural group with a distinct literary heritage), that Sani are in opposition to the Han in both political subordination and cultural (simpler but not inferior?) difference, and that Sani by their very character are open to conversion to Christianity. On this last point, he commented: ". . . these sweet, honest, naive, and likeable faces have conquered me . . ." (1894:161).

Vial interpreted ethnic relations between the Sani and other local groups as being shaped by their sociocultural "character" differences, as well as by the dynamics of political inequalities, and their physical proximity to each other. The relationship between Sani and Han was his primary emphasis. He rarely noted Sani relations with neighboring minority groups such as the Nuosu Lolo, Axi Lolo, or Miao.[8] Muslims allied with various indigenous groups including the Sani during their grueling twenty-year revolt, but, according to Vial, they

8. Vial uses the terms Ashi (for Axi) and Noeso (for Nuosu). His discussion of the Axi, among whom he also inaugurated a mission, does mention one mixed Sani/Axi village along the border of their territories (1893:283). The villagers spoke each other's Lolo dialects as well as Chinese.

often became enemies. He cites Muslim treachery as the reason there was so much post-revolt enmity between them, despite their common Han oppressor (1898:4).

Cross-references and specific comments indicate that the editors of *Les Missions Catholiques* read all of Vial's writings as one unified discourse on the people he was evangelizing. His writings do inform each other, sometimes raising questions about what he really meant, but often filling in apparent gaps or background information. However, the voice Vial used in his writings differed from audience to audience. His popular works were written as informal narrative, describing his environment and the people he worked with, offering opinions and often paraphrasing conversation. His scholarly works which are cited by his fellow Orientalists and other researchers are formally concerned with ethnographic description and linguistic analysis. Vial's greatest weaknesses for a reader today include his unorganized writing, which leaps from topic to topic, and his lack of maps, which make it difficult to locate his actions in small outlying villages. Another problem, especially in his scholarly work, is his transcription of Sani dialect into his own French-based phonetic system, rather than the International Phonetic Alphabet, which some French linguists used as early as 1886.

Vial can be portrayed as an Orientalist by quoting his views on Chinese society and his mission, and by examining his missionizing project among a "simpler people." He lauded the positive qualities of indigenous life—the love of freedom, noncoercive law, gender equality, and language complexity of "la race Lolotte"—and railed against the folly of colonial imperialism and the slander of peripheral peoples by the Han. He was very clear in his distaste for much of Chinese civilization. Often in the same letter or chapter however, Vial spoke of "mes enfants," the Sani folk he worked to convert, their pagan superstitions and simple childlike ways, and their need for enlightenment into the true faith through his colonial mission. There was thus an ironic tension between Vial's celebration and defense of peripheral people and his efforts to make them more European than Chinese. His writings imply that he believed he was empowering the Sani to deal with the modern world in the face of inevitable change, without the loss of their language and culture. Vial's theology and politics shaped his belief in continued cultural diversity within the commonality of humankind.

It is not really correct to say that this missionary-explorer-scholar was a Social Darwinist or unilineal evolutionist like many of his contemporary Orientalists. Rather, he reflected the Neo-Scholastic movement among Catholic intellectuals, which combined theology with an interest in "pagan" peoples (Arbuckle 1985). A counter-evolution theory popular at the time among Catholic scholars was the "degradation theory," which held that in many cultures (especially tribal folk) universal monotheism had been corrupted by human weakness into idol worship. Vial expressed his own theory in a paraphrased conversation with the British consul to Hainan aboard a ship running from Hong Kong to Haiphong (1902:89). He quickly determined that the Englishman was an agnostic and asked if this meant he was a disciple of Spencer. When the consul answered affirmatively, saying that agnosticism was the highest form of truth, Vial attacked with gusto:

> Oh! The highest form! Do you know *monism?* Do you know Haeckel? . . . I would say that you are ignorant of the latest pack of truths that *science* (!) has given us. ["]I believe, he responded, that everything changes and that there will come a time when the earth belongs to five or six powers.["] I find you very generous . . . for an Englishman. Is that because I am French? Well, I believe just the opposite; I believe that humankind will end by forming only one people, but a people divided into small nationalities. I have studied your "evolution" with the firm intention to admit it, if it became evident to me that it was rationally demonstrated. But, the entire system is based on pure hypotheses or on false appearances. . . . Modern science is based on the immutability of natural laws. . . . *Evolution* is nothing other than a late-model rifle which, one hopes, will vanquish the army of the Church. But this is a gun *that does not shoot* and it will end by exploding in your hands. Me, the more I study, the more I understand man, and the more I am Catholic. (Ibid.)

Vial's Popular Writing

Vial's extant letters were published in *Les Missions Catholiques* in the articles and series "Yun-nan (Chine), un tournoi chez les sauvages Lolos" (1888), "Les Gni ou Gni-p'a: Tribu Lolotte du Yun-nan" (part 1, 1893; part 2, 1894), "Deux mois chez les Miaotse" (1900), "Les Joies du retour" (1902), and "A travers la Chine inconnue: Chez les Lolos" (1917). From Vial's letters emerges the story of why and how he found the Sani. He had moved from his mission in the Dali area and spent several years administering a small, calm district which (in his own words) was not sufficient for his zeal and character—he ran out of converts (1893:160). His perception of Chinese persecution of French missionaries after the Sino-French war also spurred his search for a new, more isolated area to evangelize. He quite literally walked into Gni (Sani) country and decided to relocate there as soon as he could make the appropriate administrative arrangements. He settled for the first time in the midst of a small-scale, peripheral community, a group of Lolo with their own literary tradition and writing system.

It was through this restless, evangelizing (by means of a harmonium and magic lantern show), swashbuckling missionary with a huge desire to help the unknowing to a better future that the Sani had their first sustained experience with a European, and ultimately global, society. Vial staked out his territory, evoked Saint Benoît for the men and Saint Geneviève for the women as Sani patrons, and went about setting up a complex mission incorporating a number of villages. He constructed schools, various residences, and churches. According to another French missionary stationed later in the area, Vial was helped with his building projects by a generous French benefactress, who is described as Vial's guardian angel: "Mademoiselle the viscountess, . . . what a shame that not all missionaries have as devoted a protectress!" (Lietard 1904:105).

Vial's first letter from Sani territory is a mixture of colonial editorializing and dramatic description, and focuses mainly on local geography and Sani wrestling events (1888:445). He misidentifies limestone as granite, but his description evokes the rugged, unique characteristics of the karstic topography, and his description of wrestling matches still applies to Sani society. Vial enjoyed watching the matches and felt that wrestling was good conditioning for the rigors of agricultural labor. Bracketing these observations, he addressed his perception of the Lolo's position in China, and his own role:

> This people, dominated but not defeated, subjugated but not subdued, as are all the rest of the indigenous peoples with whom the Chinese are in contact, wait for the time when the celestial empire will disintegrate before the strength of the wind that blows from Europe. . . . Later, if it is the will of God, I will

be the historian of this humble nation. . . . Who knows? Perhaps when China dies, this humble nation of Lolo will still live
on. (Ibid.:445, 446, 448)

This theme is restated in 1893 when Vial starts a series of letters with
the following observation:

> The Lolo people, if they succeed in inoculating themselves with
> true civilization, which is that of Christianity, may be called
> upon to play an important role in the future of the Chinese race,
> which vanquished them, but [which] has not the power to
> assimilate them, and against which they [the Lolo people] hold
> a grudge as deep as it is tenacious. (Ibid.:60)

Vial's 1893 letters comprise a nine-chapter study, written mainly in
an active personal voice, expressing his feelings and opinions as an
engaged observer. These chapters are titled as follows: (1) How I
arrived among the Lolo; (2) How I introduced myself into the [Sani]
Gni tribe; (3) My installation at Loumeiyi; (4) An apostolic trip
around Gni country (different climates, rice culture, description of
Gni country, an excursion, souvenirs, a festival, the "braves" of
Voetsoe, hunting in Gni country, oil mines, the history of a Lolo
overlord, a patrician tribe, arrival at Sia poutse [to visit colleague]
Père Birbes, and return to Loumeiyi); (5) A group portrait; (6) Of
the family; (7) A word on the Axi ["Ashi" in Vial's writing]; (8)
Methods of conversion; (9) The persecution.

Each chapter is rich with detail that is sometimes difficult to distinguish as fact or opinion. Examples of Vial's ongoing themes are
found in his comparison of Sani and Han family life (1893:258), where
the Han are portrayed as opium addicts incapable of productive life,
while the Sani are seen as hard-working saints. This view was echoed
by a fellow missionary who maintained that Sani and Axi in the area
were buying up land from Han forced to sell for cash to support their
opium habits (Lietard 1904:94). Vial in another chapter wrote an
interesting variation on the Orientalist "they seem Aryan" argument
about indigenous folk:

> Thus, the Lolo is convinced that we belong to the same race as
> him; and this conviction draws him all the closer to us, as he
> hates the Chinese race. "Since we are of the same race, it is

natural," he says, "that we be of the same religion." And so he hopes to live in the safety of the protective shadow of our influence. (1893:293)

From Vial's perspective, the Lolo (i.e., Sani) saw themselves as very distinct from the Han and kindred with Europeans. Thus "his" Lolo at least sought mission protection and readily converted to Catholicism.

In his ongoing comparison of Han and Sani character, he summarized Han intelligence as strong, crafty, and mercantile. The Han were farmers only by necessity—their instinct was commercial. The hierarchical structure of Chinese society mandated that all social interaction be calculated as responses in dominant-subordinate relationships, which Vial maintained was contrary to "the European character, and especially the Catholic character" (1893:245). In comparison, in his view the Sani loved their land. They had a sense of liberty, but that was not the same as an independent character. More than the Han, Sani allowed themselves to be swayed by example, following their leaders. The Sani had their faults, but they were not haughty, jealous, or opinionated like the Han (ibid.). Vial discussed the problems resulting from exchange of identities between the Sani and the Han:

> They take on their reciprocal faults and abandon their [own] strengths. The Chinese-Lolo loses the politeness that distinguishes the yellow race in order to fall into the libertine way; the Lolo-Chinese abandons his good nature and his simplicity in order to become hypocritical and haughty. (1893:209)

He also related some aspects of Sani-Han political economy in his letters. He believed that most Han settled in Sani territory were descended from waves of migrants coming west out of the Nanjing region,[9] who took indigenous people's land by force or trickery (ibid.:179). The Han then started charging rent and administered the area as a prefecture under their jurisdiction. Vial described Sani territory as two parallel plains divided by a mountain chain running north-south (1902:160; 1917:537). In the western Loulan (Lunan) plain, the land is well irrigated and villages are tied to regional market systems and to the main road running from Kunming to

---

9. Harrell (personal communication, 1989) notes that many "minority" peoples of central Yunnan trace their descent to Nanjing. On a Lipuo case, see Harrell (1990:531).

Guangxi. The population is about half Han and half Sani, living in segregated villages. The eastern plain is much more rugged karstic topography, remote, and dry, and the population is mainly Sani. Vial reports that every year Sani women, men, and children migrate from the east, where their crops are still green, to the Lunan region, where they can work as temporary laborers harvesting rice on Han lands. Han prefer to hire Sani laborers "who talk less and work better," rather than other Han (1893:201). Vial felt that in Lunan, on the outer limits of Sani territory, "where [they are] in contact with a race whose minds are less one-track, more advanced," the Sani were more open to conversion than were the Sani in more remote areas. Hence his long-term mission strategy was to first concentrate on these people, then slowly work eastward to communities in the core of Sani territory. He wrote about this plan in 1902 and in his 1917 letters gave details of recent conversions in the remote communities. (See map 2, p. 64.)

In Vial's last letters he talked about the most remote village yet to convert, and remarked how strange it was that "the more the village seems savage to me, the more the children who live in it seem sweet. All around me I perceive such big, calm, innocent eyes, shadowed by a chestnut blond head of hair; could it be the true ancestral type?" (1917:545). There is a strong romantic sentiment in Vial's description of the Sani which usually avoided the words "primitive" or "savage" to describe *his* people of "the noble simplicity, . . . this good people which civilization has not yet reached" (1893:179). This perception shaped his conversion efforts among the Sani. Vial saw them as little babes, incapable of reason at first, and needing to be carefully guided to take their first steps toward spiritual maturity (ibid.:224). Firm paternal authority was the avowed style of his mission, with entertaining enticement in songs, "European curiosities," and outright bribes of pearls for the women. He found it remarkable that during his evangelizing, the Sani never slandered the religion he taught, even though they may not have understood it (ibid.:245).

Over the years, Vial commented on Sani character as the inspiration and challenge of his mission. His first impressions of Sani portrayed a lively, well-built, warlike people, a little rowdy, frank, of good faith, and even the women were "not frightened" (1888:446). His later observations used words such as fearful (*craintif*) and timid (*timide*) in reference to the Sani response to outsiders, which varied with both the relative isolation of Sani and the nature of the

PÈRE VIAL AND THE GNI-P'A

"other."[10] In 1893 he wrote that Sani shun (*fuient*) strangers, although he was making some progress, and had been "allowed to lift the veil that had enveloped them until now" (ibid.:160). A little later he observed that "the Gni is unfortunately fearful: his first movement is to avoid you" (ibid.:245). This could be resolved if one opened up one's heart to them, but here Vial was talking about the Sani response only to strangers like himself. In the next sentence, he wrote: "Happening suddenly upon a Chinese, he will come to you and beg you to defend him." He later expanded on this theme:

> The Gni is born timid but not fearful; he shuns strangers as if they were bringing the plague. . . . He is not afraid, but he is not daring. In front of a Chinese, he is as a dog before a tiger; it is not the man but his treachery that he dreads. . . . The most serious fault of the Gni is clearly to be a large child who follows you, but who never precedes you. He is missing the mind that makes nations and leaders, but between *headless* and *heartless*, I need not deliberate[;] I choose *headless*. (1898:26)

Vial's understanding of Sani and Han character reflected the Sani point of view about the Han and served as a rationale for his mission to convert this "simpler people" and thus arm them with ways to protect themselves from the Han.

Vial's chapter on Chinese persecution of his mission set the stage for a remarkable story retold in the "current news" section of *Les Missions Catholiques* (1894:307–308). In a verbatim report of a lecture Vial gave at a seminary in France in 1894, his continuing fight with the local mandarins unfolds like an adventure novel. His struggle with Han authorities became personally dangerous when the word went out among the Han that this priest had set himself up as king of the Gni and needed to be removed. After discovering the "mandarin's assassins" in his church late at night, Vial fought with them, receiving fourteen wounds, including damage to his right arm and a stab wound next to his heart. His followers dragged him back to his quarters, where he said to them: "You see, I will die; it is because of you and in order to defend you that I voluntarily offer my life for you; always stay faithful to the religion that I have taught you." He doused his wounds with an antiseptic, a local Sani medicine man

---

10. Vial used similar terms to indicate Sani belief in "superstitions" for explanations.

applied herbs, and Vial recovered enough to go to Hong Kong for surgery. Because he needed more medical care, he proceeded to France.

While in Europe, Vial continued work on his scholarly text, *Les Lolos*, excerpts of which he published as "Les Gni ou Gni-pa: Tribu Lolotte du Yun-nan" (part 2) in *Les Missions Catholiques* in 1894. He then returned to Yunnan, continuing his mission building and working on his Sani dictionary, which he completed in 1908. His mission grew to incorporate several other French missionaries and Chinese nuns and ultimately Sani priests serving some thirty villages throughout Sani territory.[11] When he wrote to *Les Missions Catholiques* in 1917 he spoke of his mission's progress in schools for boys and girls, and of focusing on the present moment in his work. Vial died that year in Lunan, surrounded by the Sani Catholic and French missionary community he had so carefully crafted (Zhang Wenchang 1987:31).

Vial's Scholarly Writing

Of three scholarly works by Vial, only his brief initial study, *De la langue et de l'écriture indigènes au Yû-nân* (1890), was published in Europe.[12] His 1898 book based on Sani data, *Les Lolos: Histoire, religion, moeurs, langue, écriture*, was published in Shanghai by La Mis-

---

11. Whether Vial chose to stay with his mission or was limited to it because of his confrontational stance toward the Han and Catholic Church hierarchy is an interesting question. In 1894 the peripatetic Australian traveler George E. Morrison noted that Vial "has often been in Yunnan City and is a possible successor to the Bishopric" (1895:150), but Vial remained a field missionary administrator. In 1900 he took a vacation among a Miao (Hmong) community and looked into possibly starting a new mission with a Yao group. As he later noted, he was forty-five years old then with maybe a dozen working years left, and his work with the Sani was virtually complete (1902:106). He reasoned that it would be the best use of his talents to evangelize a new group, but Mgr. Fenouil ordered him to return to his Sani "children," and there Vial stayed.

12. This study was printed less than two years after Vial moved to Sani territory, where, as he notes in his early letters, he was taking time to learn the Sani language and to build up trust among the people. As Colquhoun (1883) noted, in the early 1880s Vial was interested in Lolo writing, so he probably had accumulated information useful in his study of Sani that became the basis of his 1890 publication. While Lietard states that Vial arrived in July 1888 to start his Sani mission (1904:105), Devéria also says that by 1890 he had been there for several years (1891:360). In Vial's 1890 work, Dom Chamard writes that his young friend has been with the Sani for three years. Vial himself dates the work July 31, 1889.

sion Catholique. His largest work, the 1909 *Dictionnaire Français-Lolo, dialecte Gni,* contains a grammar and six Sani texts and was published in Hong Kong by La Société des Missions Étrangères. A detailed examination of Vial's scholarly writing and of contemporary ethnographic and linguistic critiques of these efforts shows us how the Orientalist's perspective on minority and Han cultures combined with scholarly interests. Vial's missionary goal of conversion intertwined with this Orientalist agenda to shape his Christian civilizing project among the Sani.

Several methodological issues are central to Vial's scholarship. The importance of language study permeates his writing and infused his missionary efforts. Vial perceived Christianizing the Sani as a process that must use their own language (1902:175–76). He hoped to accomplish conversion by preaching to them in Sani and, most of all, by publishing a catechism written in their own language: "Their own ways must be added there to obtain this goal [of conversion] and the methods must be in keeping with the genius of this people" (ibid.).

Vial prefered to use primary research materials. He remarked that his own translation of many Chinese texts about the Lolo proved to be useless "childishness" (*enfantillages*), and he cautioned all students of human diversity in China to firmly avoid Chinese texts on the subject. Rather than give an example of these prejudiced Chinese texts, Vial quotes Marco Polo as an early outside source on the Lolo. In response to colleagues' questions about why he did not use Chinese sources, Vial wrote: "All sinologists are legion . . . to travel through the labyrinth of Chinese literature; I would prefer to travel on foot, and gather the information myself. . . . The Chinese observe foreigners, Miao, Lolo, or Europeans only through the magnifying glass of their immense conceit, and all objects have the appearance of a grotesque caricature which seems reality to them" (1900:474).

Initial Study: De la langue et de l'écriture indigènes au Yû-nân. In his 1893 letters Vial makes a brief reference to his 1890 study: "Two years ago, I was the first, I believe, to become acquainted with the language and writing of the Gni-p'a" (p. 160). In a preface to the 1890 work, the Benedictine Dom Chamard writes that while it assuredly was not a complete study following the scientific methods of comparative philology required in Europe, "it seemed to me that, written by the first missionary to take on such a work, . . . [it] was worthy of the attention of those who are interested in the history of primitive peoples and faraway regions." This same theme—that Vial's work is incomplete but noteworthy especially because it is the first study of a Lolo dialect based on sustained fieldwork—is echoed in G. Devéria's 1891 review. Devéria draws on reports by various agents and travelers in southwest China and includes information from Edward Colbourne Baber's 1882 study to favorably assess Vial's contribution. The missionary's character also seems to be a factor, as he is portrayed in rather heroic terms:

> [T]his valiant missionary began to study their language and their writing. He is the first who made this attempt, dictated by an intelligent zeal, which places him among his scholarly predecessors of the last century, [an] attempt crowned by success which will broaden the fieldwork of Catholic missions in South China and [which] suffices from this day onward to rectify some appraisals previously too hastily published on the writing and language of the Lolo. (Devéria 1891:360)

Père Alfred Lietard, who worked in the neighboring Axi Lolo mission inaugurated and administered by Vial, provided another commentary on the 1890 study, noting that Vial is the authoritative voice on Lolo ethnography (1904:94). However, he differs with Vial on various points—including the names of the two major Lolo dialect groups constructed by Vial (the *a* and the *ou,* which Lietard calls the *o*)—and calls Vial's group Sagni, not Gni. Vial remarks of Lietard that here is a young man, much as he himself was in his earlier days, full of idealism and protectively watching over his Axi "children" (1902:149). What might have been a fruitful working relationship between the two missionaries is not reflected in their later publications.[13]

This first study of Vial's, which established him as an expert on Sani, if not all Lolo language, is seventeen pages long. It consists of an introduction, a section on spoken language, a section on writing, and the Sani text and a literal translation of the Sani story of the flood (which would be rewritten and retranslated in the 1898 study). Vial carefully cites various Europeans who had published opinions on

---

13. Vial makes no mention of Lietard in his dictionary, although Lietard published on Axi linguistics. Lietard gives one scant reference to Vial in his own well-organized, detailed 1913 study of the Lolopo, a Lolo group located in northwestern Yunnan with whom he subsequently worked.

Lolo writing, including his old friend Colquhoun and the often-quoted Terrien de Lacouperie. Much of what Vial has to say in the language sections is elaborated on in his later work. Of particular interest here is the introduction, in which he writes about ethnic relations between the Lolo and the Han and the forces of imperialism. Vial saw in European history parallels to the situation in Yunnan—the Han were like the Romans, while the Lolo were like his own people, the Gauls (1890:8):

> In their administration, their morals, their character, and their religion, the Lolo vividly recall our [fore]fathers. . . . Their tribes are as numerous as the Gallic tribes, and if their language is basically the same, the difficulty of communications has multiplied the dialects. That which has caused them to be delivered to the Chinese is the same as that which delivered us to the Romans: lack of unity. Finally, the last trait of resemblance, those same Franks who drove out the Romans and conquered our fatherland, are now at the door of Yunnan." (1890:8)

Les Lolos—Histoire, religion, moeurs, langue, écriture. Vial's 1898 study is a seventy-one page jumble of information. The subjects are generically Lolo or specifically Sani, with reference to several other indigenous groups. About one third of the content concerns language. The following brief review of the study's nine chapters and an appendix illustrates the variety of topics Vial pursued. In the preface, he writes that a desire to counter misunderstanding about the Lolo motivated his study:

> I love him [the Lolo] because he is good, I love him because he is scorned. I would like to have him known [for] pushing aside the plethora of prejudices that fill books and that are unabashedly accepted as proven facts. It seems to me that a missionary who has first of all given eight years of his apostolic life for the salvation of the Chinese, and who now has evangelized to the Lolo for as many years, has the right to carry an opinion exempt from ignorance, if not errors of partiality.

In chapter 1, "History," Vial attempts to "set the record straight" with a partial history of Lolo people, citing Sani stories and French

161

missionaries working in Southwest China since the 1600s.[14] There is a symmetry between Vial's experience with Lolo culture and Sani origin myths. Vial first came into contact with Lolo groups in the Dali area, and the Sani origin myths say that their ancestors traveled east from Dali to settle in their current territory. This chapter was critiqued by R. F. Johnston, a British colonial official stationed in Northeast China who wrote with a focus on ethnology about his own travels in the Southwest. Johnston noted Vial's conclusion that the Lolo are one and the same as the Manzi (a Chinese term for independent "barbarians" living in the Southwest) based on the linguistic research of a colleague, Père Martin. He comments that "probably no one has a better acquaintance with the Lolos than the Catholic missionary M. Paul Vial. . . . [But] his historical sketch is unfortunately too brief to be of much value. . . ." (1908:274–75).

Chapter 2, "Religious Traditions," relates Sani myths Vial collected from texts written in Lolo script, or from dictations by the writers and keepers of these texts, religious specialists called *pimo*.[15] Myths translated by Vial include "The Creation," "The Disobedience," "The Drought," "The Flood," "The Darkness," and "Redemption." Recitation of the flood myth occurs at every marriage. According to Vial, its story of the second beginning of the earth is a metaphor for the beginning of each family. The myth relates the first act of venerating ancestors (both mother's and father's parents) by decorating a small household memorial with a specific species of orchid. Vial observed this form of ancestor worship commemorating two generations (grandparents and great grandparents) within Sani homes.

In his analysis of the creation myths, Vial sees trinities of good and evil forces. From the redemption myths, he notes indigenous appli-

14. For recent Lolo history, Vial (1898:4) refers to fellow Orientalist G. Devéria's "La Frontière Sino-Annamite" as the authoritative source on the peripheral peoples' political situation in Yunnan under the Chinese, perhaps returning the favor of Devéria's favorable review of his 1890 study.

15. Vial translated *pimo* as *sorcier* (sorcerer), a male religious functionary, but noted that there are other named categories of specialists (male and female) whose activities include positive and negative sorcery and divination. About the *pimo*, who interprets sacred texts and presides over rites of passage, Vial wrote: "It would be more accurate to translate it as *prêtre* [priest], if I were not afraid to profane this word" (1898:12). Much of what Vial wrote about myths and religious specialists he applied to all Lolo, although he notes specific "tribal" differences and acknowledges the Sani source of much of his material.

cation of Jesamo or Iesou, a redeeming culture hero, to signify Jesus. Despite many potential parallels with Christian myths and symbolism, Vial does not argue for a "primitive monotheism" or actual links, as did many of his anti-evolutionist co-frères. Rather, he writes: ". . . since they became Christians, they have insisted to us that Isou and Iesou (Jesus) are the same. Myself, I still believe that this is only a fortuitous resemblance" (ibid.:11).

The next chapter, "Lolo Language," mentions a few points of grammar, then discusses three questions: Is there one Lolo language? Is it widespread? To what languages is it related? In response to the first, Vial states: ". . . the Lolo language is indeed the same everywhere in its structure and its mechanism; but it is divided into a large number of dialects by the changing of consonants or vowels—or consonants and vowels" (ibid.:14–15). Vial answers the second question by using Chinese maps and compiling word lists showing relationships over a broad geographic range, to map the distribution of Lolo. To answer his third question, he posits: ". . . the Lolo seem to me to be the brothers of the Burmese and the cousins of the Baiyi (or Tai); but they have no relationship with the Chinese, neither in language, nor in custom, nor above all in character" (1898:15).

This last answer was critiqued by Johnston (1908:277). He felt that Vial had "gone a little astray" by offering a linguistics-based argument, "which should always be accepted with very great caution. . . ." Vial's conclusion that the Lolo, Burmese, and Tai had common origins in the area between the upper Mekong and the Brahmaputra, also "does not account for the subsequent divergence of languages, customs, and traditions." Johnston's reasoned tone disappears (ibid.:279) when he turns to his own ideas on possible language links between the Lolo and "Mo-so" ("they call themselves Lashi or Nashi") living in northwestern Yunnan (ibid.:279). Any such links were denied by the Mo-so he asked, but "such denials . . . do not go for much, especially in the case of a people who are totally lacking in any historical sense."[16]

16. Upon questioning, some Mo-so "admitted" to Johnston that they had many words in common with the Lolo. Furthermore, he used a remark by Vial to fuel his own ideas, which well illustrate the perils of linguistic based arguments. Vial's 1898 book mentions that the Axi Lolo tribe lives in southeastern Yunnan. Johnston (1908:280) then tried to demonstrate that the Axi are somehow one and the same as the Naxi in northwestern Yunnan, who today, with many linguists, would still deny any close link.

Chapter 4, "Literature and Poetry," expands on Vial's view that the Sani are part of a larger linguistic tradition and repeats materials he published four years earlier in *Les Missions Catholiques*. By literature, Vial meant both oral and written traditions. He distinguished poetry from prose forms by the invariant rhythm of three or five syllables per line. Long formal chants, such as the flood epic or the nuptial chant describing the development of a girl from infancy to marriage, are part of the Sani *pimo*'s written tradition. Songs are an informal poetic form of improvised recitations following a set melody. They are more often melancholy than cheerful and are most often sung by young women while working. Vial notes that "like the song in France, the indigenous tragic ballad has its fashion, and some are even passed on to posterity" (1898:21). Sani and Lolo in general also sing geographic verses called *mifêkê*, which describe where they live as well as territory occupied in the past "which the Chinese took from them" (1894:302).

Poetic laments and geographic songs published by Vial (1898:20–23) were used with acknowledgment by the writer Paul Boell in a paper on Lolo language presented at the International Congress of Orientalists in 1899.[17] Boell began with a list of previous works on Lolo language, including those of Baber and Vial. Vial had impressed Boell with his industry and knowledge when they met in Yunnan:

> . . . the man currently best placed to furnish us with information on the language of the Lolo must be mentioned: Fr. Vial. . . . We await from him an extensive dictionary of the Gni-p'a dialect, which he knows well. . . . We are happy that Fr. Vial can find, in the midst of his demanding ministry, the necessary time to complete this great work. . . . [Vial] was on many an occasion my authorized guide during my stay in Lolo country. (Boell 1899:2)

Returning to Vial's 1898 study, chapter 5, "Lolo Morals and Customs," discusses themes found throughout his work: that the Sani are linguistically Lolo; that they are culturally and politically in

17. Boell, who had left the secretariat of the French legation in Beijing to become the special correspondent for *Le Temps,* traveled in Southwest China in 1892 (Morrison 1895:150). One of Boell's objectives on this trip was to research the Lolo language. An opportunity to "unlock" Vial's French-based orthography of Sani was lost when Boell, instead of using the International Phonetic Alphabet for the same texts, chose to use his own system based on a mixture of European languages. He even transcribed into his own system Sani words that are used in the grammar notes attributed to Vial.

opposition to the Han, and that the Sani are open to conversion to Christianity. He defends his use of the Chinese derogatory gloss Lolo as an expediency because there is no pan-linguistic-group indigenous term,[18] and then in the appendix elaborates on the possible origins of the term. Addressing the question of how to distinguish between the numerous Lolo peoples, Vial's observations prefigure issues of ethnic identity that anthropologists would focus on more than fifty years later. Noting that members of the same tribe can dress in a variety of costumes and that the same dialect can be spoken by several tribes, Vial continues:

> There is, in fact, only one way to recognize the clan to which these inhabitants with such varied costumes and dialects belong: it is to know whether they marry each other. No doubt, there are exceptions to this rule, it could not be otherwise; but the principle remains true and it alone suffices to explain many things. In short, a tribe is nothing other than a nation writ small and a family writ large. (Ibid.:25)

His argument that marriage rules reflect a group's boundaries much more accurately than language use or material culture was based on years of travel, work, and observation in Southeast Asia. Edmund Leach, in his 1954 study *Political Systems of Highland Burma* (based on his research among the Kachin), brought this type of observation to mainstream anthropology. As G. Carter Bentley has observed, ethnicity emerged as a key problem in the discipline when Leach challenged

> the conventional assumption that societies and cultures covary sufficiently that the two terms can be used interchangeably. Leach's argument . . . was that members of a social group need share no set of distinctive cultural traits. Instead . . . social units are produced by subjective processes of categorical ascription that have no necessary relationship to observers' perceptions of cultural discontinuities. (1987:24)

Once Leach's premise was fairly well accepted among anthropologists, "the issue shifted to whether subjective claims to ethnic identity

18. See Harrell (this volume).

derive from the effective potency of primordial attachments, . . . [and/]or the instrumental manipulation of culture in service of collective political and economic interests" (ibid.:25). While I would not argue that Vial was thinking along these lines, I do think that his theoretical openness about the criteria used by the people themselves to determine an ethnic group or "tribe" was ahead of its time.[19] Unlike many of his fellow Orientalists, Vial in this passage was not equating a linguistic group with a sociocultural or racial entity.

In chapter 6 of *Les Lolos,* "Birth, Marriage, and Death," one might expect to find the definitive Sani characteristics spelled out in marriage, residence, and inheritance rules, but neither in this study nor in his letters does Vial address kinship issues and authority structure coherently. Rather than describe household composition, he discusses families, which he says averaged six members (1898:27) and had an average of six children (1893:268).[20] Marriage is treated as a fact of Sani life that had been somewhat corrupted by adapting the Han practice of paternal betrothal of young children (1898:28). Sani marriage customs are shown to vary considerably from those of the Han in the following ways: either child could later refuse to enter into the marriage; the marriage was not performed until both partners were considered of marriageable age; and after marriage a young woman could visit her parents—the Sani did not practice matrilocal residence prior to birth of the first child, as did some Lolo groups (1893:268—70; 1898:28—30).[21] This last Lolo custom, Vial com-

19. Harrell (this volume) notes that while Leach was studying the Kachin, his contemporaries Feng and Shryock in China ironically were interpreting Chinese accounts of various minority groups to mean that "an ethnic group is a racial and/or cultural, but not political, group."

20. This might imply neolocal residence, although virilocal is implied by "The Complaint of the Young Bride," a song recorded by Vial in which a girl laments her separation from her mother, and living with people who make her feel like a thief or someone with the plague, and who, despite her hard work, still speak to her unkindly (1898:20—21). I have found only one reference to family authority in Vial's writings: ". . . this intimate life of a patriarchal people" (ibid.:67). Under the term *parente* in his dictionary, Vial notes that consanguines (*ts'òkò*) are thought of as a trunk, while uterine kin (*kòkeé*) are a branch off a different trunk (1909:246). He did not discuss indigenous political authority, except in a dictionary entry on *chief* described later in this chapter.

21. This was discussed by Lietard in his comparison of Sani to the neighboring Axi, who did follow distinct Lolo customs (1904:94—96). Axi youths stopped sleeping at home at about age fifteen and stayed in single-sex groups at night. Informal in-

mented, was "an abuse, but it will not go any further; and the prejudices against this people must be deeply ingrained in order to dare conclude them a monstrosity" (1898:30). The highly negative Han opinion of the position of women in many peripheral societies based in relative gender equality was an issue that Vial raised when comparing Sani ways more favorably to European than to Han mores (1893:189). Sani gender equality was also expressed in property rights,[22] rituals welcoming the birth of all children, similar funeral and ancestor rites for males and females, and the lack of patronyms.

Although Vial did not discuss marriage rules defining potential spouses, he offers a few clues in the writings discussed here. He remarks that in the Sani extended kinship system

> almost all are cousins, as is the fashion in Brittany; it suffices, for example, that [when] one old man greets another old man for all the descent relations to be acknowledged, not only direct descent [relations] but even collateral and quasicollateral [relations] if there are any. (Ibid.:270)

tervillage youth gatherings, where marriage partnerships often first evolved, were held monthly. Parental sanctions were requested for marriage around the age of twenty. Lietard does not make it clear where the young couple lived after marriage. The Sani epic poem "Ashima," popularized in China during the 1950s as folk literature, tells of a Sani maiden who, following a custom similar to that of the Axi, socializes with a group of young people prior to the time of choosing a mate. In Vial's versions of this wedding chant, prenuptial coeducational camping is not mentioned.

22. This is another underdiscussed issue in Vial's writings. In his letters, Vial mentions that "sons, daughters, sons-in-law, all are on the same footing; in addition a son-in-law has the right to a double inheritance, first his own and afterward his wife's" (1893:268). That the son-in-law has rights to his wife's property infers that males may have more male ultimate control in the system than do females. However, Vial offers more tantalizing clues in his next paragraph: "If the daughter leaves her house to enter another, her mother makes a gift of some fields which belong to [the daughter]; the young wife can always return to her parental dwelling and live there like other members of the family." So a bride is given property by her mother, and she has the option of coming back home if the marriage fails. Vial then states that the Lolo's high incidence of divorce is most likely due to women's freedom. In the same chapter he writes that partition of property occurs late in the family cycle, with siblings often staying together for a while after both parents are dead (ibid.:270). Perhaps bride-wealth and inheritance was a gender-based parallel system, with mothers giving to daughters and fathers to sons. In his comparison of Axi and Sani marriage, Lietard wrote a little on inheritance. While both groups celebrated the birth of either sex, among the Axi "parents seem to have a weakness for boys who will continue the family. A daughter, in effect, has no share in her paternal inheritance unless she has not been married" (1904:94).

If practically all are cousins, and if the Sani marry only Sani (Lietard 1913:39), then marriage partners are probably cousins. In his dictionary Vial does not define marriage partners, but he gives the terms for different kinds of cousins, aunts, and uncles. Two main types are distinguished. Ego's father's brother (FB) and mother's sister (MZ) are called in everyday usage *eebá* and *emmà* respectively, the same terms for "father" and "mother." The children of FB and MZ, parallel cousins, are called by ego the same terms as sister (*moùneù*)[23] and brother (*vìghài*). The other type, cross cousins—the children of father's sister (FZ, *àghhè*) and mother's brother (MB, *ágni*)—are distinguished by specific terms. Ego calls MB's and FZ's son *ágnizá*, while MB's, FZ's, and ego's own daughters are call *ámái*. A similar form of this Iroquoian system of cousin terminology has been recently documented by Stevan Harrell (1989) among Nuosu Yi, who practice preferred cross-cousin marriage. In Vial's day, even though marriage forms were being sinified, the choice of partners, which Vial considered critical for group identity, may have been based on the Sani kinship system, which was very distinct from that of the Han.

Chapter 7, "The Dong *jiazi* [people] and the Miao *jiazi*," is a rendition of correspondence between Vial and his colleague Père Roux, a missionary working with peripheral peoples in neighboring Guizhou province.[24] The two groups in the title are the focus of Vial's questions and Roux's answers. Vial was particularly interested in comparing Miao (Hmong) society and culture, which he saw as considerably less complex, to those of the Sani. Later, in 1900, he tried to set up a mission among a Hmong group in southern Yunnan.

"Complementary Notes," chapter 8, deals with the Lolo calendrical zodiac cycle (a system similar to that of the Han); Lolo naming practices; and "the future of these people." This last section contains Vial's urgent message about and to the Sani: they can and should persist. He relates that some fifteen years earlier an old missionary had commented to him that there was little reason to evangelize this

23. While he gives this term and explanation for this relationship, Vial also notes under *soeur* that there is no direct Lolo gloss, and relationships are age-graded in a variety of terms (1909:305). Address terms are simplified and terms of reference are often age-graded for kin relationships as well as marked by generation.

24. Roux wrote from "Tchen-lin, Koei-tcheou [Guizhou]" in 1889. While saying that he had little time to research the Miao in particular, he wrote that the numerous tribes he was aware of called themselves in their own language various types of Hmong and said they came "from the East."

race when in twenty or thirty years all their efforts would die with the Lolo. Obviously Vial thought otherwise, but he understood that this Han-derived perspective about indigenous peoples was difficult to overcome: ". . . it is evident that this people has been called upon to disappear, or rather to disintegrate. There is not a shadow of a doubt, and to think otherwise would require gall indeed" (1898:38). He acknowledged that the Han had driven back Lolo people from the plains into the mountains, that some Lolo had sinified by choice, and that even whole tribes for diverse reasons imitate the Han. But at the same time, the Han, who "have the spirit of assimilation even less than the English," scorned the Lolo and the Lolo hated the Han. Vial argued: "If the Lolo have relations with a kind, sweet, and just nation, I believe they will willingly ally themselves with it" (ibid.). He did not see the Han changing, however, and literally put his faith in Christianity as the hope for the Lolo's future: "Christianity . . . will make him understand what is beautiful, good, and true, and the Lolo will no longer think to search elsewhere for that which he will find henceforth in himself" (ibid.).

The last chapter, "Lolo Writing: Ideologic, then Phonetic," briefly describes the main characteristics of the language and what Vial theorized to be its development history. He argues that each tribe has conserved the usage of some signs and has forgotten others (ibid.: 41). The writing was used mainly by the *pimo* religious specialists to record Sani teachings. Vial lists four difficulties in translating Lolo books: (1) It is difficult to know where a phrase starts and ends because there is a "five-character rule," which adjusts the meaning of each measure. (2) Many of the locutions are of an old form, are regionalisms, or are extinct. The books are transcribed without intentional change, which is helpful to a translator trying to decipher a particular text. (3) When comparing texts, it is best to work with the oldest for the most accurate (least copied) text, but dating the manuscripts is just conjecture. (4) The actual ideographic and phonetic aspects of each character are obscure (ibid.:66–67). Despite these and other problems, Vial worked long at translating Sani writings, apprenticing himself to learned *pimo* when possible. In this chapter he offers side-by-side Sani script, pronunciation, and French gloss for three Sani myths: "The Creation," "The Universal Drought," and "The Universal Flood," and provides a textual translation.

Vial had hopes of someday discovering a book of Lolo writing that would reveal the history of this people. However, he saw no conscious need for such a book among the people with whom he worked:

> Basically, the Lolo know only the life of the family—of the village at most—and all the books with which I am familiar are written for this life: birth, marriage, illness, religious acts, death—such are the circumstances around which the literary works of these tiny republics effuse. (Ibid.:67)

The issue of "historical sense" was important in Orientalist paternalism and in the Social Darwinist argument about the position of "simpler" folk on the evolutionary scale. As Vial noted early in his work with the Sani, he hoped to become their historian. What was wrong with the Sani's own religious leaders who wrote and interpreted the sacred Yi scripts, telling their written stories and oral histories as well? In part it was the need of the Europeans to rewrite these histories so that they fit into Western schemas of how things are and should be, thus justifying imperialistic actions. Vial in fact saw himself salvaging Sani language from certain deterioration and loss in the face of cultural change that from another point of view was aggravated by his colonial mission:

> The literate Lolo no longer write, they only transcribe; it happens, however, that they add what they believe to be explanations, and the text of which I speak is one of these. I was not put off by this, out of a sense of impartiality; perhaps others will not think like me. (Ibid.:67)

The final entry in *Les Lolos* is an appendix, "Origin Problem of the Word 'Lolo,' " with comments by Vial's trusted friend Père Martin. Martin argued that a euphonic doubling of the first syllable of Noeso, the indigenous name of the "patrician" tribe they first encountered, led the Han to call them Nono, often pronounced Lolo in Chinese.[25] Vial comments:

> Particular to a tribe, this word had become the appellation of an entire people. . . . It is a scornful term only when passing from a

25. This word was very much in use as a pejorative by Han in the Kunming area in 1987.

Chinese mouth, from which, one realizes, the word European is also an insult. Later, the Chinese developed a less confused opinion of the Lolo, and they strove to designate each tribe by a particular name. (Ibid.:70)

As Vial notes with the example of "European," just because distinct cultures are known does not keep others from grouping people by perceived characteristics. Vial had already stated in chapter 5 why he used this term despite its pejorative meaning in Chinese, for lack of any other group name. His need seems to be primarily to label a linguistic group, although he lapsed into racial rambling, as his remarks on a "true ancestral type" quoted above from his letters illustrate (1917:545). In his dictionary, Vial elaborates once more on usage of the term Lolo:

> The Lolo do not have a single term that can be applied to an entire nation or a race of men, no more for others than for themselves. . . . With the Lolo, each tribe knows only the tribes around it; beyond this horizon, it knows nothing. In their books, the author uses the name of his tribe, sometimes in a limited sense, if it is a particular history; sometimes in a broad sense, if the history applies to the entire race. (1909:81)

Vial explains that he therefore translated the tribal name Gni in a Sani legend as Lolo because the story of the ancestors before the flood applies to the whole "nation or race" (ibid.).

A number of other Orientalists also wrote on the problem of using the term Lolo (see Harrell, this volume). R. F. Johnston saw it as a question of lost history that could no longer explain current conditions:

> I venture to express a doubt whether we should gain much by classing under one such designation a number of peoples who, whatever their origin, have been so long separated from one another that they refuse to acknowledge any mutual connection, and to some extent have different customs and speak different languages. (1908:274)

Other European scholars suggested substitute terms, and the Protestant missionary Samuel Pollard took Vial soundly to task for promoting the use of this epithet:

The Roman Catholics have had a flourishing mission work among the Gni, a branch of the Nosu race, and Père Vial, who has for many years been the head of this mission, gave the world some account of this people and their language. There is . . . one serious criticism to make of Père Vial's writings. He persists in calling these people Lolo. . . . One ought always to be a bit suspicious of adopting any [Chinese] name for an aboriginal tribe. . . . The ideograph which Chinese use for the word Lolo is usually written with a "dog radical at the side," thus in a concise way expressing to all who can read the supreme contempt in which the Nosu are held. . . . The name which the people prefer should rather be adopted. Nosu . . . is not an insult to a brave race, who have kept up their end of the wicket for so many centuries. (1920:264–65)[26]

Chinese imperialists, European Orientalists, and Chinese Marxists have all utilized a linguistic classification of Lolo or Yi.[27] The Chinese imperial system defined and grouped ethnic populations over the centuries as a form of political manipulation and creative historiography to control potentially dissident peoples. The Orientalists were motivated to map out linguistic and/or racial classifications as an intellectual exercise and as a way of understanding the intriguing and inferior other. The use of Marxist-Stalinist criteria of nationalities classification in the People's Republic has upheld the government's ultimate goal of incorporating all nationalities into greater China. Ethnic differences can be tolerated if the long-term goal is kept in mind.

It was during this reclassification effort that the Gni-p'a Lolo became known as the Sani Yi. The syllable *sa* had been added to *gni* (Sagni) by Lietard (1904, 1913) to name this group, while Vial persisted in combining *gni* with the suffix *p'a* to indicate male gender (1909:24). By the 1940s Chinese scholars had standardized the romanization of Sani (Ma Xueliang 1951). Linguistically, the Sani were classified by Chinese scholars in the 1950s as speaking a vernacular of the

26. A sticky wicket at that. Pollard's suggested use of (Nuosu) a group name used in Liangshan and western Guizhou, as a generic name for this "race" would of course infer a commonality that the people themselves did not acknowledge.

27. See Harrell (this volume) for a detailed discussion of this point. The term Lolo is still used in non-Chinese linguistic circles for the Loloish branch of Tibeto-Burman languages (Bradley 1987).

Southeastern dialect of the Yi language in the Yi branch of Tibeto-Burman (Bradley 1987:82), and socioculturally as part of the large Yi nationality.[28] The nonprejudiced term Yi was constructed to replace Lolo as a *minzu* name.[29]

Vial's French-Lolo Dictionary. Vial's language study, the primary focus of his scholarship, culminated in his *Dictionnaire Français-Lolo, dialecte Gni*.[30] The work is organized into two parts: an introductory text discussing various features and examples of the language, and the French-Gni lexicon itself. The introduction is addressed to outside scholars, with a preface on the distinction between Western and East Asian thinking;[31] "preliminary notes" on pronunciation, money, measurements, calculation of time; and a list of some 430 Lolo characters used in the work. The grammar section covers characteristics of articles, nouns, adjectives, pronouns, verbs, adverbs, propositions, conjunctions, interjections, sentence word order, and particular words with multiple usage. Following this are notes on numerals and six actual texts: "A Genealogy of Lolo Ancestors," "A Dream," "Why the Earth is Wrinkled," "An Elegy," "The Sacrament of the Eucharist," and "The Act of Contrition." These texts were included at the request of Vial's colleagues, who argued that these additional examples of writing would have "the advantage of making [one] grasp more precisely not only all the rules that coordinate words, but also the special genius of this language that instructs discourse" (1909:77). The genealogy and the geology story are from Sani books, the dream and the elegy are from oral tradition, and the texts on Catholic rituals were written in both Sani script and Latin by a Sani about to be ordained as a priest.

Information from Vial's dictionary has been compared in a paper by A. G. Haudricourt (1958) on uvular consonants in Tibeto-Burman to

28. Much of Sani territory was incorporated into Lunan Yi Autonomous County in 1956, although some Sani communities remained part of Luliang County.

29. This Yi 彝 is distinct from another form of yi 夷 applied through centuries of Chinese history to non-Han "barbarians." Vial wrote that Lolo as a group are composed of the independent *man* and the subjugated *yi* (1890:7).

30. Vial's dictionary is one of many sources James Matisoff is using for correlative material in his huge Tibeto-Burman dictionary project at the University of California, Berkeley.

31. For example: "We love the new; they, the ancient; we, progress, they, tradition." (Vial 1909:4). Vial thought such distinctions arose from the difference between flexible European languages and inflexible, monosyllabic Asian languages.

material from a more recent linguistic study of Sani language by the Chinese linguist Ma Xueliang (1951). In Haudricourt's analysis, both studies have their strengths and weaknesses as partial descriptions of the language's phonetic system. In Vial's lexicon, all of the words are accompanied by their written form from a syllabary, while Ma's study gives words in the international phonetic alphabet, but the lexicon is separate from the syllabary. The Chinese government has developed educational materials in the various Yi dialects and vernaculars (Bradley 1987:82), but the government-published 1984 Sani-Chinese dictionary (*Yi-Han Dictionary* 1984) using traditional Yi orthography and phonetic transcription is not used in Sani schools.[32] The wealth of ethnographic information in Vial's lexicon can also be mined for a historic perspective on the Sani (e.g., the previously mentioned kinship-system clues uncovered in the entries for *cousin, aunt,* and *uncle*). Under *hemp*, thirteen operations involved in preparing and weaving the fiber are named and described. Information on the indigenous authority structure is given under the word *chief*.[33] Many of the "holes" in *Les Lolos* are at least partially filled in this dictionary.

While the grammar section was definitely written for outside scholars, the lexicon may well have been intended for both linguists and Sani students in Vial's numerous schools who were studying French, Latin, Chinese, and Sani languages. Some entries are curious for a European scholar, such as "cupide—Voy Désirer" (1909:108). Vial also proselytized in his entries. For example, the word *comme* (as), is illustrated with the following sentence in both Sani script and French: "Le corps de Jesus-Christ nourrit notre âme *comme* la nourriture nourrit notre corps" (The body of Jesus Christ nourishes our soul *as* food nourishes our body) (1909:87). Contemporary Sani response to the Oriental other in Vial's dictionary would be extremely interesting to pursue, as a chronicle of conversion.

32. The entries in the *Yi-Han Dictionary* (1984) are in Sani script, then phonetics, with definitions in Chinese. There is also a Chinese-Sani index. Sani have demonstrated to me their ability to use this dictionary, but it is virtually unavailable to them, and it is not widely used in other research. A Chinese-Sani dictionary by Fr. Laurent Zhang, which translates Vial's French into Chinese, is discussed below.

33. For the internal direction of the village, there were two types of chief: the *boùdzé*, who forms the village council and who deliberates over current affairs, and the *sèmo*, who executes the orders of the council. One says equally "headman" and "middleman," because in reality "Village chiefs are nothing but mediators among different opinions" (Vial 1909:79).

We have seen in this survey of Vial's scholarly work interlocking themes of difference and superiority in an Orientalist's discourse, reinforced by critiques of fellow ethnographers and linguists, and shaped by a missionary's drive to convert the other. Orientalism justified Western imperialism while fostering an ironic commentary on competing (Christian vs. Chinese) civilizing projects. It was in this intellectual milieu that Vial formed his Christian civilizing project of conversion and modernity for the Sani.

MISSIONARIES, MISSIONIZING, AND IDENTITY CHANGE

Vial belonged to the Société des Missions Étrangères de Paris, which was a product of the Catholic church's involvement with expanding French colonial interests in East Asia. The Holy See's agency to coordinate missionary activity, known as the Propaganda, recruited its first apostolic vicars from Paris in 1658 for Tonkin and China. Their mission was to develop a native clergy, supervised by foreign bishops.

Instructions issued in 1659 to missionaries from the Propaganda stressed respect for local customs, as long as they did not conflict with the teaching of Catholicism.

> Do not regard it as your task, and do not bring any pressures to bear on the peoples, to change their manners, customs and uses, unless they are evidently contrary to religion and sound morals. What could be more absurd than to transport France, Spain or Italy, or some other European country to China? Do not introduce all that to them, but only the faith, which does not despise or destroy the manners and customs of any people, always supposing they are not evil, but rather wishes to see them preserved unharmed. (Quoted in Burridge 1985:153)

In 1700 a French seminary for new missions in East Asia was officially recognized as the Société des Missions Étrangères de Paris. Its goals included "the building of native churches and the training of a native secular clergy which in time would be capable of self-maintenance" (Latourette 1929:114–15). The society's missionizing project, however, was not to create a syncretic, nativistic church. During the long Catholic Rites Controversy (1640–1742) the dispute over incorporating Chinese language and ritual into Chinese Christianity was both a clash between two cultures (Imperial China and the Roman Catholic Church) and a clash between missionary societies. Ultimately, the Jesuits and others whose scholarly approach supported some Chinese cultural elements lost to a papal bull upholding the church's authority to not compromise its customs or adapt to what it deemed "superstitious" Chinese beliefs. Beginning in 1742, all Catholic missionaries in China were sworn to uphold this decree (ibid.:150–52).

Père Paul Vial was thus trained to build a native church with close ties to global Catholicism. The common bonds of set European ritual and Latin liturgy (translated into the local dialect for native comprehension) were supposed to be reinforced by changing any elements of native culture construed by the missionary to be of unsound morals or evil intent. As seen in the Rites Controversy, there was little consensus among missionaries in diverse societies, or between missionaries and peoples being evangelized, regarding what particular acts or institutions should be described as evil. This task was further complicated, for "if the evils of civilized society, whether in Europe or Asia, had much in common, first experiences with the non-literate or subsistence communities . . . provided missionaries with an entirely different set of problems" (Burridge 1985:154–55). In response to Social Darwinism, missionary doctrine from the mid-nineteenth century on saw all "inferior" (to advanced Euro-American industrial society) people as teachable, capable of reaching equivalent heights. However, goodness was represented in "progress, trade, and industrialization, . . . [while] the rural scene overseas tended to be 'wretched' or 'miserable,' at best 'simple'; the 'primitive' was bad and superstition, magic, taboo, nakedness, and other savage customs—impediments to [good] progress,—were generally described as 'evil' " (ibid.:156).

Conversion

Most missionaries, Catholic and Protestant, took on the task of determining what was evil among "their" people and then devised methods to remove it. Central to their methods have been questions of holism and social change theory: can one change a single element of a sociocultural system without affecting the whole; and should one first focus change in social circumstances, or in ideology (Beidelman 1982:16)? The missionary dealt with evil through the practice of conversion. Gerald A. Arbuckle defines conversion in the following way:

Conversion to Christianity entails, precisely, a new consciousness. But since the old consciousness was contained and maintained and renewed by the traditional institutions, the latter had
to go or be considerably modified if the new consciousness was
to have a viable ambience of action. And behind a people's
reluctance to modify or abandon their traditions and institutions one can see not only Jung's "struggle" against the light of
new consciousness, but the determination not to give up an
identity bequeathed by the ancestors, an identity which contra-
dicts the new consciousness. (1985:160)

However, the conversion process may sometimes complement a
people's identity, given the political environment of interethnic
power plays. It may be instrumentally advantageous for them to
adapt some aspects of this new consciousness into their cultural
identity, as Daniel Hughes shows in his analysis of what might be
called polysemic Christianity as a response to missionizing in several societies (1985:168–71). Hughes applies Ward Goodenough's
(1963) insight that change in both individual and community identity is experienced in religious conversion. The change comes from
within individuals as a psychological process that can transform
from individual beliefs and practices to a generalized attribute that
"any member of a community attributes to all other members of
the community" (Hughes 1985:169). This is a process, in other
words, with individual variation and group adaptation, not a wholesale substitution. The conversion strategy of a missionary, or the
"theology of evangelization" (Arbuckle 1985:181), determines whether the primary concern is community evangelization or individual
salvation supported by the missionary-implanted church hierarchy.
Those focused on individuals see "little need to understand culture
or its implications for human behavior or corporate salvation"
(ibid.). The primary goal of converting individual souls for incorporation into the Church was questioned in the late nineteenth
century by Catholic Neo-Scholastics. Returning to Aristotelian philosophy through Aquinas, theologians thought that insights about
God were obtainable through the study of humanity, not just
through the scriptures. "There emerged an openness to discover
what is valuable within the so-called heathen religions" (ibid.) and
community-based evangelizing. While some Catholic missionaries,
such as Vial, exemplified this stance (including a rejection of evolu-

tionism), ethnocentrism (entrenched for instance in the use of Latin) slowed down even the strongest intentions to build a culturally
identified converted community.

As agents of change, missionaries had a range of messages they
preached to their flocks, telling them that they were either "set in evil
ways, in ways that could be better, or in ways inadequate to a future
pressing hard on them" (ibid.:160) As we have seen, Vial's view of
Sani culture was remarkably positive, and he was sensitive to their
subjugation and the encroachment of Han society. What he saw as
evil in Sani life was limited to practices he felt were rooted in superstition, which he dealt with by replacing pagan practitioners, rituals,
and sacred objects with similar Christian ones. Vial was a firm, patriarchal figure, literally addressed as Father. He distinguished in his
tallies between those merely studying Christianity and those who
had converted, and commented that once he was convinced students
had become believers, he put them to the test by having them destroy
all of their own "superstitious objects" (1893:293–94). Vial felt that
conversion was often partial for the individual, and, as is shown in
the running record of converts in his letters, concentrated much of
his effort on family units or whole villages. In Sani religion, Vial saw
many parallels with seventh-century European paganism uprooted
by the Church, such as sacred groves, forests, stones, and trees that
were worshiped in group ceremonies (1890:7; 1893:294). He felt that
to uproot superstition, he must have long patience and prudent
reserve. His goal was to transform (his own word) rather than to
destroy Sani religiosity. He did this in many ways, such as by placing
crosses on sacred rocks, meeting in the same place at the same time of
day for celebrations, and replacing Sani charms on babies' hats with
Catholic medals.[34] His solution to Chinese corruption and domination was to arm the Sani with the sophisticated knowledge of European modernity and global Christianity. He saw reflected in the
Sani's relatively egalitarian ways and intriguing literary heritage a
good, simple basis for development into a modern society. Ultimately he hoped that they would be Sani Christians. As the evils perceived
by this missionary were outweighed by many perceived goods in the
native society, the transformation process may not have been so

34. This is reminiscent of tactics used by priests who followed the Spanish conquest in the New World, with the difference that Vial represented a secondary colonial
force in opposition to the Sani's colonial oppressors.

disruptive to the community as if it had been more radically Europeanizing. From the indigenous point of view, conversion can be a layering of distinct ideologies (Hughes 1983:168–69). Especially in the Sani case, these people who were already subjugated to Chinese rule had little to lose by adding to their worldview new ideological constructs that offered a belief and practical proof of transcendence.

Missionary as Ethnographer

The issue of whether a missionary—someone with a conversion agenda—can actually be an ethnographer producing material of any value is obviously relevant to the work of Paul Vial on the Sani. I take a stance fairly close to James Clifford's (1982) conclusions about the renowned French Protestant missionary Maurice Leenhardt. Clifford, in Paul Rabinow's analysis, saw "no unspanable gulf between Leenhardt the Ethnologist and Leenhardt the Missionary; only a field of tensions in which Leenhardt forged his life" (1983:203). Despite major differences in religion, methods, and theoretical interests (Leenhardt definitely moved beyond Orientalism in his analysis of person and myth in Melanesia), there are a number of commonalities between these two missionary-ethnographers.

To paraphrase Rabinow, both missionaries opposed exploitation but worked within a colonial system (ibid.:199–205). They believed that progress was inevitable, and that conversion to Christianity would safeguard native culture through bilingual and bicultural education. As participants they defended their flocks and basic human rights; as observers they "saw that ethnographic understanding was a linch pin both for their own mission[s] and for the survival of native culture in a healthy form. The task of the missionary-ethnographer was to gain an understanding of local custom that would enable him to change it without 'violating' its life sustaining form" (ibid.:201). They made observations for the sake of promoting change, basing their work on decades in the field, sound language ability, and "believed in the sacred as did those [they] studied" (ibid.). There were several dialectics at work between their own spirituality and indigenous tradition, and between their desire to convert and doubts about the depth of these conversions. Evolutionary sentiments about these "simpler" people contrasted with the missionaries' commitment to transform indigenous culture through conversion to transcend the inevitable destruction of their way of life. As Rabinow notes, there is no consideration in this perspective of conversion's implications for the other's political and existential realities (ibid.:202–203). While Rabinow argues that Leenhardt's ethnography was fused with conversion by using "informed transcription" by trained indigenous converts writing their own texts, Vial was somewhat different. Vial worked side by side with the literate specialists who transcribed texts, and he recorded oral traditions himself in the "usual" field method. He therefore did not foster "intertextuality" of native voices as did Leenhardt. Both Vial and Leenhardt as missionary-ethnographers can be shown to have been active agents in changing the cultures they studied. Through their efforts to convert, they hoped to foster a type of ethnogenesis—to transform the identity of their converts into a new identity that was both Christian and culturally contiguous with the converts' past.

The Other's View of Missionizing

Sani response to Vial's missionary project is a focus of my current research. Background information on Han-Sani ethnic relations and the role of the state is useful in developing an understanding of the mission between Vial's death in 1917 and the end of the mission era in 1949–1951. A series of Nanjing newspaper articles written while the mission was still functioning is one source of research questions (Fang 1939). Two examples of the competing civilizing project that followed—an early PRC scholarly work on Sani language (Ma Xueliang 1951) and a locally authored "county information" book on Lunan Yi Autonomous County (Lunan Yizu 1986)—illustrate the reaction in the People's Republic to Vial's Christian-Orientalist civilizing project.

Ma Xueliang's work (cited above in comparison to Vial's linguistic studies) provides a commentary on Christian competition with the PRC civilizing project involving the Sani. Ma does not overtly use Vial's work on Sani language, but he has a great deal to say about missionaries among Yi people. In an essay entitled "How Imperialism Destroys Our Brother Nationality's Culture"[35] Ma wrote about

---

35. The following paraphrase from the Chinese only hints at the emotion behind the words. I wish to thank Yu Sheunn-der for his help in translating this document. In an introduction to this study, Ma briefly describes working with Sani informants who were Catholic converts. They told him stories from the Bible rather than from actual Sani life. Ma also mentions Vial's scholarship. According to Ma's colleagues, it was this brief reference that caused his imprisonment during the Cultural Revolution.

his field experiences in 1942, when he first came into contact with missionary activity (1951:381–85). Everywhere he went in Yi country there were churches, schools, and hospitals organized by British, French, and American missionaries. Ma tells of being watched by the missionaries, who were particularly suspicious of his interest in Sani religious texts. The missionaries insisted that the local youths study Yi using their romanized alphabet, not traditional Yi characters. Ma studied with a group who learned both systems to placate the missionaries. Even though Ma and his Yi friends demonstrated their ability to read the missionary's transliterated Bible, the missionaries drove them out of the area with rumors of bandits. Ma went to Kunming to recover from harassment, then found a new Yi informant, who took him to his home by the Jinsha River. After studying for a while Ma was introduced to a shaman (wushi) who was supposed to have many holy books. The old man was evasive about the books, and Ma learned that people thought the old man had hidden the books away. Ma approached him as a student and asked if he might study the old stories orally with him. The "shaman" asked Ma why he, a Han, wanted to study Yi writing. Ma replied that in order to preserve Yi culture, Yi writing must not be given up. Later, the "shaman" told Ma his story. The missionaries had asked to buy the holy books. At first he thought it would be all right to sell them because his family needed money. Then he thought about how writing was given to Yi people by God, so he refused to sell them. Later he heard that the foreigners had burned Yi books secretly. The "shaman" hid his books away in the mountains. Now the youngsters no longer learned from the Yi holy stories taught by the ancestors. Everyone, even his own son, went to church to learn the foreign language and read the Bible. When the "shaman" first talked to Ma he thought he was just like the foreigners, trying to wipe out what was left of Yi culture. Even though he later trusted Ma, he would not show him his books.

At this point in the story, Ma tells about his own efforts to preserve what was left of the Yi books in the area. Trying to act before the missionaries were able to buy up the books, he requested funding from the government and was able to buy one thousand texts, which he shipped off to Beijing (via Chongqing) for safekeeping. Thus, in his own way, Ma was responsible for taking away what was left of Yi writing, but he reasoned that at least the texts would be safe for future study (if not for religious use by the Yi). In his final paragraphs, Ma argues that the missionaries destroyed local culture by creating foreign language alphabets so the natives would learn quickly and be converted to Christianity. Missionary myths from the Bible also took away their history. Some people even say they are not Chinese now, because of the story of Adam and Eve taught to them by the missionaries. Ma saw this story, which told people that they are all descendants of one family or all the same people, as typical of the kind of poison missionaries spread.

It is instructive to compare Ma and Vial on the subject of sacred writings. They were agents of distinct, competing civilizing projects that conflicted with Sani sacred teachings. Both saw Sani books as valuable links with the past, as cultural heritage, but not necessarily keys to the future. At the same time both professed concern about the maintenance of Sani identity in the face of modernization. Ma's remarks about the Christian imperialists taking culture away could be addressed to subsequent years of Communist rule, especially during the Cultural Revolution, which drove both traditional Sani and Sani Catholic religious practitioners underground.

The tension between Western missionary activity and Chinese state policy among ethnic minorities is also reflected in a muted Sani political text. In the Lunan Yi Autonomous County information book (*Lunan Yizu Zizhixian gaikuang*) there are several references to Vial and his mission. It relates that in 1889 a French Catholic missionary named Paul came to missionize in Lunan (Lunan Yizu 1986:29). He built churches in six places, including Qingshankou, which became an estate with more than twenty households of Yi peasants as tenants of the church. The mission was there for forty years, but after Liberation there was religious freedom (ibid.:46).

Although it has been decades since this mission closed, the retelling of events from Vial's era continues as a part of the new Chinese civilizing project. The story of Vial's being attacked in his church has been retold by Yunnan social scientists, but in this version the robbers are Sani jealous of Vial's wealth, certainly not henchmen of the Chinese state. This restatement of conditions between competing civilizing projects can also be seen in Vial's legacy among the Sani. In Loumeiyi, the site of Vial's first Sani church, there is a stalemate in the early 1990s between local Sani Catholics and the state. The church building was desecrated during the Cultural Revolution, and has not been used as a church since. State officials want the community to accept the rebuilding of this embarrassing structure now covered with "Long live Chairman Mao" slogans. The community has refused on grounds that this is an important monument to their martyrdom, and they want a new church built for them elsewhere, which the state refuses to fund. Another concern of the state is adoption in Loumeiyi of the official Catholic church as a replacement for the underground Roman Catholic church. The official church is controlled by the state, while the Roman Catholic church is considered by the state to be an intrusion of a foreign power—the Vatican.

The spiritual mentor of these Sani Catholics is a French-speaking Sani priest, Laurent Zhang, who was ordained in Kunming in 1947 and later imprisoned in Yunnan for twenty-six years. When not ministering to the local Catholic community, this priest carries on Vial's intellectual legacy. Zhang's first writing project when released from prison was translation of the French into Chinese and republication of Vial's Sani dictionary. Like the *Yi-Han Dictionary* (1984), this work was published by the state, but is not available to the Sani public. Zhang (1987) has also written a biography of Vial, and numerous articles with Christian or Yi folklore themes. He hopes young people will carry on his work, but is not too optimistic.

Small pockets of several hundred Sani Catholics have persisted, but their future is unsure. At the moment, there seems to be a triangle of tension between traditional Sani practicing the old ways, Christian Sani, and the majority of Sani being propelled by government action toward becoming modern Chinese with a few interesting folkloric features useful in tourism. It could well be that Vial's hope for the Sani—to become modern citizens of the world while being distinctly Sani—may be reached but as a reaction to the PRC civilizing project.

CONCLUSIONS

The subtext in Vial's missionary letters and scholarly writing about the Sani was Orientalism, mediated by his commitment to conversion and expressed in his dialectical role as missionary-ethnographer. Orientalism can be conflated with evolutionism and racism (Clifford 1988:271), but Vial's Catholic theology prevented a direct equation of race with limits to cultural development. What he saw in the Sani was a "simple" group that was more Occidental than Oriental, and for whom it would therefore be easy, he thought, to become more "like us." This was a dynamic Orientalism, committed to change through conversion or the transformation of culture. Clifford, in his essay on Orientalism, made the following observation:

> . . . collectively constituted difference is not necessarily static or positionally dichotomous in the manner of Orientalism as Said describes it. There is no need to discard theoretically all conceptions of "cultural" difference, especially once this is seen as not simply received from tradition, language, or environment but also made in new political-cultural conditions of global relationality. (Ibid.:274)

Vial believed in both cultural difference and cultural transformation, which are also basic to a dynamic understanding of ethnicity. The factors that shaped his discourse on the Sani included a concept of linguistic classification that did not dictate associated political economy (Lolo language group, with great cultural variation into diverse tribes) and an understanding of intergroup dynamics over boundaries (the opposition between Han and Sani). These factors—of language group versus political entity, and the feedback of majority culture–minority culture over boundaries—are important to the construction of Sani ethnic identity. Besides teaching his catechists Latin, Vial taught French in his schools for indigenous boys and girls. The fact that some Sani in the late twentieth century know a little French reinforces their uniqueness in Chinese society. Sani do think of themselves as Sani—it is possible, despite Vial's efforts to contextualize the Sani as Yi in his linguistic studies, for Sani of mixed heritage to think of themselves as "half Sani, half Yi" in the 1990s.

Missionary Orientalism in Southwest China was a factor in ethnogenesis among peripheral groups. Affiliation of ethnic groups with specific national/religious organizations and particular missionaries within spatial and temporal boundaries affected the groups' interactions with each other and ultimately with the state. Assessing the impact of missionary Orientalism calls for comparative study of contemporary indigenous societies with a history of missionizing. In the Sani case, reactions to Vial's scholarly study, conversion efforts, mission policies concerning gender roles (Swain forthcoming), education, and the teaching that indigenous people have "God given" rights to a distinct culture are being investigated as possible ingredients in Sani ethnic identity. It is under the subsequent Chinese civilizing project that Sani language is not taught in schools, Sani culture is commoditized for tourism (Swain 1991), and the push is toward assimilation into the mainstream modern culture. Without the Orientalist twist of "we" non-Chinese Christians against "them" of Vial's civilizing project, the Sani may again be moving into a phase of ethnogenesis as they respond to the state's project for Sani society and culture.

Voices of Manchu Identity, 1635–1935

Shelley Rigger

Three centuries after its triumphant conquest of the Chinese empire, the Qing court fled back to the land whence it had come. The Aisin Gioro chief who staggered into Northeast China under Japanese protection in 1932 was a powerless figurehead. Yet for some, Henry Pu Yi symbolized a people that once had been the preeminent military and political force in Asia. The Japanese and their collaborators spared no effort to convince the world that Pu Yi and his Manchu followers were a sovereign nation entitled to secede from the corrupt and oppressive Chinese administrations that had misruled them since the fall of the Qing. George Bronson Rea, an American who collaborated with the Japanese in Manchukuo, wrote:

> Foreign judges of Manchukuo were severely critical of the selection of Pu-Yi as Chief Executive of the new state, and now that he has been elevated to his rightful position as Emperor, they ridicule him as a "Japanese puppet," arraign him as a "traitor to China" and sneer at him as a "weakling" who dares not call his soul his own. No thought seems to be given to the fact that Pu-Yi is not a Chinese, that he owes no allegiance to China, that he and his forebears were Manchus, and that the Chinese Republic entered into a solemn treaty with his family to recognize and respect his status as a "Foreign Sovereign." (Rea 1935:186–87)

In 1935 assertions of this kind were brushed aside as nothing more than cynical Japanese propaganda. In fact, however, Rea's words—whatever their motivation—raise a fundamental question in Manchu history. Were the Manchus Chinese, or did they constitute a separate ethnic group?

The Manchus, like many communities that have been labeled "ethnic," cannot be assigned a consistent, unitary history or identity. On the contrary, to get at the truths of the Manchu experience we must

Many thanks to Dru Gladney, Kent Guy, and David Boraks for their many suggestions.

listen to a variety of voices. What they tell us ultimately calls into question the usefulness of our definitions and guides us toward a new understanding of ethnicity in general and Manchu identity in particular.

The first Manchu voice belonged to Hong Taiji, the leader of the Jianzhou Jurchen federation, heir to Nurgaci, and inventor of the term Manchu.[1] In 1635 Hong Taiji declared that all those under his command should henceforth be known as Manchus, and he prohibited the use of all previous designations (Lee 1970:7). Thus, with a word he abolished all the existing categories among his subjects and created a new, purely political designation for the people loyal to him, without regard for their ancestry or custom. Even the word itself was new; no one has ever conclusively linked it to any existing group, individual, place, or idea. Indeed, Hong Taiji seems consciously to have created an entirely new entity to carry out his ambitions of conquest.

But if the Manchus became Manchus only in 1635, who were they before? Who were the individual subjects whom Hong Taiji forged into a single people?

At the core of the Manchus were members of the Jianzhou Jurchen federation. The Jurchens were a collection of tribes living in northeastern China. They had migrated to the region together hundreds of years earlier, but their recent history had created important divisions. Beginning in the tenth century the Jurchen developed tactics of mounted warfare that allowed them to conquer neighboring tribes and, ultimately, much of China proper. In 1115, they established the Jin dynasty. The Jin rulers quickly adopted traditional Chinese governing techniques and other aspects of Han Chinese culture: a civil service examination system based on the Chinese classics, a legal code similar to that of the Tang dynasty, salt and iron monopolies, Chinese language, and Chinese surnames (Tao 1977:153–54). When the dynasty collapsed in 1234, they continued to live in settled agricultural

---

1. Traditionally, Hong Taiji was called Abahai in English, but recent scholarship questions the authenticity of that name. Hong Taiji is a more standard transliteration from Manchu-language sources. Similarly, Nurgaci is a contemporary transliteration of the traditional Nurhaci.

communities, which separated them from their nomadic Jurchen cousins (Tao 1970:121).

When the Jin dynasty's conquest elite entered China, other Jurchen tribes remained in the Northeast, primarily in the mountainous regions along the Yalu River. They retained the nomadic hunting economy that had characterized the group before the conquest (Crossley 1983a:89). After the fall of the Jin, the tribal Jurchen fell under the Yuan dynasty's frontier government in an administrative unit known as Nurgan. The land occupied by the descendants of the Jin conquerors was organized as the province of Liaodong. Liaodong also had thousands of non-Jurchen residents, including Han Chinese (Lee and Eng 1984:8).

In Nurgan, two groups of tribal Jurchens settled on opposite slopes of the Changbai Mountains. The eastern group rose to prominence in the early 1400s under the leadership of Mongke Temur, who attained official recognition from the Ming court and extended the influence of his group across the mountains. From 1400 until 1600, the eastern Jurchen gradually increased their influence over Jurchen and other tribal groups in Nurgan, forging the Jianzhou Federation.

The gradual expansion of Jianzhou power received an enormous boost with the rise of the brilliant leader Nurgaci in the late 1500s. Nurgaci knitted together the various Jianzhou Jurchen tribes by reorganizing scattered clans and cementing them under his personal leadership. At the same time, he celebrated the Jin dynastic period as exemplary of a Jurchen tradition he and his followers were determined to restore. The revitalized clan organizations helped formalize the link between the Jianzhou present and the Jin past (Crossley 1987:768).

But the link between the Jianzhou federation and the Jin dynasty was more mythological than biological; Nurgaci's followers in Nurgan were but distant blood relatives to the Jin ruling house. The actual Jin descendants lived as detribalized farmers in Liaodong (Tao 1970:121); they were not part of the Jianzhou Federation. In fact, as Nurgaci's armies began conquering Liaodong, they classified all of its residents as Han, even those of Mongol, Korean, and Jurchen ancestry. The criteria for classification were economic practice, lifestyle, and political status, not descent. To Nurgaci, a Han was someone who lived in or near the Chinese border and was not a nomad (Crossley 1983b:39).

Once his power over the Jianzhou federation was solid, Nurgaci began to reshape the peoples under his control in a form that concentrated power in his own hands and stifled diversity among his followers. The result was a new unity that made political affiliation the most basic category of identity. Nurgaci pressured his followers to reject any identity other than that of membership in the Jianzhou federation (Roth 1979:6; Li Chi 1932:38).

Nurgaci's skill as a conqueror extended beyond the military. He was a cunning diplomat as well, one who recognized the propaganda value of treating conquered people humanely and exploiting superstitions to legitimate his rule. He insisted on strict discipline on the part of soldiers and administrators to avoid offending reluctant subjects and he was known for his generous economic policies. Thus, his historians boasted, "There is no precedent to Chinese going over to another country but [because] they have heard that we take good care of our people, they have come to us to submit" (Roth 1979:10).

In 1601 Nurgaci reorganized his followers into military detachments known as banners (*qi*). Although they initially were based on the existing clan structure, banners ultimately replaced clans as the fundamental units of social organization of the Jianzhou federation. The functions traditionally ascribed to clan headmen were taken over by military officials, while individual banner members increasingly gave up all other activities in favor of military service. By taking power away from the local chiefs and headmen, Nurgaci tightened his own grip (Ch'en 1981:45). In 1615 he fixed the number of banners at eight and placed each one under the control of a member of his family.

From 1601 until 1623 anyone who surrendered to the banner forces was enrolled in a banner. Those who had Han Chinese surnames and customs traded them in for Manchu names and the banner life. From the perspective of the leadership, they were indistinguishable from those who had joined Nurgaci's army in the sixteenth century (Lee 1970:34; Lee and Eng 1984:8). But harmony did not reign long. When they captured Mukden (Shenyang) and Liaoyang—two large Ming towns in Liaodong—in 1623, the banners found it difficult to digest the sudden influx of Han. Conflicts between long-time banner members and newly surrendered subjects of the Ming forced Nurgaci to create special Hanjun (Han banners) (Liu 1981:53). The Hanjun included not only those who called themselves Han, but those members of Jurchen clans who lived among them as well. The

Hanjun were considered an inseparable part of the banner force, and Hong Taiji included them in the Manchu designation twelve years later (Shirokogoroff 1924:12).

In 1626 Hong Taiji succeeded Nurgaci as leader of the Jianzhou federation. From the beginning, he recognized that the population under his command was something new in the world. He notified the Ming empire:

> . . . you Ming nobles are not the scions of the Song emperors, and we are not the scions of the previous Jin emperors. That was one season, and this is another. This heavenly season and the mind of man have become completely distinct [from the past]. (Quoted in Crossley 1987:773–74)

Hong Taiji's subjects were not the Later Jin dynasty Nurgaci had once claimed to be, nor were they the Jianzhou federation of the distant past in Nurgan. Instead, Hong Taiji declared, the diverse and disciplined fighting force he and his ancestors had constructed were Manchus.

Hong Taiji, along with Nurgaci and the Qing emperors from the Shunzhi emperor to Henry Pu Yi, belonged to the Jurchen clan Aisin Gioro. Their mythical clan history provided a charter myth for Hong Taiji's newly named Manchus. The story of the Aisin Gioro does not purport to explain the Manchus' origins in antiquity; rather, it reinforces the idea that they were a political entity born out of the union of groups that had existed before. The purpose of the myth is to explain and justify the joining of those groups in obedience to the Aisin Gioro ruling house.[2]

According to the myth, a magically conceived Aisin Gioro ancestor named Bukuri Yongson unified warring tribes in the Northeast and was rewarded by being elected leader of the Jurchen east of the Changbai Mountains. He invented the term Manchu to describe his people. Later, the historical figure Mongke Temur was born into the clan, as was Fanca, another documented historical person. Although these two people play different roles in the myth than they did in history, they are credited with helping to unify and enlarge the Manchu population, which is, in a general sense, accurate. Thus, the myth

2. For a discussion of the Aisin Gioro myth and its role in establishing the power of the imperial clan and reorganizing the clan system, see Crossley (1985).

defines the Manchus as a creation of the Aisin Gioro clan and as a fundamentally political entity whose existence is inseparable from Aisin Gioro leadership. In practice, the charter myth also reinforced the top clan's authority by defining certain Manchu sacred sites and totems (especially the crow) as having special connections to the Aisin Gioro clan.

On the eve of the Qing dynasty, as the Manchus under Hong Taiji planned their final attack on the Chinese heartland and its crumbling Ming government, Manchu was a political designation. To be a Manchu was to be a loyal subject of the Aisin Gioro clan, living and fighting as a member of the banner force. Practicing the shamanistic rituals of the Northeast, speaking the dialect of Jurchen called Manchu, eschewing footbinding, practicing archery and horse riding, wearing side-buttoned clothing, and belonging to a clan with a Manchu name—these were cultural options most Manchus practiced. But they were not obligatory. The definitive symbolic and practical tie that bound individuals to the Manchus was loyalty.

OBOI

In 1644 Manchu forces under the regent Dorgon entered Beijing. The next few decades represented the consolidation of Manchu rule in China, and were characterized by the most fervent Manchuization efforts of the Qing dynasty.[3] To the newly installed Qing rulers, Manchu identity was rooted in the experience of conquest. Manchus were those who had taken part in the conquest, and a Manchu government was one that rested on the traditions that had propelled the Aisin Gioro clan into the Forbidden City. For example, the early leaders, Dorgon and the Oboi regents (Oboi, Ebilun, Suksaha, and Soni), insisted upon military supremacy over civilian government. The military was, by definition, entirely Manchu at the time of the conquest, so giving the military the leading role in politics meant that Manchus would occupy all the most important positions. (One of the Shunzhi emperor's most egregious offenses, in the minds of

3. The period following the Dorgon regency (1643–1650) is an exception to this generalization. The Shunzhi emperor encouraged sinification and seemed uninterested in promoting Manchu identity. But he was an aberration, and his effective reign was brief (1650–1661). The subsequent leaders (the Oboi regent clique, which ruled from 1661 to 1669) quickly reversed his policies.

the Oboi regents, was that he consulted with Han advisers on military matters [Oxnam 1975:59].)

Not all Manchu institutions were military, of course, and the early Qing rulers maintained Manchu civil institutions alongside the banner system. Administration in the first years of the dynasty rested on Hong Taiji's "majestic example": careful balancing of northeastern and Chinese institutions, judicious use of Han officials and soldiers, and dogged pursuit of the Manchus' historical mission (ibid.:30). The most important northeastern institutions, which the regents imported into China, were the Council of Deliberative Officials and the Lifan Yuan (Court of Colonial Affairs). In particular, the Council was a uniquely Manchu institution in that it was rooted in the communal decision-making of the banner heads under Nurgaci. The Lifan Yuan allowed the Manchus to continue their relations with Mongolia, Tibet, and Xinjiang along the same lines they had followed before the conquest, without the interference of the traditional Chinese agency for foreign affairs, the Board of Rites (ibid.:31).

The early rulers also followed Hong Taiji's example in regulating the role of Han in the government. Hong Taiji recognized early in his career that the Manchus would have to make concessions to the Chinese political tradition if the conquest was to succeed (Roth 1979:24). Not only were the Han unlikely to submit willingly to a radically unfamiliar political system; in addition, the number of qualified Manchus (including the Hanjun) would fill only a fraction of the administrative posts required to rule China. Thus, he and his successors made extensive use of the Han banner members as administrators after the conquest and allowed lower-ranking Han officeholders to retain their positions (Oxnam 1975:passim).

Dorgon scored a tremendous political victory upon entering Beijing when he repudiated Li Zicheng's cruel and humiliating treatment of the Ming scholar-officials and invited them to take part in the new regime (Wakeman 1979:76). But, as the requirement that they wear the queue reminded the Han, there was never any doubt that the Manchus were the conquerors.

In sum, the new Qing rulers defined Manchu administration as a government based on the martial values of toughness and loyalty and on the institutions of the conquest, and these were still the defining characteristics of Manchu identity. The idea of a Manchu historical mission sprang, in part, from the belief that China was weak and corrupt. Hong Taiji left to his successors a responsibility to purge

China of the decadent institutions and culture of the late Ming period. Robert B. Oxnam argues that the choice of Qing (Pure) for the dynastic name expresses this drive for purification:

> Whether or not Abahai [Hong Taiji] took this purification mission seriously is a moot point, for he died before the conquest was complete and never had the opportunity to develop policies from the throne in Peking. But the regents of the 1660s, and many of the Manchu conquest elite, were fervently committed to this mission and would often justify their actions as efforts to "eradicate the vile legacies of the Ming." (Oxnam 1975:35)

So far, the picture I have drawn of Manchu identity lends itself to a circumstantialist view of ethnicity. There were no ubiquitous "primordial" characteristics among the original Manchus; they shared neither heredity, language, nor custom. What they did share during this period was a willingness to become part of a conquering army. The fact that all but the core of the early Manchu population gained their identity from submission to military force reinforces the circumstantialist view.

According to Fredrik Barth's theory of boundary maintenance, what is important about ethnic groups is not what they include (their cultural content, linguistic patterns, etc.), but how they determine whom to include and exclude (Barth 1969:passim). Barth criticizes primordialist definitions of ethnicity for relying on conditional ethnic traits and cultural forms that are not definitive in terms of the social understanding of ethnicity among members of an ethnic group. Thus, he defines an ethnic ascription as one that "classifies a person in terms of his basic, most general identity, presumptively determined by his origin and background" (ibid.:13). Barth would reject the idea that a list of Manchu traits could be developed that would distinguish accurately between Manchus and non-Manchus. Instead, he would argue that the way to understand the difference between the two is to look at how each group defined the boundary between them.

The Barthian approach to ethnicity is useful in looking at Manchus in the early Qing dynasty because it doesn't require the members of the Manchu group to share any specific characteristics; rather, the fact that the Manchus maintained a consistent division between themselves and others is adequate to qualify them as an ethnic group.

Barth's understanding of ethnic boundaries as plastic and functional accommodates the Manchus. Also, his theory is not hampered by the Manchus' tendency to change the content of their culture over time. He writes: ". . . the human material that is organized in an ethnic group is not immutable, and though the social mechanisms discussed so far tend to maintain dichotomies and boundaries, they do not imply 'stasis' for the human material they organize: boundaries may persist despite what may figuratively be called the 'osmosis' of personnel through them" (ibid.:21).

The weakness of Barth's theory in this case is that, while it is inclusive enough to allow for the definition of the Manchus as an ethnic group, it is not particularly informative; it does not add much to our understanding of Manchu identity. In fact, it may make more sense to argue that the boundaries surrounding the Manchus in the mid-seventeenth century were political, not ethnic. The Manchus' very inclusiveness suggests that considerations of political efficacy were the foundation of their boundaries. For them, the most basic, general ascription that Barth would describe as ethnic was banner affiliation, which was clearly a political (and economic) category.

THE QIANLONG EMPEROR

The Qing dynasty reached its apex during the extraordinary reigns of the Kangxi (r. 1662–1722), Yongzheng (r. 1723–1736), and Qianlong (r. 1736–1795) emperors. The Kangxi emperor broke free of the Oboi regents in the late 1660s and at once began to prove himself a highly capable leader. During his reign he consolidated not only the dynasty's power and legitimacy, but the authority of the emperor as well. At the same time, he introduced a broad range of traditional Chinese institutions into the Manchu political order. As the Qing leadership opened itself to more and more ideas and practices from outside the Manchu conquest tradition, a new understanding of Manchu identity arose. The new definition centered on descent; it replaced the Qing founders' inclusive, politically based conception with an exclusive, formalized notion that sought to define the Manchu people in terms of heredity and culture. It originated in the innermost circles of government and was motivated by the drive to consolidate imperial power.

The Qianlong emperor completed two important projects designed to formalize and standardize Manchu identity. The first was the reregistration of Hanjun as Manchus.[4] Traditionally, the Hanjun were considered part of the Manchu population; membership in a banner defined a clan as Manchu. But beginning under the Kangxi emperor, the court began changing the registration of some clans from Han banners to Manchu banners (Crossley 1983b:38) if they could show biological connections to banner members from Nurgan (Crossley 1990a:228). This implies that the Hanjun affiliation extended to banner members recruited in the Ming-administered province of Liaodong was no longer considered adequate qualification for full Manchu status. If it had been, reregistration would not have been necessary. Even some Jurchen clans that traced their origins to the Jin dynasty but happened to have been living in Liaodong when they joined the banners no longer felt satisfied with the Hanjun designation and searched for (and in some cases invented) hereditary links to the Jianzhou federation. The re-enrollment process initiated during the Kangxi reign gained momentum under the Qianlong emperor; in effect, it reversed the pattern of assimilation that had prevailed up to that time. Before, the Manchu designation had absorbed Han Chinese. Now, the Manchus were beginning to push some clans back into the Han category (Lee and Eng 1984:8).[5]

The second project completed during the Qianlong period was the compilation of *Researches on Manchu Origins* (Manzhou yuanliao kao). As Crossley points out, the works included ". . . reveal at least as much about the eighteenth-century attitudes of the Qianlong emperor and his court as of the truths of Manchu origins" (Crossley 1987:762). They formalized and codified clan histories and genealogies, standardized Manchu mythology and shamanistic practices, and elevated the (fictitious) link between the Qing and Jin dynasties to the level of official dogma. The goals of the project included bringing the clans, with their individualized rituals and mythology, into an official, bureaucratic system; increasing the historical status of the Aisin Gioro house; and standardizing the Manchus' social and historical role in order to tie them into the imperial order.

The Confucian emphasis on the emperor-subject relationship, a central feature of the Chinese tradition and one of the Qing imperial

4. See Crossley (1983b) for a description of the experiences of a representative Hanjun family that sought registration as Manchus.
5. The source for this discussion of the banner re-enrollment program is Crossley (1987).

clan's favorite notions, was missing from the Manchu political tradition forged during the conquest. Manchu politics in the sixteenth and seventeenth centuries were characterized by joint decision-making, power sharing, and factionalism—not the imperial authoritarianism the Qing emperors preferred. The *Researches* project, therefore, was in part an effort to impose the Chinese concept of authority on the Manchu tradition. At the same time, the Qianlong emperor used the project to satisfy the traditional Chinese need for the "rectification of names," the orderly placement of individuals and groups in appropriate, clearly defined social roles. But the results were "rigid" and "artificial" (Crossley 1987:779).

Two important concerns motivated the search for a new understanding of Manchu identity under the Qianlong emperor. First, a century had passed since the conquest, and the link between the original conquerors and the administration in Peking had become attenuated. Moreover, through its steady adoption of Chinese traditions, the imperial court was losing its claim to the cultural inheritance of the conquest. In response, the court intensified its efforts to formalize its ties to the original historical mission that had legitimized the conquest. Lacking strong cultural and political connections, the court emphasized its hereditary links to Nurgaci and Hong Taiji (ibid.:77).

The passage of time alone probably would have been a surmountable obstacle for the Aisin Gioro clan, but the loss of uniqueness of the Manchu administration posed a serious threat to Qing legitimacy. This blending of Manchu and Chinese culture demanded a noncultural definition of Manchu identity if the separation between Manchus and Han was to remain coherent. Beginning with the fall of the Oboi regency, the Qing rulers increasingly absorbed aspects of Chinese tradition into their life in the Forbidden City. The Manchu language was rarely heard in Beijing by 1800, and even the traditional Manchu pursuits identified in the *Researches on Manchu Origins* no longer commanded much interest. The influence of Han at court is also reflected in imperial marriage patterns. Although officially the Manchu emperors practiced marital endogamy, taking only Manchu women as their primary wives, they were perfectly willing to accept Han women as concubines and to promote their offspring as heirs; apparently, the mothers of the Kangxi, Jiaqing (1796–1820), and Daoguang (1820–1850) emperors all were Han women.

Manchu political life also integrated many aspects of Chinese tradition by the end of the Qianlong reign. Hong Taiji's Council of Deliberative Officials lost influence during the Kangxi reign, and the Qianlong emperor abolished it altogether. He established the Grand Council to advise him. At the same time, the number of Han officials serving the dynasty was increasing, until by the end of the Qianlong reign more than 80 percent of provincial officials were Han (Kessler 1969:498). These officials were selected through the traditional Confucian examination system, one of the bulwarks of the Chinese political tradition. As the Han gained power in the civilian administration they also began to expand their military role. The banner troops decreased in importance while the Chinese regular army, known as the Army of the Green Standard, gained in stature (Feuerwerker 1976:54).

Given the degree to which the culture of the Manchu elite had come to resemble that of the Han, the idea of Manchuness had to get its significance from a noncultural source if it was to mean anything at all. The push to define Manchu identity in terms of descent was one way the court tried to resolve this dilemma. Another was the formalization of Manchu culture—a kind of cultural taxidermy that stifled cultural growth and gave the Manchu elite a static "tradition" to which it could pay lip service while ignoring contemporary developments in Manchu life.

Standardizing Manchu culture meant choosing symbolic elements and treating them as definitive Manchu traits. The *Researches* project formalized the shamanistic rituals of the early Jurchen and removed them from the influence of living religious practice. At the same time, the court adopted a policy of preserving the martial tradition—the essence of Manchu identity prior to the Kangxi reign—by mandating for the emperor and his Manchu advisers occasional ceremonial and recreational hunts. The banner forces were also preserved, but in an equally distorted form. They were forbidden to take part in any economic activity other than military and government service. Thus, the ordinary Manchus were locked into stereotypically "traditional" roles.

Nowhere was the effort to freeze Manchu culture more apparent than on the frontier. The Oboi regents opened the frontier to Han immigration in the hope of strengthening and repopulating it, but the Kangxi emperor closed it again in 1668 (Lee 1970:78–79). From then on, the frontier was maintained as a preserve or reservoir of "pure" Manchu culture. According to Lee, "The imperial policy was to keep the frontier unchanged. . . ." (ibid.:77), even though doing so meant condemning the frontier Manchus to a life of backwardness and poverty. Cultural purity was not the only objective of the policy. The Aisin Gioro remembered their own history and took pains to insure that the frontier did not develop independent power that could threaten their authority. Thus,

> . . . the material and cultural primitiveness of the frontier region became a political asset rather than a liability. The frontier Manchus, in the eyes of their imperial masters, should be isolated from the corrupting influence of Chinese culture and be content to serve in the frontier banner force all their lives. The privilege of delving into the Chinese classics and becoming members of the civil bureaucracy was to be reserved for the sophisticated Manchus in China proper. (Ibid.:21)

Paradoxically, the Qianlong emperor's efforts to clarify Manchu ethnicity ended up confusing it. The Qing elite undermined those aspects of their heritage that actually held some promise as meaningful, unified cultural traits (such as a political tradition built on the example of the conquest). What they preserved were little more than quaint artifacts, empty rituals, and stereotypical social roles.

In effect, the Qianlong emperor was trying to transform a group forged by circumstance into one held together by primordial attachments. He sought to create a Manchu identity based on hereditary links to the Jianzhou Jurchen federation. He defined the federation territorially and linguistically, as the Jurchen-speaking banner members in Nurgan, rather than culturally (which would have included non-Jurchen banner members and Jurchen in Liaodong). In forcing Manchu identity to conform to such a model, the Qing scholars encountered many of the same obstacles that plague the primordialist school of ethnicity theory. They sought to identify constellations of cultural traits—what Clifford Geertz called " 'givens' of place, tongue, blood, looks, and way-of-life" (Geertz 1973:277)—to define the Manchu identity. But this model established arbitrary categories; it excluded people for whom there was no other coherent identity. Above all, it provided too static a picture. The "slice of life" that the *Researches* portrayed, with its permanently fixed array of clans and rituals, was so contrived as to betray reality altogether.

But the arbitrary, artificial aspects of the new definition did not prevent it from becoming an important touchstone of Manchu identity in the nineteenth century, because the Qing court's sponsorship gave it the force of law. As Gladney's studies of contemporary Hui ethnicity have shown, official endorsement of certain traits can actually make those traits more prominent in practice and enhance group members' attachment to them (Gladney 1991:passim). Among the Manchus, the officially recognized characteristics became accepted as accurate markers of identity. Still, ordinary Manchus were not merely passive recipients of the Qing elite's ideology. They had their own conceptions of Manchu identity, which were influenced, but not dictated, by the official policy. It is in the intersection of these popular understandings with the Qing definition and the realities of Manchu life that the essence of Manchu ethnicity is to be found.

THE FRONTIER MANCHUS

The Qing leadership pointed to Manchus living in the northeastern frontier—the Manchu place of origin—as the true, pure Manchus. Yet those Manchus were the most invisible and most silent of all. They were also the least aware of the meanings and conditions of Manchu identity that were being defined at court. By the end of the Qing period, the "Manchu preserve" in the Northeast had become an ocean of Han immigrants in which the tiny, impoverished Manchu banner population was not merely submerged, but drowning. The misfortunes these Manchus faced were in no small part the result of deliberate policies designed at the center to promote the interests of the dynastic elite.

During the conquest, the majority of Manchu banner troops entered China proper, leaving the Northeast largely depopulated (Li Chi 1932:37; Shirokogoroff 1924:15). Soon thereafter, the frontier was legally closed to Han immigration, leaving the Manchus who remained there on their own. In order to preserve their way of life, the court denied them access to education, opportunities to develop with the rest of the Qing state, and self-government (Lee 1970:22,66). It also segregated them from other groups living in the Northeast.

Economically, the frontier Manchus had few opportunities other than military service. Efforts to develop agriculture in the Northeast had little success. Unlike the Hanjun of Liaodong, most banner members on the frontier were descendants of tribal Jurchen whose livelihood was based on hunting (Crossley 1983a:89) and trade (Crossley 1983b:30). These Jurchen began to develop agriculture only under Nurgaci, and then only because he recognized the need for a food surplus to sustain the conquest (Liu Chia-chu 1981:49). Usually, the Jurchen themselves did not perform agricultural labor, but used Chinese and Korean captives as slaves (Oxnam 1975:24). This arrangement benefited the Jurchens in two ways: the slaves provided both agricultural labor and know-how.

The Nurgan banner members' economic weakness was apparent even during the early part of the conquest. For example, when the rate at which their territory increased slackened in the 1620s and 1630s, there were famines. The soldiers could not support themselves without a constantly expanding land base.

The policy of forcing Manchu banner members to adopt stereotypical roles exacerbated their economic problems. After the conquest, Manchus were forbidden to practice trades or take part in commerce (Crossley 1990a:51), and the court established monopolies over the traditional luxury products of the Northeast (furs, ginseng, and pearls). Thus, there were few economic niches left open for them outside of government service and agriculture. Given their record as farmers, the frontier Manchus were truly at a loss.

Even with these disadvantages, the frontier Manchus might have learned to exploit the rich resources of the Northeast successfully had it not been for the competition provided by the thousands of illegal immigrants who flooded into the area over the course of the dynasty. Unable to compete with the Han in trade or agriculture, most banner members retreated into towns, where they lived as absentee landlords. Although the Manchus initially owned all the farmland in the Northeast, they often lost it to savvy Chinese tenants and merchants (University of Washington 1956:113). Often the Han exiles confined in the region's towns had more education than frontier Manchus could hope to achieve, and they soon set the tone for the whole community. Within 150 years after the conquest, even the Manchu language was dying out in Jilin (Lee 1970:82).

One consequence of their failure to develop an independent economic base was that the frontier Manchus came to depend on government handouts for survival. Beginning in 1656, the Qing court paid stipends to banner soldiers throughout the empire. Few banner members had any other income. By the twentieth century, there were virtually no frontier Manchus who practiced the Jurchen economic traditions of hunting, ginseng gathering, and pearl collecting. Those who were farmers mostly occupied marginal niches in the northeastern agricultural economy, raising pigs and horses for a dying market (Shirokogoroff 1924:128–30). The Manchus' sad economic situation prompted an early twentieth-century scholar to lament:

> Intellectually . . . the Manchu is no match for the Chinese. The former lacks the intelligence and capacity which are characteristic of the latter. . . . As a merchant or farmer, too, the Manchu lacks the business qualities and industry of the Chinese. This intellectual inferiority is due, in the main, to the grant by the State to the majority of Manchus of mature age of a monthly subsidy which, while keeping them from actual want, precludes that stimulus to earn a living and better their condition which goes to make men and nations. . . . (Hosie 1904:157–58)

The economic crisis facing frontier Manchus illustrates the superficial nature of the Qing court's concern for the Northeast. While it is true that there was enormous pressure within China to allow immigration into the frontier, the dynasty did not exhaust its options for reducing immigration or softening its impact on the frontier Manchus. In fact, for economic and strategic reasons (at the time, Russian incursions into the Northeast threatened Qing security), the court began in the mid-nineteenth century to encourage immigration (Lee 1970:103).

The contradiction in Qing frontier policy between celebrating the Northeast as the Manchu homeland and allowing the conditions of life there to deteriorate seems to have confused frontier banner members' sense of identity. Even after the fall of the Qing dynasty they continued to believe in their special status and proudly asserted their Manchu identity, but they had little understanding of its history or official definition. For example, when the ethnographer S. M. Shirokogoroff visited members of an isolated Manchu community in the Northeast in the 1920s, he found that:

> Several purely Chinese institutions they now consider to be their own and some Manchu institutions and customs they ascribe to the Chinese. For example, as soon as the revolution broke out the Manchus of the Aigun District cut off their long plait. They seriously asserted that this is a "Chinese fashion."

But at the same time they were sure that the Chinese spirits,
Confucianism, and so on are purely Manchu ancient ideas.
(Shirokogoroff 1924:148)

On the frontier, being Manchu meant being part of the banner
organization, serving in the military, and receiving a military stipend.
The cultural manifestations of ethnicity so important to the Qing
court were meaningless on the frontier, ostensibly the source of Manchu culture but in fact heavily influenced by Chinese customs and
ideas. The standardized Manchu culture promulgated in Beijing was
irrelevant to frontier Manchus whose material culture and educational deprivation left them at the mercy of the Han dominating the
frontier. The Beijing version of Manchu identity simply was not
salient to the Manchus of the Northeast, so they did not absorb it in
any consistent way. Meanwhile, their evolving experience of Manchu
life failed to capture the attention of the court "ethnographers" and
gained little recognition in the official canon. But the court's enthusiasm for maintaining a unique Manchu identity—manifested both in
its codification of Manchu culture at the center and its policy on the
frontier—reinforced the frontier Manchus' own feelings of uniqueness and prevented them from assimilating altogether.

IN THE MANCHU GARRISONS

The Manchus who entered China proper during the conquest were
quartered in banner garrisons (known as Tatar cities) until the twi-
light years of the dynasty. Within the garrisons, legally and physically segregated from the Han and from their frontier cousins
(Crossley 1990a:47–49; Feuerwerker 1976:55), the garrison Manchus
constructed a culture and way of life different from both the "pure"
and the "official" traditions. In a sense, theirs was the most authentic Manchu experience because it was shared by the majority of
Manchus during most of the group's history (267 out of 354 years).

Lao She's final, unfinished, autobiographical novel, *Under the Red
Banner* (Zheng hong qi xia) opens a window on the Manchu community in the last decades of the Qing dynasty. His protagonists are
his neighbors and relatives, a proud but destitute circle of banner-
members living in Beijing in the 1890s. The novel reveals the ambivalence, uncertainty, and pathos of garrison life. What comes through
most clearly, however, is the centrality of Manchu identity to the lives

of the Beijing bannermen. As we compare the insights of this extraordinary book with other accounts, the nature of Manchu identity within the garrison communities emerges.

The garrison system, like many aspects of Manchu life, had its roots in the conquest. When they conquered Ming cities, the Qing rulers attempted to provide a livelihood for the banner troops stationed in them by confiscating nearby farmland and giving it to the soldiers. Some of the land had been part of Ming imperial estates, but much of it belonged to Han farmers who were relocated in other parts of North China. Before long, however, the same conditions that were displacing the Manchu farmers on the frontier forced most of the Manchus in conquered China to give up their agricultural efforts and lease or sell their plots.

While economic factors made farming unfruitful for the garrison Manchus, legal restrictions kept them out of most other vocations. At first, they were forbidden by law to engage in trade or manufacturing. Later, most found it impossible to break into the competitive Chinese commercial life in the garrison cities; moreover, they tended to see such activities as unworthy of imperial bannermen (Shirokogoroff 1924:129). Lao She illustrates this point in his description of his much-admired cousin, Fuhai:

> This experienced bannerman was actually only half of one; you could even say only a third. This had nothing to do with blood. . . . But the thing that most surprised people was this: he was a housepainter! My uncle was a third ranked colonel. . . . but since his son learned to paint houses, one could hardly argue that he was anything but a half a bannerman. (Lao She 1987:31–32)

Denied access to agriculture, trade, and commerce, garrison Manchus without high official posts or large landholdings were forced to rely on their subsidy payments for survival. As Lao She puts it, "By then, buying on credit was our system" (ibid.:22). The garrison Manchus' dependence on subsidies from Beijing enhanced the court's power over them (Crossley 1983a:10–11) and eroded their incentive to find an economic niche outside the garrison walls. Writes Lao She: "Under this system [the Manchus] swept the South and cleared out the North, beating down everything in their path. It was under this same system that the bannermen gradually lost their freedom and

their self-confidence and under it many spent their whole lives unem-
ployed "(Lao She 1987:33). Eventually, with the rise of the Army of
the Green Standard, even the garrisons' military functions lost their
importance (Feuerwerker 1976:54). Similarly, the dynasty phased out
its policy of preferentially hiring Manchus for government posts,
making that professional avenue more difficult.

The economic hardships of life in the Manchu garrisons were
supportable because of the status afforded by Manchu identity, at
least within the community. Lao She leaves no doubt that the divisions among Manchus, Han, and other ethnic groups were clearly
drawn, although individual Han might be welcomed into the Manchu community. The garrison troops were devoted to the idea of
Manchu identity (Crossley 1983a:138, 273). They saw themselves as
heirs to the conquest tradition and relatives of the Qing elite. Many
who retreated to the Northeast after 1911 considered the trip a return
to their ancestral homeland (Crossley 1990a:186). But this sense of
connection to the Manchu past (and to the imperial and frontier
present) was based almost entirely on notions received from history
and the state:

> The garrisoning of the Manchus is an enigmatic feature of Qing
> life. On the one hand, it destroyed completely the traditional
> economic and social contexts of Manchu life; on the other
> hand, it demanded that Manchu life continue, segregated from
> the Chinese and with few cultural resources apart from the
> Court and history. (Ibid.:270)

Despite their self-identification as Manchus, the garrison troops
were heavily influenced by the Han communities around them.
Many bannermen studied the Confucian classics and took part in the
civil service examination system, while others studied Chinese arts
and culture for their personal enjoyment. The fact that legislation
regulating almost every area of garrison life was necessary to maintain segregation suggests that most Manchus were open to outside
influences. The dynasty outlawed intermarriage of Han and ban-
nermembers, required Manchus to live within the Tatar cities, prohibited them from learning trades or engaging in commerce outside the
garrisons, and forbade bannermen to own property. With the cultural differences between the two groups fading and de jure segrega-

tion persisting, the difference between Han and Manchus came to be understood in terms of descent (Crossley 1983a:271). (For example, Lao She's characters have no trouble recognizing that Fuhai, the "half-bannerman" housepainter, is still a Manchu and that the Hui butcher who buys himself an imperial post is still a Hui.)

The conventional wisdom among scholars of the Qing dynasty once held that the Manchus were completely assimilated by the turn of the twentieth century. Crossley has shown that this assumption was inaccurate, that in fact the Manchus in many ways preserved both an independent way of life and a unique culture within the garrison communities (Crossley 1990a:71, 91). Lao She's work reinforces this conclusion. Clearly, the Manchus were different from their Han neighbors. But were the differences ethnic ones?

In many ways, the characteristics of ordinary Manchus in the postconquest generations appear to fit the primordialist definition of ethnicity. The Manchus felt as if they were part of an elite, hereditary group, and they clung to that status even when it was to their economic disadvantage to do so. In other words, they felt attachments that defied circumstantialist logic. G. Carter Bentley's theory of ethnicity as an interactive phenomenon including elements of "habitus" (unconscious "schemes and dispositions" common to all members of a group) and domination offers an explanation of this situation (1987:29). Bentley argues that neither "circumstantial" nor "primordial" describes this kind of attachment adequately. Instead, he looks to the shared experiences of people living in evolving groups set in real political and social contexts. Members' ethnic identity can change in such settings, yet remain coherent throughout the group. Moreover, Bentley's theory acknowledges the role played by the state in molding members' experiences, and therefore the group's habitus.

Part of the value of the Manchu case to the study of ethnicity lies in the fact that, while it appears to satisfy conventional primordialist and (in the pre-Kangxi period) circumstantialist criteria, a close examination produces reservations that call those criteria themselves into question. The group began as a pragmatic coalition formed to accomplish a particular task, and later the state redefined it in terms of primordial traits. But the traits the Qing leaders put forth as "ethnically Manchu"—such as horsemanship, speaking Manchu, hunting, and the appreciation of martial skill—had little resonance within Manchu communities, where few of these traits could be practiced. Bentley rightly argues that elements of habitus are coherent only if they touch a chord in the common experience of group members; state-sponsored ethnic traits will not necessarily penetrate. It is true that many of the traits defined in the Forbidden City as Manchu did not "take" in the garrisons and on the frontier, and those traits that were salient could well be said to have been nonethnic. Once we remove from the description of Manchu life the results of the Qing dynasty's political and economic policies, most of the obvious visible differences between Manchus and Han disappear. The idea that differences in political and economic function are inadequate to define ethnicity is explored theoretically in Judith Nagata's work. She argues that both primordial and circumstantialist criteria can be satisfied by associations that are clearly nonethnic, such as kinship and gender groups. In order to differentiate ethnic divisions fully, she suggests that

> the final factor seems to lie in the institutional self-sufficiency and self-reproducing capacity of the ethnic community, in its ability to cater to the needs of both sexes, all ages and stages of the life cycle, which makes them [sic] potential "candidates for nationhood. . . ." (Nagata 1981:97)

In a fundamental way, the Manchus were neither self-sufficient nor self-reproducing. Their identity as a group depended upon performing particular functions: first that of the conquering army, then those of military occupation and political leadership. Those Manchus who learned to play other social roles—as farmers, tradesmen, or merchants—could be expelled from the community. Moreover, Manchu values denigrated social and economic roles outside military and political life, so that full status as a bannerman required eschewing such roles. Given that so many differences between Manchus and Han were political and economic, must we reject the idea of Manchu ethnicity altogether?

We can pile up evidence against the Manchu claim to ethnic status, but we will ultimately fail to extinguish the spark of self-awareness and community cohesion that united Manchus in the garrisons, on the frontier, and in the Forbidden City. The clarity with which Lao She's characters categorize themselves and their neighbors, the pride with which Manchus throughout China spoke of their imperial connections, and the construction of unique Manchu goals and values point to a Manchu habitus and ethnicity. Over the course of three centuries, the descendants of the diverse tribes united under Nurgaci came to view their relationship to one another as the definitive category in their understanding of self. Their contradictory positions as the ruling political organization and a minority people conspired to hold them apart from other groups—and in the process, welded them together.

Ultimately, any definition of ethnicity that does not rest on this combination of sociopolitical recognition and self-awareness cannot make sense of the Manchus. One definition that does recognize the interaction of social and political factors with group members' understanding of self is what Dru Gladney has called a "dialogical" definition.[6] Such a definition acknowledges that Manchu was, for many years, a fundamentally political category. Thus, it allows us to include people of widely divergent origins in the group, just as Nurgaci did when he organized the banners of the 1500s. It allows us to recognize the Hanjun as full members of the Manchu community, whatever their ancestral origins, language, lifestyle, or customs. It allows us to interpret the fundamentally political nature of Manchu "tradition" (the tradition of conquest) as an adequate description of Manchu culture, regardless of the diversity of belief, custom, and language within the original group. Finally, the notion of Manchu as a political category that gradually took on an ethnic character explains how the group could continue to exist long after the uneven adoption of Chinese ways had opened wide gaps between those living in different places and times.

The Qing dynasty certainly strove to create the impression that the Manchus were a descent-based community. What were the results of their efforts? Did their political distinctiveness and internal cohesion convince outsiders of their ethnic uniqueness? To answer these questions we must listen to voices from outside the Manchu community.

HAN VOICES

The first 150 years of the Qing dynasty were marked by a mostly cooperative relationship between Han and Manchus. During that period, the Han generally subscribed to the axiom "Use Chinese meth-

6. Gladney developed the idea of dialogically defined ethnicity in a series of seminars at Harvard University, in the spring of 1989.

ods to transform barbarians" (*Yong Xia bian yi*) (Wiens 1969: 2, 7). The traditional Confucian definition of barbarianism stressed cultural factors, not hereditary ones (ibid.:2, 6) and most scholar-officials believed that the Manchus generally met those cultural requirements. The late Ming period was a disaster in the eyes of Confucian moralists, and the Qing emperors exploited its weaknesses to enhance their dynasty's prestige (Oxnam 1975:35). Leaders such as Dorgon and the Shunzhi, Kangxi, and Qianlong emperors consciously courted Han favor by stressing Confucian virtue in their administrations (Oxnam 1975:34). Indeed, late-nineteenth-century protestations to the contrary notwithstanding, the harsh, discriminatory treatment meted out by the Oboi regent clique was the exception in Qing history, not the rule (ibid.:8), as the widespread willingness and ability of Han scholars to serve the dynasty attest.

Of course, the Manchus did not meet with automatic or universal approval when they invaded China and took over its government. Immediately after the conquest of Beijing they battled Ming restorationists; later, the rebellions by the Three Feudatories in the Southwest and pro-Ming pirates along the Fujian coast challenged their legitimacy as well. But as a rule, these rebellions were political rather than racial or ethnic. Wiens has shown that race-based anti-Manchu ideas existed in the early Qing period, but argues they had little influence, both because they were suppressed and because they did not resonate with most Han at the time (Wiens 1969:passim). Still, anti-Manchu sentiments continued to surface from time to time throughout the dynasty, and repressing them was a regular feature of Qing policy. Anti-Manchu thinkers rejected the Manchus as outsiders and usurpers. According to R. Kent Guy, "Almost constant Manchu efforts to suppress the racist idiom of political protest make it difficult to tell how widespread such thought was or what end it served, but there is no question that it represented an extremely powerful political weapon" (Guy 1987:17).

As Qing power began to decline in the nineteenth century, more and more Han sought to tap the potential of that weapon. Several factors combined to nourish a flowering of ideas rejecting Qing legitimacy and defining the Manchus as a foreign, alien people. The Qing elite's decision to emphasize descent in its self-definition reinforced the notion of racial differentiation by the Han. In addition, the declining power of the dynasty undermined its authority and promoted dissent.

A major premise of Taiping ideology was a virulent hatred of the Manchus which included both political and ethnic dimensions. An early Taiping manifesto stated:

> All the bamboo groves in the Nanshan Mountains . . . would not suffice to recount their dirty deeds on our land. The turbulent waters of the Eastern Sea would not suffice to wash away the traces of their enormous crimes and evil deeds that shut out the sky. . . . A campaign is beginning that will bring the barbarians inevitable extermination. The Manzhou scum, which have ruled for two hundred years, are doomed, their fate is sealed. (Quoted in Ilyushechkin 1983:260)

The Taiping rebels' wrath was not limited to the Qing leadership; rather, their race-based hatred extended to all Manchus, regardless of their station. A British missionary made this point in his description of the Manchu garrison in Nanjing after a Taiping attack in 1863: "A walk in the Manchu city helped us appreciate the intense hatred of the Tartar rulers felt by the Taipings. Only one house was left standing in a city of 25,000 inhabitants" (Rev. Joseph Edkins, quoted in Clarke and Gregory 1982:293).

Late in the nineteenth century Western influences came to play a prominent part in anti-Manchu agitation: with the idea of modern nationalism came the thought that China, too, could and should become a modern nation with a unitary ethnic composition. Nationalists such as Sun Yat-sen combined elements of Chinese tradition, including the early anti-Qing racial critiques, with Western concepts of nationalism to create anti-Manchu justifications for their own revolutionary ambitions (Wiens 1969:17).

In general, these critics did not attack the Manchus on the grounds of Manchu culture or specifically Manchu behavior. The confession of Lu Haodong, one of Sun's coconspirators in the early Revolutionary party, the Xingzhonghui, illustrates the kinds of objections the rebels had against Manchu rule:

> It is common knowledge that the Manzhou dynasty of Qing, the bandit spawn from Jianzhou, established itself in China, seized our lands, killed our ancestors, took our children, and the gems and silks of our wives. Ponder, who lives on whose land, and who eats whose fruits? The ten days of Yangzhou, the three

massacres in Jiaqing, the invasion of two Wangs in Guangdong—history contains innumerable instances of the killing of
our countrymen. We know and remember this. Can all this be
called virtuous? It must be understood that today, without exter-
minating the Manzhou Qings, the Han nation can under no
circumstances be restored. (Quoted in Borokh 1983:298)

Clearly, Lu's hatred of the Manchus was racial. Rather than objecting
to the behavior and policies of the current rulers, he attacked the Qing
founders, then demanded the extermination of living Manchus as
retribution. This mentality, which blamed China's problems on alien
rule and traced them to the beginning of the dynasty, pervaded the
anti-Qing rhetoric of the nineteenth and early twentieth centuries.

One consequence of the racialism of these attacks was that—like
the Taiping Rebellion—they failed to differentiate between the Qing
elite and ordinary Manchus. As a result, revolutionaries often directed their violence at the garrison residents, who by that time were
intimately tied to the Chinese communities surrounding them and
virtually defenseless. Thus, in Xi'an alone, as many as twenty thousand Manchus were massacred during the 1911 Revolution (Crossley
1990a:197).

Throughout most of the dynasty, the prevailing Han conception of
Manchu identity was based on the Manchus' political role and conduct, but the suspicion that the dynasty was illegitimate and foreign
simmered below the surface, held in check by repression and relative
satisfaction with Manchu rule (Guy 1987:6). But as the Qing's ability
to minimize anti-Manchu sentiment disintegrated in the dynasty's last
years, political aspirants jumped at the chance to exploit ethnic tension
to justify political rebellion and a nationalist strategy for the Chinese
state. The idea that race served as a cover for other motives for oppos-
ing the Manchus gains strength from the fact that the racial attacks had
little resonance for those Han who were not disadvantaged under the
Qing. It is also instructive to note how quickly the Chinese reversed
their position on the issue when Japan began to use the idea of a
Manchu-Chinese schism to justify their Manchukuo policy. Suddenly
the Northeast was an inalienable part of China, and the Manchus were
once again full-fledged members of the Chinese nation (Li Chi
1932:passim). Yet appeals to ethnic divisions would have been far less
successful had they not resonated with a genuine perception of ethnic
difference between Han and Manchus.

CONCLUSION

After the 1911 Revolution, some Manchus attempted to revitalize the group's identity. They organized schools and clubs to promote the Manchu language and traditions. But, as one commentator put it, "They were never in danger of being effectual" (University of Washington 1956:193). The language was too long neglected to be revived and even the teachers of Manchuness were at a loss to define it. The Japanese, too, tried to breathe new life into the Manchus in Manchukuo, since their puppet state's legitimacy rested on the idea of a Manchu nation. But Manchukuo, like the earlier Manchu revival movement, didn't take hold. The search for a Manchu identity linked to traits the Qing court had promoted turned up little enthusiasm among ordinary Manchus.

The Manchus existed as a group only because of their experience as conquerors. In the beginning, all they had in common was that experience. As they became generations removed from the events that had brought them together, their original identity lost relevance. Had the Qing followed different policies, Manchus might well have taken the path of their Jurchen Jin relatives, settling into the Han communities around them and gradually assimilating. But the Qing goverment aborted this process by enforcing the legal segregation of Manchus and Han. Why? The best explanation seems to be that they needed to preserve ethnic differentiation in order to sustain their legitimacy as the ruling house. But the Aisin Gioro and their cronies in Beijing did not want to play the part of traditional Manchus. Instead, they used their cousins in the banners to create the illusion of a connection to the original Manchu historical mission.

Thus the Qing leadership entered into a dialogue with the Manchu people. It forcibly prevented them from becoming Han, but at the same time it provided them with a justification for their separate status. Manchus outside the Forbidden City, for their part, answered by constructing a group identity centered on their common history as conquerors and their current fate as servants of the regime. Had they not been segregated, the Manchu people might well have lost their cohesion, tenuous as it was. Had they not looked to their common history and life together to understand themselves, they might not have defined their identity in terms of their Manchu heritage. It was these two factors—political influences and a unique, shared experience of life—that, acting in concert, created the Manchu people.

EPILOGUE

The dialogue between the Manchu people's shared experience and the Chinese state continues to shape Manchu identity to this day. During the Republican period anti-Manchu sentiment prevailed, and many Manchus "went underground" to protect themselves. Adding to their insecurity was the Nationalist policy of encouraging minority-group assimilation. Even today, self-identified Manchus living under the Nationalist government on Taiwan long for acknowledgment. In 1981, a group of such Manchus founded the Manchu Association (Manzu Xiehui) (see Crossley 1990a:216–18). Their purpose was to work toward achieving recognition both as Manchus and as full members of the Chinese nation. They also wanted to lift the shroud of secrecy and shame in which many of their older relatives had hidden their Manchu identity.

The decision to organize the Manchu Association in Taiwan coincided with a period of heightened ethnic awareness throughout Taiwanese society. Since the mid-1970s, opposition politicians in Taiwan have stressed ethnic difference in their political appeals, shattering the Nationalist Party's insistence that all Chinese are one. Their calls for a renovation of Taiwan's political institutions (and in some cases for Taiwan's independence) are based on the distinction between the "native" Taiwanese majority and the Mainlanders (Waishengren, or those who came to Taiwan with the Nationalists after 1945), who have held political power. In response to the mainly Minnan-speaking opposition movement, members of other ethnic communities—the Hakka (Kejiaren) and Aboriginal people (Yuanzhumin)—began staking out their own cultural (and political) territory. It is not surprising, then, that Manchus living in Taiwan in the early 1980s, who were almost certainly fed up with being thrown into the unpopular Mainlander category, wanted to define their experience on their own terms.

In the People's Republic of China, too, the political context has interacted with Manchus' own experiences to shape ethnic identity. Chinese Communist Party ideology teaches toleration for minority groups. In the long run, national distinctions will disappear with the birth of a new, communist society. But before national differences fade away, class barriers must be broken down. The Party took the position that antagonisms between nationalities should be muted in order to concentrate on eliminating class differences. The result was a policy that included space for minorities to continue their distinctive ways of life, as well as efforts to win them over gradually to the socialist cause.[7] It was a policy of integration (or amalgamation), as opposed to assimilation.

Although nationalities policy in the People's Republic has vacillated considerably, being at times favorable to minorities and at other times less so, certain aspects of the policy clearly increased the salience of ethnic identification. For example, the government instituted an elaborate program of ethnic labelling. Groups were invited to apply for status as minority nationalities. They were then examined by ethnographers to see whether they met the criteria for minority status.[8] Those whose status was upheld were eligible for certain privileges and exempted from a number of regulations, including the one-child rule. Individual membership is largely a matter of personal choice, but once a person wears an ethnic label, his or her political status changes in subtle ways. For example, programs to encourage minority students and cadres make it easier to gain admission to schools and institutes.

As of 1965, 2.43 million persons in the People's Republic were registered as members of the Manchu nationality (Dreyer 1976:145); by 1989, the number had grown to approximately 4.3 million (Ma Yin 1989:41). June Teufel Dreyer speculates that the Manchus may have been granted recognition to repudiate the Nationalists' assimilationist agenda (Dreyer 1976:145–46). As the Manchus' garrison experience amply illustrates, ethnic labeling—the official acknowledgment of ethnic difference—can intensify group identification. For example, Lao She, the "voice" of the Manchu garrisons, revealed little awareness of his Manchu roots in his early novels. Yet after he

7. Dreyer (1976) gives a thorough account of minorities policy in the People's Republic. This summary is based on her work.

8. The definition of a nationality, which is based on Stalin's criteria for nationhood, is as follows: "A nation is a stabilized community, formed by man in history, which has a common language, a common territory, a common economic life, and a common psychological make-up that find expression in a common culture" (quoted in Hsieh Jiann 1984:4). The integrity of the evaluation process is open to debate. Obviously, it is difficult to see how the Manchus could have achieved nationality status under this definition, strictly applied. For a thorough discussion of Chinese Communist views of ethnicity, see Heberer (1989).

was "labeled," he "was designated chief spokesman for [the Manchus]" (ibid.:271) and went on to write the story of the Beijing garrison in *Under the Red Banner.* Part of recognition is legitimation. In 1987 a school for the study of the Manchu language opened in Beijing. Its goal was to train readers to translate old Qing documents before the documents disintegrated. Pamela Kyle Crossley describes Manchu reaction to the school:

> Its faculty of eleven—ten Manchus and one Mongol—expected to have to recruit students for the school, but instead they ended up accepting 90 of 150 applicants. Of those accepted, more than half were formally registered as Manchus, but it is clear that only a small minority of the students saw themselves as without Manchu ancestral affiliation. . . . "The school helps to boost the sense of pride for an entire people," said the founder. "[Since the end of the Qing] many Manchus, though they had nothing to do with the toppled ruling class, have hidden their origin. Today we are excited that our Manchu culture is beginning to be well recognized and our Manchu descendants enjoy equal status in our motherland." (Crossley 1990a:218–19)

As Crossley eloquently explains in the conclusion to *Orphan Warriors,* defining Manchu identity in the modern states of the People's Republic of China and the Republic of China on Taiwan is extremely difficult. Most of what non-Manchus view as "characteristically Manchu" is arbitrary and unauthentic. Yet what remains, now that the frontier and garrison communties have been dissolved, their populations scattered? What is left is habitus, a worldview learned at the knee of parents and grandparents who can never expunge the memory of garrison life, and the recognition of the state. In Taiwan, where the state is silent, Manchus join the chorus of voices pleading for acknowledgment. In the People's Republic, those who feel their Manchu identity welcome each new piece of evidence that the dialogue between habitus and power has not been broken off.

PART II
The History of Ethnic Identity
The Process of Peoples

Millenarianism, Christian Movements, and Ethnic Change among the Miao in Southwest China

Siu-woo Cheung

In the early twentieth century the Hua Miao (Flowery Miao) peoples of northeastern Yunnan, western Guizhou, and southern Sichuan experienced both mass conversions to Christianity and rapid development of a Miao ethnic identity.[1] Among the Hei Miao (Black Miao) of southeastern Guizhou, however, Christian missionaries were largely unsuccessful, and there was no major change in the basis of ethnic identity. The thesis of this chapter is that the different nature of capitalist penetration in the two areas goes far toward explaining the radical differences in ethnic and religious change. Specifically, in the socioeconomically homogenous Hua Miao society, millennial Christian movements arose out of a realization of the transcendent political power of Western missionaries over the Miao's traditional adversary, the Chinese state. In the Hei Miao areas, in contrast, where indigenous social stratification was intensified by capitalist commoditization, such a realization was impossible, and millennial movements did not occur. (See map 3, p.93.)

THEORETICAL CONSIDERATIONS

Most previous works on millenarianism place discrete emphasis on one or another aspect of millennial movements, such as ideology,

1. I use the Chinese designation Miao to refer to the various groups of people in Southwest China who call themselves Hmong, Mong, Hmu, or Xioob, and whose languages are closely related. The Hmong and Mong speak the Western branch of their language family, and were known in Chinese as Bai Miao, Qing Miao, or Hua Miao. The Hmu speak the southeastern branch, and are known as Hei Miao; the Xioob speak the northeastern branch, and are known as Hong Miao. The related people in Vietnam, Laos, and Thailand are usually designated Hmong or Meo. It should be noted that since the term Hmong refers to only some of these people, I have used the term Miao, which is the most inclusive, as a matter of convenience. For a more detailed account of the various peoples subsumed under the category Miao, see Diamond (this volume).

collective action, individual emotional response, or extrinsic political-economic conditions.[2] The approach in this chapter is a synthetic one that understands millennial movements as a process of articulation of the various aspects of religious phenomena. While most writers recognize that millennial movements are transitory in nature (Keyes 1977b:284; Worsley 1968:xxxvi–xxxviii), they do not adequately address the mechanism of the transformation. Worsley, for example, gives a detailed typological sequence of the developmentmental stages of following, movement, and organization (1968:xxxvi), but the processual study of millennial movements still lacks an analytic scheme that accounts for the development from one phase to another, as well as for the transformation of the movement into other forms.

C. S. Peirce's semeiotics (see Greenlee 1973 and Peirce 1960) can be used to formulate an analytical framework comprehensive enough to understand the relationship between millennial ideology, political action, emotional agitation, and the extrinsic political-economic conditions of Miao millenarianism, as well as the relationship between individual experience and collective phenomena and the developments and transformations in the history of a movement. A scheme of progression of different modes of interpretation can be shown to develop from emotion (a quality of feeling toward a sign) to action (interpreting a sign through muscular effort or dialogic thought) to conception (formulation of a concept or general understanding produced by the sign). Applied to the process of a millennial movement this scheme shows that the savior of the oppressed people (in the form of supernatural agency encompassing millennial ideas, usually represented or indicated by a prophet) works as a sign. The interpretation of such a sign initially arouses enormous emotional agitation among the oppressed people as a response to the contradiction between the power order proposed in the religious fantasy and that experienced in reality. This sign next incites people to take action in

2. Approaches emphasizing intrinsic factors include Norman Cohn's sociopsychological approach (1962:31), George Shepperson's distinction between pre- and post-millenarianism (1962:44–45), and Charles Keyes's proposal that millennial ideology is formulated in the cultural terms with which a population is most familiar (1977b:283–302). Approaches emphasizing extrinsic factors include David Aberle's relative deprivation theory (1962:209–14), Cohn's specification of circumstances that may give rise to millennial movements, and Keyes's idea that millennial movements are caused primarily by crises surrounding political power (1977b: 293–302).

order to resolve the contradiction and bring about realization of the desired power order. Finally, it generates a conception of the resultant power order as the resolution of the contradiction. If the movement has successfully changed the power order, the conception generated will be a reformulation of the original millennial belief into more secular ideology or a new religious belief that supports the new power order, since the millennium of the original religious fantasy will never come true. If the movement fails to change the old order, the original millennial belief, which reflects the predicaments of the people, will be reinforced and remain as a latent force that can erupt again.

Another fundamental principle of Peircian semeiotics is that the interpretation of a sign depends on one's goals and experience; whether different people can undertake synchronized interpretations of a sign depends on whether they share common goals and experience, whether they form a community of inquirers. A millennial movement can be seen as a process of sign interpretation undertaken by a group of people who share common experience of subjugation and oppression by a dominant group and common goals of escaping structural restraints or effecting radical structural change, transforming the power order. These common experiences and goals are, of course, shaped by the political-economic factors that constitute their relationship with the dominant power.

A major problem in the study of millennial movements concerns the formulation of ideology. The formulation of millennial beliefs appears to always involve some kind of conceptual transformation of the power order in reality. The hinge of such transformation is the idea of salvation, which is a process leading from the subjugation of the oppressed people in the existing order to their participation in an ideal power order in the coming millennium. The central idea of salvation is the arrival or emergence of the savior, who is thus the core sign in millennial movements. If, as Keyes proposes (1977b), millennial beliefs do not emerge ex nihilo, but are formulated in cultural terms with which people are already familiar (either from their own indigenous beliefs alone or from a syncretic combination of these and an outside religion), then the savior is usually formulated after the sign of paramount power in the dominating group, which is usually manifested in the mystification of the prevailing religion or ideology of that group. For example, Keyes (1977b) shows that in millennial movements in northeastern Thailand, the conception of the savior centers around the Theravada Buddhist belief in Maitreya, the Buddha to come, and "persons with merit" (*chu mi bun*), both of which are ideological buttresses of Thai cosmocratic kingship. Correspondingly, the Miao conception of the savior, the Miao King (Miao Wang), can be shown to center around the idea of Chinese emperorship.

In a millennial movement, oppressed groups usually formulate their sign of the savior as a mirror image of the sign of paramount power among the dominating group, a power so strong that it can be opposed only by such an image. In fact, the participation of the oppressed group is repeated and futile millennial resistance reinforces the idea of the savior as a counterforce. The peculiar formulation of the savior thus precipitated in the history of resistance will then become a sign of habitual millennial response to crises of political power; in a sense the savior thus becomes a "sign of habit" in the culture of the oppressed group. Usually unnoticed in daily life, it comes to consciousness in times of crisis. And, as E. V. Daniel (1984) notes, such signs of habit are also generative of other, more conscious ideological signs. In the case of millennial movements, the sign of the savior generates related millennial beliefs, such as the idea of salvation.

Being generative, the peculiar formulation of the savior as a habitual sign for millennial response is usually unduly abstract. As a matter of fact, the actual form of paramount power in the dominating group, after which the sign of the savior is modeled, is usually obscure to the oppressed group, existing beyond their direct experience of everyday life. Such an abstract formulation of the savior thus serves in the initial phase of a millennial movement mainly to arouse habitual emotional response and to incite action. When the movement has developed to the stage of confrontation, some more concrete formulation of the savior is necessary for guiding specific action. In the course of a movement, new formulations of the savior may be adopted according to the needs of specific phases, but these are largely shaped by the generative scheme of the habitual sign.

We now need to apply this semeiotic model to millennial movements instigated by ethnic confrontation. It is recognized that millennial movements in the context of ethnic conflict often give rise to increased ethnic cohesion in the oppressed group (Hinton 1979:92; Keyes 1979:22; Worsley 1968:227). If ethnic identity is a kind of collective self-consciousness about who one is and to whom one is related, then ethnic consciousness will develop through a process of gradually changing modes of interpretation of the sign of the savior among members of an ethnic group who share highly resonant experience and goals in the context of confrontation against dominant ethnic groups.[3] The process starts with an upsurge of emotion in the form of primordial sentiments among members of an ethnic group, a feeling of closeness taken as given. Then common actions are taken in ethnic confrontation against the dominant group. Finally, the nondominant group formulates the conception of a common ethnic identity. Such a conception is always related to a people's view of the structure of power in the context of ethnic interaction. As a consequence of millennial movements against the dominant group, the cultural basis of the nondominant group's ethnic identity will be constituted in the notion of the savior and the encompassed millennial belief, in accordance with their conception of the resultant power order.

Usually, millennial movements fail to change the experienced power order, and the conception of being a deprived people is recurrently confirmed in the cultural basis of the oppressed group, perpetuated in the ideal of the awaited savior and the encompassed millennial belief, modeled after the paramount power of the dominant group. But if the oppressed group is able to adopt a new sign of power in a savior who transcends the dominant group and enables the oppressed group to combat them effectively in ethnic confrontation, the old cultural basis of their ethnic identity will be superseded by a new one that is constituted in the idea of the new savior and its related beliefs in accordance with their conception of the new power order. The new cultural basis of ethnic identity will then be further manipulated to enhance their sociopolitical position relative to the dominating group, and will subsequently transform the original power order of ethnic interaction. This kind of cultural transformation is, in fact, what happened when Christian missionaries entered the power equation of the relationship between the Miao and the Chinese state.

---

3. Following Bentley (1987), Bourdieu's notion of "habitus" can be used to account for the highly resonant experiences and goals among members of an ethnic group, guiding the semiotic process of development of ethnic consciousness in the context of ethnic interaction.

CHINESE EXPANSION AND THE MIAO
MILLENNIAL TRADITION

There have been countless uprisings among non-Han people in South China, but massive insurrections by Miao and other groups became particularly endemic after the founding of the Ming dynasty.[4] This resulted from further expansion of the Chinese empire toward the Southwest through military colonization and, later, through implementation of the policy of *gai tu gui liu,* or replacing former *tusi* with ordinary Chinese civil magistrates. This policy was begun in northeastern Guizhou in 1413; in the following year Guizhou was designated a province. Since then, serious Miao insurrections have occurred intermittently; for example, there were eighty uprisings in central Guizhou between 1416 and 1426 (Concise History 1985:95). The most devastating of the Ming period were those of 1426–1433, 1436–1460, and 1536–1551, mainly in the regions of northeastern Guizhou–western Hunan and southeastern Guizhou–southwestern Hunan. The Qing dynasty implemented *gai tu gui liu* even more thoroughly, often using massive military action to bring tribal people under civil administration. This led to a series of Miao uprisings in 1734–1737 in southeastern Guizhou, and in 1795–1806 in northeastern Guizhou–Western Hunan. The dynasty's two-hundred-year campaign of suppression and sometimes extermination culminated in a series of massacres during the Miao insurrection of 1854–1872, which spread over the whole province and wrought havoc upon the population and the economy.

In confronting the crisis of political power brought on by the forceful implementation of civil administration by the Chinese state, the Miao were driven to desperation, and thus relied on millenarianism to resist Han domination. Chinese sources describe the process in which the Miao King emerged (Miao Wang *chushi*): at the beginning of an uprising, shaman-sorcerers, or simply people who had given in to hysterics, appealed to the public with the prophecy of the Miao King's emergence. These prophets exhorted people to abandon

4. In ancient Chinese records, Miao was used alternately with such terms as San Miao, Nanman, *man* and Mao to designate non-Han people in South China (Wiens 1967:67–77). Those people inhabited the middle reaches of the Yangtze River in the second millennium B.C. Since then, they have migrated southward under Chinese pressure. Not until the twelfth century did the term Miao designate a specific cluster of ethnic groups, by that time settled in western Hunan and northern Guizhou (Ruey 1972:146).

their daily activities and join the ceremonies to receive the Miao King, who was sometimes said to be somewhere near (e.g., in a cave). The ceremonies usually involved offering sacrifices, disseminating amulets, demonstrating magic powers, and so forth. The prophets also promised that the Miao King's arrival would bring improvements in life, such as discovering hidden treasure, getting land back from the Han, and obtaining official posts. Meanwhile agitation continued, with those who had entered trances wielding arms and threatening to kill the Han. Before long, someone would declare himself the Miao King and appeal to the public for support. Messages of revolt—often in the form of engraved pieces of wood and taboo objects such as chicken feathers and charcoal, or sometimes in written form—would be disseminated to the villages in the vicinity. If they had not done so earlier, imperial troops would often arrive at this point, and confrontation would erupt.[5]

The religious fantasy of Miao millenarianism was in fact a reversed image of the people's conception of their lot of subjugation in the contradiction between state and stateless societies. The ideas of kinship and accession to officialdom, and belief in military superiority ensured by magic, and the hopes of finding treasure and recovering land were simply the reflection of the powerful Chinese state.

The notion of the Miao King and its derivatives were the most prominent signs of Miao uprisings, from both the Miao and the Chinese points of view. The Miao millennial movements developed in a semeiotic process of interpretation of the sign "Miao King." The Miao, who shared common experiences and goals, would first respond collectively to this sign with enormous emotional agitation, aroused by the contradiction between the conception of the power order proposed by the religious fantasy and that experienced in reality. Such emotion would then trigger the second mode of interpretation, collective efforts to actualize the ideal power order. The people rose up to loot, kill Han settlers, and organize resistance against the consequent state repression. As a matter of course, the insurrection was bound to fail, and the people would undertake the third mode of interpretation, resolution of the contradiction between the religious fantasy and reality. This was accomplished by reformulating the con-

5. This description of the incipient state of the Miao millennial movement is a composite of numerous examples appearing in various sources, most notably Number One Historical Archives (1987).

ception of the power order that resulted after the rebellion was suppressed; the original power order was reconfirmed after the failure to alter the people's lot of subjugation.

Such conceptions have been recounted in myths that tell of the Miao as a deprived people who have lost their kingdom and await their savior. H. A. Bernatzik (1970) claims that the memory of times when there was a much larger political unit has been kept alive to this day among the Miao in Thailand. The tradition there tells of a powerful Miao kingdom whose last military king was defeated in battle against Chinese forces menacing their settlements, after which the Miao subjects fled southward before the pursuing enemy. Even today, they believe that sometime and somewhere a Miao King will rise again, unite his people, and lead them against the hated oppressors. In fact, this kind of myth is not simply rationalization of the people's present subjugated lot; it is also a reservoir of millennial ideas and beliefs.

Invoking the emergence of the Miao King and related millennial beliefs was a habitualized Miao response to Chinese expansion; the notion of Miao King is thus a "sign of habit" in Miao culture. Hiding in myths, it was usually unnoticed in daily life, but was evoked and brought to consciousness in crises of political power. It also generated such millennial elements as the religious fantasy of an ideal power order and other forms of the savior. These variant signs of paramount power might be reinterpretations of history or formulations of indigenous or foreign religious ideologies. For example, the title Lord of the Sky was popular in Miao and Hmong millennial movements in Hunan, Laos, and northern Vietnam. It was proclaimed as a title by the leaders of Miao insurrections in 1501 (Concise History 1985:98) and 1802 (Ma Shaoqiao 1956:47). In western Hunan Heavenly King (Tian Wang) is also the name of a local deity of uncertain origin who is popular among the Miao (Ling and Rui 1947:163; Shi 1986:481).

The Miao King also was sometimes seen as the reincarnation of a legendary historical character (of either Miao or Chinese origin) who had once assumed a kingly title and fought the Chinese state. The most prominent of these was Li Tianbao, who claimed the title Martial King (Wulie Wang) and led a Miao uprising in western Hunan in 1455–60, becoming a prominent hero in that region's oral Miao tradition (Concise History 1985:97). In some cases, Li was referred to as Great Ancestor (Taizu), in a certain sense becoming a mythical ancestor of the Miao people in that region (Number One Archives 1987, 2:59–63, 82–89).

In other cases, leaders of Miao revolts claimed to be reincarnations of non-Miao leaders. For example, Wu Sangui was a Chinese warlord whose betrayal of the Ming dynasty was instrumental to the Qing conquest in 1644, was honored as a feudal lord in the Southwest, and later rebelled against the new regime. Leaders of a major Miao insurrection in northeastern Guizhou–western Hunan in 1795–1797 claimed the title King Wu (Wu Wang) as reincarnations of Wu Sangui (Number One Archives 1987, 3:252–56).

The detailed records of that particular insurrection illustrate nicely the process of adopting a new sign of power based on the generative model of Miao King. The rebellion had five major leaders, the first two of whom simply claimed the title of Miao King in the initial stages of the movement as they went into trance, proposed millennial ideas, and aroused popular emotional agitation. The last three leaders, a father and his two sons, claimed the title of King Wu later in the movement in a seemingly more rational and conscious manner, without the initial process of trance and arousal of agitation. By the time the first King Wu appeared, the rebellion had developed to a stage of massive confrontation with the imperial quelling forces, and the leader who claimed the title had gained paramount authority in the movement. He formally appointed some officials, including one of the original Miao Kings (the other had been captured), and when he himself was captured, he was succeeded by one of his sons, who was then killed and succeeded by his younger brother, in a manner resembling ordinary monarchic succession.

On the whole, the process of institutionalization of power in the later stage of the insurrection corresponds aptly to the substitution of a new sign of power for the original one. As a mirror image of the vague Miao conception of Chinese kingship, the idea of the Miao King is highly abstract, and its interpretation in the early stages of the movement relied on habitualized response, arousing collective emotions. Later on however, as the insurgents became more conscious of their undertaking and the insurrection reached the stage of massive confrontation against quelling forces, they actively adopted more concrete signs of power in order to sustain their combative action. These signs were derived from their immediate realm of experience, such as interpretations of history and religious ideologies.

SIU-WOO CHEUNG

WESTERN EXPANSION AND CHRISTIAN MISSIONS
AMONG THE MIAO

The first Christian missions among the Miao in Southwest China were begun in the final years of the nineteenth century by Protestants operating under the aegis of the China Inland Mission, which launched missions among two different Miao groups in Guizhou: the Hei Miao in the Southeast and the Hua Miao in the Northwest. The work among the Hei Miao commenced in 1896 with the founding of a small mission station near Panghai, a market town in southeastern Guizhou. Despite years of effort by successive missionaries, the scale of the enterprise remained limited. The mission was generally considered a failure, a reflection of hardship and discouragement, as it cost the lives of a missionary and the first Miao convert in an anti-Christian murder case (Broomhall 1940:237–41).

This failure stands in sharp contrast to the highly glorified success of the mission among the Hua Miao in the Northwest initiated in 1895 by James R. Adam, who was in charge of a China Inland Mission center in the city of Anshun in western Guizhou. At the beginning of the twentieth century, a remarkable Christian movement was begun among the Hua Miao; it quickly spread over northwestern Guizhou and, in 1904, northeastern Yunnan. Under the leadership of Samuel Pollard, an American missionary in charge of the United Methodist Mission center at Zhaotong, another spectacular Christian movement was triggered among the Hua Miao in both northeastern Yunnan and northwestern Guizhou, and spread even to Wuding in north central Yunnan under the leadership of Arthur Nicholls of the China Inland Mission. In the following years, a significant proportion of the Hua Miao were converted. By 1920 the China Inland Mission had established nine centers in northwestern Guizhou and adjacent areas of southern Sichuan, as well as at Wuding; the United Methodist Mission had established over thirty outstations in the region encompassing northwestern Guizhou, northeastern Yunnan, and southern Sichuan. There were about seventy thousand Miao Christians, with fifteen thousand baptized; scores of churches and over sixty schools were opened (Hudspeth 1922:702–705).

The contrasting responses of the two Miao groups to Christian missionization need to be understood through two factors: the contrasting impacts of Western political power and capitalist development of commodities in the two areas, and the relationship of the conversion process to traditional Miao millennial movements.

Political and Economic Aspects of Western Incursions

Western expansion and the arrival of missionaries in the second half of the nineteenth century brought new and disturbing elements to the power order of China. The unequal treaties of 1842, 1844, 1856, and 1860, signed when China lost a series of wars to Western powers, granted rights to Christian missions in China. With political and military backing of Western governments, missionaries gained the upper hand in their confrontation with Chinese officialdom and the gentry class. They insisted on equal status with Chinese officials (Lu Shiqiang 1966:84–91), interfered with Chinese jurisdiction by claiming foreign protection for Chinese Christians (Latourette 1929:279–90, 309–11), pursued exemptions for Christians from contributing to local religious activities (Latourette 1929:475; Lu Shiqiang 1966:132–37), and supported the division of non-Christian religious properties between Christians and the rest of the community (Lu Shiqiang 1966:137–39). These undertakings aroused tremendous conflicts with the Chinese elite class, as well as with Chinese communities in general.

The conflict between Christian missions and Chinese society also found its manifestation in ideological disputes and groundless rumors. Among educated people, the question of compatibility between Confucianism and Christianity was a protracted debate (Levenson 1965:117–25, Lu Shiqiang 1966:12–45). Among the general public, there were numerous rumors concerning missionaries (Latourette 1929:346–53). In general, Christian missions were considered subversive to Chinese society and the ruling regime. They were thought to be similar to sectarian groups that had fomented religious rebellions in the past, and the influence of Christianity on the ideology of the Taiping Rebellion—the most devastating insurrection of the nineteenth century—offered support for these convictions.

Under these conditions, confrontation between Christian missions and Chinese society was inevitable. Persecutions of Christians were so epidimic that even regions far from China proper were affected. Each time, missionaries asked their home governments for protection against riots and for redress of injuries. Western governments vigorously supported the treaty rights of their nationals and often brought pressure on behalf of missionaries, sending gunboats and exacting indemnities (Latourette 1929:475). Moreover, constant threats of military action were brought in the process of negotiation and enforcement of agreements. Social and ideological conflicts, constant persecutions, and foreign government interference all blended together and reinforced one another. The pressure of anti-Christian confrontation escalated to its zenith and contributed greatly to the outburst of the Boxer Uprising in 1900, a general antiforeign catastrophe that wrought tremendous havoc upon Christians throughout China. Not surprisingly, a united military force of eight foreign powers was launched in retaliation, and once again the Powers had China at their mercy (Latourette 1929:519–20).

Chinese officials generally considered Christian missions one of the most troublesome and obnoxious features of their intercourse with the West. With the political and military backing of their governments, missionaries usually prevailed in the settlement of persecution cases, with those involved in the mobs being executed, officials degraded or banished, provincial leaders sometimes transferred, and usually a huge indemnity paid. As a result, Western missionaries became a new form of political power in Chinese society. Chinese officials, afraid of making trouble for themselves, usually avoided disputes with them.

The political prestige of Western missionaries was also based on the general Chinese conception (gained in numerous losing military confrontations) of the technological advancement of the West. Thereafter, as the state sought to combat the Western challenge, it focused on importing Western technology, and a fundamental aspect of this effort was the establishment of new-style schools that emphasized Western technological knowledge. In these circumstances, mission schools and missionary educators were highly regarded for their instruction in Western knowledge.

Western commodities and capitalistic activities also affected the Chinese conception of Western people. Motivated by capitalism, Western expansion aimed at exploring overseas markets for commodities and extracting resources for manufacturing industries at home. Western capitalist activities had a huge impact on the native economy. On the one hand, cheap, high-quality Western goods replaced many native commodities in Chinese markets; on the other hand, capitalist penetration instigated the transformation of much of the native economy from a largely subsistence economy to a commodity economy. In the Southwest, imported cotton and silk cloth began to dominate the local market, and the household-based native weaving industry withered in the Miao region; at the same time increasing foreign demand made tung oil an important crop in some Miao areas, attracting investment from both Han capitalists and Miao landlords. In addition, opium became an important cash crop for the Miao, meeting the demand (originally instigated by foreign importation of the drug) among the Chinese. Finally, the mining and timber industries also grew rapidly (Concise History 1985:182–85). Many new market centers developed with the gathering of merchants and capitalists, among whom were wealthy Miao landlords. With the growth of capitalist commoditization came the development of socioeconomic classes; within the Miao regions, landlords' involvement in capitalist activities deepened their exploitation of their tenants, and subsequently widened the socioeconomic gap between them.

Despite the magnitude of these changes, however, the specific impact of capitalism and people's conceptions of the political power of missionaries varied with regional political-economic structure. The political-economic structure of ethnic interaction in the Miao region of northwestern Guizhou–northeastern Yunnan was very different from that in southeastern Guizhou.

The Miao Christian Movement in Northwestern Guizhou and Northeastern Yunnan

In the northwestern Guizhou–northeastern Yunnan region the policy of *gai tu gui liu,* instituted in 1644 (Guizhou) and 1728 (Yunnan), did not demolish the *tusi* system entirely. Instead, the removal of the apex of the original structure resulted in an acephalous system of Yi chieftains.[6] Relatives of the former Yi *tusi,* along with their retainers and agents (generally called *tumu*), became semi-independent overlords ruling over their own estates. Although they acknowledged the sovereignty of the Chinese state and paid taxes, throughout their region the state's authority was only partial. Also, they were often rich enough to buy the connivance of the nominally powerful magistrate.

Almost all the Hua Miao living in the small hamlets and villages of this region were tenants of Yi overlords. The terms of tenancy included rents, levies, corvée, and various other obligations (Concise

6. The term Yi here refers to the group who call themselves Nasu and reside in northwestern Guizhou and northeastern Yunnan.

History 1985:128; Fei 1985:57; Samuel R. Clarke 1911:123–24). Rent was a portion of the harvest or a levy of animals, such as chickens, pigs, or goats. Besides the nominal rent, the Yi overlord had the right to exact other levies on special occasions, such as funerals or weddings, or when he incurred litigation costs in the magistrate's court. Each Hua Miao tenant also owed the Yi overlord a certain number of days of labor during the year, paid in tilling land, gathering crops, or other activities. When their lord was in dispute with another lord, the tenants would be summoned to fight for him.

The Han, Yi, and Hua Miao in this area thus constituted a political-economic hierarchy somewhat like a pyramid. At the top were the Han, concentrated in walled cities, towns, marketplaces, and villages along the main transport routes, and subject to direct rule of the state. The middle stratum was the Yi, concentrated around the strongholds of their overlordly estates, who formed an acephalous system of chieftainship semi-independent from the rule of the Chinese state. At the bottom were the Miao, living in discrete villages scattered around among the Yi strongholds, and subject to tenancy and oppression at the hands of the Yi lords. The following story illustrates this system of power:

> Many of the lairds are called by the name of their estate. At So-i, thirty or forty miles from Weining, the laird, a young man whose family name was Yen, died three or four years ago. His heir was a child: some say it was the son of the widow. But that child died after the death of the laird, and the widow adopted another. The next of kin was So-do, laird of a neighboring estate of that name, whose family name was also Yen. There has been very much litigation of the Chinese Yamen at Weining over the matter. The civil magistrate at Weining is changed about once a year. One magistrate decided in favour of So-do, and another in favour of the widow, for what reason we don't presume to say. Meanwhile, the tenants are between the hammer and the anvil. If they pay rent to So-i, So-do with his people comes and carries off their cattle and beats them; if they pay rent to So-do, So-i's people plunder them in the same way. (Samuel R. Clarke 1911:255–56)

In this power order, the lot of the Hua Miao was deplorable. Economically, they were subjugated to a marginal livelihood; any accumulation of wealth could not escape the eyes of the rapacious overlords, who would eventually seize it through nasty measures (Pollard 1928:152; Kendall 1954:83–84). Sociopolitically, they were deprived of control of their own lives. Their children were sometimes seized by the lord to work as household slaves (Kendall 1954:133), they were conscripted to military service for the overlord, and they were sometimes treated as private property of the lord in land transactions (Zhou et al. 1982:336; Fei 1985:58) or as dowry for a bride in a marriage between lordly families (Concise History 1985: 128). They were even forced to submit spiritually: on the last day of the Yi year, they were obliged to prostrate themselves in reverence before the overlord's family gods (Pollard 1928:130; Kendall 1954: 111). In short, the Hua Miao tenants were subjugated totally to their Yi lords.

The arrival of Western capitalist commoditization had not had much impact on the basic economy of this region, probably because of the rugged terrain, lack of natural resources, and marginal agricultural productivity. However, there was a great influx of Western commodities to the cities and market towns, such as Anshun (the second-largest city in Guizhou, located on the margin of the Hua Miao region) and Zhaotong (located on the main transport route linking Yunnan and Sichuan). Han merchants and capitalists concentrated their commodities in these cities to meet the needs of the local people, including Han settlers and Yi landlords. The Hua Miao tenants lived such a marginal, exploited existence that they could hardly share in the new material prosperity (Concise History 1985:187).

The relative lack of Western commodities among the Hua Miao in this region was largely due to their exploitation at the hands of the Han and Yi. This was exacerbated by new taxes, imposed all over the empire by the Chinese government in order to pay the costs of putting down rebellions and paying indemnities to Western powers. The Yi overlords transferred their increased tax burden to the shoulders of their Hua Miao tenants (Concise History 1985:176–77). This formidable and escalating exploitation, combined with their relative deprivation of Western commodities, probably pushed them beyond the limits of endurance and unleashed the upsurge of their indignation. Their encounter with Western missionaries and their perception of the missionaries' political power finally triggered a massive movement to resist the power order through conversion to Christianity. The process of this movement largely followed the traditional pattern of millennial movements in Miao history.

In 1903 missionary James R. Adam visited some Hua Miao people twenty miles north of Anshun. The prologue of the Christian movement among this group was Adam's attendance at a Hua Miao funeral in a place called Ten-ten, along with his sharing a meal with a group of Hua Miao hunters there. His sympathetic and friendly attitude impressed the people, who were so despised by the Han and the Yi, and some of them started attending church services in Anshun. However, the turning point of the movement was the emergence of the notion of the Miao King and its spread among the people:

> One old man among them, the first of that tribe to hear the Gospel, said: "It is not good for us to keep such good news to ourselves, let us go and tell our kinsman at Lan-lung-ch'iao." So this old man at once went there and told the people about the Lord Jesus. His name for Jesus was *Klang Meng*, the Miao King. (Clarke 1911:184)

One Chinese account of this turning point (Wang and Li 1986: 206) states that the Miao hunters who shared a meal with Adam then went hunting again and killed a boar. But a local landlord seized the boar, and the hunters went to Anshun to ask Adam for help. Adam brought the case to the magistrate of Anshun, and successfully forced the landlord to pay for the boar. The Miao hunters were enthused by Adam's help, and the event was recounted widely, together with the rumor that the Miao King had emerged in Anshun. Before long, one of the hunters attended a big gathering of kin for ancestor worship in Weining, held every thirteen years. There he announced the emergence of the Miao King, and urged his relatives to join the church. This news agitated the whole region, and the people sent delegations to Anshun. As more and more people flocked around the mission center there, Adam referred those who came from distant Weining to Samuel Pollard in Zhaotong.

With the exception of Clarke's remark quoted above, the notion of the Miao King seldom appears in missionary accounts, but it may be implied in certain missionary usages of terms such as Jesus or God. Moreover, it is clear that in the beginning of the movement, missionaries were often identified as the Miao King, as in these descriptions of Pollard's first encounters with the Miao:

July 12, 1904 was a red letter day for Pollard. On that day four tired tribesmen walked into the wide open gates of the mission at Chaotung. . . . [The] first question was interesting. Could they see Jesus? . . . Pollard spent the next four days talking about this great friend, Jesus, and when the oatmeal was finished, the Miao said good-bye. Pollard saw them go with a feeling that they were so ignorant that they had mistaken him for God. (Castleton 1948:17)

So little did they know that sometimes they took the foreign missionary for God, and addressed him as such. (Pollard 1928:27)

The story of Adam's helping the Hua Miao hunters secure payment for the boar has never appeared in Western sources, even the missionaries' own accounts, although it is mentioned frequently in Chinese sources (Wang and Li 1986; Yang 1981, 1982; Zhang 1988). I suspect that this is a myth generated among the Hua Miao in association with the message of the emergence of the Miao King. The myth worked as a millennial belief about a hoped-for new power order in which the expected savior would free the people from domination and oppression by the Han and the Yi.

The millennial nature of this movement is also reflected in other cases in which Hua Miao shamans played the role of prophets and announced that the end of the world was imminent (Pollard 1919:50; 1928:92–93). Although some of these messages were in the idiom of Christian millenarianism, it is clear that the beginning of the Hua Miao Christian movement modeled its shape upon traditional Miao millennial movements. At this stage, the contradiction between the awaited new power order and the existing reality unleashed an upsurge of emotion. In Peircian semeiotic terms, the mode of interpretation of the sign Miao King at this point was emotional agitation— solely a kind of feeling, rather than a comprehensible conception. This is why Pollard found it so difficult to convey the meaning of Christian concepts to them, even in common parlance:

. . . I spoke to them for some time; as simply as I could, and tried to tell them the Gospel story. As I spoke to them of God as the Father and Mother of all races their faces brightened up and they nodded assent. Presently I was called away. When I returned I questioned them on what I had just told them and they answered, "We cannot remember." It is so difficult to know how to teach these primitive folk. (Kendall 1954:73)

They could not remember what the missionary had told them because they did not respond with rationality. Rather, they reacted with emotion, as shown in their bright faces.

Such response was particularly prominent when the people came across notions or images that were emotion-laden in themselves, such as the crucifixion of Jesus:

> Tonight I went alone to a Miao village where there is only one family of believers. I took the magic lantern [to show slides] and called on them all. Most of the others came and we had a crowded service. There was not much said about the pictures until we came to the picture of the Crucifixion. As soon as that appeared there was a general cry of surprise and pain all over the room. Then a great silence broken by nobody for awhile. I said nothing. Then one of the believers spoke up and exhorted the others to believe with true hearts. (Kendall 1954:110)

To the Hua Miao the image of the Crucifixion was particularly moving as it reminded them unwittingly of how they were tortured and oppressed by Yi overlords, and of their predicaments in general. Thus a kind of resonance was sounded.

The strong emotion aroused by the contradiction between reality and millennial fantasy incited the Hua Miao to take action to resolve the contradiction and realize the hoped-for power order. In Peircian semeiotic terms, the mode of interpretation of the sign of the savior in this stage was action and reaction with the Han and Yi, a process of suppression and resistance in which the Miao challenged the old power order and the missionary exerted his paramount political power.

As the Christian movement started, the Hua Miao gathered in huge groups around the mission centers in the cities (which they otherwise seldom entered) and traveled incessantly to and fro. This aroused the attention, the suspicion, and finally the opposition of the Han, and before long it was whispered about that the Miao were contemplating rebellion and wholesale massacre. The rumor was rife that foreigners were supplying each band of Miao with bags of potent poison, which the Miao were casting into wells to kill the Han and Yi and leave the land for the Christians (Clarke 1911:186; Pollard 1928:42–43). The magistrate of Weining even sent a report to the governor accusing the foreigners of drilling the Hua Miao, who were contemplating harmful action against the state (Pollard 1928:43–44).

The Han then tried to stop the Hua Miao from visiting the missionary; they beat and robbed them on their journeys, blocked roads leading to the city, and molested those Miao who managed to enter. But more severe persecution brought ever more people into the marches on the city. As unrest increased, Yi overlords also became agitated, especially as cases of persecution against tenants were brought daily to the missionary. Some tenants were put to the treadmill or were beaten, while others had money extorted, were driven from their land, or thrown in prison. Later, they were even forbidden to attend weekly markets.

In the face of escalating confrontations, which would sooner or later fulfill the allegation of his leading the Miao rebellion and instigate massive official repression, Pollard decided to intervene. Invoking treaty rights, he urged the magistrate to post proclamations all over the county declaring that no one was to be molested for reading Christian books or for becoming a Christian, or to forfeit land for those reasons. Special dispatches were also sent commanding Yi overlords to obey. Pollard and his helpers, under official escort, visited market places to announce the proclamation, and he and Adam called on Yi overlords to respect the rights of the Hua Miao Christians.

Although Pollard's and Adam's efforts largely calmed the crisis in 1904, persecutions of Hua Miao Christians recurred intermittently in the following decade, especially on Yi overlords' estates. Another crisis came in 1906 and 1907, when Yi overlords throughout the region burned villages, seized property, and imprisoned and tortured many Hua Miao Christians. The missionaries continued to have proclamations sent from the magistrate to these overlords, and Pollard and Adam frequently visited the Yi lords in order to curb their behavior.

This Miao Christian movement flourished in a process of constant combat, especially between Miao tenants and Yi overlords. Indeed, the more severe the persecutions, the more energetically the Miao embraced Christianity:

> By severe persecution [the Yi overlord] attempted to turn [the Miao] away from the Truth, but failed. It seemed, on the con-

trary, as if his arbitrary actions only increased the loyalty and independence of our people. (Pollard 1928:104).

> Contrary to our expectation, we find that the villages where they refuse the Gospel are on the lands of good landlords, and that most of those who have turned to Christianity are in the domains of bad landlords. (Kendall 1954:103)

This is comprehensible if we consider the movement as an effort by the Hua Miao to resist the Yi and Han, and to change their lot of subjugation.

A crucial factor in this process of resistance was the missionaries' intervention in cases of persecution. Their actions were backed in the end by Western political power based on treaties and military force. For example, when two local officers talked openly in the market about driving out the foreigners, Pollard quickly went and threatened them. Later, he received word that the officials would guarantee that if he would not argue the matter any further, no Hua Miao would be harmed. Probably they would have been removed from their posts if Pollard had reported the case to higher authorities. It was the interpretation of this paramount form of power as the sign of their savior that supported the Hua Miao Christian movement.

The Failure of Christian Missions in Southeastern Guizhou

The political-economic structure and mode of ethnic interaction in southeastern Guizhou were very different from those in northwestern Guizhou and northeastern Yunnan. The Miao in this region, generally designated as Hei Miao, are primarily concentrated along the upper and middle course of the Qing Shui River. In the Yuan and Ming periods, the rule of the state flowed primarily though a number of military colonies and a few *tusi*. In the middle of the Ming this region became largely independent of state control, which was not reasserted until the late 1720s, when civil administration was implemented by force, inciting a large-scale insurrection in 1735–1736 (Concise History 1985:88, 109–110).

Civil administration in this region was backed by military stations and supplemented with a system of minor native officials. Following the implementation of civil administration came a tremendous influx of Han, including soldiers, landlords, merchants, and ordinary immigrants, who seized the best farmland from the Hei Miao and induced numerous ethnic conflicts (ibid.:118–19, 124, 125–27, 148–49). In addition, the system of minor native officials gave rise to economic stratification within Hei Miao society: the Miao officials eventually became landlords and exploited their own people. The resultant ethnic and class conflicts culminated in 1854–1872 with a devastating Miao insurrection.

After the insurrection, the political-economic structure and mode of ethnic interaction remained more or less the same, but the administration increased its reliance on minor native officials and landlords (ibid.:177–78). In a policy of assimilation, the state made much effort to improve the school system, and also encouraged Hei Miao scholars to participate in the examination system (ibid.:178–79). Usually only the rich could afford to pursue a civil degree, which would in turn further enhance their social and economic standing. This policy probably caused further stratification within the Hei Miao community.

Because of its rich natural resources and favorable transport, the eastern part of Guizhou had already developed a rudimentary commodity economy by the mid-nineteenth century. The arrival of Western capitalists in the second half of the century brought about greater exploitation of resources and commodity exchange, and further exacerbated stratification. Timber and mining industries and cash crop plantations developed rapidly. Western commodities, such as cotton cloth, dominated markets and replaced local products. Landlords and merchants continued to emerge, mainly in market towns. At the same time, more and more people lost their land, were forced to sell their labor, and found themselves deprived of access to commodities.

The emergence of Hei Miao merchants and landlords raised a challenge to Han capitalists, giving rise to ethnic conflicts. In 1898 a dispute arose between the Han and the Hei Miao over the site of a market at Panghai. Failing to control the market, the Han retaliated by burning Miao stalls. Not long afterward, the disaffected Hei Miao seized and looted the town, and then burned it to the ground. China Inland Missionary W. S. Fleming, as well as Pan Shaoshan, the first Miao convert in the area, were murdered by Han who suspected the missionaries of instigating the revolt (Broomhall 1940:239; Clarke 1911:155–59).

The British consul demanded an investigation which resulted in execution of the murderers, demotion of local civil and military officials, and withdrawal of examination degrees from local graduates

(Clarke 1911:159). In fact, this was not the first time Westerners had exerted their political power in support of the Christian mission among the Hei Miao. When the mission began in the Panghai area, the missionaries had been constantly under threat of beating and looting by the local Han leaders, who were afraid the missionaries might incite unrest among the Miao. After the missionaries asserted that they were there by treaty rights and with the approval of prefectural and provincial authorities, the local Han leaders did not dare to take action (ibid.:114–45).

Here, as in the Hua Miao area in northwestern Guizhou and northeastern Yunnan, the missionaries were ready to exert their political power in ethnic conflicts involving their missions. Why was there no comparable Christian movement in the Hei Miao area? The China Inland Mission offered one explanation:

> As a people they are especially prone to rebellion, and have in consequence been much harried by the Chinese soldiers, who have destroyed their villages from time to time. Further, they have been intimidated by what the early inquirers suffered, and have probably been deterred by the succession of trials and sorrows which have beset the work. (Broomhall 1940:241)

The Hei Miao did rebel, then; the question is why they clung to traditional forms of rebellion rather than using conversion to Christianity as a means of resistance. The answer lies in the interpretation of the Western missionary as a power form and as the savior.

According to Peircian semeiotics, the interpretation of a sign relies on people's experience and goals. Therefore, whether a group can achieve a common interpretation of a sign depends on whether they share common experiences and goals. Those who do are a "community of inquirers." For the Miao to share an interpretation of the Western missionary as a sign of paramount power and of the savior would require that they have common experiences and expectations not only of the missionary himself, but also of other things related to him. Particularly important here were the people's experience of capitalist commoditization and of Western political and military power. Their interpretations of these related phenomena would affect their interpretation of the mission and the missionaries.

In northwestern Guizhou and northeastern Yunnan, Hua Miao society was highly homogeneous, with little socioeconomic stratification either within or among villages. People's experiences and expectations of Western capitalist commoditization were highly uniform, with access to Western commodities and the related commodity economy largely limited to the Han, and to some extent the Yi. Thus capitalism was associated with the power elite; the Hua Miao were deprived of access to it and longed for it. Their common experience with and expectations of Western capitalism thus guided in part their common interpretation of the Western missionary as a sign of paramount power; they were members of a community of inquirers.

The Hei Miao social structure, on the other hand, was more complicated. Stratification had already begun with the implementation of civil administration in the 1720s, and was intensified by the arrival of Western capitalism in the late nineteenth century. People's experiences and expectations of Western capitalism diverged greatly among different socioeconomic strata. For Hei Miao native officials, commodities and the commodity economy were readily accessible. They could compete with the Han, rather than simply be dominated by them. Thus the association between power and Western capitalism was not strong, and the Westerner was not so easily interpretable as a sign of paramount power. The Hei Miao common people did feel deprived. They found access to commodities and the commodity economy limited to the Han and the Hei Miao dominant upper class; thus Western capitalist elements were always associated with the powerful, and the common people did interpret the missionary as a sign of paramount power. There was differential interpretation of the Western missionary between social classes (or communities of enquirers) within Hei Miao society.

Furthermore, due to the richness of natural resources and better transport conditions, the commodity economy in southeastern Guizhou was much more developed than in the northwest, and the impact of the commodity economy on the Hei Miao lower class was much greater than that on the Hua Miao tenants. For the Hei Miao lower class, the breakdown of local indigenous commodity production in the face of Western commodities' domination of the market, along with exploitation resulting from the commodity economy, made their experience of Western capitalist commoditization much more bitter than that of the Hua Miao tenants, who experienced little change in their economic life except relative deprivation of access to Western commodities. This bitter experience of the Western

presence in general may have hampered the Hei Miao's conceptualization of the Western missionary as the savior among them.

CHRISTIANITY AND ETHNIC CHANGE
AMONG THE HUA MIAO

Through the process of confrontation—of interpretation by action
and reaction—the Miao conception of the missionary as paramount
power form changed, gradually reaching the stage of conception
formation, in which a new conception of the missionary as a paramount power form took shape. The missionary was now seen in the
context of Christianity, and the sign of paramount power had its
basis in this foreign religion. The political power of the missionary
was rationalized though Christian doctrine as the power of the leader
of the church and the servant of God, from whom the power was
derived and who was the ruler of the heavenly kingdom to which the
saved would finally go. At this stage the conversion of the Hua Miao
to Christianity succeeded. As a consequence, the Hua Miao conception of the power order in ethnic interaction changed from their
being a people who had lost their kingdom and were waiting for
their Miao King, to their being a people who had been redeemed
through conversion to Christianity and who had gained access to the
heavenly kingdom in eternity, access that the dominant heathen
groups were denied.

This reformulated cultural basis for Hua Miao ethnic identity was
manifested in collective endeavors to change cultural practices to
conform to Christian standards. In addition to renouncing traditional religious practices (such as spirit worship and dealings with
religious practitioners), they also changed various mundane aspects
of their lives. Free sexual liaisons among young people were severely
prohibited, bride-wealth was reduced, the marriage age was raised,
and bride-kidnapping and polygyny were condemned. Practices such
as whisky drinking and opium smoking were also banned. But the
most apparent signs of the people's new identity were their adoption
of Christian names and changes in body adornments, such as
women's hairstyles.

Perhaps the most significant contribution of the Christian mission
to the reformulation of the cultural basis of Hua Miao ethnic identity, however, was promotion of literacy. Before the Christian movement, Hua Miao society was largely nonliterate. In order to facilitate

their missionary efforts, missionaries began very early to experiment with writing systems for the Hua Miao language (Kendall 1954:82; Clarke 1911:248–49), eventually devising a system of phonetic signs, later called the Pollard Script. Passages of scripture, hymns, and simple Christian doctrines were then translated, and training courses in the new script were offered. *The New Testament in Hua Miao* was published, and by the late 1920s ten thousand copies were in circulation (Hudspeth 1937:44–45).

The significance of the writing system for Hua Miao ethnic identity is reflected in legends about their own ancient script. One tells that the ancient Miao script was banned after the insurrection in Hunan in 1741 was suppressed by the state (Concise History 1985:3). Another tells that when the Miao were crossing a river in their escape from Han encroachment, they swallowed a 'great deal of water together with all the characters of their script (Clarke 1911:39–40); another version tells that while they were crossing the river, their books were washed away and swallowed by fish (Hudspeth 1937:39). When the first translated Gospels were printed and distributed, it was said that the lost books had been found in the White Man's country, and they were treated as testimony that Jesus loved the Miao.

The significance of literacy in ethnic confrontation was also reflected in a rumor circulated among the Han that the Miao could read splendidly when the missionary put a drop of water into their mouths and that their memory became marvelous after the missionary stroked their hair (Kendall 1954:76). Writing and literacy had long been upheld by the Han as testimony of their own cultural superiority, and the invention of Hua Miao writing by and for Christians thus certainly contributed significantly to the incorporation of Christianity into the cultural basis of Hua Miao ethnic identity.

The missionary effort to promote literacy among the Hua Miao was also manifested in the founding of schools for them. By the beginning of the 1920s there were fifty to sixty elementary schools and one secondary school in the district of the United Methodist Mission, with a Hua Miao student body of around three thousand. Some of the graduates were sent to secondary schools in Sichuan, and two studied at West China Medical College in Chengdu (Hudspeth 1922:703; Pollard 1928:146–47). By the early twentieth century, Western knowledge had become highly valued, and the new-style school system was gaining in popularity; thus missionary schools

enjoyed extraordinary prestige. The schools for the Hua Miao immediately became the best-known educational institutions in the region,
and they aroused much respect and admiration from other ethnic
groups; Han officials recommended them to the local gentry as models for their own schools, and many Yi overlords sent their children
to study there. In fact, the schools became one of the most important
signs of the Christian mission among the Miao (Qiu 1982; Wang
Jianming 1982; Chen 1982) and contributed enormously to the im-
provement of Hua Miao political status in regional ethnic interactions (Yang 1982:10–11).

The advancement of Hua Miao political status was also related to
changes in their social organization. Before the missions, they had an
egalitarian society, with individual villages led by elders with very
limited authority, based on sex and age. These elders' lack of political
and judicial authority is indicated by the fact that when disputants
could not settle their conflicts, they took the case to their Yi overlord,
even though he might be unjust or extort payment from the disputants (Clarke 1911:122; Pollard 1928:37). Moreover, there was little
connection between the scattered villages, except for some kinship
ties. In the course of the Christian mission, a new leadership system
developed, with authority held by church leaders, who had the competence to acquire knowledge of the Bible, as well as physical and
mental ability to preach.

As Christianity spread throughout the region, church leaders were
appointed in each Hua Miao village to guide services in the absence
of the missionaries, who visited individual villages only once in several months or even less frequently (Kendall 1954:109). The church
leaders in separate villages, unlike elders in the past, had close contact
with one another, frequently gathering to discuss matters concerning
the Christian community beyond the village level. For example, the
United Methodist Mission regularly gathered its Hua Miao deacons
for conferences in Shimenkan, and also held a district conference in
Zhaotong once a year (ibid.:114). The church also provided training
and promotion opportunities for its personnel. For example, in 1909
the China Inland Mission held monthly meetings of village church
leaders for prayer and Bible study at Gebu, and fourteen of those
leaders were then chosen to attend a two-month Bible school in the
mission center in Anshun, the graduates of which subsequently became important church personnel (Clarke 1911:229–30). Through
training in the church, the Hua Miao leaders were initiated into a

formal administrative system. They acquired decision-making skills through formal processes, such as using voting to determine a change in marriage customs (Pollard 1928:128).

The church administration bestowed upon the Hua Miao leaders considerable powers not formerly possessed by village leaders. In the first baptismal service Pollard conducted for the Hua Miao, eleven elders were appointed as examiners, and all candidates were submitted for these examiners' final approval (ibid.:95–101). Not infrequently, church leaders were summoned as references for baptismal candidates (e.g., Clarke 1911:208, 259), and sometimes they were called together to exercise discipline in cases of backsliding (Kendall 1954:109, 120–21).

One remarkable feature of the Christian mission among the Hua Miao was the people's own self-reliance in spreading the message of Christianity, without which the extremely limited missionary work force could never have achieved such a massive movement. In the beginning, this depended on kinship ties among Hua Miao in different areas. When the church was fairly well established, formally trained Hua Miao preachers were sent on tours to other villages (ibid.:102–103, 114, 117, 166; Hudspeth 1937:60). Across the broad region of northeastern Yunnan, northwestern Guizhou, and southern Sichuan, the Hua Miao belonged to diverse groups with distinctive customs, dialects, and other features, though some of them were related in other ways (Clarke 1911:227–28). As the church sent out preachers in all directions, frequently people preached to other groups, enhancing contact among them and promoting the development of a common ethnic identity (Kendall 1954:162, 166, 168–69; Hudspeth 1937:80).

In sum, the Christian mission had an enormous impact on Hua Miao social organization. The small, scattered, loosely related villages became connected through the church network. Diverse Miao groups came into more frequent contact. The leadership of village elders who previously had only very limited authority was replaced by that of church leaders, who exercised substantial power through a formal administrative system. On the whole, after conversion the Miao in this region became a unified, well-organized people, able to handle their own affairs through formal administration. These changes in social organization enhanced the development of a common ethnic identity, and increased their ability to overcome their subjugation to the Han and the Yi.

The Hua Miao then sought to actualize their aspired-to sociopolitical status in ethnic relations with the dominant groups, for example by refusing to offer whiskey to the Yi overlords' family deities on the last day of the Yi year (Kendall 1954:111–12; Pollard 1928:130–34). One of those overlords insisted upon an old custom that required his Hua Miao tenants to prostrate themselves before his family deities when offering their oblation. After much persecution and negotiation, the lord finally agreed to accept money instead of the whiskey offering, but he fixed the sum exorbitantly high, threatening dire punishment to all who proved obstinate. Finally the missionary called upon the overlord, who agreed to accept a reasonable sum of money in place of the whiskey. There were similar cases concerning opium. Some Yi lords accepted opium as rent, but after conversion, the Hua Miao tenants refused to give opium. Finally, the overlords agreed to payment in silver (Kendall 1954:102). In another case, Hua Miao Christians asked the missionary whether they should continue to help their Yi overlord harvest opium; he told them that if the overlord ordered them they might do so, as it was her own business (Kendall 1954:104).

The authority of the Yi overlords was further challenged in a case involving polygyny. A lord was going to marry a second wife, and levied his Hua Miao tenants for the expenses. In a church meeting, the Hua Miao Christians decided that they would respect the law of the land, but recognized their responsibility only for his first wedding (Kendall 1954:110–11). The observance of the Sabbath provided the Christians with another way to express their defiance. Overlords were probably perplexed about what resting from labor meant, but in at least one case a firm and insistent request by the missionary made them concede to release Hua Miao tenants from corvée on Sunday (Clarke 1911:190). In a church conference some asked whether the Hua Miao Christians should comply with military conscription to fight for the Yi overlord. Finally they decided they would not go if the muster were on a Sunday (Kendall 1954:133).

These cases show how the Hua Miao manipulated Christian beliefs, which had become the new cultural premises of their ethnic identity, to enhance their sociopolitical status in ethnic interactions according to their conception of the new power order. The result of these endeavors is aptly reflected in the following remark by a Yi overlord and the missionary's comment on it:

[I was] talking to a Nosu [Yi] landlord recently, [and] he said, "How much better off the Miao are now than they previously were." I asked, "In what way?" "Oh," he said, "No one dare molest them now as they formerly did; they are able to keep their cattle and horses; the people of the neighborhood think twice before they interfere with the Miao now they have joined the Church." This is not because of what the Church actually does, but because the Chinese and Nosu are fearful of what might be done. (Pollard 1928: 149)

The cause of the Hua Miao advancement in sociopolitical status was much more intricate than the missionary understood. It certainly involved the missionary's political power, but also important was the people's effort to change the cultural basis of their ethnic identity, and their manipulation of this new formulation to actualize their desired sociopolitical status. After conversion, the Hua Miao developed a strong social organization; they were equipped with writing and education, and were willing to assert their power to alleviate sociopolitical predicaments. The Han and the Yi found themselves confronted with a vigorous people who would no longer submit to domination.

DISCUSSION AND CONCLUSION

For Clifford Geertz (1973 [1966]), religion is a cultural system that is both a model of and a model for reality. In this case, Miao millenarianism served throughout history as a model of the reality (although usually in reverse form), of a stateless people's power relationship with neighboring groups, particularly the dominant Chinese state. Yet at the turn of the twentieth century millenarianism was able to serve the Miao as a model for their acceptance of Christianity and their effort to change their subjugated lot; the Miao millennial tradition thus constituted a precondition for their response to Western Christian missions.

Seeing religion merely as an ideational system may undermine our understanding of other aspects of religious phenomena, such as action, emotion, and political-economic conditions, and the relations among them. Unless we hold a comprehensive view of a religious movement as a process involving the articulation of various aspects of individual religious experience that constitute the collective religious phenomenon, it is sometimes difficult to systematically explain particular cases, such as the differential acceptance of Christianity among the Hau Miao and the Hei Miao.

A similar case was described by John Shepherd, who told of the remarkable movements in which plains aborigines in Taiwan adopted Christianity. Shepherd (1988) explains that the aborigines' low status and their inability to resist Chinese encroachment led to their desire for a new set of values that would confer both power and prestige, and to them the Western missionaries appeared to offer just that. He repudiates cultural explanations, such as the comparative lack of obstacles to accepting the foreign religion among the aborigines, their character, and the decay of their culture, all of which presume an active role for the missionaries and a passive one for the aborigines. He maintains instead that the aborigines found the foreign religion attractive and actively pursued it. However, if his argument is generalized to different cases of Christian movements among other minority groups in China, it should be stressed that there might be cultural factors that would enable some groups to react more actively to missions than others. Compared with the Hua Miao case, the scale of the plains aborigine and other Christian movements among minorities in China was rather small. Perhaps the vigorous millennial tradition developed throughout the long history of fighting against Han encroachment was one of the most important preconditions that allowed the scale of the Hua Miao Christian movement to dwarf all others.

In his work on the impact of missionary Christianity upon marginalized ethnic minorities, Nicholas Tapp (1989) identifies awareness of nonliteracy, reflected in the myth of lost writing, as an invariant in Christian movements among upland peoples in China and Southeast Asia. He also points out the significance of the concept of a returning king in Miao Christian movements. It seems that this concept appears in the millennial traditions of all Miao groups, but the legend of lost literacy is limited to speakers of the Western (Hmong) branch of Miao language, who inhabit the northwestern Guizhou–northeastern Yunnan–southern Sichuan area, and who constitute the great majority of Miao outside China.[7] Does this varia-

7. A similar legend is found among the Shuitian people in southernmost Sichuan. These people are classified by the current government as Yi, but most are unhappy with this designation; to them, Yi are barbarians who live in the hills, while they themselves are a civilized people, as indicated, for example, by the writing they once had (Harrell 1990).

tion in millennial beliefs among different Miao groups account for the differential responses of the Hua Miao and Hei Miao groups? Surely the Christian movement among the Hua Miao received legitimation from mystifying the Scripture and from the invention of writing against the background of legendary lost literacy. If we consider the legend as a confirmation of the transcendent political power of Western missionaries, its significance still relies on the common interpretation of power among group members. Still, the comparison of the Hua Miao and Hei Miao responses to Christianity deserves further scrutiny, especially as regards variation in the millennial tradition and the internal socioeconomic conditions of the two groups.

In a more general sense, a thorough understanding of the differential responses of various groups to Christian missions requires an approach that includes variation in both pre-existing cultural traditions and socioeconomic conditions. Such an approach can clarify the power relations among the dominant majority, the Western missionaries, and the minority group.

Chinggis Khan
From Imperial Ancestor to Ethnic Hero
Almaz Khan

Although problems of ethnicity are becoming increasingly important among Mongols, especially in China and the former USSR, where they find themselves a disadvantaged minority, the topic has been little explored in Mongolian studies. This chapter examines the emergence and evolution of Mongol ethnicity by looking at how it is related to a particular Mongolian cultural symbol: Chinggis Khan, the highly mythologized Mongol conqueror of the thirteenth century. By exploring the evolutionary history of this symbol and its signification, I hope to unveil the processes through which the cult and symbolism of Chinggis Khan evolved from a privileged ruling ideology manipulated predominantly by the imperial house, or Golden Descendant , during the premodern period of Mongolia,[1] into a popular universal discourse containing an increasingly wider and deeper sociopolitical significance in modern and contemporary times. While serving today as one of the basic identity symbols for both the Inner and Outer Mongols (and other Mongol groups as well),[2] this unique cultural form carries different meanings for the two groups.

For the Inner Mongols, Chinggis Khan has come to serve specifically as a symbol of ethnic/cultural survival of their group in relation to the overwhelmingly dominant Chinese state and society, which they more or less have to deal with on an everyday basis. The symbolism of Chinggis Khan functions as an increasingly salient identity boundary marker that sets them off from the dominant Han group in today's Inner Mongolia, where due to the overwhelming Han presence in social,

---

1. The term Mongolia, if not otherwise specified, refers here to Mongolia as a historical, cultural area that includes both present-day Inner Mongolia (in the People's Republic of China) and Outer Mongolia (the Mongolian People's Republic).

2. Included here are Mongols in Xinjiang, Qinghai, and other parts of China; the Buryat Mongols of the Lake Baikal region; the Kalmyk Mongols of the lower Volga region; and, as an intriguing extension, some non-Mongol Central Asian groups today, such as the Kazaks and the Kirghiz of Soviet Central Asia.

MAP 5. Inner Mongolia and neighboring regions

political, and economic structures, formal/physical boundaries between the two groups are becoming more and more arbitrary (while,
as a result, symbolic boundary markers are increasingly important).

For the Outer Mongols, on the other hand, the Chinggis symbolism has been closely linked to the nature of their relationship with
the Soviet Union, a relationship in which the issues of Mongol
national/cultural survival have seemed to be rather insignificant if not
irrelevant—even though they have sacrificed dearly in terms of their
dependency on the USSR for economic aid and protection in the
international arena.[3] This differential signification of the symbolism

3. Founded in 1924, the Mongolian People's Republic was, until the breakup of the
Soviet Union and its empire in 1991, the oldest Eastern Bloc country as well as the
second oldest socialist country in the world—after the USSR. Despite its political and
economic dependence upon the USSR, however, the national culture of the country
enjoyed autonomy and protection as well as growth.

of Chinggis Khan appears to be a direct consequence of different sociopolitical contexts, particularly since the founding of today's Mongolian People's Republic.

We must first examine the symbolism of Chinggis Khan in premodern Mongolia (from the Yuan dynasty to the mid-nineteenth century), and then in the modern and contemporary periods (from the mid-nineteenth century to the present), with Inner and Outer Mongolia as two separate political entities. This is in consideration of the fact that the founding of the Mongolian People's Republic in the early 1920s created two fundamentally different sociopolitical contexts—two social and ethnic entities that share the same cultural traditions and primordial ties.

What makes the cult of Chinggis Khan so different in the premodern and modern periods is the emergence of ethnicity as a feature both uniting Mongols and distinguishing them from others. The concept of ethnicity, as defined in anthropology, may refer to ethnic identity or the phenomenon of "political assertion of cultural differences" (Anthony P. Cohen 1985:104). The problem of identity implies not only self-perception, but also an interactional relationship with another group or groups whose perception or identification of the group in question exerts significant impact on the latter's self and total identity (Harrell 1990). "Ethnicity" refers here to the political assertion of cultural differences (see Crossley 1990c). Ethnicity is intrinsically relational; primordiality (either as a genuinely biological or fictive, "imagined" construction) provides one of the crucial bases of ethnicity, but by itself does not automatically give rise to ethnicity. In a larger sense, ethnicity can be the product only of circumstances, particularly adverse ones (Nash 1989). Further, there is a direct correlation between the nature of the relationship a group has with another group (or groups) and the degree of saliency and intensity of the group's self-consciousness and political assertion of its cultural differences. Within such a context, contrary to the melting-pot or assimilationist point of view, the more intensive and extensive the relationship, the stronger the ethnicity of the group in question becomes. This process is further intensified when the group in question suffers overwhelming sociopolitical-economic encroachment from the other group and therefore faces the issues of cultural survival. Here the experiences of the Mongols in China are a most telling testimony.

THE EARLY PERIOD: GOLDEN DESCENDANTS
AND THE LACK OF ETHNICITY

Following the above theoretical framework, let us examine the history of the cult and symbolism of Chinggis Khan. We begin with the period after the fall of the Yuan dynasty, when the symbol of Chinggis, though often invoked by members of the Chinggisid line in tribal power struggles, could not serve as a rallying point in preventing killings among brothers or creating a united front against external threats. The most important reasons for this were: the tendency to constant shifting of alliances and loyalties that seems to be an intrinsically easily available tactic in the politics of nomadism (Bawden 1968:40, 44);[4] the absence of a strong bond to specific locality or territory—something characteristic of powerful centers of sociopolitical-economic civilization with high degrees of adhesiveness, integration, and homogeneity; and, most importantly, the relatively high degree of independence and autonomy in economy and politics during the period from the Yuan dynasty to the mid-nineteenth century, which was characterized by, among other things, the absence of significant external threat to the survival of the Mongols as a group, thereby lending a free reign to a phenomenon of chronic intertribal fighting.[5] In fact, to talk about Mongol group survival in this period makes little sense, since there was in reality no such a category as the Mongol community or nation, but rather various local groups, whom the Chinese conveniently referred to as Mongols, probably because of their common linguistic and other cultural traits. Therefore, the concept of group survival at this time applies to historical reality only in reference to a certain tribe, whether it be the Khalkha, Khorchin, or Oirat.

4. Here the split of Temujin's (Chinggis Khan's personal name) tribe upon the death of Yesugui (his father) seems to be uncannily allegorical and prophetic of patterns of events to come. See Cleaves's translation of *The Secret History of the Mongols*.

5. The relatively comfortable position the Mongols perceived or found themselves in is reflected in Mongolian folklore, which has it that the founding emperor of the triumphant Ming was in fact the son of a Mongol princess (Chan 1989); in the minds of the folklorist and the Mongol popular imagination, the Ming to some extent had become a continuation of Mongol reign. On the practical level during the period in question, the Mongols remained politically and militarily remarkably powerful. During the Qing period, many "Mongolic" tribes did not perceive the Manchus as enemies.

According to *The Secret History*,[6] the early Mongols had traditionally practiced a form of ancestor worship. After the establishment of
the Mongol Yuan dynasty in China under Qubilai Khan, grandson of
Chinggis, the traditional practice of ancestor worship was officially
institutionalized and transformed—largely within the confines of the
Imperial House—into a state-sponsored imperial ancestor worship
in relation to Chinggis Khan. In 1266 an imperial ancestral temple
was constructed and regulations were implemented regarding genealogies, offerings, and temples of the "four great emperors" (Chinggis, Ogedei, Guyug, and Mongke). Moreover, the well-known Eight
White Halls (Naiman Cagaan Ger), a worship institution specifically
devoted to Chinggis, was later officially established; after the fall of
the Yuan it evolved into what is now known as the Cult of Chinggis
Khan, with its traditional site in Ordos, in the western part of today's
Inner Mongolia (see Jagchid 1988:300–315).

From this rather sketchy review of the origin of the cult, it seems
safe to conclude that the symbolism of Chinggis Khan came into being
as a result of the direct participation and manipulation of the Imperial
House, namely, the extremely prestigious Chinggisid khans, otherwise known as Altan Uragh—Golden Descendants. In other words,
the cult was more a state-implemented sociopolitical form than one
that grew out of the spontaneous reaction of the masses. This top-
down nature and origin of the cult to a large extent determined its
particular efficacy as a symbol of prestige, privilege, and political
legitimacy—issues and parameters that were removed from and irrelevant to the commoners of the time. From their retreat back to the
steppes after the fall of the Yuan up until the mid-eighteenth century, a
period during which the survival of the various "Mongolic" groups as
social and political units encountered little if any external threat,
Chinggis Khan was invoked as a symbol again and again in intertribal
wars among the princely power contenders who strove to gain control
of land, animals, and subjects. Thus, during the beginning years of the
seventeenth century, when the Chinggisid Ligden Khan of the Chahar
tribe (who at the time stood as the third power between the rising
Manchus and the declining Ming dynasty) declared himself emperor

---

6. *The Secret History* (Nuuchi tobchi), is the earliest known native-written history
of the Mongols. Compiled in the mid-thirteenth century, it tells in a combination of
mythology and historical facts of the origin and rise of the Mongol tribe and of
Chinggis Khan's life and conquest. See Saunders (1971:Appendix 1).

of the Mongols, he made the announcement of his accession "according to old custom, before the relics of Chinggis Khan . . . in the Ordos Region" (Bawden 1968:45). On top of that, he subsequently took the relics with him so as to "use the possession of them to substantiate the legitimacy of his reign, and as a device to rally support in the Kukunor area [today's Qinghai] for which he was making" (ibid.:45–46). Another instance of such symbolic manipulation occurred when, in a letter he sent to Nurgaci, the Manchu khan, Ligden "boasted of his title of Genghis Khan, the Lord of forty tumen [myriads] of Mongols" (ibid.: 43). In 1635, after the death of Ligden and his son's surrender to the Manchus, Ligden's imperial seal went into the possession of Hong Taiji, Nurgaci's son and the second ruler of the Manchu alliance. The transfer of the Chinggisid seal might have been a Manchu practice legitimizing Hong Taiji's succession to the inheritance of Chinggis Khan (ibid.:47; Crossley 1990a:16). This symbolic assertion of political legitimacy by evoking the symbolism of Chinggis Khan must have considerably smoothed the process of change of power.[7]

The symbolism of Chinggis Khan was also manipulated during the introduction and spread of Tibetan Buddhism in Mongolia and in the relationship between the Mongolian secular and religious aristocracies. As early as the Yuan period, when Buddhism was first brought to the attention of the Mongol ruling class, Tibetan Buddhologists and historians had drawn upon the theories of reincarnation to link the Mongol imperial lineage directly to Buddhism. They claimed that Khorichar-Mergen, Chinggis Khan's ancestor of twenty-one generations before, was the reincarnation of Padmasambhava, a great master of Tantrayana and founder of the Buddhist faith in Tibet. Later, as the influence of Buddhism expanded, Mongolian Buddhist historians linked the Khan's genealogy to Tibetan and Indian legendary kings and to the Buddha himself. Still later, during the Manchu reign, it was claimed that the Manchu emperor was the bodhisattva

---

7. After the collapse of the Mongol reign in China "Khan," the highest political title, continued to be restricted to the descendants of Chinggis Khan—in Mongolia as well as in other parts of the Mongol-controlled world. After the fall of the Yuan domination on the steppes there emerged non-Chinggisid tribal leaders, such as Mahmud of the western Mongols and Arughtai of the eastern Mongols. These leaders, though they exercised effectual rule themselves, nevertheless found it necessary to maintain a facade of political legitimacy by naming a Chinggisid descendant as the formal, symbolic khan, while leaving to themselves the title of *tayishi,* a position formally inferior to the khan.

Manjushri, while Chinggis Khan was the reincarnation of the bodhisattva Vajrabani (Jagchid 1988:306–307). It is highly alluring to hypothesize here that this incorporation of Chinggis Khan into Buddhist historiography might have been a successful maneuver on the part of the Tibetan missionaries to make the alien belief more acceptable to the Mongols, while the coupling together of the Manchu emperor and Chinggis Khan as reincarnations of bodhisattvas might have helped significantly, as did the transference of Ligden's Chinggis seal, to maintain the Manchu-Mongol alliance and legitimize and facilitate Manchu domination of Mongolia. However, whatever the real intentions and consequences might have been, given the fact that by the nineteenth century the Mongols had been turned into a thoroughly Buddhist nation, it may not be far-fetched to assume that the incorporation of Chinggis Khan into Buddhism helped to a large extent the popularization of the Chinggis symbol in the lives of the common people.

Toward the latter part of the seventeenth century, when Tibetan Buddhism became popularized, the first Zebtsendamba Khutuktu (the highest ranking Buddhist leader in Mongolia) was chosen from the Golden Descent line, and after his death in 1723, his successor was manipulated so that he was reborn once again in the imperial line of Chinggis Khan (Bawden 1968:58).[8] This joining of the secular with religious prestige and legitimacy brought about a potentially highly powerful political force among the Mongols, as seen in two newly emerged powerful sociopolitical classes, the noble lamas, religious practitioners who were born into the Chinggisid line, and lama nobles, great lamas who enjoyed the confidence of the khans (Jagchid 1988:146, 157). As soon as the Manchu court realized the danger generated by such a union, it decreed that the reincarnation of Khutuktu no longer be sought in Mongolia, but rather in Tibet (Moses 1977).

In short, during this period, the symbolism of Chinggis Khan was principally manipulated by different members and factions among the Golden Descendants as a symbolic measure to gain prestige and legitimation of power over the various tribes (or in relation to such groups as the Manchus and the Chinese). Put differently, there seemed at this time to be little sense of common national/ethnic

---

8. Jagchid (1988:300–315) discusses the deification and mythification of Chinggis Khan and the processes of his incorporation into Buddhist folklore.

identity among the different groupings identified as Mongol in historical records. The symbol of Chinggis Khan as a rallying point
seems to have been restricted mainly to the privileged members of
the Golden Descent, and certainly was ineffective in preventing
genocidal cross-tribal wars. A most telling and ironic case in point
involved the late-seventeenth-century Khalkha tribes (the majority
group in today's Mongolian People's Republic), which handed themselves over to Manchu domination in order to escape annihilation by
the Oirat tribes.[9] In his letter to the Kangxi emperor (r. 1662–1722)
requesting that his followers be received as subjects of the Manchus,
the Khutuktu of Khalkha graphically described the sense of crisis:
"Suddenly the Oirats have come and burned my temples and destroyed my scriptures. . . . My serfs are many. If I could live in the
protection of the Holy Emperor, my desires would be satisfied. I beg
the Holy Emperor to show mercy on me" (Bawden 1968:77). Many
more such cases can be found in the period after the fall of the Yuan
dynasty (see Barfield 1989:187–297; Li Jingping 1982:131). In fact, the
whole period seems to have been filled with frequent fighting and
changes of alignment among these various tribes known to us
through historical records as Mongol, and their varied relationships
to the Manchus and the Chinese only further complicate the picture.
Indeed, it ironically proves rather difficult to establish the interaction
among these various parties as one of a triadic structure. The reason
for this lies in the troubling fact that the so-called Mongol tribes in
effect had not acted as a unified single nation/ethnic entity in relation
to the other two groups.

THE QING PERIOD:
THE EMERGENCE OF MONGOL ETHNICITY

Owen Lattimore divided his discussion of the history of the Manchus' Mongol policy and Han colonization of Mongolia into several periods. The first starts before the Manchu conquest of 1644
and ends in 1748 (Lattimore 1934:73), and is characterized by the
Manchu government's preoccupation with consolidating its power

9. The Oirat, also known as the Zungar or the western Mongols, traditionally
resided in the Altai Mountain area of Central Asia. Unlike the majority of the tribes in
eastern Mongolia, they were not related to the line of Chinggis Khan. See Halkovic
(1985:1–20) and Du and Bai (1986).

structure over Khalkha and China; its lengthy and costly military endeavor to quell the danger of the establishment of a new Mongol empire by the Zungars; and implementation of its frontier policy of preventing the spread of Han infiltration into Mongolia so that the Mongols would not become "softened" and would remain a reservoir of military forces to be used in times of need. Han colonization during this phase, according to Lattimore, was "a luxury which the Mongols themselves introduced" (ibid.:71). In general, in Sino-Mongol interaction of this period, the Mongols were the "privileged people" (ibid.:63). On various levels the lack among the various Mongol tribes of a what we today call ethnic/national consciousness and solidarity can be seen, but this was also a time when seeds were sown for the emergence of such consciousness in the future, through such major developments as the loss of political independence of the Inner Mongolian princes (1636) and later of Outer Mongolia (1691) to Manchu dominance (see Bawden 1968:47, 80).

It was in Lattimore's second period, beginning in the mid-eighteenth century and extending toward the end of the nineteenth century, that Mongol ethnicity really began to emerge. This period was crucial in that it was the time during which the Mongol social, political, and economic life finally saw its inevitable drastic decline and decay. To start, the year 1748 saw a major hardening of Manchu policy toward the Mongols (Lattimore 1934:75). The traditional Mongol land tenure, which asserts that all land belongs to all the tribes, was formally replaced by the Manchu banner administrative system, which created territorial identity among the Mongols by assigning definite, rigid boundaries to each tribe. The prince was accordingly made responsible for the handling of Han colonization.[10] The direct consequence of this divide-and-rule policy was the disappearance of the fluid quality of traditional nomad politics that had time and again given rise to formidable steppe empires (Togan 1990; Barfield 1989: 275–76). Even though the Mongols still went on to be the politically "privileged" people (as defined by Lattimore), hard times had unmistakably set in. The widespread practice of Tibetan Buddhism under the active sponsorship of the Manchus, who themselves shunned it, is

10. Many of these princes later became rather corrupt, selling large amounts of Mongol pastureland to the encroaching Han colonists for personal gains, thus speeding up the decay of Mongolian society.

seen by many historians as having greatly damaged the productivity and vitality of Mongol society, since monks could not marry or engage in economic activities (Jagchid 1988:234–37; Moses 1977:7–8). It is reported that by the early decades of the twentieth century every family with three sons offered one of them to "serve and glorify the Buddha" (Almaz Khan 1988; Moses 1977:8). In the economic sphere, the Manchu government opened the steppe for the first time to severe exploitation by profiteering Han merchants through such devastating means as credit and compound interest.[11] An important event indicative of trouble was the mid-eighteenth-century rebellion of some of the Khalkha princes against Manchu rule only about fifty years after Khalkha's voluntary subjugation to Manchu overlordship in 1691 as a result of invasion from the Zungar (or Oirat) Mongols (Barfield 1989: 282–83). According to C. R. Bawden, the main causes of the rebellion were the irritation of the Khalkha nobility at their high-handed treatment by the Manchu emperor, the war-weariness of the people (from military campaigns againt the Zungar Mongols), and their exasperation at high taxation and commercial exploitation by the Han merchant community (Bawden 1968:112–14, 117; Barfield 1989: 301–302). The course of events leading to and surrounding the rebellion (which, for example, included Kalkha traffic with the Zungar Mongols, whom the Khalkha princes were supposed to fight against [Bawden 1968: 110–34]), reveals quite a few interesting points concerning the symbolism of Chinggis Khan and the rise of Mongol ethnicity. Galdan Tsering, the new khan of the Zungars who succeeded to the position in 1727 (and who was also the grandson of the brother of Galdan Khan, whose invasion of Khalkha forced the latter to become incorporated into the Manchu state [Barfield 1989: 282–84]), decided to expel the Manchus from Khalkha and to organize a united Khalkha-Zungar state. What is of interest to our discussion is that both Galdan Tsering and the Manchu emperor tried to win over the Khalka as their allies by evoking the symbolism of Chinggis Khan. The emperor, addressing the Inner Mongolian nobility, stressed the fact that they (like the Khalkhas) were descendants of Chinggis Khan, while the Zungars, not descended from Chinggis, had always been traitors to the Mongol imperial house (Bawden 1968:113). Galdan, too, sought help through

---

11. For studies of Han merchant exploitation of Mongolia, see Barfield (1989:301–302); Lu Minghui (1988:87–94; 1982:94–95). NMQW (1984) provides a detailed case study.

this kind of symbolic discourse. In his letter to a Khalkha prince from whom he hoped to win collaboration, he wrote:

> We are of one religion, and dwell in one place, and have lived very well alongside each other. . . . Considering that you are the heirs of Chinggis Khan, and not wanting you to be the subjects of anyone else, I have spoken with the emperor of China about restoring Khalkha and Kukunor as they were before. But now the emperor of China wants to organize us, too, like Khalkha and Kukunor, into banners and sumuns [traditional communes], and grants us titles, wherefore I am going to oppose him by force by arms. If all goes well, I shall restore Khalkha and Kukunor. May it soon succeed! Move over to the Altai, and dwell together with us in friendship as before. If war comes, we can face it together, and not be defeated by any men. (Bawden 1968:114)

Several important observations can be made of this document. First, it indicates that the symbolism of Chinggis Khan had undergone subtle but important changes: that Galdan does not bother to attribute to himself political legitimacy by claiming connection to the line of the Chinggisid in order to become the "natural" emperor of the Mongols suggests that the privileged exclusiveness of the symbol of the Golden Descent had become somewhat diluted.

Second, even though evoked here as one way to rationalize a concerted effort in the possible establishment of a united states of Khalkha and Zungaria, Chinggis Khan was still more a symbol of exclusive prestige and imperial political legitimacy than of unity among various tribes, as Bawden would have it (Bawden 1968:115). To say Chinggis Khan was a symbol of Mongol unity at this point in history would imply a general sense of national/ethnic identity cutting across and overriding regional, descent, and class boundaries among the Mongols of the time and in relation to non-Mongol groups perceived as a common source of threat. We really do not, however, find such a sociopolitical context in existence during the period in question. The symbolism of Chinggis Khan, when invoked, was for the power struggle among the Golden Descendants and other imperial pretenders (including, in a sense, the Manchus) rather than as a rallying point for a self-conscious effort to restore the Mongol empire or unite the Mongols as a nation of solidarity. In fact, upon a closer look at the semantics of the above-cited document, we cannot but notice Galdan's alienating tone and phraseology. Instead of employing the idea that "we are of one stock—Mongolian," Galdan claimed only that the Zungars and Khalkhas were "of one religion," and "have lived very well alongside each other [in one place]." Indeed, disregarding the conventional wisdom that the groups involved here were Mongols, we could hardly see them as such—not simply on the basis of common religion and proximity of territory, or mutually intelligible languages (which seem to have been ignored by Galdan in his discourse). The apparently inevitable, unorthodox conclusion would be that these two groups did not perceive themselves as belonging to what we today call a common ethnic group or nation. The appellation Mongol might have been externally imposed on various "Mongolic" groups by such neighboring peoples as the Chinese, who perceived them to be nondistinguishable in terms of objective, visible culture: Mongols were people who lived in yurts, "followed water and grass" (*zhu shui cao er xing*), and spoke languages that were more or less mutually intelligible. With this in mind we can see why Bawden missed the point when he regretfully pointed out that, in spite of Galdan Tsering's appeal to the symbol of Chinggis and his interest in a "united Khalkha-Zungar state," he and his followers

> in particular seem to have been obsessively determined to allow their own internal jealousies and ambitions [to have] priority over their resistance to the common enemy, the Manchus, and right up [until] the very end they persistently and perversely turned aside from the struggle for their national survival to indulge in palace revolutions and civil war. (Bawden 1968:115)

Leaving alone the problematic concept of "nation" here, the reasons for this lack of solidarity and a common course are not difficult to detect: apart from the factors mentioned earlier, the absence of common experiences (particularly adverse ones) and of action against a common enemy are important factors.

Mongol ethnic identity and solidarity and their political assertion in social and political movements came about only with the advent of the modern historical period. This development was closely connected to changes in the Manchus' Mongol policy and the related drastic escalation of Han colonization of Mongolian land in the latter half of the nineteenth century. The shift in policy from protection and isolation to allowing vast colonization of the Mongol frontier was caused by several factors, including the gradual sinification of the Manchu ruling class, which resulted in their conception of the empire as basically Chinese; the unprecedented threat and damage by the "barbarians from the sea," which had begun in the mid-nineteenth century and caused a shift of the frontier from North to the sea coast, thus reducing the former's political importance in national politics; and the intrusion by Russians from the North, which necessitated not the re-enforcement of the Mongols as a people, but the dispatching of large numbers of Han Chinese to colonize Mongolia.

As a result of these changes, there was a sudden, radical increase in the degree and amount of interaction between the Mongols and China, not only on the official level, but—in many ways more importantly—on the individual level as well. Compared with the period from 1644 to the first half of the nineteenth century, during which the Mongols had more or less patronized Chinese farming activities, they now not only found themselves fast declining in sociopolitical status and importance, but feared for their livelihood as well. They were pushed farther and farther back into remote, inhospitable areas, at times under military coercion.[12] Furthermore, Mongols found their cultural traditions threatened and their identity stigmatized by Han ethnocentrism and ethnic chauvinism.

It was under such circumstances that a sense of Mongol national/ethnic identity and solidarity began to emerge and develop. This was expressed, starting in the late nineteenth century, in numerous popular uprisings launched against corrupted Mongol aristocrats who sold Mongol pastureland for personal gain and against Han colonists who cultivated Mongol land.[13] Other turn-of-the-century manifestations of Mongol nationalism include the introduction of modern

12. There are few detailed studies of Han colonization of Mongolia. For Han migration during the Qing, see Tsai (1983); for the period after 1949, see Ji (1986). For a personal account of the processes through which the Mongols were increasingly pushed into inhospitable hinterland by the onslaught of Han migration and colonization, as experienced by one Mongol family during the first three decades of the twentieth century, see Khan (1988).

13. For more detailed information on popular uprisings, see Onon (1976), Jagchid (1988:186–93), Underdown (1980), and, for a Chinese official representation, MJS Writing Group (1985:292–308, 323–36, 347–66).

education,[14] the invention of modern printing in Mongolian and the resultant surge in Mongolian publications,[15] the birth of Mongol civil and cultural organizations, and, needless to say, the founding of the Mongolian People's Republic in 1924, the series of attempts at independence and autonomy in Inner Mongolia, and the plans and actual endeavor for a great pan-Mongolian nation-state for Mongols of all lands, including (in addition to Inner and Outer Mongols) the Buryats of Siberia, the Zungars of the Central Asian Altai regions, and the Kalmyks of the Lower Volga region (Jagchid 1988:244).[16]

CHINGGIS KHAN IN MODERN POLITICS: A DOUBLE-EDGED TOOL

Nationalism and Soviet Repression: The Mongolian People's Republic

With the decline of the feudal order in Mongolia and the awakening of Mongol ethnicity in the face of an ethnic survival crisis, the symbolism of Chinggis Khan went through important changes in its signification and application. In Outer Mongolia the Cult of Chinggis Khan was abolished in the 1930s and Chinggis Khan as a symbol became problematic. In 1962, encouraged by the relaxed atmosphere of the post-Stalinist era, the Mongolian ruling party and government held grand celebrations on the occasion of the eight hundredth anniversary of the birth of Chinggis Khan. As expressions of the commemoration, a stone monument was erected at the Khan's putative birthplace and the government issued commemorative stamps decorated with his portrait, the *sulde* (his mili-

---

14. For a study of Gungsannorbu (1871–1931), the pioneer of modern Mongol education, see Jagchid (1988:207–33). For more general information on education during this period, see MJS Writing Group (1985:459–60).

15. The first lead-type printing press for Mongolian was invented in 1922 by Temgetu (1887–1939), a nationalist who received his education in Japan. In 1923 he founded one of the first Mongolian printing houses, the Mongol Bichigiin Khoroo, and proceeded to publish numerous books, newspapers, and journals in Mongolian. For a biographical account of Temgetu, see Lu Minghui et al. (1981:310–18); for a study of the publications of the Mongol Bichigiin Khoroo, see Krueger (1966). For more information on early twentieth-century Mongolian printing and publishing, see MJS Writing Group (1985:461–64).

16. The drastic deterioration of Mongol society and of the Mongol-Han relationship were also evidenced by anti-Mongol movements among the Chinese settler/colonist populace.

tary standard, which embodied magic and legendary power), and other historical artifacts linked with him.

In addition to the above activities, the Academy of Sciences held a special conference devoted to Chinggis Khan, during which Natsagdorji, head of the Historical Committee, gave a speech entitled "Chinggis Khan, Founder of the Mongol State," in which he confirmed the positive contributions of Chinggis Khan. He asserted that only forces such as the Chinese Nationalists, who tried to deny Mongolia's statehood, would wish to misinterpret Chinggis Khan's historical role. The anniversary celebration immediately drew fire from Moscow, which attacked Chinggis as a "reactionary" (Sanders 1968: 40). Then, at the third plenum of the Mongolian People's Revolutionary Party Central Committee, Tomor-ochir, a secretary responsible for organizing the commemorative event, was suddenly dismissed from office for, among other things, his "tendencies directed at idealizing the role of Chinggis Khan" (Rupen 1964, 1:320–21). Other officials were expelled two years later for similar or related charges (Sanders 1968:40–41; Rupen 1963: 77–78).

Scholars of Mongolian studies have explained the suppression of the symbol of Chinggis Khan in Outer Mongolia by pointing out that the symbol, easily invoked as a rallying point for Mongol nationalism, ran counter to the Communist ideology of international proletarianism (Bawden 1968: 417–19). But this does not seem to have been the main reason. The Chinese Communist Party certainly has never refrained from evoking its nationalistic symbols of *long de chuan ren* (descendants of the dragon) and Yan Huang *zi sun* (children and grandchildren of Yan Huang), or even the Great Wall. The Mongolian People's Republic's suppression of the symbol of Chinggis was probably mainly for the sake of international survival in its relationship with the Soviet Union and the People's Republic of China, both of which were trying to win over the Mongols to their own side in their bilateral dispute. By totally depending on the USSR in opposition to China, the Mongolian People's Republic had to follow the Soviet Party line; in that era, the USSR allowed no dissent within its bloc. In addition, Chinggis Khan as a historical figure has never been popular among the Russians (Saunders 1970:391).

But history has shown once again the amazing endurance of the Chinggis symbol. The dramatic political changes in the Mongolian People's Republic that started toward the end of 1989 indicate that despite official suppression, the symbol of Chinggis Khan has remained alive in the minds and hearts of the people. One central theme of the present democratic movement centers around the restoration of the symbol, Chinggis Khan, and for the first time in decades people can freely talk about Chinggis Khan in public (*SR* 1990). The title "Lord" has started to be used in front of his name in the officially run news media, a new hotel and vodka have been named after him (*NYT* 1990b), and mass-produced memorial buttons have appeared.

In conjunction with a nationwide celebration of the 750th anniversary of *The Secret History,* an international academic conference was held in August 1990. This was not only the first such anniversary celebration ever held, it was also the first time a pan-Mongol congregation was held with a keen sense of a common Mongol nationality unbounded by political/geographic boundaries: the conference was attended by representatives from both Inner and Outer Mongolia, and from the Buryat and Kalmyk Mongolian Autonomous Soviet Socialist Republics of the USSR.

Apart from official reassertions of the symbol of Chinggis Khan, there have also been various popular expressions. A famous Mongolian rock group, Hongk (Bell), composed a song about Chinggis Khan that well expresses the sentiments of the people. According to the *New York Times,* the song, entitled "Forgive Us," "brought the house down at a packed-to-the-wall concert" in March 1990. It is addressed to Chinggis and runs as follows:

> Forgive us for not daring
> To breathe your name.
> Though there are thousands of statues,
> There is none of you.
> We admired you in our hearts
> But we dared not breathe your name.
> (*NYT* 1990a)

In short, for the Mongols in the Mongolian People's Republic, the meaning of the Chinggis symbol has been closely linked to their particular relationship to the Soviet Union, a relationship that provided them with international protection as well as political suppression and economic exploitation. Within such a context Chinggis Khan came to be a symbol of opposition and of yearning for a strong Mongol fatherland and independent nation-state. It is no wonder that one of the first matters taken up by the Mongolian democratic movement as soon as *glasnost* allowed was reviving his status as a national hero.

The Manipulation of the Chinggis Khan Symbol by Outside Political Forces: The Case of Inner Mongolia

Throughout Mongolian history, we see many instances where non-Mongol groups have tried to evoke, eulogize, and/or even incorporate the Chinggis symbol in an effort to achieve political ends, and it can be argued that in modern times such non-Mongol efforts have corresponded with or even predated the increased popular identification among Mongols with Chinggis Khan as a common ethnic—or even biological—ancestor of Mongols of all lands, and have added to the Mongols' consciousness of a shared past. The multivocal nature of symbols has meant in the Chinggis case not only multi-interpretation but also multisignification. The process of foreign influence is best demonstrated in twentieth-century Inner Mongolia.

The earliest instance of foreign manipulation of the Chinggis symbol appears to be Hong Taiji's taking possession of Ligden's imperial seal so as to bring legitimacy to his rule. Throughout the Qing dynasty the Manchu rulers used the Chinggis symbol. The imperial court created a special *zasaq* administrative unit for the care of the shrine of Chinggis Khan in Ordos. In addition, it provided an annual budget of five hundred taels of silver for preservation of the Chinggis relics (MZWYH 1962:26).

During the Second World War, the Japanese invaders also showed a great deal of enthusiasm for the symbol of Chinggis; after occupying Manchuria and eastern Inner Mongolia, they constructed a temple in his honor in a city known today as Ulaanhot (formally Wanggin Sume, in today's Hinggan League, in northeastern Inner Mogolia) (Jagchid 1988:300).[17] In an act strongly reminiscent of Ligden Khan, they had plotted in 1939 to abduct the shrine and relics of Chinggis from Ordos—probably to the planned Ulaanhot temple (Bawden 1968:417). But, according to current Chinese official history, the abduction plot was somehow revealed to some Mongol

17. According to an official travel guide, this Chinggis temple, occupying an area of about sixty-two thousand square meters, was constructed in 1940. Interestingly, the book does not mention the Japanese sponsorship of its construction.

"patriotic [i.e., pro-Chinese] princes," who at once appealed to the Chinese Nationalist government for protection of the shrine. The Nationalist regime lost no time in dispatching a "special commission on shrine evacuation" to Ordos (Xu Cheng 1985:80).

The Chinese Communist Party did not miss out in this curious competition for the symbol of Chinggis Khan. As early as 1935, in order to win over the Inner Mongols (who were by then becoming more and more involved in the power struggle between the Nationalists, Communists, and the Japanese invaders), Mao Zedong issued his "Declaration to the People of Inner Mongolia," in which he warned against the Japanese intention to dominate Inner Mongolia by invoking "Mongol chauvinism," thus paving the way for further Japanese attacks on the "Chinese Soviet Republic." After going on at great length about the Mongols' allegedly pending "national annihilation" by the Japanese imperialists and the Nationalists, Mao declared that the "only way out" for the Mongols was to "cooperate with the Chinese Soviet regime and the Red Army." This way, "who then dare entertain the thought that *the sons and grandsons of Chinggis Khan* can be humiliated!" (Wang Tingdong 1985:395 [my emphasis]).[18]

With the above discourse in mind, it should be no surprise that upon the shrine's arrival in Yan'an en route to its evacuation destination in Gansu, the Chinese Communist Party "held a grand sacrificial ceremony which was attended by about ten thousand people from various walks of life in Yenan." In addition, high-ranking Party and military officials attended the ceremony, and sacrificial wreaths were offered in the name of the Party Central Committee, Headquarters of the Military Forces, and the local Chinese Soviet government. The following day, representatives from various institutions including the Party and the government paid their respects to the shrine and the relics, and then escorted the team on its journey to Gansu (Xu 1985:80). In the following year a Mongolian cultural exhibition and a Chinggis memorial were set up in Yan'an, with a plaster statue of the Khan expressly sculptured for the latter project. Chairman Mao Zedong personally wrote the tablet identifying the Chinggis Khan Memorial Hall (*MJS* Writing Group 1985:421).

18. It would be interesting to find out whether this phrase is a translation from Mongolian or a Chinese coinage, in which case it would be a Chinese representation and conceptualization of the Mongols that might have helped reinforce Mongol historical consciousness and national identity.

Chinese manipulation of the Chinggis symbol has continued after the Communist victory. Shortly after the founding of the People's Republic in 1949 and the incorporation of Inner Mongolia as an autonomous region, according to a Chinese official account, "in order to forever commemorate this great historical figure of the Mongolian nationality, the Party Central Committee invested a huge fund to reconstruct Chinggis Khan's mausoleum in Ordos. Two years later a magnificent and sacred new mausoleum was set up standing solemnly on the Ordos steppes" (Xu 1985:80). In Taiwan, the Nationalist regime sponsors an annual celebration and veneration of Chinggis Khan "with traditional memorial services" (Jagchid 1961).

FROM GOLDEN DESCENDANTS TO "SONS AND GRANDSONS OF CHINGGIS KHAN": THE TRANSFORMATION OF AN ANCIENT SYMBOL

When Mao Zedong appealed to the Mongols of Inner Mongolia, using the the term Menggu (Mongol) *minzu,* and referring to them as "sons and grandsons of Chinggis Khan," he was apparently conscious of the emotional appeal of such a symbol to the struggling Mongols. More importantly, this novel appellation indicates both that there was a folkloric idea among the Chinese that the Mongols were actually the descendants of Chinggis Khan and that the original Chinggis symbolism, with its absolute blood/kinship connection, had receded from the sociopolitical arena. The old, exclusive, prestigious Golden Descendants had been replaced and transformed into "sons and grandsons of Chinggis Khan": an all-inclusive appellation transcending differences in descent, class, and tribal or regional affiliation. A kinship bond had thus evolved into an ethnic tie, and a new tradition had been invented (Hobsbawm and Ranger 1983)—or an old one redefined—to accommodate a new community of imagination (Anderson 1983).

Throughout the history of the Inner Mongolian Autonomous Region, the symbolism of Chinggis Khan has remained highly important, for the central government in Beijing as well as for the Mongols. This is demonstrated by the fact that the symbol has experienced (as has senior leader Deng Xiaoping) at least three ups and downs: up in the early 1950s (as symbolized by, among other things, construction of the Chinggis Khan Mausoleum in Ordos);

down during the Great Leap Forward (as a "historic casualty" in the Campaign against Local Nationalism [Connor 1984:414–15]); up in the early 1960s (as evidenced by the highly conspicuous eight hundredth anniversary of the birth of the Khan); down during the Cultural Revolution (when non-Han minority cultures, together with the "four olds" [old culture, thought, customs, and habits], suffered great devastation); and up again since the end of the Cultural Revolution (as signaled by an official statement in *People's Daily* early in the summer of 1980 that the Khan was a "leader of Chinese and foreign peoples,[19] an outstanding military strategist and statesman" [ibid.:466–57]).[20]

The ratio of the Mongol population to that of the Han in Inner Mongolia, in contrast to the ups and downs of the Chinggis symbol, has seen a steady, drastic decline: despite a tripling of its absolute number, its percentage has ironically dropped from roughly 40 percent to today's 12 percent of the total population of over twenty million. This has been caused by huge waves of hunger-induced inmigrations of Han peasants (tacitly approved by the central government); by rigorously implemented transference of large numbers of Han administrators, educators, and industrial workers under the policy of "constructing the frontier" (*jian she bian jiang*); and finally, by forced replacement of the border Mongol population with specially transposed Han peasants, a practice strongly reminiscent of Ming dynasty policy. Many pastures were lost due to cultivation by the Han immigrants, and huge areas of pastureland degenerated into deserts due to overuse. On top of that, the Cultural Revolution proved to be irrevocably devastating to the relationship between the Mongols and the Han. Numerous Mongol lives were lost in a frameup purge that affected almost every Mongol family.[21]

19. It is interesting to note here that Chinggis Khan is not identified as Mongolian.

20. In another ostentious expression of the current policy, in the mid-1980s the Chinese government allocated more than three million yuan (U.S. $800,000) for extensive restoration of the mausoleum (*LAT* 1987), partly in order to celebrate the fortieth anniversary of the Inner Mongolian Autonomous Region in 1987.

21. The purge was with regard to the long-dead Inner Mongolian People's Revolutionary Party (otherwise known as the Inner Mongolian Nationalist Party), which was alleged to be recruiting new members with an independent Inner Mongolia or United Mongolia as its goal. See Jagchid's articles "The Inner Mongolian Kuomintang of the 1920s" (1988:262–80) and "The Inner Mongolian Autonomous Movement of the 1930s" (ibid.:281–95). There has been only one study of the purge (Jankowiak 1988).

While these unfortunate events have greatly increased and strengthened Mongol ethnicity in relation to the dominant Han sociocultural
structure, the structural boundaries between the two groups have
been reduced: the old sociopolitical institutions of aristocracy and
Tibetan Buddhism were abolished in the 1950s, many people have
stopped wearing traditional costumes, and (in urban areas at least)
many can speak only Chinese. In areas of mixed residence such as
towns and cities, intermarriage has not been uncommon. In short,
the culture of the Mongols is confronted with unprecedented pressure toward and a real prospect of integration into the dominant
culture.

Out of these historical circumstances have emerged both a new
generation of Mongols with a keen sense of Mongol ethnicity, and
those overwhelmed by defeatism. Particularly since the end of the
Cultural Revolution and the implementation of official reforms in the
late 1970s, efforts to reassert and maintain Mongol culture and identity
have seen a remarkable surge. And, in response to the blurring structural boundary between the Han and Mongols, symbolic devices are
becoming increasingly crucial and common for the Mongols in drawing ethnic boundaries (Khan 1989). Thus the Mongolian language, a
cultural form and communicative tool, has again been emphasized as a
symbol—even in areas where its practicality is minimal at best.[22]
Along with this tightening of the ethnic boundary through a symbolic
means has been a palpable and paradoxical loosening of the qualifying
criteria regarding Mongol ethnicity—knowledge of the language, for
example, is no longer a must, just as "pure" blood is no longer an
absolute prerequisite. In fact, urban Mongol youth (most of whom
speak no Mongolian) and the children of mixed Mongol-Han marriages are often the most adamant advocates of Mongol ethnic asser-

22. For example, the Mongols of the Tumet Banner, crop-growers who stopped
speaking Mongolian as early as three generations back, have now started Mongolian-
language schools for their children, with teachers from pastoral areas specially hired at
high pay. An even more remarkable case is a Mongol community in Yunnan, left
behind when the Mongols retreated back to the steppes upon the collapse of the Yuan
dynasty seven hundred years ago. For practical reasons they had concealed their
identity and adopted local ways hundreds of years ago, and today speak a language
that is neither Bai nor Yi (their ethnic neighbors), nor Chinese (see He Jiren 1989:36).
In the early 1980s their identity was reconfirmed through the ancestral tombstones
they have kept through the ages. Subsequently they recruited Mongol-language teachers from Inner Mongolia and started Mongol-language schools for their children.

tion. Here we see an uncanny parallel between the evolution of the semantics of the Chinggis symbol and symbols and traits qualifying membership to the Mongol ethnic group. While Chinggis Khan has evolved from an exclusive symbol of imperial political legitimacy grounded in kinship to a symbol of ancestry for all Mongols, the general criteria for being a Mongol have moved from the physical to the ideational and imaginative.

The achievement of the unprecedented popularity of the symbol of Chinggis, along with a much stronger enthusiasm and emotional intensity in promoting the symbol in Inner Mongolia, has been achieved through considerably improved modern forms of communication, which have been easily available to the masses (NMZG Writing Group 1983:173–85, 192–94). During the forty years in question publications about Mongolian culture and history, as well as about Chinggis Khan himself, have seen a tremendous increase. A feature film about the life of the Khan was released in 1988, and the Chinggis Khan Mausoleum in Ordos has become a site of pilgrimage for Mongols not only from all parts of Inner Mongolia, but also from various regions across China, reminding people of and reinforcing their connectedness through the invocation of a shared proud past mediated by the symbolism of Chinggis Khan.

The Chinggis Tahilga

According to tradition, the Chinggisiin Tahilga (Chinggis Khan Sacrificial Ceremony) is held at least seven times annually on occasions such as the Khan's (putative) birthday, enthronement, victory over enemies, and so forth (Jagchid 1988:303–305). In May 1988 I attended one of these commemorative occasions and was moved by the tremendous effort the Mongols have exerted in preserving their culture and identity, as expressed in the course of this traditional event. I was particularly struck by the general efficacy of the rituals—and, indeed, of simply being there—on festival-goers as well as on serious pilgrims.

The Tahilga, which lasted through most of the day, apparently consisted of four major proceedings: the *oboo* ceremony, which took place early in the morning; the official sacrificial offering later in the morning; and, for the rest of the day, individual offerings consisting of two separate, simultaneous, ritual events—the *kumiss sacuuli* in the open, and worship sessions executed in front of the shrine of the Khan inside the mausoleum.

The *oboo* ritual, originally a shamanistic offering to various local gods, to exorcise evil spirits or to invoke rain,[23] took place on top of a hill outside the compound housing the mausoleum. Seven or eight monks (some wearing secular clothing) sat chanting by the *oboo* (a pile of rocks roughly resembling a stupa), which was decorated with tree branches and silk ribbons and streamers bearing images of the Heavenly Horse (Hii Mori) and Buddhist prayers written in Tibetan. The *oboo* ritual is a striking example of interaction between indigenous shamanism and the victorious Buddhism (Moses 1977:118–19).

The official sacrifical offering took place in the square in front of the mausoleum, where tens of thousands of worshippers and visitors had assembled by late morning. A sheep was taken into the main hall of the mausoleum, killed, boiled, brought back out, and placed on a long rectangular table on the platform leading to the main entrance to the mausoleum.[24] Before long, a Darhad[25] ritual master standing on the platform started chanting sacrificial prayers. At the end of the chanting, troops of Party and government officials, social dignitaries, and celebrities marched in a long rectangular formation toward the platform with long silk *hadag* (sacrificial silk scarves) and streamers (some with words of praise written on them) held in their outstretched hands. One after another they placed their offerings on the table.

After the official offering began, the "informal" worship sessions were held inside the mausoleum, with mostly common people as participants. The mausoleum consists of three halls. In the central hall facing the main entrance was a five-meter white marble statue of the Khan, dressed in civilian costume and assuming a calm sitting pose, his face appearing serene and amiable.[26] In the other two halls glass cases contained saddles, a sword, and other items supposedly used by the Khan, as well as the *sulde* (Jagchid 1979:169–70; 1988:306, 311–15). On the walls

23. For discussions on shamanism among the Mongols, see Banzarov (1981 [1846]); Jagchid (1979:164–75; 1988:322–32); and Moses (1977:112–118).
24. The mutton, known as *heshig* (blessed food) is as a rule distributed among worshippers and consumed toward the end of the *tahilga*. This is one of the ways of establishing a sense of commonality among the pilgrims.
25. A special name for members of the five hundred hereditary families designated to guard the shrine of the Khan.
26. During a visit to the Chinggis Khan Mausoleum in 1986, I noted a differently styled statue of the Khan: he was wearing an armored combat costume with helmet, his pose showing vigilance and tension, his hand resting on the handle of a long sword, and his facial expression awe inspiring.

were huge murals depicting the Khan's life and political and military feats. Behind the main hall is the Chamber Hall, where the shrine of the Khan rests, together with those of his three wives and his brothers. The shrine of his youngest son, Toli, is in the east hall. It was in front of these shrines that the worshippers, kneeling, paid their respect to the Khan and received in return blessings from him. The shrine of the Khan himself attracted the most people. Here there were worshippers of all descriptions: gray-haired pastoralist men and women in the traditional robe with sash and boots, urbanites in their Western style clothes, college students, government officials, teenagers, children led by their parents, and Buddhists of advanced age. Many brought with them sacrificial items such as butter, cheese, distilled liquor (Chinese style *baijiu*), kumiss, bread, and *hadag*. Many also offered money.

The general atmosphere of the worship session was not rigid, excessively formal, or stiflingly solemn. Depending upon the number of people present at a particular moment, it could be a one-person affair or a collective one involving twenty or thirty people. The group could be composed entirely of friends and acquaintances or of strangers or a mixture of both. The Darhad ritual master, dressed in traditional costume, occasionally would organize the crowd.

The structure and content of the ritual are fairly simple: the worshipper approaches the shrine, which consists of a golden silk yurt in which is contained the *onggon* ("object of worship," i.e., the casket) of the Khan[27] and a sacrificial table in front of the entrance to the yurt. The worshipper kneels on the floor facing the shrine, with arms stretched out holding *hadag* or other offerings, while the ritual master chants a psalm. Composed in a flowing, epic style, the prayer is basically an invocation to the Khan, with an account of his life, his superhuman ability, and his feats. The beginning stanza runs as follows:

Born with the mandate of Supreme Heaven,
Bearing majestic fame and divine title,
Governing all nations of the universe,
Chinggis Khan, you were born of Heaven!

27. According to Jagchid (1988:305–306), the *onggon* is unlocked only when it is necessary to change the satin covering the relics. Before carrying out this task, the Darhad officials involved must make a solemn oath that they will never reveal to anybody what they see or experience.

Then, after a lengthy account of his life and conquests:

This day we offer effusive prayer to you,
preparing various offerings we entreat you:
Grant mercy and provide for the well-being of your
    descendants, offspring of your Majestic Borjigin line,
Oh Chinggis Khan of divine birth!

And, toward the end of invocation of some one hundred lines:

We pray, your own—the Mongol masses.
Extend their lives and longevity.
Enlarge the size of their herds and animals.
Cause to flourish your own descendants and offspring.
(Quoted in Jagchid 1988:308–310)

Finally, the prayer ends with the name of the worshipper (to signify personal blessing from the Khan), as the ritual master sprinkles liquor from a bowl on the head of the worshipper and ties a *hadag* around his neck.[28] Following that, and after dipping his right middle finger into the bowl and flicking the liquor into the four directions and toward the sky, he offers the bowl of liquor to the worshipper, saying something to the effect that it is a blessed drink from the Khan. After repeating the same sprinkling ritual, the worshipper drinks from the bowl. When there is a group of worshippers, the bowl is passed around until every person has partaken of the same blessed drink.

While the worshipping went on inside the mausoleum, the *kumiss sacuuli*[29] ritual was carried out not far from the *oboo*. The kumiss offering, according to the regulations set by Qubilai Khan regarding the imperial ancestral temples, is one of the rituals practiced by the Golden Descendants in honor of the four great ancestral emperors

28. This scene was witnessed by Frank Bessac, an American anthropologist who attended a Chinggis Tahilga in the 1940s (Jagchid 1988:318:n. 64). Jagchid (1979:109; 1988:308) interprets the tying of the *hadag* as symbolizing that the worshiper has "pledged himself to the cause of Chinggis Khan"; receipt of the *hadag* means "the acceptance of vassalage of an individual to the Mongols, and with it . . . a certain degree of national identity."

29. Or *cacuuli* (lit., "to sprinkle"). Here it refers to the activity of offering liquid such as milk or liquor.

(Jagchid 1988:303). Unlike the worship at the shrine of the Khan, the *sacuuli* must be performed collectively (although excluding women, probably because it was originally a rite of ancestral worship). The *sacuuli* is carried out by a group of nine, each of whom takes a ladleful of kumiss from a huge wooden bucket and runs along a route marked by sticks with cotton heads, while sprinkling the milk along the way. Upon returning to the starting point with the emptied ladle, each runner is replaced by a new person, thus ensuring that there are always nine people on the run. The structure of the ritual remains unchanged (i.e., the number of people and the manner of performance), while the body of actual performers changes constantly. Throughout the performance the kumiss sprinkling is accompanied by the chanting of two ritual masters.

This rather simplified description of the form and content of the rituals of the Cult of Chinggis Khan demonstrates how the Cult has evolved from an imperial ancestral institution exploited as a symbol of political legitimacy, to a popular ethnic tradition pregnant with contemporary signification. In terms of the structure of the Cult's rituals, little seems to have changed from its earliest version. The original procedures set forth by Qubilai Khan upon establishing the Eight White Halls still are observed: "the sacrifice of animals, the offerings of kumiss and the words of prayer," as recorded in *Yuan shi* (History of the Yuan dynasty) (Jagchid 1988:303). In terms of signification, however, changes are remarkable and unmistakable: while the specific rituals are still those originally designed and practiced by the Golden Descendants for the purpose of worshipping the four ancestral emperors (as evidenced by the repeated invocation of the phrase "your own offspring," "your own Borjigin line," and so forth, in the prayer cited above), participants in today's Chinggis Tahilga have come to include all Mongols,[30] even regardless of sex if we look at the event as a whole. (This aspect can be viewed as a structural change in the Tahilga.) While the offering of *hadag*—a practice that probably came with Tibetan Buddhism—remains, the epithets written on them have come to include such lines as "Long live the unity of all the nationalities in China!" "Long live the unity between the Mongolian and Han peoples!" and "Mongolians and Han are one family"—

---

30. As well as many fun-seeking Han tourists who arrive with their picnics and boom boxes blasting Chinese disco music—something inconceivable only a few decades ago.

a reminder of the Chinese government's tremendous interest in the Cult and its symbolic efficacy, and efforts invested in its manipulation. While it is largely a matter of interpretation to try to determine the significance of such symbolic acts as the tying of the *hadag* around the neck of the worhsipper or of the sprinkling of kumiss on the ground, there should be little doubt about the emotional, psychological effects the Cult and its rituals have on the participants, or about its impact as a powerful tool of socialization and acculturation. Indeed, at a time when the Mongols have come to find themselves a tiny minority in their own land, a social gathering such as the Chinggis Tahilga is one of the rare occasions on which Inner Mongolians can physically assemble in large numbers without causing political suspicion. Therefore, for a Mongolian person, suddenly finding him/herself amidst thousands of others sharing the same primordial sentiments is by itself a tremendously powerful emotional experience. Although few people can or even try to understand the intricate symbolic meanings of specific ritual acts (as would an anthropologist), the participants nevertheless return home with their historical consciousness enhanced through the proud symbol of Chinggis Khan, and with their sense of identity and community created, recreated, or reinforced. For no one in his right mind would leave the occasion without pondering at least a little the reality and future of the Mongols as a group, when the whole arrangement of the Cult forces them to confront history. As Durkheim sums up such phenomena eloquently in his discussion on totemism, sacred beings "attain their greatest intensity at the moment when the men are assembled together, when they all partake of the same idea and the same sentiment" (Durkheim 1915:230). The Chinggis Tahilga, as such, is more than a physical assembly: it is also a congregation of the minds and hearts of the participants.

That Chinggis Khan has in the latter part of the twentieth century become a symbol of ethnicity in the consciousness of the Mongol populace is evident in many examples. The logo of a Naadam Festival[31] held by the Mongols of Beijing a few years ago, for example, bore, among other traditional ethnic symbols, the image of the Chinggis Kahn Mausoleum. A member of the recently "rediscov-

---

31. This festival, traditionally a trade and entertainment occasion, became an officially sponsored activity after the founding of the People's Republic of China.

ered" Yunnan Mongol community[32] composed a poem that testifies
to the power of the primordial tie when (and only when) it is awak-
ened and put to practice by the pressure of reality. The poem, published in a university paper in Inner Mongolia, is entitled "We Are
the Sons and Daughters of the Steppes: Children and Grandchildren
of Chinggis Khan":

> We are the sons and daughters of the steppes,
> children and grandchildren of Chinggis Khan.
> Under the military standard of Zandan,[33]
> riding horses and holding bows, we fought
> across vast lands of the North and South.
> Passing the steppes on our magical horses
> and crossing the Jinsha River on [inflated] leather bags and
>   bamboo rafts, we
> camped at the Ka Qu Tuo Frontier, under the military
>   standard of
> Zandan.

> We are the sons and daughters of the steppes,
> children and grandchildren of Chinggis Khan.
> We planted trees and set up schools and promoted
> culture and civilization, and our awesome
> cavalry maintained peace and harmony.
> Under the leadership of Zandan
> we guarded the Southern Frontier.

> We are the sons and daughters of the steppes,
> We are the children and grandchildren of Chinggis Khan.

32. The Yunnan Mongols, whose term for themselves is Khatso, number about
6,400 (He 1989:25). Their identity as Mongol came to the full attention of Chinese
officialdom and academia only in the late 1970s. Since then, they have maintained
an active relationship with the Mongols of Inner Mongolia. Their renewed interest
in genealogy is similar to that inspired by the novel *Roots* among African
Americans in the United States. They have sent several delegations to Inner
Mongolia and have invited teachers to come to Yunnan to teach their children
Mongolian.

33. Zandan was the son of Altemur, commander of the Mongol Yuan troops
headquartered at Qutuo Pass (also mentioned in the poem), Yunnan, during the Yuan
dynasty. For a detailed study of the Yunnan Mongols, see Schwarz (1984).

Looking into the distant North we could see
in our mind's eye the fresh pasturelands,
the healthy sheep and cattle, and the galloping horses.
We miss the fine liquors and kinsmen.
Ah, we miss our ancestral land of the faraway North.
(NMDXRB 1982, my translation)

As mentioned above, the signification of the Chinggis symbol often differs according to the parties involved. If the fall of the Qing dynasty had meant the end of an era of some sort of official institutional sponsorship of the cult and symbolism of Chinggis Khan, then half a century later the construction of the Chinggis Khan Mausoleum by the Chinese government signified the resumption of state sponsorship, albeit one of much greater vigor and with new official meanings injected into the symbol and sponsorship. These novel elements include the official slogan that the Menggu *minzu* is a great nationality of China, and the similar discourse that Chinggis Khan is a hero of the Zhonghua *minzu* (Chinese nation) (Ma Yin 1984: 113);[34] and finally, the statement that sponsorship of the Cult of Chinggis Khan has been a proof of "concern and love" for the Mongols on the part of the government (NMZG 1983:244). As for the function of the Chinggis Khan Mausoleum and its annual commemorative rites, they (along with officially incorporated traditional practices such as the Naadam Festival) have "greatly benefitted the unity among the various *minzu*" (Xu Cheng 1985: 82)[35] and have proudly become "one of the greatest resorts for tourism" (CKMa), attracting visitors from both home and abroad due to their "peculiar historical value" (CKMb).

34. This can be traced back to both Sun Yat-sen and Chiang Kai-shek. Chiang, in particular, was remarkably candid about his view: "Our Republic of China is founded by the whole Chinese nation. The 'Chinese nation' is composed of five lineages or Zongzu—Han, Manchurians, Mongolians, Hui, and Tibetans. The reason I use the term 'lineage' instead of 'nation' is because all of us belong to the Chinese Nation. It is just like several brothers in a family" (quoted in Hsieh Shih-chung 1989:146).

35. A few years ago the Chinese State Council listed the Chinggis Mausoleum as "one of the key units of cultural relics of nationwide historical significance to be protected by the state" (CKMb). In another ironic turn, officials have discovered the economic value of the Chinggis symbol. Thus a rather posh tourist hotel designed in the style of yurts and named, not surprisingly, Chengjisi Han Jiujia (Chinggis Khan Inn) has recently been completed on the eastern outskirts of Beijing.

CONCLUSION

Since its emergence seven centuries ago, the symbolism of Chinggis Khan has gone through a complicated history of change in signification and application, just as Mongolian culture and society and their relevant international contexts have undergone tremendous changes. The symbol as such has shown not only an amazing level of tenacity but also a high degree of adaptability in taking on new meanings in relation to different historical contexts and different sociopolitical entities. For the Mongols, it has evolved from a symbol of imperial political legitimacy and privilege grounded in absolute kinship ideology and relevant exclusively to the Golden Descendants, to a potent symbol of ethnic/national identity shared by Mongols all over the world, just as the historical Mongols have gradually evolved from an empire of tribal confederation to a nation and ethnic entity of solidarity. Thus the claim "we are the children and grandchildren of Chinggis Khan," which used to be an exclusive self-reference of the Golden Descendants, can now be exercised by the Mongol populace in general; such a claim would have sounded absurd or even dangerous centuries ago. This fictive biological ancestry, and its symbolic value as an identity marker (which came into being as the conscious or unconscious creation and imagining by various non-Mongol groups as much as by the Mongols themselves), proves eloquently that ethnicity is fundamentally ideational, relational, and historical. Arguing along a similar line, Eric Hobsbawm points out that an invention of traditions occurs "when a rapid transformation of society weakens or destroys the social patterns for which 'old' traditions had been designed, producing new ones to which they were not applicable, or when such old traditions and their institutional carriers and promulgators no longer prove sufficiently adaptable and flexible, or are otherwise eliminated; in short, when there are sufficiently large and rapid changes on the demand or the supply side" (1983: 4–5). The case of Chinggis Khan and the Mongols proves again this intricate interaction between social context and cultural tradition. Indeed, if ethnicity can be viewed as an "imagined" tradition as well as a body of specific social practices, then the evolution of the cult and symbolism of Chinggis Khan has mirrored the processes through which Mongol ethnicity has emerged in accordance with the changed and changing Mongol social milieux.

The Impact of Urban Ethnic Education on Modern Mongolian Ethnicity, 1949–1966

Wurlig Borchigud

> Ethnic identity is the product of forces operating on the individual and group from within, and those impinging on them from without. In other words, identity has both a subjective and an objective dimension.
>
> Kuen Fee Lian, "Identity in Minority Group Relations"

In modern China, "ethnic unity" (*minzu tuanjie*) is the basis upon which the state seeks to build a multi-ethnic nation. In this project of "creating putative homogeneity out of heterogeneity" (Williams 1989: 439), the state-controlled education system is assigned an important role. But even though Chinese national education emphasizes communist and socialist ideologies and Han traditions as bases for a unified national culture for all Chinese ethnic groups, in practice education is divided into regular and ethnic programs. Han students are part of the regular education (*zhenggui jiaoyu*) network; minority students in areas where they are concentrated attend ethnic education (*minzu jiaoyu*) schools. The essential result of ethnic education is thus paradoxical: intended to promote "ethnic melting" (*minzu ronghe*), in practice it creates a visible ethnic boundary within Chinese society. Thus special education for ethnic minorities has created a contradiction between the goal and the concrete result. The discussion here of the aims of ethnic education, and the presentation of practical examples from pre-1966 Inner Mongolia illuminate the ways in which ethnic boundaries are created and show how interaction in diverse contexts in and out of school heightens Mongol students' ethnic awareness. (See map 5, p. 249.)

THE AIMS OF ETHNIC EDUCATION

In order to unify all ethnic minorities into a single nation, the Chinese state has tried to find a historical attachment to legitimize its

This chapter is based on studies of Chinese official documents, personal interviews, and the author's twenty-years' living experience in Inner Mongolia.

Chinese national culture (*Zhonghua minzu wenhua*) by including all Chinese ethnic groups. The state uses its educational system to formulate a common Chinese culture in terms of shared descent. In schools and through news media and publications, people learn that all modern Chinese ethnic groups are natives of China's common territory; that throughout history ethnic integration has been an important trend in the nation's development; that according to history, the modern Han group is an ethnic mix of various ancient and modern ethnic groups, as are the minority ethnic groups; and that therefore, all these groups are able to trace back their origins to the founding father of China—the Yellow Emperor. Symbolically, this version of common culture has been further explained in terms of a family relationship. The state is directly responsible for taking care of the whole nation-family; the relationship of the state (the Communist Party) to the people is that of parents to child and that of the Han majority to other minorities is that of older brother to younger brother with the older brother responsible for helping the younger.[1]

Since the Chinese state maintains that authentic ethnic integration can be realized only after the achievement of communism throughout the world (Chen Yongling 1987:353), assuring that individuals adopt communist ideology is essential during the socialist period. In order to retain political power and prestige after the Communist victory in 1949, the Party put large amounts of effort into training loyal cadres. Throughout China, training schools for state cadres sprang up overnight, as did nationalities institutes (*minzu xueyuan*), which trained ethnic minorities for the same purpose. By means of such training, the Party has been able to normalize its homogeneous model into institutional practice among both Han and minorities.

The institutional establishment of national ethnic education was an attempt to implement this ethnic integration policy in light of Chairman Mao's mandate: "It would be impossible to solve the nationalities problem and completely isolate the reactionaries among the minority nationalities without a strong contingent of minority cadres committed to communism" (quoted in Kwong 1989:8). In 1951, the First

---

1. Since the inception of China's post-Cultural Revolution open-door policy to the Western world and domestic economic reforms, this particular version of Chinese national culture has been emphasized more than ever because of the state's desire for international economic benefit through its historical and cultural ties with Taiwan and Overseas Chinese populations.

National Ethnic Education Conference concluded: "The revolutionary content of ethnic education 'should be adopted with advanced and appropriate ethnic forms from the people of all ethnic groups,' and ethnic education 'should be taken to nurture ethnic minority cadres as its first task'" (quoted in NMZJT 1981:24). In 1957 Premier Zhou Enlai also emphasized the significance of ethnic languages: "We should respect all ethnic minority languages and help those whose languages do not have written forms by creating their written languages according to their own will. In the minority autonomous areas, the first language should be the language of the main ethnic minority group" (quoted in NMZJT 1981:19). Accordingly, ethnic language teaching initially played a vital role in the system of national ethnic education. However, in 1957 and 1958, when Han regions experienced the Anti-Rightist Campaign and the movement toward communist distribution of production (*gongchan feng*), minority areas were subjected to the Anti–Local Ethnic Chauvinism Campaign (Fandui Difang Minzu Zhuyi) and the implementation of "ethnic melting." Since then, the state has carried out a bilingual training (*shuangyu jiaoxue*) policy—using Mandarin Chinese and the ethnic minority language—by following another of Mao's orders: "The Han Chinese cadres working in the minority areas must learn the local minority's language. Minority cadres should also learn Chinese language" (in Zhang Gongjin 1980:46). This language policy has been interpreted by state-oriented intellectuals as an egalitarian practice leading toward the natural transforming process of ethnic melting.

The state thus sees ethnic education, both in its linguistic medium and in its substantive content, as an ideal tool with which to implement the model of ethnic melting in local practice among all minority ethnic populations. This analysis of educational practice in Inner Mongolia serves as a concrete example of the way this policy has been carried out, and of its unintentional result—the heightening of ethnic consciousness among minority peoples.

GUIDELINES FOR ETHNIC EDUCATION
IN INNER MONGOLIA

Ethnic education has been carried out formally in the Inner Mongolian Autonomous Region since 1953.[2] Before then, except in some

---

2. In 1953 a complete official set of Mongolian teaching materials was finally available to elementary-level Mongolian-speaking students (NMZJJ 1979, vol. 1:3).

pastoral areas, there were no separate official Mongolian schools, and Mongolian students in regular schools at all levels comprised less than 30 percent (NMZJJ 1979:2). Mandarin was the primary teaching language for Mongol students.

In the new ethnic education project, the state model of ethnic integration was reinterpreted in more detailed guidelines and rules, which remained in effect until 1966. These guidelines addressed both the general goals and the specific methods of the ethnic education project. The basic aims of the project were clear:

> It is crucial that education with socialist content be carried out in ethnic forms for the development of Inner Mongolian ethnic education. (Ibid.:24)

> The development of ethnic education is an efficient tool for overcoming economic and cultural backwardness due to ethnic minorities' long-term suffering and past oppression. (Ibid.:31)

> The only way to wipe out actual economic and cultural inequality between ethnic groups is through the achievement of nationwide socialist industrialization. (Ibid.)

> In order to change the backwardness of ethnic minorities, we must make ethnic education serve the socialist construction of the Chinese nation. (Ibid.)

To meet these goals of socialist development, national integration, and the elimination of "backwardness," the state proposed ethnic education with heavily ideological content:

> Political, literature, and history courses and textbooks for ethnic education should emphasize government policies toward *min-zu,* patriotism and internationalism, real-life stories symbolizing national unity and great historical contributions from every ethnic group to the Chinese motherland, and criticism of the ideas of nonhistorical materialism and narrow-minded local ethnic chauvinism. (Ibid.:12)

> We should educate students to understand the class nature of ethnic problems, the relationship between the ethnic group and

281

the nation, and the distinction between the proletarian national perspective and the bourgeois national perspective. (NMZJJ 1979, vol. 3:71)

The linguistic tools of this education process were also specified, with a heavy emphasis on the use of Chinese:

> Chinese is the primary language of China and is also one of the most important languages in the world. It is the language used not only by the Han but also by brother–ethnic groups for interethnic communications. For this reason, all ethnic minority schools should set up Chinese-language study programs. (Ibid., vol. 1:106)

> In order to enrich and develop Mongolian culture, Mongols should learn from the advanced [Han] ethnic culture and its experience with production. Therefore, fifth graders in Mongolian elementary schools should start learning Mandarin. (Ibid.:80)

> Through the study of the Han language, Mongolian students will clearly understand that the Inner Mongolian Autonomous Region is an inseparable part of the People's Republic of China, and that the Mongolian ethnic group is a member of a big family in which all the ethnic peoples of China love and cooperate with each other. Moreover, if the Mongolian people want to achieve an advanced level of social status, they should understand the significance of assistance from the Han people. (Ibid.:112)

> In general, Mongolian textbooks in social sciences, arts, sports, biology, and geography should accept special terms from the Chinese language. However, loan terms in chemistry and mathematics should follow common international usage. (Ibid.:102)

Through these and other specific guidelines, the regional Inner Mongolian government intended to direct future generations of modern Mongols toward a new, unified development of their homeland.

There were, however, practical problems to be solved. By 1953 the Inner Mongolian population was about six million (*NMR*, October 19, 1959), but Mongols in the region numbered only 1.46 million, or

24 percent of the total, with Han Chinese constituting the majority (Zhao Hongci 1976).[3] At that time, the regional Mongolian population inhabited economic areas of four different types: pastoral, semi-agricultural/semipastoral, agricultural, and urban (NMZJJ 1979:21). Most Mongols made their living in a semiagricultural/semipastoral economy, living in compact villages. Pastoral Mongols usually knew little Mandarin or the local Han dialect. The Mongols from semi-agricultural/semipastoral areas were almost all bilingual but spoke one language better than the other. Mongols from agricultural areas could neither speak nor understand Mongolian, since their older generations had lost their native tongue centuries before; the local Chinese dialect was their only language for daily communication. For urban Mongols, Mandarin was the basic language for public communication. Most adults could understand and speak both Mongolian and Chinese, and some could even write both languages, while others could speak and write only Chinese. Almost all members of the younger generation were good at speaking Chinese, and some could understand Mongolian but could not speak it; very few spoke both Mongolian and Chinese well (NMZJJ 1979, vol. 1:114; vol. 2:21, 132).

Due to these different linguistic configurations, it was impossible for the state to conduct ethnic education in a uniform way, so the Inner Mongolian government established four types of practical programs: (A) separate Mongolian schools for Mongol students who could speak only Mongolian (Mongolian as the basic teaching language at both elementary and junior-secondary levels); (B) separate Mongolian schools for Mongol students who could not speak Mongolian (Chinese as the basic teaching language at both elementary

3. In 1902 the Qing government officially opened Mongol land to Han immigration. According to incomplete figures, during the high tide of the Han migration (1902–1908), over 7.57 million *mu* (1.24 million acres) of Mongol land were converted into farmland in western Inner Mongolia, as were over 2.45 million *shang* (6.05 million acres) of Mongol land in eastern Inner Mongolia (Wang Tingdong 1985). Han immigration continued in the Republican period:

> In 1914 the Peking government declared that all Mongol lands belonged to China and that consequently all Mongol land titles were invalid unless ratified by its local authorities. . . . it was not now applied to lands held by Han, and the net result of the 1914 decision was to deprive Mongols of their land. This led to the land booms of 1916–1919 and 1926–1928, at the end of which Han had come to outnumber Mongols in the Mongols' own homeland. (Dreyer 1976:19)

and junior-secondary levels, with Mongolian learned as a second language); (C) classes of Mongol students in Mongolian-Han joint schools (Mongolian as the basic teaching language for Mongolian-speaking students at both elementary and junior-secondary levels); and (D) classes of Mongol students for both Mongolian-speaking and Chinese-speaking Mongol students in Mongolian-Han joint schools (Mongolian as the basic teaching language for Mongolian-speaking students, Chinese as the basic teaching language and Mongolian as the second language for the Chinese-speaking Mongol students) (ibid. vol. 2:112). The Type A program was normally found in pastoral and some semiagricultural/semipastoral areas, Type B in urban and a few agricultural areas, and Types C and D in urban and many semiagricultural/semipastoral areas. By drawing a line between Mongolian and Chinese schools and classes, the Inner Mongolian government guaranteed the practice of regional ethnic education as well as the creation of visible boundaries between Mongols and Han, and between Mongols from diverse economic areas.

EXAMPLES OF INSTITUTIONAL PRACTICE
IN AN URBAN SETTING

Examples from different schools should give us an idea of how the state model functions in actual practice and how students react to the state-proposed "work of culture." The state's aim is to achieve ethnic integration among the younger generations by translating an idealized national culture into a set of coherent messages in the curriculum. The following portraits of three urban secondary schools as they operated before the Cultural Revolution are derived from interviews and documentary materials. (Type A schools, which do not exist in urban areas, are not considered here.) The first case is a Type B program in which the majority of Mongol students came from nearby agricultural areas. The second includes Type C and D programs enrolling Mongol students from pastoral areas and both Han and Mongol students from the city. The third is a Type B program enrolling Mongol students from elite urban social backgrounds as well as ordinary urban and suburban backgrounds. In this city, the Han are an overwhelming majority. Public interactions between city residents of different ethnic identities are conducted in either Mandarin or the local Chinese dialect. Therefore, the ethnic educational programs have created opportunities for non–Mongolian-speaking

Mongol students to practice their unfamiliar or forgotten native tongue outside the home.

Temut Secondary School

Temut Secondary School[4] was officially converted from two regular schools into a special Mongolian school which also accepts students from other ethnic groups. By 1953 the school had 13 classes with 584 students, of whom 428 (73 percent) were Mongol, 113 (20 percent) Hui, 29 (4.7 percent) Manchu, 13 Han, and 1 Korean. There were 31 teachers, of whom 6 were Mongol, 3 Hui, and 22 Han (NMZJJ 1979:10).

Being a majority of the student body, the Mongol students played an important role distinct from those of students from other ethnic groups. After 1956 most Mongol students came from the city's nearby agricultural areas, and ate and lived on campus while school was in session (NMJCB 1987:39–40). Most students from other ethnic groups lived in the city and spent their time after school at home. Courses were taught in Mandarin; Mongol students also took a Mongolian language course. This special treatment for Mongol students unintentionally caused differential attention to their unequal ethnic status and to the awareness of ethnic identities among the students.

Most of the Mongol students identified themselves as Temut Mongols, the original residents of the area. Centuries ago, as a result of losing wars against Han conquerors, market trade with Han merchants, and farming by Han immigrants, the Temut Mongols had gradually transformed their way of life from animal husbandry to agriculture. As the Han population encroached further, the Temut Mongols also lost their native language. However, during the pre-Liberation days, a few young Temut Mongols were the first Inner Mongolian Mongols to join the Communist Party, and later went on to become the highest representatives of the modern Inner Mongolian government. As fellow natives and kin of these modern Mongol VIPs, the Temut Mongols shared in their revolutionary glories and ethnic prestige. Before the Cultural Revolution, many Temut Mongol students in this secondary school were also

4. The description of this school is based on documentary studies and on personal interviews with three urban Mongols in 1990.

graduates of the Temut Elementary School in the city, the history of which went back to 1724, when it was established as a Mongolian official school (Yu 1986:49). During the Republican period many of the earliest Mongol communists graduated from and later led Inner Mongolian revolutionary movements in this school (ibid.). After Liberation, Temut Secondary School was established as a higher level extension of the original Temut Mongolian School. The families of all the Temut Mongol students were better off economically than the local Han villagers. Because of their special contribution to the revolution, the Temut Mongols had not only achieved power and glory, but had also gained more personal land than their Han neighbors in the same villages. Outsiders who went to visit the Temut rural area often heard Han farmers complain about this. Although the Temut Mongols were recognized by the Han Chinese as acculturated, they still thought of themselves as Mongols. Many Temut Mongol farmers had retained their traditional belief in Tibetan Buddhism, for the ancestral Temut Mongols were the first Mongolian carriers of Buddhism from Tibet. Since many counties in the Temut area did not have their own Mongolian schools or separate classes of Mongol students before the Cultural Revolution, most Temut Mongolian families persisted in sending their children to the city's two Temut Mongolian schools, saying, "We should let our children regain our own language, which we lost in the past when we suffered" (NMZJJ 1979, vol. 3:20).

The young Temut Mongol students were proud of being close ethnic relatives of the earliest Inner Mogolian communist leaders, yet they were somehow uncomfortable about the special practice in school of their lost Mongolian language—many felt that it lowered their otherwise equal social status with the Han and other ethnic groups. Moreover, they felt less confidence about their practice of their lost native tongue outside the school. In the larger society of Inner Mongolia, many official organizations used only Chinese language in their daily business. Some organizations and enterprises refused to hire Mongolian-school graduates, and some even treated as illiterate the Mongol cadres who were literate in their own language and culture but not in Chinese (NMZJJ 1979, vol. 1:26). Compared with those Mongols who could speak only Mongolian, many Temut Mongol students felt that they were better off, since Chinese was their first language. Therefore, under the influence of the state's ethnic integration model, some Temut Mongol students concluded that "the Mongolian language is a backward language—we should not use it," "without learning Mongolian, in the future we still will find jobs no differently from the Han," or "it is no use learning Mongolian in order to get into higher education—on the contrary, learning Mongolian actually causes a conflict with promotion to higher learning" (ibid.:11).

The Hui students constituted the second-largest ethnic group in the school during the early and mid-1950s. In their eyes, they had not received equal treatment from the Inner Mongolian government, so some Hui students asked the school to offer Arabic language courses taught by *ahongs* (priests) from local Hui mosques (ibid.:11). By 1956 the city government had set up a separate Hui secondary school, which solved the problem of equal treatment for the local Hui people, but the school did not offer Arabic (NMJCB 1987:45).

Many of the local Han, on the other hand, were dissatisfied with the local government's letting the Mongols use and study their own language. Some complained that "minorities do not have many special characteristics. To emphasize their ethnic characteristics is to offer them privileges" (NMZJJ 1979, vol. 2:32).

The Joint Boarding School

This secondary school was a Mongolian-Han joint boarding school.[5] During the first six years after its establishment in 1956, the school had separate classes at every grade level for Mongol and Han students. All students were from the same city, however, many Mongol students had spent their childhood in pastoral or semiagricultural/semipastoral areas before their parents were assigned official jobs in the city. Because these students were bilingual, with better knowledge of Mongolian than of Chinese, they were required to take most of their junior-secondary level courses—such as Chinese history, philosophy, biology, chemistry, and physics—in Mongolian, with only Chinese and mathematics taught in Chinese. Nevertheless, the requirements for the senior-secondary level Mongol students heavily emphasized instruction in Chinese. In contrast, the Han students could speak only Chinese, and took all their courses in Chinese. The school did not require that Han students learn Mongolian or any

5. This case study is primarily based on personal interviews with four former Mongolian students of the school in 1990.

other Chinese ethnic language as their second language; they instead learned Russian or English. At the junior-secondary level, the Han students were divided in separate classes by gender in each grade. When they were promoted to the senior-secondary level, their classes were rearranged into sexually mixed classes, but they were still separated from Mongol students; even the boarding arrangement had kept them separate. There was only one sexually mixed class of Mongol students in each grade at both the junior- and senior-secondary levels.

In 1963 the school started enrolling one hundred Mongol students from pastoral and semiagricultural/semipastoral areas each year for both junior- and senior-secondary level classes. Except for Chinese language courses, all courses for these students were taught in Mongolian (ibid.:20). Unlike the urban Mongol students from families of cadres and intellectuals, most of these new students came from ordinary herding families. They were selected through the regional examinations from Mongolian elementary and secondary schools at lower administrative levels. Since their lifestyle and eating habits were different from those of both urban Mongol and Han students, the school offered them a separate dining hall.

By adding another group of Mongol students at each grade level, the school created a visible triadic structure as well as a dynamic hierarchical relationship between the three kinds of students. Because of this arrangement, each group functioned as an independent unit and acted diversely upon a cognitive hierarchical order under the regular routines of institutional practice. The students of each group formed a separate cultural circle, within which they gradually built up mutual trust by sharing similar experiences of language, ethnicity, and economic status. As for their outside status, the students of each peer group first developed a sense of otherness because of their experience of ethnic and class divisions within the school structure.

In 1963 almost all the first-year students in classes for urban Mongols were city-born. Their language ability in Mandarin was much better than in Mongolian. Since most of their parents originally came from pastoral or semiagricultural/semipastoral areas and some had long been engaged in professional and special technical work—such as Mongolian linguistic and historical studies, and Mongolian-language journal and newspaper editing—these urban Mongol students had opportunities to practice Mongolian language with their parents, but they always spoke Mandarin outside the home with the local Han and their young urban Mongol friends. Even at school, they spoke with their classmates in Mandarin outside the classroom. Unlike the earliest urban Mongolian students of the school, they preferred to label themselves as "modernized" or "advanced," rather than "traditional," Mongols. On the other hand, many Mongol students from pastoral areas liked to label themselves as "pure" or "authentic" Mongols, in contrast to urban Mongols, whom they saw as "impure" or "inauthentic."

This distinction between urban and pastoral Mongols caused painful experiences for many of the latter. Before they came to the city, ethnic identity had never been an important issue in their daily lives. To them, to be a Mongol was to live, as they had for generations, the herding life. Although ethnic education in their homeland had interrupted their lives in certain ways, the idea that Mongols should learn Mongolian encouraged them to stay in the boarding schools in their local areas.[6] But after 1958, when the Inner Mongolian government changed its language policy in ethnic education from stressing Mongolian-language practice to Mongolian-Chinese bilingual training (*Meng-Han jiantong*) for all Mongols, the total time spent studying Mongolian language was reduced from three thousand to one thousand hours per year in all Mongolian schools for Mongolian-speaking students (ibid.:37). The Mongolian-Han joint schools also increased in number (ibid.:24). Some Mongolian schools offered all courses for Mongol students in Chinese, except for Mongolian language (ibid.:25). As a result, the dropout rate in pastoral Mongolian schools increased from 50 percent to 70 percent (ibid.:24). Examples are numerous:

In the No. 2 High School of Alshan Left Banner, 40 students in each class in 1960 dropped to 20 in each class in 1962; in Wushen Banner High School, Yehzhao League, 34 freshmen dropped to 8 sophomores the following year . . . ; in Jingpeng Second

6. These pastoral Mongolian children had some experiences similar to those of Native American children in boarding schools. School life, including meals and daily activities, was completely different from their nomadic lifestyle. The major difference between the two boarding systems is that Mongolian children were taught to read and write in their own language, whereas Native Americans were forbidden even to speak their own language.

High School of Zhowood League, 100 freshmen dropped to 49 sophomores the next year . . . ; in No. 2 High School of Hulenbor League, 330 freshmen dropped to 180 seniors . . . ; in Ethnic Minority High School of Wujim League, 50 freshmen in each class dropped to 20 or so graduates from each class; in Yellow Banner High School of Shilingol League, 34 freshmen dropped to 17 sophomores. . . . In many pastoral areas the main reason that Mongol students dropped out was that they could not handle the difficulty of learning Chinese without help in their native language. (Ibid.:26, 34)

By 1963, when the regional government realized the actual results of its bilingual training policy, teaching Mongolian was restored for both Mongols and local Han cadres. It was in this new situation that pastoral Mongol students came to the Joint Boarding School from their remote homes. Compared with their previous Mongolian schools, where they had visualized the larger society through their own imaginations of the "proposed world"[7] in their textbooks, this new school was an unfamiliar world. Their sense of togetherness changed into a sense of alienated otherness in their new city school and its surrounding world. In this real and new living world, they felt like strangers to the urban Mongols and Han. Outside their school they had to use Mandarin, which they could not speak at all well. City people often laughed at their heavy Mongolian accents and called them "old Mongols" (*lao Menggu*).[8] Their treatment in this new, changing world made them doubt their self-worth and caused painful feelings of stigmatized identity. At the same time, they strongly perceived the special meaning of their Mongolian identity.

In contrast to the pastoral Mongol students, most new urban Mongol students had grown up in the city and thought of it as their home. They had been used to living with a large number of Han since childhood. In addition, they all had graduated from the same Mongolian elementary school (not the Temut Mongolian school) in

7. Charles Keyes defines this "proposed world" as "one known not through the experience of actual social relationships but through a set of coherent messages presented through . . . a 'work of culture' that open up in the possibility of engaging in relationships that may be established in the future" (1991:90).

8. This is a popular derogatory term applied by the local Han to express their disdainful feelings toward the Mongols.

the city. The new peer-group tie of the class of Mongol students was in fact a heritage from their previous school experience. Their sense of Mongolian identity was produced by communicating with their parents about the history of the Mongols and by their mutual experience in the present world. When they encountered the pastoral Mongol students, they admired their ability to speak perfect Mongolian, but felt awkward at being unable to share experiences and feelings with their pastoral brothers and sisters. They realized that to them, the meaning of Mongolian tradition was only a memory of the past, but to the pastoral Mongols, it was the true life of the present world. At the same time, the urban Mongols developed a sense of superiority based on the state model of ethnic integration, which contrasted the "modernized" urban Mongols with the "traditional" pastoral Mongols. The relationship between the two had come to be viewed in a new hierarchical order.

In the eyes of Han students, Mongols as an ethnic groups were categorized as "backward," although they felt they had more in common with urban Mongols than with pastoral Mongols in language and cultural behavior. However, they saw their commonalities with urban Mongols as resulting from sinification at an individual level. They considered themselves to be ethnically superior to all Mongols, but in practice treated them differently depending on individual degrees of acculturation.

The Elite Mongolian Boarding School

As a result of the local government's restoration of the Mongolian Language Learning Movement in 1963, a new elite Mongolian secondary boarding school was founded in 1965.[9] Before the Cultural Revolution nearly half of the school's students were the children of local high-ranking Mongolian officials and professional intellectuals, and nearly half were the children of ordinary Temut Mongols from the city and its suburban counties. In addition, between 1 and 2 percent were Han students who lived nearby. Most of the Mongol students had graduated from the local Han elementary schools. Since most of their parents were either bilingual with better knowledge of Chinese language or monolingual in Chinese, the Mongol students could not

9. This case study is based on personal interviews in 1990 and 1991 with three Mongol former students of the school.

speak Mongolian, although a few perhaps understood some of their parents' daily conversations in Mongolian. (Many high-ranking Mongolian officials were Temut and other non–Mongolian-speaking Mongols.) Before 1965 most high-ranking Mongolian officials had sent their children to the best local Han schools. When the new elite Mongolian boarding school came into being, the local government ordered the transfer of these students to the new school. Mongolian-Chinese bilingual training was to be the key link in operating the whole school system. All students were required to take ordinary courses in Chinese and Mongolian language in Mongolian. Students were promised advanced political and governmental training after their secondary education, but, due to the arrival of Cultural Revolution in 1966, this goal never was realized.

Before this political movement, the students from high-ranking families often unconsciously related their ethnic pride to their superior family status and public acknowledgment of their capable performance in the larger Han society. Because of this and their better academic achievement compared to Temut Mongol classmates from ordinary families, they tended to despise the latter. To many of them, the Temut Mongol students were unintelligent, lower-class people.

This situation changed during the first three years of the Cultural Revolution, when the school was accused of being a "revisionist black nursery"[10] for modern Mongol anticommunist elites. After high-ranking parents of Mongol students were purged from the local government, the lower-class Temut Mongol students played an important role within the school. They identified themselves as the descendants of proletarians, in contrast to the students from the previously high-ranking families, who were the descendants of the bourgeoisie. By the end of 1968 a political purge of the so-called Inner Mongolian People's Revolutionary Party (IMPRP) was launched throughout the region. This dramatically transformed the class struggle between proletarian revolutionaries and bourgeois revisionists into an ethnic struggle between local Han and Mongols. Consequently, almost all Mongol students' families had at least one member accused of being an IMPRP member (counter-revolutionary) and many had close relatives brutally

10. In contrast to the color red, which symbolized luck, loyalty, and the proletarian revolution, black represented evil and the bourgeois spirit.

tortured or killed during this particular purge.[11] In the face of this tragedy, Mongol students from different family backgrounds finally confirmed their common identity in opposition to ethnic discrimination and Han chauvinism.

In these three cases, we have seen how interactions in specific social contexts within the schools affected Mongolian students' perceptions of the state-proposed work of culture. We have also seen how in each case the ethnic division of school programs influenced identity awareness of Mongol students in various ways. This school-based ethnicity often conflicted with Mongolian family identity.

THE ETHNIC BOUNDARY BETWEEN HOME AND SCHOOL

Due to early education at school, the superethnic image of the modern Chinese state and its communist ideology became a fundamental part of modern Mongolian children's worldview.[12] However, the Chinese nationalism they learned in school contradicted the mythical history of Mongols learned at home. What they learned from textbooks were in fact the traditions of the Han.

For instance, many school textbooks presented ideas such as: people from different ethnic groups in China all are called Chinese, and China is their motherland; the main trend of ethnic relations in Chinese history has been the peaceful coexistence of various ethnic peoples; and all the suffering, conflicts, and struggles in history were due to class relations rather than ethnic relations. The military hero Yue Fei (1103–1141), for example, is known to every student as a national hero. But many Mongolian children learned from Mongolian adults that this heroic figure was a Han killer of Mongols. According to school textbooks, Yue Fei was a loyal twelfth-century marshal who bravely led troops in defense of the Southern Song dynasty against invasion by a northern regime, the Jin or Jurchen. Later, at the instigation of a

11. Ten years after the purge was stopped by a document from the Central Committee of the Chinese Communist Party on May 22, 1969, a report in *People's Daily* indicated that over 10,000 Mongols had died and over 100,000 were injured in the purge of the IMPRP in Inner Mongolia (Ulanfu 1979). In 1981 at the third Chinese National Ethnic Education Conference, a government official announced that as many as 340,000 had been harmed (NMZJT 1981:12).

12. This section is based on the memories of many urban Mongols of myths learned and shared at home in contrast to the state culture learned in school.

traitor, the Southern Song emperor had Yue Fei killed. In his own time, Yue Fei was seen as a dynastic loyalist, but in modern China he symbolizes national patriotism. In contrast, among many Mongols, Yue Fei is considered a representative of the Han and a symbol of the Han humiliation of Mongols. In their eyes the Jin was a multi-ethnic nation whose army included many Mongols, so the war between the Southern Song and the Jin can be seen as a Han-Mongol conflict. Some claimed that Yue Fei was the reason Mongols do not celebrate the Mid-Autumn Festival. They told their children that on the evening of a big victory on the fifteenth of the eighth lunar month Yue celebrated his victory with Mongols' heads under the light of the full moon. Although the Han now display or eat watermelons and moon cakes instead of Mongols' heads on the fifteenth day of the eighth lunar month, the symbolism for many Mongols remains clear.

Similarly, a Chinese myth about the Mid-Autumn Festival, though it does not concern Yue Fei, also mentions killing Mongols. This is a story about southern Han led by Zhu Yuanzhang (who later became the first emperor of the Ming dynasty), who killed Mongols during one Mid-Autumn Festival at the end of the Yuan dynasty:

> After the usual festival activities had been completed, midnight struck and the whole city lit up the lanterns, raised flags, and beat drums and gongs. Breaking open their moon cakes, they all found slips of paper bearing the message: "Kill the Dazi [a humiliating term for Tartar Mongols]." The people armed themselves with kitchen knives and wooden sticks, and just at that moment, Zhu Yuanzhang's army, which had stealthily approached the city, filled the air with deafening battle cries, beat on their drums and gongs, and lit a multitude of torches. The Yuan defenders had no idea of the strength or numbers of their attackers; they saw only the brightly burning lanterns, the fluttering flags, and heard the wild beating of drums and gongs. They fled in fear and confusion. Those who lingered were killed or made prisoners. (Latsch 1984:80)

Reflecting upon this Han myth, some modern Mongols still do not celebrate the Mid-Autumn Festival, even though it has become a Chinese national celebration of family reunion.

In school, everything Mongolian children learned about Han culture or the history of China was labeled as unified Chinese culture and history. It was hard to find Mongolian or other minority stories in school textbooks, even those written in Mongolian. At home Mongolian adults often told their children that all the modern Mongols were the offspring of Chinggis Khan and that the expanded territory of modern China was due to his contribution. Although whenever they talked about him they expressed their feelings with pride and admiration, they could hardly find this Mongolian historical figure in their children's school books.

In the eyes of Mongols, Chinggis Khan expanded land through wars against others, whereas the Mongol hero Gada Meilin (1893–1931) defended Mongol land against Han immigration and conversion of pasture into cultivated farmland (Lu Minghui et al. 1981). Gada Meilin was an officer of Prince Zasaak's army at Darhan Banner, in northeastern Mongolia. (Meilin was an official title for the commander of the army.) When Zhang Zuolin, the northeastern Han warlord, came to northeastern Inner Mongolia, he forced Prince Zasaak to give up three quarters of the land in Darhan Banner to the Han rulers. As a result, more and more Mongolian herding families were driven out of their homeland, and in 1929 Gada led an uprising of Mongol herdsmen. His force was finally defeated by Han warlord troops in the spring of 1931, and Gada himself was killed. Many myths and legends of this hero rapidly spread among the Mongols, and for years a paean to Gada has been the most popular Mongolian song, the refrain of which is: "Gada Meilin who led the uprising was for the land of Mongolian people / Gada Meilin who led the uprising was for the benefit of Mongolian people." But no matter how great and popular the image of Gada is in the hearts of Mongols, this Mongolian ethnic hero is still unable to share the stage with Han ethnic heroes in formal education.

THE DOMINATION OF HAN CHAUVINISM IN INNER MONGOLIA

Whether in the specific arrangements of ethnic division between local Mongolian and Han schools, or in the classes of Mongol and Han students in a joint school, the only readily visible difference between Mongol and Han students was that Mongols had to learn Chinese, but Han did not have to learn Mongolian.[13] One often

13. The general information and most examples in this section are from NMZJJ *Nei Menggu Zizhiqu minzu jiaoyu Wenjian huibian* (Selected documents of ethnic education in the Inner Mongolian Autonomous Region), vols. 1, 2, and 3.

heard Mongol students and teachers ask: "Why do we have to become bilingual, when they [the Han teachers and students] have never bothered to learn Mongolian?" (NMZJJ 1979, vol. 2:32). Although the local government's new language policy in 1963 also encouraged the local Han cadres to learn Mongolian for better communication with the Mongolian populace, the regional regular education programs have applied the policy to only a few classes of Han students in joint schools. The socialist idea of nationalism has not been introduced to the Han students in the name of ethnic integration, but in direct connection with the historical civilization of the Han Chinese nation.

During the first seventeen years after the founding of the People's Republic, the domination of Han chauvinism played an essential role in the ethnic education and larger society of Inner Mongolia. Within the ethnic education system, actual leadership of Mongolian and joint schools often was in the hands of Han cadres. In Mongolian schools, headmasters were Mongolian, but the school Party secretaries were Han. Everyone in China knows that the Party is the true ruler of the entire nation, and therefore of every single unit within it. In most Mongolian-Han joint schools, both headmasters and Party secretaries were Han, Han students outnumbered Mongol students, and the management of school activities stressed Han styles (ibid.:35). Many Han headmasters and Party secretaries paid great attention to classes of Han students, but did not like to deal with ethnic questions, and gave little attention to classes of Mongol students. For instance, when a Han Party secretary in a joint school found a Mongol teacher using Mongolian to introduce the school background to his new Mongol students, he unhappily questioned the teacher's use of Mongolian with students who could understand Chinese. Some joint schools required announcers at student performances to speak only Chinese. The Han leaders and faculty in joint schools generally felt that it was a symptom of backwardness when Mongolian faculty members could not speak Chinese (ibid.:39), and the Education Bureau of Inner Mongolia encouraged such teachers to learn the language:

> At present, we do not have enough supplementary teaching and reading materials in Mongolian. Therefore, learning Chinese is the way to open the door for the Mongol teachers to broaden their sources of knowledge. (Ibid.:130)

The quality of Mongolian teaching materials is poor. The main problem is that the contents of texts lose contact with present social and political reality. The teaching materials of Mongolian literature inadequately adopt too many works from the People's Republic of Mongolia. Because of this, the ideas of "ethnic nationalism" and "uniqueness of Mongolian art and literature" are emphasized to a certain extent. (Ibid.:127–28)

Mongol students—especially those who spoke only Mongolian or Chinese—suffered greatly with unexpected policy changes in Inner Mongolian ethnic education. When Mongolian language training came into favor, non–Mongolian-speaking Mongols were often forced to transfer from higher-grade Chinese classes to lower-grade Mongolian classes. On the other hand, when the teaching policy emphasized Mongolian-Chinese bilingual training, Mongolian-speaking Mongols came under attack for their language and cultural behaviors in everyday life. When they realized that what they had learned in school was not based on the needs of their daily practice but on the needs of a larger and unfamiliar social sphere, they tended to drop out of school.

Mongolian-speaking graduates of separate Mongolian elementary and secondary schools could usually go on to Mongolian teachers' training schools or Mongolian language and literature departments of ordinary colleges in Inner Mongolia (ibid.:36). Since there was no college in the whole region with only Mongol students, almost all disciplines except Mongolian language and literature were taught in Mandarin. For this reason, most Mongolian-speaking graduates from secondary Mongolian schools were excluded from the higher education system. Those students were often viewed by the authorities and Chinese faculty as low-quality or problem students. Very often, such students even had a hard time finding jobs as accountants, work-point recorders, or storekeepers in their pastoral or rural communities. For example, when 396 Mongolian-speaking high school graduates in Holenbor League applied in 1961 for these jobs in different pastoral communes, only ten of them were successful. Many parents of Mongolian graduates complained that their investment in selling ten cattle to send their children to Mongolian schools gained them nothing in return. As a result, more and more local Mongol cadres started sending their children to local Han schools (ibid.:36).

In consequence of these educational policies, the Mongolian language was neglected in the larger social domain. Some Han leaders thought that Mongolian translation work was only a "form of decoration" for the government's minority policies, and did not carry it out. In fact, many local translation offices at various administrative levels existed solely in name, while carrying out irrelevant tasks such as maintaining archives, delivering official documents, providing secretarial assistance, and writing reports. In the entire year of 1956 one administrative district, one league, and over six banners translated only a handful of Chinese official documents into Mongolian (NMZJJ 1979, vol. 1:51). By the end of 1963 there were still compact Mongolian areas in which the Mongolian language was seldom used in regional official documents and orders. In some pastoral Mongolian production teams, work-point records and accounts were kept only in Chinese by Han accountants, rather than by literate local Mongols. Some communes even held meetings in Chinese for Mongols who did not understand the language, and some local government offices and official organizations refused to accept official documents and public letters written in Mongolian (NMZJJ 1979, vol. 3:3).

The direct cause of the above phenomenon was the influx in the early 1960s of numerous Han immigrants. According to the immigration figures for 1960, 945,000 Han settlers moved into the region that one year (Liu and Zheng 1979), and "Mongols soon found themselves outnumbered in their autonomous region by a ratio of one to ten" (Schwarz 1979:144). This unbalanced population ratio caused various problems for the political management of the region. In many pastoral areas, the division of labor differentiated by assigning Mongols to herding and Han to building houses, digging wells, and administration. It was impossible for Mongols to enjoy their autonomous rights with an overwhelming majority of Han living on their land.

CONCLUSION

In the cases presented here, ethnic school programs helped unorganized Inner Mongolian Mongol youth form their own ethnic entities under the protection of ethnic education in school. In particular, the boarding school system increased opportunities for peer group activities and for coherent ethnic experiences outside the classroom. Unlike some Native American boarding schools (McBeth 1983), most

Mongolian or joint schools did not set strict after-school rules for the students. For this reason, the students gradually set up their own residential routines based on ethnic-oriented age or grade peer groups. Such groups were "much more important than the family as a principal mediator of social identity. The peer group is certainly a most exacting socializer, which demands continual symbols of allegiance from those participating" (De Vos 1982:31).

We have seen that the Mongolian language played a crucial role in the learning process of Mongol students at school. Although the state and the local governments' language policies highlighted the significance of ethnic minority languages in achieving national ethnic integration, actual language practice varied even within a single ethnic group. We have also seen that programmed Mongolian-language learning for young Mongols in school was discouraged by the fact that Mandarin was dominant and Mongolian was rarely used officially in the larger society of Inner Mongolia. The political authority of Mandarin in fact laid down the dividing line between the acceptable and the unacceptable, so that Mongol students who spoke only Chinese were often reluctant to learn Mongolian and did not take the language as an important marker of their Mongolian identity. Those who had better knowledge of Mongolian, especially students from pastoral areas, were eager to learn the language as a part of their way of life, and later many of them also took it as an essential marker of their Mongolian identity in competition with the Han and with non-Mongolian speaking Mongols. Therefore, when we talk about the ethnicity of modern Mongols in China, various social contexts have to be taken into consideration.

Carter Bentley accurately observes:

> Since ethnic identity derives from situationally shared elements of a multidimensional habitus, it is possible for an individual to possess several different situationally relevant but nonetheless emotionally authentic identities and to symbolize all of them in terms of shared descent. (1987:35)

According to these case studies, the meanings of Mongolian identity to the young Temut Mongols were closely related to the idea of shared descent through their place of birth, their older generation's historical contributions to the revolution in Inner Mongolia, and the class division in landholding between themselves and the local Han.

299

To the pastoral Mongol youth, their nomadic way of life was a basic foundation of Mongolian identity. However, only when they found themselves alienated in their own land and unaccepted by the larger society was their sense of Mongolian identity formed. Very often they took the Mongolian language as a crucial boundary between themselves and both non–Mongolian-speaking Mongols and the Han. As for the young urban Mongols, ethnic education created a cultural space for their own ethnic peer groups and evoked visions of family ties shared through common mythical history with the entire Mongolian group.

On the Dynamics of Tai/Dai-Lue Ethnicity

An Ethnohistorical Analysis

Shih-chung Hsieh

The Tai-Lue, a Tai-speaking people who now live mostly in Xishuang-banna Dai Nationality Autonomous Prefecture, Yunnan,[1] are unlike other non-Han ethnic groups in this frontier province, most of whom are divided into distinct, noncentralized units. Although the Tai-Lue have had the full experience of running a state, in their case a kingdom, at present they are counted as a subgroup of the Dai*zu* (Dai nationality)—recent contact between the Dai-Lue and the Han has transformed the Dai-Lue from an independent kingdom to a sub-group of a minority *minzu*. To understand the relationships between the Dai-Lue and Chinese state, we must adopt an ethnohistorical approach, exploring changes in the ethnic status of the Dai-Lue.

The Dai-Lue are an example of how a minority ethnic group, whose former state is not recognized by the dominant group, copes with an actual nation-state that does not recognize itself as such, but claims instead to be multi-ethnic. The Dai-Lue story can be used to explore the universal effectiveness of the framework of official "nation-state" (cf. Anderson 1983) versus "minority ethnic group" in shaping ethnicity in Socialist China, and to demonstrate that the model of one "ethnic-state" (a premodern state established by a single ethnic group) among others can be a fruitful approach for understanding processual ethnic relationships.

SIPSONG PANNA AS A TAI KINGDOM

To determine whether Sipsong Panna was once a kingdom is not so silly a task as determining whether China was an empire before it was a

---

1. Both anthropologists and linguists agree to using "Tai" to refer to all peoples who speak the Tai language. "Thai," on the other hand, is reserved for the majority of the Tai-speaking peoples in Thailand, or citizens of the kingdom of Thailand. In 1951 the Chinese government created "Dai" to name the Tai-speaking ethnic groups who were mostly called Baiyi by the Han. "Dai" is used here only in the context of Chinese manipulation and domination under the People's Republic.

MAP 6. Yunnan and neighboring areas

republic. After all, "Chinese empire" is a bit of historical common knowledge, while "kingdom of Sipsong Panna" awaits our investigation and verification. The "state of Sinsong Panna" may vanish permanently under the conservative interests of certain Western Southeast Asianists and the never-ending distortions of Chinese Xishuangbanna studies. If such is the case, it not only will be unfair to the people of Sipsong Panna, but also probably will distort future studies of Sipsong Panna society and culture.

Because the kingdom of Sipsong Panna never received recognition from the world's "legitimate" powers, it completely disappeared from the network of international affairs, except when Siam[2] attempted to unify all Tai peoples (including the Tai-Lue in Sipsong Panna) during the 1930s and 1940s. No one knew where

2. In 1939 Phibun Songkhram, a powerful general who controlled national politics, changed the name from Siam to Thailand.

Sipsong Panna went, how it had been treated, or whether it survived.[3]

The Role of the Chao Phaendin: *Ethnic Identity as Subjecthood*

The symbolic significance of the *chao phaendin* (king) is crucial to understanding ethnic solidarity among the Sipsong Panna Tai. Like the Japanese imperial family, the royal house of the kingdom of Sipsong Panna was one unbroken family line since 1180. The Sipsong Panna kingship maintained an effective centralized government through a native network of dominance that had nothing to do with the imaginative authority of the Chinese-appointed Cheli *junmin xuanwei shi* (lord of the Cheli [i.e., Sipsong Panna] pacified administrative region for governing people).[4]

3. Mitsuo Nakamura (1969) and Shigeharu Tanabe (1988) referred to Sipsong Panna, or Lue, as a "kingdom". Their use of this term did not give rise to any noticeable interest in Western academic circles, even though the study of relations between the Dai-Lue and the Communist polity and economy is a proposed research priority in the newly founded Thai-Yunnan Project of Australian National University. At the same time, neither Nakamura nor Tanabe is concerned about the symbolism of Tai kingship as a mechanism of ethnicity, nor do they attempt to reconstruct a more detailed and integrated configuration of the kingdom of Sipsong Panna. All we know about Sipsong Panna is that it was an "illusory community," a term borrowed from Marx by Tanabe, or an "illusory kingdom," a term employed by anthropologists and historians with conservative interests.

4. Shigeharu Tanabe argues that "the power of the kingship [in Sipsong Panna] was largely restricted to the capital and adjacent *moeng* [*meeng*, 'local principalities']" and adds that "the instability of the kingship was also a prominent feature, as the perennial usurpations and succession disputes show" (1988:5). However, he fails to explain how the royal family could exist for more than seven hundred years if, as he suggests, it was plagued by both the weak centralization of the kingdom and "perennial usurpations and succession disputes" (ibid.:15). Here we should distinguish between the external and internal political operation of Sipsong Panna. The Tai-Lue kings indeed were weak when China and Burma, the two suzerain states of Sipsong Panna, used the small kingdom as an arena in which to compete with each other, and separately appointed two different kings (ibid.:5). In other words, to China and Burma, the kings of Sipsong Panna appeared to be as powerless as the people. All the Sipsong Panna Tai were required to call the commissioners from China and Burma *da ren* (my lord). In internal affairs, however, the king did have stable power. All the local princes or chiefs of *meeng* knew that the authority of the king was granted by the powerful emperor of China. The king not only controlled the area around the Jing Hung, the capital, but could suppress any revolt by having his messengers report to Simao, Puer, or Kunming, Yunnan. The army would be sent immediately. For the most part, however, the king was not seriously concerned about internal conflicts in the *meeng*.

The ideology and behavior patterns of people under a king and those under a chief or tribal head are fundamentally different. People ruled by a king are passive with respect to the state. The king's people know they are living in a secure or fixed area because of the king. The king both ensures the survival of his populace and is the emblem by which the people identify who they are and what they belong to.

This explains the existence of strong nostalgia among the Lue of northern Thailand (cf. Moerman 1967, 1968): the people miss their home country with its royal *chao phaendin*. It is not surprising that in 1986 tens of thousands of Lue people came to kowtow to Chao Hmoam Gham Le (Dao Shixun), the last king of Sipsong Panna, when he visited the Lue community in Nan, northern Thailand, after presenting a paper as an ethnolinguist at an international conference in Chiang Mai.

Sipsong Panna was not a protectorate of China and Burma; it had absolute rights in military action, foreign affairs, economic activities, and internal governance, and neither China nor Burma ever signed a treaty for its protection. Sipsong Panna recognized that the great powers standing by it possessed a sort of superiority, but she was out of the range of the Middle Kingdom (Zhongguo, i.e., cultural and ethnic China).

Both Le Bar (1964) and Moerman (1965:1219; 1967; 1968:154) found that various northern Thai groups, whose dialects were mutually intelligible, nevertheless maintained airtight ethnic boundaries. They hypothesize that the remembrance of disappeared states to which those peoples belonged—such as Lan Na (northern Thailand) for the Tai-Yuan, Lan Zhang (Laos) for the Tai-Lao, and Sipsong Panna for the Tai-Lue—still perform a critical function of distinguishing selfness and otherness in daily ethnic interactions. Both Le Bar and Moerman are basically right, but there is more to the question than this. In Sipsong Panna, members of a particular lineage could live in several villages. Each person was expected to fulfill obligations to his lineage and village, receiving benefits and enjoying rights from both sides as a result. The name of the head of a lineage was used as the name of the lineage. When the head of a lineage died and a new leader was selected, the lineage name changed. There were no surnames in Tai-Lue. In other words, a Tai-Lue lineage did not form a cultural unit or have a cultural identity, because the lineage is not the same as the village, the village being a political unit. Membership in a lineage does not confer benefits, but membership in a village does.

MAP 7. Historical Tai kingdoms and modern states

The general principle of egalitarianism among commoners in Sipsong Panna assures that in regard to obligation to the *chao* ("king," "noble," or "master"), every village is equal and every non-*chao* person is equal. Because each household raises the same amount of money or crops for the *chao,* rather than sharing payment from every lineage, the lineage never developed into the clan, nor was primordial ethnic identification sought from the lineage or descent line.

Despite the political importance of the village, however, a person rarely belonged specifically and permanently to a particular village, but could move back and forth freely. A village thus was a location for lodging and doing one's obligation only, and was not important in forming group indentity because no matter where one stayed, one was always a *xa* (slave) of the *chao. Chao,* in this sense, refers only to the *chao phaendin,* because people could also migrate among different *meeng* (local principalities). A particular *chao meeng* (prince) might not mean anything in the process of ethnic identification to most of the people in Sipsong Panna. The only predominant symbol of unity in the Lue area was the *chao phaendin*. He was the greatest *chao* wherever a person traveled (as long as that person was a Lue), in his effect on ethnic psychological boundaries (De Vos 1982:6). Such boundaries, according to De Vos, "are maintained by ascription from within as well as from external sources which designate membership according to evaluative characteristics which differ in content depending on the history of contact of the groups involved" (ibid.:6). In other words, in the case of the Tai-Lue, the more the people interact with the other Tai-speaking groups (e.g., in Lan Na, Lan Zhang, and Keng Tung [northeastern Burma]), the more the *chao phaendin* is strengthened as a symbol of Lue group unity.

The *chao phaendin* is unique to the Dai-Lue, differing from the *chao jiang* of Lan Zhang, the *chao praya* of Keng Tung, and the *chao yuan* of Lan Na. These four small Tai kingdoms frequently interacted with one another, both in interstate affairs and in popular contact, before modern nation-states were formed. People speaking mutually intelligible dialects felt free to move to and fro. This was an adaptation to encirclement by powerful neighbors: Burma, Siam, Mons, Cambodia, and China. When one of the four northern Tai states was attacked, people could move quickly and safely to other territories to reside temporarily.[5] This "tacit alliance" functioned as political unification, although a formal agreement was not conducted. However, each state's members maintained the identity of their origin, because they had their own supreme *chao*.

It is clear that members of this ethnic group had their original identity, no matter where they were living. This basically answers Moerman's questions about the nostalgia of the Lue toward Sipsong Panna and about the dynamic relations between various northern Tai

5. For example, in 1765 the Burmese captured the king of Keng Tung, Chao Meeng Jung, but his son escaped to Lan Zhang first, and then hid himself in Meeng Jie, Sipsong Panna (Li Foyi 1984:97). In 1886 many northern Tai princes and headmen fled from the uncertain social order in their own territories to the capital of Sipsong Panna (Zhu Depu 1987:203). Chao Long Pha Sat, uncle of the last king, told me: "When Chao Hmoam Siang Meeng [the prince regent and father of the last king] and I fled to Keng Tung in the 1940s, we said to the ruler, 'You should help us, because we aided your ancestors several times before, and found a place for them to live in Jing Hung when they came as refugees.' "

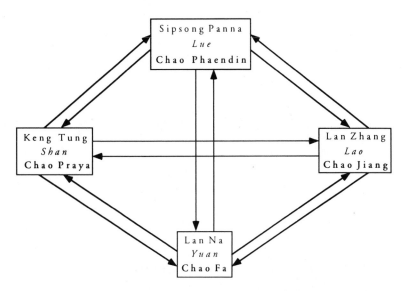

FIGURE 1. An interactive network of the four Tai kingdoms in northern Southeast Asia, showing geographic areas, ethnic groups, and titles of rulers

ethnic identities and historical states (fig. 1). These four states also established their own regimes based on one or several particular principalities and separately received four different official titles from China. Today they belong to four independent nation-states. These four units were never combined in any way by any power. Table 1 illustrates these relationships. The political situation thus strengthened the formation and maintenance of ethnic boundaries among these northern Tai groups.

The *chao* in the Lue area became a major symbol of identification, which was reflected in the equal distribution of the common people's obligation to him. Although the people were classified into two categories, *tai meeng* and *kun hen tsau,* it was expected that they do the duties expected of their class. *Tai meeng* ("Dai of the *meeng*"—similar to the *khon myang* of Chiang Mai [cf. Hanks 1983]) were responsible for the public affairs of the state as well as for the external business of the king. *Kun hen tsau* (people of the *chao*) were responsible for managing the internal affairs of the king. In sum, *tai meeng* devoted themselves to making the *chao*'s state strong, and the *kun hen tsau* provided a comfortable life for the *chao*. We can thus boldly interpret the term Dai-Lue as meaning "the people who call themselves Dai, live in Lue, and share equally in making their *chao phaendin* a satisfied king."

TABLE I

The Changing Political Positions of the Four Northern Tai Kingdoms

	Before 13th Century		13th–18th Century	19th Century	20th Century
People	State	King	China's Appointments	Colonial Suzerain	Nation-State
Tai-Yuan	Lan Na	Chao Yuan	Babai da dian junmin xuanwei shi si	Siam	Thailand
Tai-Lao	Lan Zhang	Chao Jiang	Laowo junmin xuanwei shi si	France	Laos
Tai-Shan	Keng Tung	Chao Praya	Mengheng tuzhi fu	Britain	Burma
Tai-Lue	Sipsong Panna	Chao Phaendin	Cheli junmin xuanwei shi si	China and France	China and Laos

The Tai-Lue View of China

Even before the Tai-Lue, led by Chao Bhaya Cheeng (r. 1180–1192 C.E., first king of the Tai-Lue) established the state of Golden Palace of Jing Rung in Sipsong Panna at the end of twelfth century (cf. Wang Jun 1982), the rulers of Lue knew well that there was a powerful state to the north. The name of this state was the Heavenly Dynasty and its leader was the *chao wong, chao lom fa,* or *chao fa wong* (great emperor of heaven). Although over time the state of Tai-Lue developed an effective strategy to cope with this powerful entity, which hypothetically might destroy it at any time, the Tai rulers were not aware of the political situation in China at all. The principle was that whenever anyone came from the north in a certain capacity, accompanied by a powerful army, and claimed his status as a representative of the Heavenly Dynasty, the Tai rulers immediately showed their loyalty and steadfast good faith to the *chao wong.* When the envoys or generals of Nanzhao (Dali or Houli) came to Sipsong Panna, Nanzhao was treated as the Heavenly Dynasty. It is thus not surprising that Tai records concerning Houli mention that the *chao lom fa* was named *bodhi gnian* (king of Houli) and that he conferred a golden seal in the shape of a tiger head upon Chao Bhaya Cheeng. Nor is it surprising to read that Ghae Neeng (1192–1211), the second king, pledged allegiance to the *chao fa wong* of the Haw (Hok) dynasty (Li Foyi 1947:1–4).[6] Many Chinese ethnologists and historians still insist that the *chao fa wong* whom Bhaya Cheeng and Ghae Neeng contacted was one of the emperors of the Song dynasty of China, even though details of the relationships between Yunnan's kingdoms and the Lue state established by Bhaya Cheeng are unknown. Even for the Yuan empire, which presumably controlled the whole of Yunnan including the Tai-Lue, details of the interactive process between China and the Lue state are obscure. The thirteenth and fourteenth centuries seem to have been a period of adaptation by the Dai in order to get along with China, formation of a centralized Lue kingdom out of the domain of Bhaya Cheeng's descendants, and establishment of formal relations between the Dai kingdom and China.

At this time, the rulers of the Lue state, or other indigenous chiefs in Yunnan, might have made some observations concerning the great Heavenly Dynasty's response to unrest in vassal states: (1) To pacify a fight, attack, or rebellion occurring in an indigenous area, the Heavenly Dynasty always simply handed down imperial instructions to conciliate. If an indigenous leader raised armies for purposes such as expanding territories, or avenging a blood feud, he stood only about a 50 percent or smaller chance of causing China to send a punitive expedition. (2) If the Chinese army did come, a rebellion might be unsuccessful, but because of fighting in unfamiliar geographical circumstances, or because of sweeping malaria epidemics, many Chinese soldiers might be killed. Experience had shown that troops always withdrew very quickly, mainly because of malaria, so indigenous states or tribes were not too anxious about being destroyed. (3) Still, the political and military strength of China impressed the non-Han aborigines. The best strategy was to declare oneself a vassal first, then do as one pleased. (4) If that behavior went against the Heavenly Dynasty's wishes, envoys should

6. In Sipsong Panna and probably most Tai-speaking communities in northern Southeast Asia Han Chinese are called Haw or Hok.

be sent with gifts to appease the emperor. Indigenous leaders who behaved thus not only rarely received punishment from China, but usually received more valuable return gifts from the Chinese emperor through the returning envoys.

If we review the materials of the Ming and Qing periods carefully, we will find that the Lue state followed these guidelines in dealing with China ever since the eighth king, Chao Gham Meeng, began formal contact with the Heavenly Dynasty in 1382 and accepted the title of Cheli *junmin xuanwei shi*. However, after the kingdom of Kausambi (Chinese-Shan)[7] in western Yunnan was destroyed in 1448 by the Ming army after a sixty-three-year-long rebellion against China (cf. Yang Yongsheng 1986:44–47; Huang Huikun et al. 1985:82–86), the Tai-Lue rulers understood that the only way to survive was to serve as a *xuanwei shi*.[8]

THE CHINESE INTERPRETATION OF THE STATE OF LUE

The statement that "China has been a united state composed of multiple nationalities" is both a popular, dogmatic statement of

7. The Tai-speaking people living in what is now known as Dehong Daizu and Jingpozu Autonomous Prefecture are called Chinese Shan because of the similarity of cultural and linguistic traits with Shan in northern Burma.

8. The only time a ruler of the Lue state attacked Chinese territory was in 1403. Chao Si Rda Gham, the ninth king, marched to Weiyuan (Jinggu) and captured its head and people. China immediately warned him. The king was afraid of Chinese punishment. Not only did he send Weiyuan's people back to their hometown, he also dispatched envoys to apologize for the offense to the Chinese emperor (Li Foyi 1984). In 1386 Ming emperor Hongwu wrote to the eighth king of Meeng Lue, Chao Gham Meeng (father of Chao Si Rda Gham): "I will follow the order of heaven and dispatch strong troops to suppress the evil Lu Chuan" (China gave the title Lu Chuan *xuanwei shi* to the king of Kausambi) (cf. Huang Huikun et al. 1985:83–84). It seems that Chao Si Rda Gham attempted to expand his territory and, considering the case of Kausambi, was ambivalent. He could not but give up his desire. In addition, because his father, the twenty-eighth king, Chao Hmoam Thao, was removed from the position of Cheli *xuanwei shi* by China on account of incompetency, in 1773 the twenty-ninth king, Chao Nam Peng, on the advice of his son-in-law, took a group of his relatives and officials and left Sipsong Panna to reside in Meeng Yong (Burma). In 1775 Chao Nam Peng went back to Sipsong Panna, but the Yunnan governor captured him in Kunming. His descendants were not given the right to inherit the position of Cheli *xuanwei shi* (see Li Foyi 1947 and 1984). This unhappy series of events caused subsequent kings to become more circumspect when dealing with China.

political propaganda (e.g., Art. 4 of the 1978 Constitution of the People's Republic of China) and a universal Chinese academic conclusion (e.g., Ma Yin 1981:1–25; Zhang Quanchang 1984:330). Socialist ethnologists, following the Communist Party's philosophy and policy, have expended a great deal of energy explaining the relationship between the key concepts "united state" and "multiple nationalities." Tibet is a good example of Chinese scholars' attempts to verify that contemporary non-Han ethnic groups have always lived in territories of the Chinese state (Liu Shengqi 1988:11–15). The anti-Han movement there in the 1980s and 90s is accused of betraying the "Chinese *minzu*" (*Zhonghua minzu*). All non-Han states of the past have been classified as "local regimes" (*difang zhengquan*). The central regime is always China, although it may reasonably include several local units.

The term "regime" (*zhengquan*) does not refer only to a form of government, such as a socialist or autocratic regime. In socialist China, all levels of administrative units—such as villages, townships, autonomous counties, autonomous prefectures, and provincial governments—are separately called regimes. All regimes other than the central one are referred to as local regimes. This arrangement and interpretation serves to make the traditional relationships between non-Han and Han more rational, acceptable, and congruent with the contemporary situation. By this logic, non-Han states of the past, such as Tufan (Tibet) and Nanzhao, have not changed, but are now considered to be completely under the control and domination of the central government.

It is not hard to imagine the political status that Sipsong Panna, a much smaller state than either Tibet or Nanzhao, is accorded in this analysis. According to *The History of the State of the Lue,* "Chao Bhaya Cheng came to be the leader of Meeng Lue in the Cula Calendar [Chulasakkharaja, a kind of Buddhist calendar used by the Sipsong Panna Tai and the other Buddhist societies of Southeast Asia] year 542 [1181 C.E.]. . . . Chao Lom Fa Bodhi Gnian granted him a golden tiger-head-shaped seal, and appointed him master of this area. . . . He was called Shomrdieb Bra Pien Chao [Greatest Buddha] or Meeng Jing-Rung Meeng Huo-Gham [the Golden Palatial State of Jing Rung]. Bhaya Cheng went on to rule Lan Na, Meeng Gao [Vietnam], and Meeng Lao [Laos]. At that time, the emperor of the Court of Heaven was the world leader" (see Li Foyi 1947:39). Based on this account of Tai history, we now have alternative interpretations by four Chinese scholars:

1. Li Foyi: "The term *zhao long fa* [*chao lom fa*] was usually used to address emperors of China. However, here it should refer to Duan Zhixing, king of the state of Houli [one of the regimes of Nanzhao]" (1984:4).

2. Zheng Peng and Ai Feng: "In the Tang and Song periods the area of Xishuangbanna was within the jurisdiction of Nanzhao and Dali, two local regimes of the Tang and Song" (1986:16)

3. Huang Huikun, vice-president of the Yunnan Institute of Nationalities and an influential ethnologist in China, and his coauthors: " 'Court of Heaven' here should refer to the Song dynasty. Bhaya Cheeng became the master of this particular area because he received the golden tiger-head-shaped seal from the Court of Heaven. . . ." (1985:56)

4. Jiang Yingliang, a professor at Yunnan University and a famous Dai specialist: "We must keep in mind that since ancient times Xishuangbanna has been a part of the territory of our mother country. The state of Jing Rung established by Bhaya Cheeng was a local regime under the domination of the Song dynasty of China. The master of Jing Rung accepted a rank of nobility from the Song government" (1983:182). Jiang also explains that the term *chao lom fa* might be related to the lord of the state of Dali. *Lom* in Dai means "below" or "down." *Fa* means "heaven," which comes from the term *chao fa wang* (king of heaven), used to address the emperor of China. *Chao lom fa* should thus be translated "the king who is smaller than the king of heaven." *Chao lom fa,* according to Jiang, refers to either the lord of Dali or an emissary from *chao fa wang,* the emperor of China (ibid.).

Except for Li Foyi, all the authors cited here are socialist scholars. Their interpretations clearly reflect the contemporary dogmatic theory of relationships between non-Han and Han peoples. These scholars and others who are familiar with historical accounts of the Tai-Lue and the state of Jing Rung know that no information on the Tai can be found in Song historical records. They also know that the evidence suggests that Nanzhao, Dali, and Houli were independent kingdoms.[9]

9. When General Wang Quanbin established control over the whole of Sichuan in 965, he asked first Song emperor Zhao Kuangyin for permission to march into Yunnan to conquer the state of Dali. The emperor thought that Nanzhao's continuous attack had caused the decline of the Tang dynasty. He thus took a jade axe to a point on the

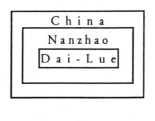

FIGURE 2. The Chinese official view of the relationships among China, Nanzhao, and the Dai-Lue

Yet they still neglect or distort the evidence. According to many Chinese Communists, including academic scholars, all research should serve the unification of the socialist motherland. In their view, the relationships among China, Nanzhao, and the Dai-Lue take one of the forms illustrated in figure 2. They do not recognize any of the networks illustrated in figure 3.

Since the fifteenth century, when the Ming dynasty swept the whole of China, Sipsong Panna[10] and the Chinese government have interacted much more. However, the new relationships were just like those between China and Burma, Laos, and other areas.[11] Cheli or Sipsong Panna was one of the appointed *Xuanwei shisi* whose sole responsibility was to submit tribute to China's emperor and to not commit aggression against China's borderlands. Statistics indicate that in the 543 years of the Ming and Qing dynasties, Sipsong Panna sent troops to occupy a region of Yunnan only

Dadu River (in southwestern Sichuan) and said, "The areas beyond here are not mine" (cf. Ruey 1972:344) During the Song dynasty, aside from a few times when they sent special envoys to the Song court, the regimes of Yunnan had almost no contact with China. Chinese scholars know this, but never cite it because it does not illustrate the morality of the socialist philosophy of China's unification.

10. According to *The History of the State of Lue,* in 1570 the nineteenth king of Meeng Lue, Chao Yin Meeng, divided his kingdom into twelve *panna* (administrative units), each of which could contain one or several *meeng.* Since then, the term Sipsong (twelve) Panna has been used popularly used for the original Meeng Lue.

11. The Ming government set up ten *junmin xuanwei shisi* in the southwestern part of the territory.

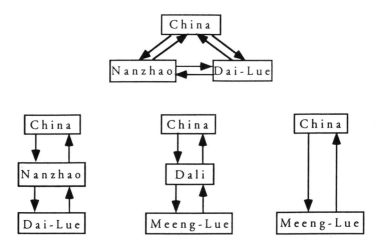

FIGURE 3. Alternative historical interactive relationships among China, Nanzhao, and the Dai-Lue

once,[12] sent tribute at least eleven times, received gifts and rewards from Chinese emperors more than seven times, and was never invaded by China. All this gives the impression of a long-lasting, stable, and peaceful relationship between Sipsong Panna and China.

Only after China's Cheli *junmin xuanwei shisi* had been established for 650 years (from 1293 until the "liberation" of Xishuangbanna in the 1950s) did the Chinese government learn about the political and social features of the Dai-Lue state. China finally understood that Cheli *xuanwei shisi* was also known as Sipsong Panna, that Cheli was Jing Hung to the Tai, and that the Cheli *xuanwei shi* appointed by the Chinese government was *chao phaendin* (the lord of the broad territory—i.e., the king) to the people of Sipsong Panna. The Chinese also realized that the twelve *panna* or thirty-odd *meeng* were local executive units managed by the *chao panna* (lord of *panna*) or *chao meeng* (lord of *meeng*) of the centralized hierarchical government in Jing Hung, the capital of Sipsong Panna. The position of

12. In February 1430 Chao Si Rda Gham attacked Weiyuan Prefecture, captured the prefect and a number of other people, and returned to Meeng Lue. Yongle, the third Ming emperor, asked the provincial official of Yunnan to warn Chao Si Rda Gham to send the prisoners back and return the land; otherwise the Chinese army would attack Cheli. Chao Si Rda Gham immediately complied and sent envoys to submit horses in apology for the offense. The emperor forgave Chao Si Rda Gham (Zhang Tingyu 1739:chap. 315).

Cheli *xuanwei shi,* in sum, was not, as the Chinese had thought, simply an appointed indigenous office under the *tusi* system of Chinese political organization.

Although Chinese interpreters have never considered Sipsong Panna to be an independent state, we know that the remembrance and imagination of the previous Lue state in northern Thailand is an important element affecting both the Tai-Lue's daily life and the process of their ethnicity (Moerman 1967, 1968). But what kind of state was it? Why do the Lue miss their home country so much? And how was image of that state formed in the Lue mind's eye? The Lue living elsewhere talk freely about their state, whereas those in Xishuangbanna are not allowed to think of it as a formerly independent state. Is there another significant or dominant symbol that can replace identification with a past state as a marker of group identity among Xishuangbanna Dai under Communist rule?

THE XISHUANGBANNA DAI
UNDER CHINA'S ETHNIC POLICY

According to empirical observation, and learning from the experiences of the Soviet Union on ethnic problems, since very early in the history of the Chinese Communist Party, differential treatment of Han and non-Han peoples has been part of the general ideology.[13] Although a number of strategic resolutions, announcements, and promises made by the Party regarding minorities—such as "freedom to be independent," "freedom to break away from China's rule," or "freedom to build their own state"—were deliberately omitted after 1949 from all kinds of published materials, including official documents, a separate policy agenda for minorities was maintained at all times. It was referred to as "regional national autonomy" (*minzu quyu zizhi*). The Sipsong Panna area is one such autonomous unit, referred to as Xishuangbanna Dai Nationality Autonomous Prefecture. This prefecture, which includes neither the Dai nationality outside Xishuangbanna nor any historically non–Sipsong Panna district in the territory, was founded on January 24, 1953. It includes three

13. For the Han people, "Chinese culture" (*Zhonghua wenhua*) definitely means Han culture. Even in academic circles, the Han have never developed any motivation to distinguish Han culture from Chinese culture.

counties: Jinghong, Menghai, and Mengla. The capital is Yunjing-hong, in Jinghong County.

The Dai-Lue have been living in the Xishuangbanna Dai Nation-ality Autonomous Prefecture with the same Dai prefect, Zhao Cunxin, for nearly thirty-five years. During this period slogans, official documents, personal speeches, and journalists' reports—similar to those about other minorities elsewhere—have given wide publicity to the huge success of Dai national autonomy. People have become used to praising the liberation by the Communists. A poem "composed" by *dang jia zuo zhu de* (master) Dai singers is representative of this:

> Since the Communists came,
> Fortune has landed on the frontier.
> The great kindness of the Communists is endless.
> When the autonomous region was founded,
> Fresh flowers blossomed,
> The fragrance of the flowers spreads hundreds and thousands
>   of miles,
> The nationality policy warms our hearts.
> (Zheng and Ai 1986:74)

However, the uncertainty of the political status and social structure of Xishuangbanna under Chinese rule is reflected in the fact that it was not until 1984 that the Law of the People's Republic of China for Regional National Autonomy (the first formal law on ethnic auton-omy) was promulgated, followed in 1987 by the Law of the Yunnan Xishuangbanna Dai Nationality Autonomous Prefecture for Self-Government.

RELATIONSHIPS BETWEEN THE DAI-LUE AND OTHER TAI-SPEAKING GROUPS

"Ethnic identification" is another process through which the Chinese government deals with the world of non-Han peoples. However, this process cannot be regarded simply as ethnic identification as the term is commonly used in anthropology. Fei Xiaotong, a leading sociolo-gist and anthropologist in China, states that "ethnic identification is a scientific task for the purpose of serving 'work among ethnic mi-norities' [*minzu gongzuo*]" (1981a:30). It is therefore a political strategy serving the aim of stable domination (for more discussion of its process see the Introduction to this volume).

During the process of ethnic identification, several groups were said to "not require ethnic identification because they have been universally acknowledged" (Lin 1987:1; Fei 1981a:6). The Dai, along with Mongolians, Manchurians, and Tibetans, were convinced that they were such a group. The problem was that, although the "obvious" status of the Dai came about because they were easily observed and frequently interacted with the Han, all identification work was conducted from the Han point of view. The various groups of Dai thus were asked to accept all the officially identified Dai outside their own homelands as "brothers" even though the majority of Dai groups had rarely or never contacted each other before.

Dai population since the 1950s and the percentage who are Xishuangbanna Dai are illustrated in table 2. Despite the absence of figures concerning the Xishuangbanna Dai for 1964, we can conclude that they have made up approximately one-third of the Dai population of China since the end of 1970s. The non-Xishuangbanna Dai— the majority—must be seriously considered if we are to understand the official Communist and Han concept of "the Dai."

The Dai are for the most part found in Yunnan. Besides Xishuangbanna, the major Dai areas include Dehong Dai and Jingpo Nationality Autonomous Prefecture, Gengma Dai and Wa Nationality Autonomous County, and Menglian Dai, Lahu, and Wa Nationality Autonomous County. There are also Dai communities scattered in Jingdong, Jinggu, Puer, Lancang, Xinping, Yuanjiang, and Jingping (Ma Yin 1981:339), and in a few counties in southern Sichuan.

The Dai were classified as a *minzu* that did not need to be reidentified. This is not only because all Dai groups—such as the Dai-Lue, Dai-Duan, Dai-Beng, and Dai-Ya—call themselves Dai, but also because they have been called by the same name (Baiyi) by the Han since the thirteenth century (cf. Jiang Yingliang 1983:109–121).

When the Han began contact with the Tai, the feature of Dai society most apparent to Han eyes was the *bai* (also known as *bui*). The most important social activity for both communities and individuals among the Tai, the *bai* is similar to the potlatch, its central purpose being economic redistribution. "Doing *bai* is a major focus of Tai cultural life; people sacrifice greatly for it, working hard and saving money just to be able to do *bai*" (Li Jinghan 1942:52).

TABLE 2
Relative Populations of the Dai Nationality and the Xishuangbanna Dai

Year	Dai Nationality	Xishuangbanna Dai	Xishuangbanna Percentage of Dai Nationality	Sources
1950s	260,000	118,421	45.50	Jiang Yingliang 1950:44–45
1964	536,000	—	—	Ma Huiqing 1988:830
1978	760,000	207,841	27.30	Ma Yin 1981:339; Song 1986:274
1982	839,797	225,488	26.90	Chen Yongling 1987:1091; Zheng and Ai 1986:22
1985	839,496	252,000	30.00	Minzu Tuanjie 1986:39

NOTE: The number of Xishuangbanna Dai was provided by the vice-prefect of Xishuangbanna Autonomous Prefecture

It is my opinion that because the sound *bai* cannot be represented by a single Chinese character, the Han combined the characters *bai* and *yi* to form Baiyi. Almost all Chinese ethnologists and Dai specialists, however, such as Huang Huikun and Dao Shixun (Chao Hmoam Gham Le, in conversation) and Jiang Yingliang (1983), contend that Baiyi came from the Chinese term *bai* (white) *yi* (clothing). However, the character used to write the homophone *yi* 夷 in Baiyi means "barbarian." The Communist government, in keeping with its policy of "ethnic equality," severely criticized former reactionary feudalistic regimes' use of the insulting name *Baiyi*. But it is true that the Han have used the name contemptuously.

When the Han moved to Yunnan in greater numbers they recorded the general activities and some features of the Baiyi, and by the fourteenth century they had a fairly complete view of where the Baiyi were distributed. The Han adopted terms such as Han Baiyi (Dry Baiyi), Shui Baiyi (Water Baiyi), and Huayao Baiyi (Colorful-Belt Baiyi) to distinguish between various "styles" of Baiyi. Ironically, quite late—in the 1940s and 1950s, when the Dai nationality was formed—members of one group of Dai typically knew little or nothing about other Dai groups, though most individual Dai knew of their identification as Baiyi. As a result, the Chinese Communist Party introduced Dai groups to one another during the process of defining ethnic distinctions.

DAI-LUE ETHNICITY TODAY

As mentioned above, most groups who call themselves Dai and were earlier called Baiyi did not have recorded historical contact with one another. The two major Dai groups today, the Xishuangbanna and the Dehong Dai, use completely different written languages, and speak mutually unintelligible Tai languages. Their styles of dress, patterns of settlement, and original political systems are disparate. The kingdom of Sipsong Panna and the principalities of Dehong had almost no contact with each other. Chao Hmoam Gham Le told me, "I didn't know that there were Tai people living in the Dehong area until I passed through there in June 1947." When the Chinese communist process of nationality creation was in full force, it was the first time those two major Dai groups were face-to-face, recognizing a possible relationship as "siblings."

In 1951 the representatives of various Dai groups met in Beijing to discuss the Chinese name of their people. The representatives of Dehong suggested using Tai 泰 (as their name for themselves still is pronounced), but the Xishuangbanna members wanted to adopt a word with the sound *dai*. Finally, to settle the quarrel, Prime Minister Zhou Enlai synthesized the character 泰 and the radical 亻 (which means "people") to create Dai 傣. Thus the word Baiyi was replaced by Dai, and Dai people began learning the Chinese character and calling themselves Dai*zu* (Dai nationality). Because there is just one Dai nationality in China, the Xishuangbanna Dai, for example, must realize that they have many new brothers and sisters whose numbers are about three times the population in Xishuangbanna.

Nevertheless, it appears that relationships among various Dai groups did not change at all. Rather than sending invitations to one another for New Year's Day, Dai groups still have nothing to do with one another. This is not only because of traditional lack of contact or rivalries, but also because the Chinese government pursues regional national autonomy instead of a single nationality autonomy. Xishuangbanna and Dehong have never had a chance to combine into

an autonomous political unit, because they belong to different regions. This policy presumably can prevent the Dai from unifying to
form a threatening nationalism. For Xishuangbanna Dai, there are
no benefits in pursuing common identity with other branches of this
artificially constructed Dai *minzu*. Each knows the others are members of the Dai nationality, and that is about all.

In sum, the Dehong Dai do not mean anything, in a cultural or
social sense, to the Xishuangbanna Dai. If we take Keyes's definition of ethnic groups (1981:3–30), these two groups of Dai lack
both the sense of sharing the same origin, and a common motivation to pursue social interest, and thus should not be classified as
belonging to the same ethnic group. The instrumental approach
(Barth 1969; Duran 1974:43; Nagata 1974; Hinton 1983; Lal 1983;
Burgess 1978), which says that a particular group of people claims
ethnic status in pursuit of immediate interests, seems to be better
able to explain the Dai*zu* as an ethnic group. The officially created
Dai nationality is a meaningful term for individuals only when it
has a practical application. Although Dai status is based on recognition by the government, Dai often skillfully manipulate the ethnic component involved in a situation, revealing their identity in
order to receive particular benefits (such as extra points on school
entrance examinations), or concealing it if it does not have practical function (in daily life). Although when the Dai*zu* was created
and defined the name may not have meant anything to most Dai
people, it is possible that the Dai may begin to function as an
ethnic group in the future if situations offering advantages from
such status occur. For the present, Dai*zu* is more like an ethnic
category, as defined by James McKay and Frank Lewins (1978) and
Peter Kunstadter (1979:119–63), in that either "there is no sense of
belonging" (McKay and Lewins 1978:418) or there exists nothing
that creates similar consciousness and mutual interests (Kunstadter
1979:119).

Tai/Dai or Lue ethnicity has been persistently shaped by the processes of ethnic-political interaction between the Lue and China/the
Han, the Lue and non-Tai hill tribal peoples, and the Lue and the
other Tai-speaking groups. The Dai have identified themselves as
such for at least several hundred years. However, they have adjusted
their ethnic positions in a historical process that depends on changing political environments. As present, the Han, the hill tribes, and
the other Tai-speaking peoples still comprise an ethnic network with

the Xishuangbanna Dai, affecting their attitudes and interpretation of their ethnic position.

In the Chinese mind, the Xishuangbanna Dai are not an independent group of people, but rather the members of the Dai*zu* who live in Xishuangbanna.[14] Since the concept of Dai*zu* is absolutely concrete, Chinese scholars who study the Dai usually proceed from the conception of Dai nationality. For example, when they compare the Dai in Dehong and the Dai in Xishuangbanna without considering the essential interactive relationship between the two groups, they conclude that the Dehong Dai*zu* are more sinicized than the Xishuangbanna Dai*zu*, because the former contacted the Han much earlier (see Huang Huikun et al. 1985; Jiang Yingliang 1983). Thus one chapter in any book dealing with Dai history or culture inevitably deals with the Dehong Dai*zu*, and another with the Xishuangbanna Dai, even though the contents of the two chapters are mutually irrelevant.

The Chinese government's policy of regional national autonomy revolves not around individual *minzu,* but rather around locality. This policy prevents Dai subgroups from forming one ethnic group, because they have no common interest. At the same time, this policy keeps the Xishuangbanna Dai an ethnic group as before. In the past, Sipsong Panna interacted with China as one state to another (Sipsong Panna to China) or one ethnic group to another (Tai to Han). Although Sipsong Panna's state status has disappeared, China, represented by the Han people, still faces a single ethnic group in Xishuangbanna—the Dai-Lue—instead of dealing with the entire Dai*zu* at once. The Xishuangbanna Dai have always acted as a unique ethnic group in their relationship to China/Han people, but outwardly, the Xishuangbanna Dai are now only *part* of a minority *minzu,* even though essentially they are an independent minority people to the Chinese administration that has relations with Xishuangbanna. In order words, the Dai*zu* as a whole are still an "initial *minzu*" that does not function as an ethnic group.

Although from the perspective of the Han in Beijing or even in Kunming the Xishuangbanna Dai may appear to be a very weak minority people because they are just a subgroup of one of the fifty-five minority *minzu,* in Xishuangbanna they still hold the majority position.

14. Harrell (this volume) makes the same point with regard to the Yi.

The term Xishuangbanna is a Chinese transliteration of the Dai term Sipsong Panna. This prefecture is an autonomous political unit whose prefect must be Dai, according to the Self-Government Law of the Yunnan Xishuangbanna Dai Nationality Autonomous Prefecture. The Dai are still the largest *minzu* in the prefecture. Dai writing is visible everywhere—in public buildings, markets, bookstores, and other shops in towns, and on plates on private houses in villages. Most villages reached by road are Dai. In *minzu* middle school only Dai students wear ethnic clothes.[15] If one did not observe carefully, one might think the Dai were the only indigenous people in Xishuangbanna, due to the fact that transportation to hill tribal communities is not convenient, so most tribal people neither come to town often nor are willing to wear their traditional costumes in public, especially the younger generation.

On a deep psychological level the Han in Xishuangbanna probably feel somewhat pressured or even threatened by the supposedly minority but actually majority Dai people. This is suggested by the fact that many Han in Xishuangbanna complained to me about everything concerning the Dai, and by the government's praise of the hill tribes (such as the Jinuo and the Hani) as "*minzu* who have leapt across evolutionary stages" (*kua shiji de minzu*)[16] because they encourage their children to get more education. Moreover, the chairman of the People's Congress in Xishuangbanna is a Jinuo. Some Dai informants felt that the above phenomena showed that the government was deliberately attempting to restrain the Dai and extol other *minzu*. Nevertheless, both the Han and the Dai, according to my investigation in Jinghong, consider the Jinuo and Hani to be the most backward *minzu,* a status of which the Hani and Jinuo are well aware. The strong Jinuo and Hani support of government policy may well reflect both an effort to

15. The government has set up one or more *minzu* middle schools in each autonomous area, admitting minority students by examination. All students are non-Han, but most teachers are Han. The curriculum is the same as that in ordinary schools (see Borchigud, this volume, on schools). Several students at Minzu Middle School of Xishuangbanna in Jinghong told me that only the Dai were willing to dress up in their ethnic costumes to celebrate the anniversary of the school. Students complained that their costumes were ugly, and that they were ashamed to wear them.

16. The Jinuo were originally categorized by the Communists as belonging to the first stage of human social development, that is, they were very "backward." So it is especially admirable that the Jinuo are eager to send their children to learn modern scientific knowledge—they appear to be a *minzu* of high achievers.

deal with their problem of stigmatized identity, and anti-Dai senti-ments.[17] In Xishuangbanna the only non-Dai civilization that the hill tribes can contact is Han. It is not surprising to see Jinuo and Hani who are eager to learn Chinese, to study in schools, and to acquire so-called advanced scientific knowledge—all symbols of high culture—in order to adjust themselves to the environment of Dai supremacy. Traditionally, the Tai were the superior people in the political, eco-nomic, and social dimensions of Sipsong Panna. At present, though the political power of the Dai no longer exists formally, in reality the design and arrangement of administrative autonomy in official ap-pointments still indicates that the preeminence of the Dai is recog-nized by the Chinese government. Even though the Han criticize the "laziness" and "backwardness" of the Dai, and it is rumored that the government purposely restrains the Dai, many former Tai aristocrats hold appointments as vice-chairperson or prefect—in effect people of high rank have been transferred to another high level. The tribal people who are assigned official positions are insignificant to the Dai. One of my informants said, "Such an *aka* [slave] can be a vice-prefect—what a joke!"[18] Another stated, "The chairman of the Peo-ple's Congress in Xishuangbanna is a Jinuo*zu*. He is very bad—I hope he dies immediately."

After the kingdoms of Lan Na, Keng Tung, and Lan Zhang were disconnected from Sipsong Panna one by one, Lue-ness lost its critical position in the ethnic identification of the Dai-Lue in Xishuangbanna. The Dai-Lue no longer need to show their Lue identity in the interac-tive network of Tai-speaking groups in northern Southeast Asia, since those peoples who equated Lue with Sipsong Panna Tai have with-drawn from the original northern Tai-speaking ethnic network. When the Dai in Xishuangbanna face the hill tribal peoples, they need to

17. In Taiwan the aborigines' almost universal belief in Christianity (which is presumably more advanced than Chinese Confucianism or Buddhism), can be seen as a means of releasing long-term anxiety about Han domination and of coping with the impact of the Han civilization (see Hsieh Shih-chung 1987). Similar cases are found in the relationship of the Kachin of northeastern Burma to Shan civilization (Leach 1954) and that of the Karen of the Burma-Thailand border areas to both Thai and Burmese civilizations (see Kunstadter 1979; Keyes 1977a), as well as in the relationships between Sani (Swain, this volume) or Miao (Cheung, this volume) and missionaries.

18. There are five vice-prefects in the Xishuangbanna Dai Nationality Autonomous Prefecture: two are Dai, one is Hani (Aka), and two are Han.

emphasize their Dai identity, since Dai-ness is the traditional emblem of superiority in the ethnic context of the area.

CONCLUSION

In the twentieth century, the Sipsong Panna Dai began to be affected by the changing interstate political environment. Members of the northern Tai "tacit alliance" were absorbed into various independent modern nation-states. The relatively isolated kingdom of Sipsong Panna immediately faced strong pressure from direct rule by the Han and from the constitution of the "Chinese *minzu*." Chinese nationalism was constructed and developed in the first half of the twentieth century in response to continuous setbacks in contacts with the Western powers and industrialized Japan. Chinese intellectuals and politicians felt that emulating the Western model of the nation-state was the best way to overcome China's weakness. The Tai leaders at that critical moment did not observe clearly the unusual situation in international affairs and in China's politics. According to proponents of Chinese nationalism, because all residents of China originated from the same ancestor, everyone became a member of the "Chinese minzu." Assimilationism was thus at that time the preferred philosophy among politicians and intellectuals. It was not so easy for the Dai to get along with the new China; they could no longer refer to themselves as "we stupid Baiyi" in their official petitions toward the occupying Chinese army in hopes that the troops would be withdrawn and that Han officials would not be sent to govern Sipsong Panna.

Originally, the Han strictly distinguished between Han and *yi* (barbarians). From the time when Chinese nationalism was formed, Chinese came to believe that *yi* (Baiyi and others) and Han belonged to the same family. All territories around the border, populated by *yi* but not occupied by Western powers, thus became the areas that Chinese were eager to dominate. At the same time an idea of an "indivisible mother country" was forming. The Han still called the Dai *"Baiyi,"* but, from that time on, the Baiyi were a member of the "Chinese *minzu*"—they were a kind of Chinese. The Chinese people and government could not tolerate the existence of an independent polity such as the kingdom of Sipsong Panna within China's territory. Baiyi could survive, but the state ruled by the Baiyi should not be allowed to exist.

The political crisis of the Tai kingdom brought on a serious crisis of ethnic identity for the Tai, because of their homogeneous polity and ethnic identity. Instead of seeking a position in which they could survive politically in the new international circumstances, the Dai isolated themselves in an effort to cope only with the Chinese ideological and territorial invasion. When the traditional social norms and ethnic order within Sipsong Panna had disintegrated after the Chinese invasion, many tribal peoples revolted against the Han in order to restore their original condition—to maintain Sipsong Panna as an ethnic-state. The Tai, the dominant people there, did not appear to be as impetuous as the hill tribes, owing to long experience in dealing with the Chinese state, and knew the unchallengeable power of China. In the traditional mode of Tai-Han political relations, the Tai had always supported what the Chinese state preferred in conducting bilateral affairs. Now in jeopardy of losing their ethnic-state, the Tai were still following, at the time of the struggle between the Nationalists and Communists, their accustomed practice of supporting either of those two powerful Chinese regimes. They thought this was the only way for the Tai state to survive, not realizing that their ability to decide their own ethnic-political fate had disappeared forever.

The Dai have become politically and ethnically passive. Chinese ideology and policy toward non-Han peoples appear to be directing the future of the Dai and perhaps influencing creation or selection of the symbolism for their ethnic identification. The Chinese government established the Xishuangbanna Dai Nationality Autonomous Prefecture in the same location as the Tai kingdom. They also created a new ethnonym. The old name, Baiyi, a term popularly given and then officially used by the Han, had been accepted by the Dai in order to preserve peaceful and safe relations with China. Several hundred years later, it was prohibited by the Chinese government, and the Dai were given the Chinese name Daizu—instead of only Dai, or Dairen (Dai people). The Dai immediately used Baiyi no more, never arguing with the Han about the matter of their ethnic name. Daizu, like Baiyi or even Lue, definitely refers to the Dai only; such names did not threaten the basic identity of the Dai.

In Communist China, Daizu is an unchangeable concept. Daizu, no matter where they live, to the Han are all the same. The Chinese government and academic circles put those identified as Daizu into one category, so that a universal Daizu culture has been created by

Chinese official writers. This inclusive Dai*zu* group, however, has been divided on the basis of original ethnic-political aspects into several administrative units. Xishuangbanna Dai*zu* Autonomous Prefecture and Dehong Dai*zu* and Jingpo*zu* Autonomous Prefecture are two of the major units. Each prefecture, according to the Constitution, is allowed to formulate laws encouraging regional identity.

A common interest among various groups classified in the Dai*zu* is obviously lacking, as are strategies and institutions for promoting mutual integration under China's ethnic minority policy. Many Dai college students distinguish between the Dai from Xishuangbanna and those from Dehong by means of the abbreviated names Xidai and Dedai. Xidai seems to be a newly created symbol of primordial identity; it is like ancient Baiyi and modern Dai*zu* in their own interpretation that only the Xishuangbanna Dai themselves can share it.

Although the *chao* class no longer exists in Xishuangbanna, and traditional political ethnicity provides no symbols to identify with any more, the Dai's ethnic boundary is still well kept. The fact that the Xishuangbanna Dai form an individual administrative unit reflects their common historical origin. The only change—a major one—is that this Dai area is an ethnic autonomous prefecture governed by Chinese bureaucracy, and no longer an independent kingdom. The conceptualization of Xishuangbanna and Dai*zu*, which has created the new symbol Xidai, prevents the Xishuangbanna Dai's ethnic boundary from being blurred. A passive ethnic-political identification has now been formed, based on manipulation by the Han. The Dai have to indicate their ethnic background in the section entitled *minzu* on all official forms. A Dai*zu* person will remain so permanently under the political theory of multinationalities.

During the period when ethnicity was being suppressed (i.e., from 1957 to 1976), claims of ethnic identity by non-Han peoples seem not to have been allowed, yet the Han were qualified to emphasize the ethnic backgrounds of others if needed. The Dai responded very quietly toward Chinese sensitivity about so-called local-nationality chauvinism (*difang minzu zhuyi*). Ironically, the government was always doing things to keep the Dai from losing Dai identity. An important government-mandated activity was criticism of traditional ethnic leaders who were counted as the worst exploiters. All *chao* were forced to realize their aristocratic status (since the decline of the Tai kingdom, the *chao* class did not exist any more), and Dai commoners were compelled to speak out against the *chao*. The two major traditional classes in Dai society were thus artificially emphasized by the Chinese government. Both the *chao* and the Dai peasants thus found no way to hide themselves in the atmosphere of opposition to local-nationality chauvinism. And the *chao* became a negative symbol for the Dai people. Originally, the Tai were Tai because they shared a universally respected *chao phaendin;* later the Dai*zu* were Dai*zu* because they shared a disgraced *chao phaendin*. The *chao phaendin* and the other *chao meeng* were still significant symbols for Dai ethnic identification, but their status had changed from positive to negative.

Class struggles manipulated by the Communist Party ended after the Cultural Revolution. The *chao* as a negative ethnic symbol was no longer pointed out or emphasized, and the Chinese government adopted another strategy to stabilize the position of the Dai*zu*. First of all, traditional expressions of ethnicity—such as pagodas, temples, Buddhist images, monks, ethnic scripts, festivals, and other customs—began to be restored. Dai*zu* and Xishuangbanna were restressed as two major emblems of the Xishuangbanna Dai as a distinct group. Further, most of the previous *chao* were appointed as either provincial or local officials. The former ethnic-state—with its territory, people, dominant ethnic group, and ethnic leaders intact—seems to be re-emerging. Ethnic boundaries and geographical (or perhaps even political) boundaries are operating once again. The maintenance of Dai ethnic identity is probably based on an essentially unchanged set of boundaries, along with fixed patterns of interaction between the populace and traditional ethnic leaders.

The Chinese government unintentionally helps the Dai keep their identity, even while it practices a covert strategy of making China into an imagined nation-state. The Communist Party imagines that a nation should act as a family, members of which obey one head (the Han), share the same blood (as descendants of the Yellow Emperor), use only one language (Chinese), and behave according to one set of norms (Han cultural ways). The Party automatically criticizes big-nationality (i.e., Han) chauvinism in order to rationalize the oppression of ethnicity of the non-Han people, and requests that all peoples identify with the "Chinese *minzu*," yet the main symbols representing this inclusive *minzu* are taken from Han culture. The nature of sinicization is Hanification.

Nevertheless, because the mechanisms that maintain Dai identity are still strong, the ethnic boundary of the Xishuangbanna Dai is tenacious. The Dai always distinguish themselves clearly from the Han wherever they are in contact. The lack of motivation on the part of the Dai in Xishuangbanna to understand their own role in the framework of the "Chinese *minzu*" is similar to the attitude of the Lue toward the "Thai nation." The Lue in Thailand have shown strong hostility to the Thai-Siamese. Their maintenance of Lue identity is based on an imagination of the previous kingdom (their homeland in Sipsong Panna) and of the living *chao phaendin*. An impression and remembrance of governing an ethnic-state, which was a major mechanism for traditional Dai ethnicity, appears to exist in the minds of the Lue.

Much unsystematic information about Taiguo/Meeng Thai/Thailand began to spread into Xishuangbanna when China's door was opened in the late 1970s. Their tragic experience during the Cultural Revolution directed the Dai to seek release from psychological and spiritual pain by imagining Thailand as "a great and wealthy Buddhist country"—a fundamental transformation of the Dai opinion of Thais as "brutal Siamese." The Dai thus imagine that they have a respectable and proud brother country called Thailand. There seems to be no similar sentiment among the Dai toward the Chinese. It is possible that conflict could arise if the Chinese government perceives its nation-state building and "Chinese *minzu*" creation to be a failure in comparison with the successful maintenance of a Dai boundary. The closer the Dai approach to Thailand under such circumstances, the more dangerous the possible reaction from the Chinese government becomes.

Glossary

anfushi 安抚使

azhu hunyin 阿注婚姻

baijiu 白酒

Baiyi 摆夷

baoliu 保留

chi yi shan, guo yi shan 吃一山，过一山

chuantong wenhua 传统文化

Da Yao Shan 大瑶山

Dedai 德傣

Dong jiazi 侗家子

dongbu fangyan 东部方言

fandui difang minzu zhuyi 反对地方民族主义

fangyan 方言

fengjian shehui 封建社会

fengjianhua 封建化

fengsu xiguan 风俗习惯

fenzhi 分支

fu zi lian ming 父子连名

funü 妇女

gai tu gui liu 改土归流

gongchan feng 共产风

guizu 贵族

Han Baiyi 旱摆夷

hanhua 汉化

Hei Miao 黑苗

Hua Miao 花苗

Huayao Baiyi 花腰摆夷

Jiefang hou 解放后

jieji guandian 阶级观点

jieji maodun 阶级矛盾

jihu shoutian 记户授田

jikou jitian 记口给田

jimi zhengce 羁縻政策

junxian zhidu 郡县制度

lao Menggu 老蒙古

lao ya wu shu zhuang, Miaozu
    wu difang 老鸦无树桩，
    苗族无地方

lishi shang de xueyuan lianxi
    历史上的血缘联系

lishi zhuyi 历史主义

liu zu 六族

luohou 落后

Luoluo 猓猡

lusheng 芦笙

mabi 麻痹

manguan 蛮官

Manzi 蛮子

Miao 苗

Miao jiazi 苗家子

Miao Wang chushi 苗王出世

minzu 民族

minzu gongzuo 民族工作

minzu jiaoyu 民族教育

minzu quyu zizhi 民族区域自
    治

minzu ronghe 民族融和

minzu shibie 民族识别

minzu tuanjie 民族团结

minzu wenti 民族问题

Minzu Xueyuan 民族学院

minzu yiyuan 民族意愿

mixin 迷信

moyao 莫徭

neibu 内部

nongcun gongshe 农村公社

nuli shehui 奴隶社会

Pan Hu 槃瓠

qi 旗

qing 清

qiuzhang 酋长

ren 仁

renleixue 人类学

Sani 撒尼

shaoshu minzu 少数民族

shehui lishi diaocha baogao
    社会历史调查报告

shehuixue 社会学

sheng 生

sheng ren 生人

Shiwan Yao Shan 十万瑶山

shu 熟

shu ren 熟人

shuangyu jiaoxue 双语教学

Shui Baiyi 水摆夷

sizhipin 丝织品

Taizu 太祖

tedian 特点

tongyi duominzu guojia 统一多民族国家

tuguan 土官

tuhua 土话

tumu 土目

tusi 土司

wenhua 文化

xian 县

xiandaihua 现代化

xiang 乡

xibu fangyan 西部方言

Xidai 西傣

xiongdi minzu 兄弟民族

Yao 瑶

Yaozu jianshi 瑶族简史

yi (barbarian) 夷

Yi (Yi *minzu*) 彝

yi yi zhi yi 以夷制夷

Yijia 夷家

Yiren 夷人

yong xia bian yi 用夏变夷

yuanshi shehui 原始社会

yuyan jianzhi 语言简志

zangfa 脏法

zhaoan 招安

zhaofu 招抚

zhenggui jiaoyu 正规教育

zhengquan 政权

zheshumin 谪戍民

zhixi 直系

Zhongguo minzu wenhua 中国民族文化

Zhongguo ren 中国人

zhou 州

zhu shui cao er xing 逐水草而行

zizhiqu gaikuang 自治区概况

zongzu 宗族

zouhun 走婚

References

Aberle, David F.

1962 "A Note on Relative Deprivation Theory as Applied to Millenarian and Other Cult Movements." In Sylvia L. Thrupp, ed., *Millennial Dreams in Action: Essays in Comparative Study*, 209–14. The Hague: Mouton.

Ahern, Emily M.

1975 "The Power and Pollution of Chinese Women." In Margery Wolf and Roxanne Witke, eds., *Women in Chinese Society*, 193–214. Stanford: Stanford University Press.

Anagnost, Ann S.

1991 "The Politicized Body." *Stanford Humanities Review* 2 (1): 86–102.

1992 "Socialist Ethics and the Legal System." In Jeffrey N. Wasserstrom and Elizabeth J. Perry, eds., *Popular Protest and Political Culture in China: Learning from 1989*, 177–205. Boulder: Westview Press.

n.d. National Past-times: Narrative, Writing, and History in Modern China. Unpublished MS.

Anderson, Benedict

1983 *Imagined Communities: Reflections on the Origin and Spread of Nationalism*. London and New York: Verso.

Arbuckle, Gerald A.

1985 "Inculturation and Evangelism: Realism or Romanticism?" In D. Whiteman, ed., *Missionaries, Anthropologists, and Cultural Change*, vol. 1: 171–214. College of William and Mary Studies in Third World Societies, no. 25. Williamsburg: College of William and Mary.

Aziz, B. N.

1978 *Tibetan Frontier Families: Reflections of Three Generations from D'ing-ri*. Durham: Carolina Academic Press.

Baber, Edward Colbourne

1882 *Travels and Researches in Western China*. London: Royal Geographical Society Supplementary Papers.

Banzarov, Dorji

1981 (1846) "The Black Faith, or Shamanism Among the Mongols." Translated by Jan Nattier and John Krueger. *Mongolian Studies* 7 (1981–82): 53–91.

Barfield, Thomas J.

1989   *The Perilous Frontier: Nomadic Empires and China.* Cambridge, Mass: Basil Blackwell.

Barlow, Tani

1990   "Theorizing Women: *Funü, Guojia, Jiating.*" *Genders* 10: 132–60.

Barth, Fredrik

1969   "Introduction." In Fredrik Barth, ed., *Ethnic Groups and Boundaries,* 9–38. Boston: Little Brown and Company.

Bawden, Charles R.

1968   *The Modern History of Mongolia.* New York: F. A. Praeger Publishers.

Beidelman, Thomas O.

1982   *Colonial Evangelism: A Socio-Historical Study of an East African Mission at the Grassroots.* Bloomington: Indiana University Press.

Belov, Y. A.

1983   "The Xinhai Revolution and the Question of Struggle Against the Manzhous." In *Manzhou Rule in China,* 325–37. Moscow: Institute of Oriental Studies, USSR Academy of Sciences.

Bentley, G. Carter

1987   "Ethnicity and Practice." *Comparative Studies in Society and History* 29 (1): 24–55.

Bernatzik, H. A.

1970   *Akha and Miao: Problems of Applied Ethnography in Further India.* New Haven: HRAF Press.

BMGSL *(Beifang minzu guanxi shi luncong)* Writing Group

1982   *Beifang minzu guanxi shi luncong* (Collected papers on the history of relationships among the northern *minzu*s). Hohhot: Nei Menggu Renmin Chubanshe.

Boell, Paul

1899   *La Langue Lolo.* Paris: Ernest Leroux.

Borokh, L. N.

1983   "Anti-Manzhou Ideas of the First Chinese Bourgeois Revolutionaries (Lu Haodong Convention)." In *Manzhou Rule in China.* Moscow: Institute of Oriental Studies, USSR Academy of Sciences.

Bradley, David

1979   *Proto-Loloish.* Scandinavian Institute of Asian Studies Monographs, no. 39. London and Malmo: Curzon Press.

1987   "Language Planning for China's Minorities: The Yi Branch." In D. Laycock and W. Winter, eds., *A World of Language: Essays*

Presented to Professor S. A. Wurm on His 65th Birthday, 81–89. Canberra: Department of Linguistics, Australian National University.

Bridgeman, E. C.
1859 "Sketches of the Miau-tsze." *Journal of the North China Branch of the Royal Asiatic Society* 3: 257–86.

Broomhall, Marshall
1940 *Some a Hundredfold: The Life and Work of James R. Adam Among the Tribes of South-West China*. London: China Inland Mission.

Burgess, M. Elaine
1978 "The Resurgence of Ethnicity: Myth or Reality?" *Ethnic and Racial Studies* 1 (3): 265–85.

Burridge, Kenelm
1985 "Missionaries and the Perception of Evil." In D. Whiteman, ed., *Missionaries, Anthropolgists, and Cultural Change*, vol. 1, 153–70. College of William and Mary Studies in Third World Societies, no. 25. Williamsburg: College of William and Mary.

Cai Fuyou
1987 "Analysis and Appraisal of Stalin's Definition of 'Nation.' " *Social Sciences in China* 8 (1): 209–21.

Cai Junsheng
1983 "Group Marriage." *Social Sciences in China* 4 (2): 189–212.

Cameron, Nigel
1970 *Barbarians and Mandarins: Thirteen Centuries of Western Travelers in China*. Chicago: University of Chicago Press.

Castleton, A. B.
1948 *On the Roof of the World: Samuel Pollard of China*. New York: Friendship Press.

Chagnon, Napoleon
1983 *Yanomamö: The Fierce People*. 3rd ed. New York: Holt, Rinehart and Winston.

Chan, Hok-lam
1990 "A Mongol Legend About the Building of Peking." *Asia Major* 3rd ser., 3 (2):63–94.

Chen Guojun
1982 "Shimenkan de Miaomin jiaoyu" (Education among the Miao in Shimenkan). In Zhang Yongguo et al., eds., *Minguo nianjian Miaozu lunwenji* (Collected essays on the Miao in the Republican period). Guiyang: Guizhou Minzu Yanjiusuo.

Chen Shilin et al.

1984 *Yiyu jianzhi* (A short account of the Yi language). Chengdu: Sichuan Minzu Chubanshe.

Chen Tianjun

1985 "Lun Yizu gudai fenqi" (Discussing the division into historical stages of the ancient Yi). In He Yaohua, ed., *Xinan minzu yanjiu, Yizu zhuanji* (Research on Southwest nationalities, special Yi collection). Kunming: Yunnan Minzu Chubanshe.

Chen Yongling

1987 "Minzu ronghe" (Ethnic integration). In *Minzu cidian* (Ethnic dictionary). Shanghai: Shanghai Baikequanhu Chubanshe.

n.d. "The Practice of Ethnology in China." Unpublished manuscript.

Ch'en Wen-shih

1981 "The Creation of the Manchu *Niru*." *Chinese Studies in History* 14 (4): 11–46.

Cheng Deqi

1986 "Notable Case Studies of Matriarchal Societies." *Social Sciences in China* 7 (Spring): 219–29.

Chinggis Khan Mausoleum

n.d.a *Chinggis Khan Mausoleum*. An official brochure published in the mid-1980s.

n.d.b *Chinggis Khan Mausoleum*. An set of official postcards published c. 1988.

Clark, G. W.

1883 "Translation of Manuscript Account of the Kwei-chau Miao-tzu." In A. R. Colquhoun, *Across Chryse*, vol. 2: 365–94. London: S. Low, Marston, Searle, and Rivington.

Clarke, Prescott, and J. S. Gregory

1982 *Western Reports on the Taiping: A Selection of Documents*. Canberra: Australian National University Press.

Clarke, Samuel R.

1911 *Among the Tribes of South-West China*. London: China Inland Mission.

Clifford, James

1982 *Person and Myth: Maurice Leenhardt in the Melanesian World*. Berkeley and Los Angeles: University of California Press.

1988 "On Orientalism." In *The Predicament of Culture: Twentieth Century Ethnography, Literature, and Art*, 255–76. Cambridge, Mass.: Harvard University Press.

Cohen, Abner
　1981 "Variables in Ethnicity." In Charles F. Keyes, ed., *Ethnic Change*, 306–31. Seattle: University of Washington Press.

Cohen, Anthony P.
　1985 *The Symbolic Construction of Community*. London and New York: Tavistock Publications.

Cohen, Paul A.
　1988 "The Post-Mao Reforms in Historical Perspective." *Journal of Asian Studies* 47 (3): 518–40.

Cohn, Norman
　1962 "Medieval Millenarianism: Its Bearing on the Comparative Study of Millenarian Movements." In Sylvia L. Thrupp, ed., *Millennial Dreams in Action: Essays in Comparative Study*, 31–43. The Hague: Mouton.

Colquhoun, Archibald
　1883 *Across Chryse*. Vol. 2. London: Low, Marston, Searle, and Rivington.

Comaroff, John
　1989 "Images of Empire, Contests of Conscience: Models of Colonial Domination in South Africa." *American Ethnologist* 16 (4): 661–84.

Concise History
　1985 *Miaozu jianshi* (Concise history of the Miao). Guiyang: Guizhou Minzu Chubanshe.

Connor, Walker
　1984 *The National Question in Marxist-Leninist Theory and Strategy*. Princeton: Princeton University Press.

Cooper, Frederick, and Ann L. Stoler
　1989 "Tensions of Empire: Colonial Control and Visions of Rule." *American Ethnologist* 16 (4): 609–21.

Crossley, Pamela Kyle
　1983a "Historical and Magical Unity: The Real and Ideal Clan in Manchu Identity." Ph.D. diss., Yale University.
　1983b "The Tong in Two Worlds: Cultural Identities in Liaodong and Nurgan During the 13th–17th Centuries." *Ch'ing shih wen-t'i* 4 (9): 21–46.
　1985 "An Introduction to the Qing Foundation Myth." *Late Imperial China* 6 (2): 13–23.
　1987 "*Manzhou Yuanliu Kao* and the Formalization of the Manchu Heritage." *Journal of Asian Studies* 46 (4): 761–90.

1990a *Orphan Warriors: Three Manchu Generations and the End of the Qing World*. Princeton: Princeton University Press.

1990b "Ming Ethnology." Paper presented to the China Colloquium of the University of Washington.

1990c "Thinking About Ethnicity in Early Modern China." *Late Imperial China* 11 (1): 1–35.

Curwen, C. A.

1977 *Taiping Rebel: The Deposition of Li Hsiu-ch'eng*. Cambridge: Cambridge University Press.

Cushman, Richard

1970 *Rebel Haunts and Lotus Huts: Problems in the Ethnohistory of the Yao*. Ph.D. diss., Cornell University.

Daniel, E. Valentine

1984 *Fluid Signs: Being a Person the Tamil Way*. Berkeley and Los Angeles: University of California Press.

Davies, H. R.

1909 *Yun-nan: The Link Between India and the Yangtze*. Cambridge, England: at the University Press.

de Beauclair, Inez

1960 "A Miao Tribe of Southeast Kweichow and Its Cultural Configuration." *Bulletin of the Institute of Ethnology, Academia Sinica* (Taipei) 10: 127–99.

Dessaint, Alain Y.

1980 *Minorities of Southwest China*. New Haven: HRAF press.

Devéria, G.

1891 "Les Lolo et les Miao-Tze: A propos d'un brochure de M. P. Vial, missionaire apostolique au Yun-nan." *Les Lotus* 3: 356–69.

De Vos, George

1982 "Ethnic Pluralism: Conflict and Accommodation." In George De Vos and Lola Romanucci-Ross, eds., *Ethnic Identity: Cultural Continuities and Change*, 5–41. Chicago: University of Chicago Press.

Diamond, Norma

1988 "The Miao and Poison: Interactions on China's Southwest Frontier." *Ethnology* 27 (1): 1–25.

Dirlik, Arif

1978 *Revolution and History: The Origins of Marxist Historiography in China, 1919–1937*. Berkeley and Los Angeles: University of California Press.

Dreyer, June Teufel

1976 *China's Forty Millions*. Cambridge, Mass.: Harvard University Press.

Du Rongkun and Bai Cuiqin
    1986   *Xi Menggu shi yenjiu* (Studies on the history of the western Mongols). Urumchi: Xinjiang Renmin Chubanshe.

Duara, Prasenjit
    1988   "Superscribing Symbols: The Myth of Guandi, Chinese God of War." *Journal of Asian Studies* 47(4): 778–95.

Duran, James
    1974   "The Ecology of Ethnic Groups from a Kenyan Perspective." *Ethnicity* 1: 43–64.

Durkheim, Emile
    1915   (1974) *The Elementary Forms of the Religious Life.* Translated by Joseph Swain. Glencoe, Ill.: Free Press.

Eickstedt, Egon von
    1944   *Rassendynamik von Ostasien.* Berlin: Walter deGruyter.

Eidheim, Harald
    1969   "When Ethnic Identity Is a Social Stigma." In Fredrik Barth, ed., *Ethnic Groups and Boundaries,* 39–57. Boston: Little, Brown.

Engels, Friedrich
    1972   (1883) *The Origin of the Family, Private Property, and the State.* Translated by Alick West. New York: International Publishers.

Fairbank, John King, ed.
    1968   *The Chinese World Order.* Cambridge, Mass.: Harvard University Press.

Fan Yitian
    1944   *Yunnan gudai minzu zhi shi de fenxi* (Analysis of the history of the ancient peoples of Yunnan). Chongqing: Shangwu Chubanshe.

Fang Guoyu
    1944   "Moxie minzu kao" (Investigation of the Moxie [Mosuo] *minzu*). *Minzuxue yanjiu jikan* (Ethnological quarterly [Shanghai]) 4.

Fang He
    1939   "Lunan Sani Axi er zu xianji" (Communities in two Lunan groups: Sani and Axi). *Yishibao* (Nanjing), July 24.

Fei Xiaotong (Fei Hsiao-t'ung)
    1980   "Ethnic Identification in China." *Social Science in China* 1: 94–107.
    1981a "Guanyu wo guo minzu de shibie wenti" (On the question of ethnic identification in our country). In Fei Xiaotong, *Minzu yu shehui* (Nationality and society), 1–31. Beijing: Renmin Chubanshe.
    1981b *Toward a People's Anthropology.* Beijing: New World Press.
    1985   *Xiongdi minzu zai Guizhou* (Brother nationalities in Guizhou). Beijing: Sanlian Chubanshe.

Feng Han-yi and John K. Shryock

1938 "Historical Origins of the Lolo." *Harvard Journal of Asiatic Studies* 3: 103–27.

Feuerwerker, Albert

1968a (ed.) *History in Communist China.* Cambridge, Mass.: MIT Press.

1968b "China's History in Marxian Dress." In Albert Feuerwerker, ed., *History in Communist China,* 14–44. Cambridge, Mass.: MIT Press.

1976 *State and Society in 18th Century China: The Ch'ing Empire in Its Glory.* Ann Arbor: Center for Chinese Studies, University of Michigan.

Francis, E. K.

1976 *Interethnic Relations: An Essay in Sociological Theory.* Leiden: Elsevier.

Gates, Hill, and Robert P. Weller

1987 "Hegemony and Chinese Folk Ideologies: An Introduction." *Modern China* 13 (1): 3–16.

Geertz, Clifford

1973 (1966) "Religion as a Cultural System." In Clifford Geertz, *The Interpretation of Cultures,* 87–125. New York: Basic Books.

Gladney, Dru C.

1987 "Qing Zhen: A Study of Ethnoreligious Identity among Hui Muslim Communities in China." Ph.D. diss., University of Washington.

1988 "Muslim Tombs and Ethnic Folklore: Charters for Hui Identity." *Journal of Asian Studies* 46 (3): 495–532.

1991 *Muslim Chinese.* Cambridge, Mass.: Harvard University Press.

Goldstein, Melvyn C.

1971 "Stratification, Polyandry, and Family Structure in Central Tibet." *Southwestern Journal of Anthropology* 27 (1): 64–74.

Goodenough, Ward

1963 *Cooperation in Change: An Anthropological Approach to Community Development.* New York: Russell Sage Foundation.

Gramsci, Antonio

1971 (1930s) *Selections from the Prison Notebooks.* Translated and edited by Quintin Hoare and Geoffrey Nowell Smith. New York: International Publishers.

Greenlee, Douglas

1973 *Peirce's Concept of Sign.* The Hague: Mouton.

Guangxi Bianjizu (Guangxi Editorial Group)

1983 *Guangxi Yaozu shehui lishi diaocha* (An investigation of the social history of the Yao in Guangxi). Nanning: Guangxi Minzu Chubanshe.

Guizhou-Hunan Shaoshuminzu Shehui Lishi Daiochazu (Guizhou-Hunan Minorities Social-Historical Investigation Group)

1958 *Guizhousheng Congjiang Xian Jiamian Xiang Miaozu diaocha ziliao* (Research materials on the Miao of Jiamian Township, Congjiang County, Guizhou Province), no. 7. Beijing: Zhungguo Renmin Daibiao Dahui Minzu Weiyuanhui. Now available in a new edition: Guizhousheng Bianjizu (Guizhou Editorial Board), *Miaozu shehui lishi diaocha* (Guiyang: Guizhou Minzu Chubanshe, 1987), vol. 2, 1– 144. Pagination may vary from original source.

Guojia Minwei (Central Nationalities Commission)

1984 *Zhongguo shaoshu minzu* (Minority nationalities of China). Beijing: Renmin Chubanshe.

Guy, R. Kent

1987 *The Emperor's Four Treasuries*. Cambridge, Mass.: Council on East Asian Studies, Harvard University.

Halkovic, Stephen A., Jr.

1985 *The Mongols of the West*. Uralic Altaic Series, vol. 148. Bloomington: Indiana University.

Hall, H. Fielding

1913 *A People at School*. London: Macmillan.

Han, Jinchun

1987 "Shi lun wo guo Xinhai Geming qian zai minzu lilun wenti shang de yixe sixiang guandian" (On some of the concepts in Minzu theory before the 1911 revolution). *Minzu yanjiu* (Nationalities reasearch [Beijing]) 6.

Hanks, Lucian M.

1983 "The Yuan or Northern Thai." In John McKinnon and Wanat Bhruksasri, eds., *Highlanders of Thailand*, 101–111. Oxford: Oxford University Press.

Harrell, Stevan

1989 "Ethnicity and Kin Terms among Two Kinds of Yi." In Chien Chiao and Nicholas Tapp, eds., *Ethnicity and Ethnic Groups in China*, 179–97. Hong Kong: New Asia College.

1990 "Ethnicity, Local Interests, and the State: Yi Communities in Southwest China." *Comparative Studies in Society and History* 32 (3): 515–48.

1993a "Linguistics and Hegemony in China." *International Journal of the Sociology of Language* 103: 97–114.

1993b "The Nationalities Question and the Prmi Prblem." Paper presented to the Colloquium on Comparative Studies in Ethnicity and Nationality, University of Washington, May.

Haudricourt, A.-G.

1958 "De Consonnes uvulaires en Tibéto-Birman." *Bulletin de la Societé Linquistique de Paris* 53 (1): 257–67.

He Guojian

1982 "Luetan Miaozu xingchengde jige wenti" (A discussion of some questions about the formation of the Miao). *Guizhou minzu yanjiu* 2: 47–51.

He Jiren

1989 "Yunnan Mengguzu yuyan jiqi xishu wenti" (The language of the Yunnan Mongols and the question of its classification). In *Minzu yuwen* (Nationalities languages). Beijing: Zhongguo Shehui Kexue Chubanshe.

——— and Jiang Zhuyi, eds.

1985 *Naxiyu jianzhi* (Concise account of the Naxi language). Kunming: Yunnan Minzu Chubanshe.

He Xuewen

1991 "Yongning Mosuo ren de hunyin, jiating xisu" (Marriage and family customs among the Yongning Mosuo people). In Ma Jidian, ed., *Ninglang wenshi ziliao xuanji* (Collected literary and historical materials of Ninglang [County]), vol. 1, 255–64. Ninglang, Yunnan: Ninglang Xian Zhengxie.

Heberer, Thomas

1984 *Nationalitätenpolitik und Entwicklungspolitik in den Gebieten nationaler Minderheiten in China* (Ethnic Politics and Development Politics in National Minority Areas of China). Bremen: Universität Bremen.

1989 *China and Its National Minorities: Autonomy or Assimilation?* (partial translation of Heberer 1984). Armonk, N.Y.: M. E. Sharpe.

Hinton, Peter

1979 "The Karen, Millennialism, and the Politics of Accommodation to Lowland States." In Charles F. Keyes, ed., *Ethnic Adaptation and Identity: The Karen on the Thai Frontier with Burma*, 81–98. Philadelphia: Institute for the Study of Human Issues.

1983 "Do the Karen Really Exist?" In John McKinnon and Wanat Bhruksasri, eds., *Highlanders of Thailand*, 155–68. Oxford: Oxford University Press.

Hobsbawm, Eric, and Terence Ranger, eds.

1983 *The Invention of Tradition*. Cambridge: Cambridge University Press.

Hosie, Alexander

1904 *Manchuria: Its People, Resources, and Recent History*. New York: Charles Scribner's Sons.

Hsiao, Kung-chuan

1960 *Rural China: Imperial Control in the Nineteenth Century.* Seattle and London: University of Washington Press.

Hsieh, Jiann

1984 *China's Policy toward the Minority Nationalities in an Anthropological Perspective.* Honolulu: East-West Center.

Hsieh Shih-chung

1982 *Luoluo zu de chubu yanjiu* (Preliminary research on the Lolo). Master's thesis, National Taiwan University.

1987 *Rentong de wuming* (Stigmatized identity). Taibei: Zili Wanbao.

1989 "A New Voice of Self-Interpretation: Han Chinese Ideology on National Territory vs. Territorial Rights of Non-Han Aboriginal People." In John R. Jacobson, ed., *The Territorial Rights of Nations and Peoples,* 144–57. Lewiston, New York: The Edwin Mellen Press.

1994 "The *Daiyan* Identity of the Wulai Atayal." In Stevan Harrell and Huang Chün-chieh, eds., *Cultural Change in Postwar Taiwan,* 184–201. Boulder: Westview Press.

Hsü, Francis L. K.

1948 *Under the Ancestors' Shadow: Kinship, Personality, and Social Mobility in Village China.* New York: Columbia University Press.

Hu Qiwang and Fan Honggui

1983 *Pan Cun Yaozu* (The Yao of Pan Village). Beijing: Minzu Chubanshe.

Huang Huikun et al.

1985 *Daizu jianshi* (A short history of the Dai nationality). Kunming: Renmin Chubanshe.

Huang Shubao and Liu Zhonghe

1987 *Ethnic Costumes from Guizhou.* Beijing: Foreign Languages Press.

Huang Shumin

1989 *The Spiral Road: Changes in a Chinese Village Through the Eyes of a Communist Party Leader.* Boulder: Westview Press.

Huang Shupin

1989 "Minzu Shibie ji qi lilun yiyi" (Ethnic identification and its theoretical significance). *Zhongguo shehui kexue* (China's social science) 1989 (1): 107–116.

Hudspeth, William H.

1922 "Work Amongst the Miao in South-West China." *Chinese Recorder* 53: 702–705.

1937 *Stone-Gateway and the Flowery Miao.* London: The Cargate Press.

Hughes, Daniel
   1985   "The Effects of Missionization on Cultural Identity in Two Soci-
          eties." In D. Whiteman, ed., *Missionaries, Anthropologists, and Cul-*
          tural Change, vol. 2: 167–82. College of William and Mary Studies
          in Third World Societies, no. 25. Williamsburg: College of William
          and Mary.

Hummel, Arthur W., ed.
   1964   (1943) *Eminent Chinese of the Ch'ing Period.* Taipei: Literature
          House.

Hunter, Jane
   1984   *The Gospel of Gentility: American Women Missionaries in Turn-of-the-*
          Century China. New Haven and London: Yale University Press.

Ilyushechkin, V. P.
   1983   "Anti-Manzhou Edge of the Taiping Peasant War." In *Manzhou*
          Rule in China. Moscow: Institute of Oriental Studies, USSR Acad-
          emy of Sciences.

Jackson, Anthony
   1973   "Tibetan Bon Rites in China: A Case of Cultural Diffusion." *Ethnos*
          38: 71–92.

   1975   "The Descent of Man, Incest, and the Naming of Sons: Manifest
          and Latent Meanings in a Na-khi Text." In Roy Willis, ed., *The*
          Interpretation of Symbolism, 23–42. London: Malaby Press.

   1979   *Na-khi Religion: An Analytical Appraisal of the Na-khi Ritual Texts.*
          The Hague: Mouton.

Jagchid, Sechen
   1961   "Chengjisi Han Da Ji Ri de lishi yiyi" (The historical significance of
          the Great Offering Day of Chinggis Khan). *Zhongyang ribao* (Cen-
          tral daily news [Taipei]), May 5.

   1986   "Mongolian-Manchu Intermarriage in the Ch'ing Period." *Zentral-*
          asiatische Studien 18: 68–97.

   1988   *Essays in Mongolian Studies.* Provo: David M. Kennedy Center for
          International Studies, Brigham Young University.

———, and Paul Hyer
   1979   *Mongolian Society and Culture.* Boulder: Westview Press.

Jankowiak, William R.
   1988   "The Last Hurrah? Political Protest In Inner Mongolia." *Australian*
          Journal of Chinese Affairs 19/20: 269–88.

Jenks, Robert Darrah
   1985   "The Miao Rebellion, 1854–1872: Insurgency and Social Disorder in
          Kweichow During the Taiping Era." Ph.D. diss., Harvard University.

Ji, Ping
  1986   "Recent Migration to Inner Mongolia." Master's thesis, Brown
          University.
Jiang Yingliang
  1948a   *Xinan bianjiang minzu luncong* (A discussion of the minorities of
          the southwestern frontier). Guangzhou.
  1948b   "Liangshan Yizu de nuli zhidu" (The slave system of the Liangshan
          Yi). *Zhuhai xuebao* (Zhuhai journal) 1: 17–53.
  1983   *Daizu shi* (The history of the Dai). Chengdu: Sichuan Minzu
          Chubanshe.
Jiang Yongxing
  1985   "Cong Guizhou minzu shibie gongzuo tanqi" (Discussion on the
          basis of Guizhou's ethnic identification work). *Minzu yanjiu jikan*
          (Nationalities research quarterly [Guangxi]) 2: 303–316.
Johnston, R. F.
  1908   *From Peking to Mandalay: A Journey from North China to Burma
          through Tibetan Ssuch'uan and Yunnan.* London: John Murray.
Jones, F. C.
  1949   *Manchuria since 1931.* London: Royal Institute for International
          Affairs.
Kandre, Peter
  1967   "Autonomy and Integration of Social Systems: The Iu Mien ('Yao'
          or 'Man') Mountain Population and Their Neighbors." In Peter
          Kunstadter, ed., *Southeast Asian Tribes, Minorities, and Nations,* 583–
          631. Princeton: Princeton University Press.
  1976   "Yao (Iu Mien) Supernaturalism, Language and Ethnicity." In Da-
          vid J. Banks, ed., *Changing Identities in Modern Southeast Asia,* 171–
          97. The Hague: Mouton.
———, and Lej Tsan Kuej
  1965   "Aspects of Wealth Accumulation, Ancestor Worship Household
          Stability among the Iu-Mien-Yao." In *Felicitation Volumes of South-
          east Asian Studies Presented to His Highness Prince Dhaninivat
          Kromamun Bidyalabh Bridhyakorn,* vol. 1, 129–48. Bangkok: Siam
          Society.
Kendall, R. Elliott
  1954   *Eyes of the Earth: The Diary of Samuel Pollard.* London: Cargate
          Press.
Kertzer, David
  1988   *Ritual, Politics and Power.* New Haven and London: Yale University
          Press.

Kessler, Lawrence D.
1969   "Ethnic Composition of Provincial Leadership During the Ch'ing Dynasty." *Journal of Asian Studies* 28 (3): 489–511.

Keyes, Charles F.
1976   "Toward a New Formulation of the Concept of Ethnic Group." *Ethnicity* 3: 203–213.

1977a *The Golden Peninsula: Culture and Adaptation in Mainland Southeast Asia.* New York: Macmillan

1977b "Millennialism, Theravada Buddhism, and Thai Society." *Journal of Asian Studies* 36 (2): 283–302.

1979   "Introduction." In Charles F. Keyes, ed., *Ethnic Adaptation and Identity: The Karen on the Thai Frontier with Burma,* 1–23. Philadelphia: Institute for the Study of Human Issues.

1981   "The Dialectics of Ethnic Change." In Charles F. Keyes, ed., *Ethnic Change,* 4–30. Seattle and London: University of Washington Press.

1991   "The Proposed World of the School: Thai Villagers' Entry into a Bureaucratic State System." In Charles F. Keyes, ed., *Reshaping Local Worlds: Formal Education and Cultural Change in Rural Southeast Asia,* 89–130. New Haven: Yale University Southeast Asian Studies.

Khan, Almas (Almaz)
1988   "Autobiography of a Mongol Farmer." Unpublished manuscript based on an interview with a Mongolian man born at the turn of the century.

1989   "Hegemonic Discourse Versus Symbolic Resistance: A Case Study of Mongol-Han Relationships in Inner Mongolia, People's Republic of China." Paper presented at the Annual Conference on Central Asian Studies at the University of California, Berkeley.

Krueger, John R.
1966   "The Mongol Bicigiin Qoriya." In Walther Heissig, ed., *Collectanea Mongolica,* 109–116. Wiesbaden: Otto Harrassowits.

Kuhn, Philip A.
1980   (1970) *Rebellion and Its Enemies in Late Imperial China: Militarization and Social Structure 1796–1864.* Cambridge, Mass.: Harvard University Press.

Kunstadter, Peter
1979   "Ethnic Group, Category, and Identity: Karen in Northern Thailand." In Charles F. Keyes, ed., *Ethnic Adaptation and Identity,* 119–63. Philadelphia: Institute for the Study of Human Issues.

Kwong, Julia, ed.
1989   "Education of Minorities." *Chinese Education* 22 (1): 8–14.

Lal, Barbara Ballis
1983 "Perspectives on Ethnicity: Old Wine in New Bottles." *Ethnic and Racial Studies* 6 (2): 154–73.

Lao She
1987 *Zhenghong Qi xia* (Under the Red Banner). Beijing: Renmin Wenxue Chubanshe.

LAT (*Los Angeles Times*)
1987 "Genghis Khan Not So Bad, China Feels." March 28.
1990a "Changing Mongolia Rediscovers Its Soul." March 28.
1990b "Mongolia Reform Group Marches to Rock Anthem." January 24.

Latourette, Kenneth S.
1929 *A History of Christian Missions in China*. London: Society for Promoting Christian Knowledge.

Latsch, Marie-Luise
1984 *Chinese Traditional Festivals*. Beijing: New World Press.

Lattimore, Owen
1934 *The Mongols of Manchuria*. New York: John Day Company.
1935 *Manchuria, Cradle of Conflict*. New York: Macmillan.
1955 *Nationalism and Revolution in Mongolia*. New York: Oxford University Press.

Leach, E. R.
1954 *Political Systems of Highland Burma*. London: Athlone Press.

Le Bar, F. M., G. C. Hickey, and J. K. Musgrave
1964 *Ethnic Groups of Mainland Southeast Asia*. New Haven: HRAF Press.

Lee, James, and Robert Y. Eng
1984 "Population and Family History in 18th Century Manchuria: Preliminary Results from Daoyi, 1774–1798." *Ch'ing shih wen-t'i* 1: 1–55.

Lee, Robert H. G.
1970 *The Manchurian Frontier in Ch'ing History*. Cambridge, Mass.: Harvard University Press.

Legendre, A.-F.
1906 *Le Far-West Chinois: Deux années au setchouen* (The Chinese Far-West: Two years in Sichuan). Paris: Plon-Nourrit et Cie.
1913 *Au Yunnan et dans le massif du Kin-ho (Fleuve D'or)* (In Yunnan and on the highlands of the Kin-ho [Yalong River]). Paris: Plon-Nourrit et Cie.

Lemoine, Jacques
1982 *Yao Ceremonial Paintings*. Bangkok: White Lotus Co.

Levenson, Joseph R.

1965 *Confucian China and Its Modern Fate: A Trilogy.* Berkeley and Los Angeles: University of California Press.

Levine, N. E.

1988 *The Dynamics of Polyandry: Kinship, Domesticity, and Population on the Tibetan Border.* Chicago: University of Chicago Press.

Lévi-Strauss, Claude

1967 (1949) *The Elementary Structures of Kinship.* Translated by J. H. Bell, J. R. von Sturmer, and R. Needham. Boston: Beacon Press.

Li An-che

1947 "Dege: A Study of Tibetan Population." *Southwestern Journal of Anthropology* 3 (4): 279–93.

Li Chi

1932 *Manchuria in History.* Peiping: Peking Union Bookstore.

Li Foyi

1984 *Shi'er banna jinian* (A chronology of the twelve *banna*). Taipei: Li Foyi.

Li Jinghan

1942 "Baiyi de Bai" (On "Bai" of the Baiyi). *Bianzheng gonglun* (Border administration bulletin) 1 (7 and 8): 51–63.

Li Jingping

1982 "Qing chu minzu zhengce chu tan" (Preliminary studies of the minzu policies of the early Qing). In BMGSL Writing Group eds., *Beifang minzu guanxi shi lucong* (Collected papers on the history of relationships among the northern *minzu*s), vol 1. Hohhot: Nei Menggu Renmin Chubanshe.

Li Lin-ts'an

1984 *Mosuo yanjiu lunwen ji* (Collected essays on [Naxi] research). Taipei: Gugong Bowuyuan.

Li Shaoming

1986 *Minzuxue* (Ethnology). Chengdu: Sichuan Renmin Chubanshe.

Lian, Kwen Fee

1982 "Identity in Minority Group Relations." *Ethnic and Racial Studies* 5 (1): 42–52.

Lietard, Alfred

1904 "Le District des Lolos A-chi." *Les Missions Catholiques* 1811: 93–96; 1812: 105–108; 1813: 117–20.

1913 *Au Yun-nan: Les Lo-lo p'o.* Münster: Aschendorffsche Verlagsbuchhandlung.

Lin Yaohua (Lin Yueh-hwa)

1940–41 "The Miao-Man Peoples of Kweichow." *Harvard Journal of Asiatic Studies* 5: 261–325.

1961 (1947) *The Lolo of Liang Shan.* Translated by Ju-shu Pan, from *Liangshan Yijia.* New Haven: HRAF Press.

1987 "Zhongguo xinan diqu de minzu shibie" (Ethnic identification in the southwestern region of China). In *Yunnan shaoshu minzu shehui lishi diaocha ziliao huibian* (Collection of materials from historical and sociological investigations of minority nationalities in Yunnan). Kunming: Yunnan Renmin Chubanshe.

Ling Chunsheng and Rui Yifu (Ruey Yi-fu)

1947 *Xiangxi Miaozu diaocha baogao* (Report on an investigation of the Miao in western Hunan). Shanghai: Human Relations Area Files.

Lipman, Jonathan N.

1990 "Ethnic Violence: Hans and Huis on the Northwestern Frontier." In Jonathan N. Lipman and Stevan Harrell, eds., *Violence in China: Essays in Culture and Counter-Culture,* 65–86. Albany: State University of New York Press.

Liu Chia-chu

1981 "The Creation of the Chinese Banners in the Early Ch'ing." *Chinese Studies in History* 14 (4): 47–75.

Liu Jingping, and Zheng Guangzhi, eds.

1979 *Nei Menggu Zizhiqu jingji fazhan gailun* (A general study of economic development in the Inner Mongolian autonomous region). Hohhot: Nei Menggu Renmin Chubanshe.

Liu Shengqi

1988 "Yici guanyu Xizang wenti de tanhua" (A discussion of the Tibet question). *Minzu yanjiu* (Nationalities research) 1: 11–15.

Long Yuanwei

1987 "Minzu diqu nongcun shangpin jingji fazhan zhong de feijingji zhang'ai wenti" (The question of noneconomic obstacles in the development of the commodity economy in villages in minority areas). *Minzu yanjiu* (Nationalities research) 5: 17–22.

Lu Minghui

1982 "Qingdai Menggu diqu yu zhongyuan diqu de jingji maoyi guanxi" (The economic and trade relations between Mongolian areas and central China during the Qing dynasty). In BMGSL Writing Group, eds., *Beifang Minzu guanxi shi luncong* (Collected papers on the history of relationships among the northern *minzu*s). Hohhot: Mei Menggu Renmin Chubanshe.

1988   "Jindai Menggu shehui jingji bianhua de jige wenti" (Some questions about economic changes in modern Mongolian society). *Minzu yanjiu* 1: 87–93.

——— et al.

1981   *Mengguzu lishi renwu lunji* (Collected papers on Mongolian historical figures). Beijing: Zhongguo Shehui Kexue Chubanshe.

Lu Shiqiang

1966   "Zhongguo guanshen fanjiao de yuanyin, 1806–1974" (The origin of anti-Christian [activity] by Chinese officials and gentry, 1806–1874). Taipei: Institute of Modern History, Academia Sinica.

Lu Simian

1933   *Zhongguo minzu shi* (History of the peoples of China). Shanghai: Shijie Shuju.

Lue shi

1947   *Lue shi* (The history of the state of Lue). Translated from the Dai by Li Foyi. Kunming: Yunnan Daxue Chubanshe.

Lunan Yizu (The Yi Nationality of Lunan)

1986   *Lunan Yizu Zizhixian gaikuang* (General account of Lunan Yi Autonomous County). Kunming: Yunnan Minzu Chubanshe.

Luo, Biyun

1990   "Mongolia: Democratic Reforms Through Positive Interaction." *China Spring,* October.

Ma Changshou

1930   "Sichuan gudai [Lao] zu wenti" (The question of the Lao people in ancient Sichuan), *Qingnian zhongguo jikan* (Young China quarterly) 2 (1).

1985   *Yizu gudai shi* (The ancient history of the Yi). Edited by Li Shaoming. Shanghai: Shanghai Renmin Chubanshe.

Ma Hetian

1932   *Nei Wai Menggu kaocha riji* (Diaries of study tours in Inner and Outer Mongolia). Nanjing: Xin Yaxiya Xuehui.

Ma Huiqing, ed.

1988   *Minzu zhishi shouce* (A handbook of knowledge about *minzu*). Beijing: Minzu Chubanshe.

Ma Shaoqiao

1956   *Qingdai Miaomin qiyi* (Miao insurrections in the Qing period). Wuhan: Hubei Renmin Chubanshe.

REFERENCES

Ma Xueliang

1951 *Sani Yiyu Yanjiu* (Research on the Sani Yi language). *Yuyanxue zhuankan* (Special publications in linguistics), no. 2. Beijing: Zhongguo Kexue Yuan.

Ma Yin, ed.

1981 *Zhongguo shaoshu minzu* (The minority nationalities of China). Beijing: Renmin Chubanshe.

1984 *Zhongguo shaoshu minzu changshi* (General knowledge about Chinese minority nationalities). Beijing: Zhongguo Qingnian Chubanshe.

1989 *China's Minority Nationalities.* Beijing: Foreign Languages Press.

McBeth, Sally J.

1983 *Ethnic Identity and the Boarding School Experience of West-Central Oklahoma American Indians.* Washington, D.C.: University Press of America.

McKay, James, and Frank Lewins

1978 "Ethnicity and the Ethnic Group: A Conceptual Analysis and Reformulation." *Ethnic and Racial Studies* 1 (4): 412–27.

McKhann, Charles F.

1988 "Naxi-Han History and the Transformation of the 'Meebiuq' (Sacrifice to Heaven) Ritual." Paper presented at the annual meeting of the American Anthropological Association, November, Phoenix.

1989 "Fleshing Out the Bones: The Cosmic and Social Dimensions of Space in Naxi Architecture." In Chien Chiao and Nicholas Tapp, eds., *Ethnicity and Ethnic Groups in China,* 157–77. Hong Kong: New Asia College.

1992 "Fleshing Out the Bones: Kinship and Cosmology in Naxi Religion." Ph.D. diss., University of Chicago.

McLellan, David, ed.

1977 *Karl Marx: Selected Writings.* Oxford: Oxford University Press.

Man shu (Book of the southern barbarians)

1961 Translated by H. Luce and edited by G. P. Oey. Southeast Asia Program, Cornell University, Data Paper 44. Ithaca: Southeast Asia Program, Cornell University.

Mao Zedong

1949 "*Xibei shaoshu minzu diqu shiwu de jianghua*" (An address on the affairs in northwestern minority areas). In Wu Shalu, ed., *Minzu zhengce wenxuan* (Selected documents on national minority policies), 87. Urumchi: Xinjiang Renmin Chubanshe.

1976 *Poems.* Beijing: Foreign Languages Press.

Meng Xianfan

1989 "State of the Field: A Survey of the Development of Ethnology in China in the Past Decade." *Social Sciences in China* 10 (2): 206–223.

Michael, Franz

1974 "Original Manchu Rule in China." *Journal of Asian Studies* 34 (2): 443–53.

Mickey, Margaret Portia

1947 *The Cowrie Shell Miao of Kweichow.* Papers of the Peabody Museum of American Archaeology and Ethnology, Harvard University, vol. 32, no. 1. Cambridge, Mass.: Peabody Museum of American Archaeology and Ethnology, Harvard University.

Minzu Gongzuo Editorial Board

1985 *Minzu gongzuo shouce* (Handbook for minority work). Kunming: Yunnan Minzu Chubanshe.

Minzu tuanjie (Nationalities unity)

1986 "Quanguo ge minzu renkou tongji biao" (Tabulated population statistics of the *minzu*s of the whole country). *Minzu tuanjie* (Nationalities unity) 6: 39.

Minzu yanjiu (Nationalities research)

1986 "Minzu lilun zhuanti xueshu taolunhui fayin zaiyao" (Abstracts from a conference on minority nationality theory). *Minzu yanjiu* 4: 2–18; 5: 1–24; 6:1–17.

MJS (*Mengguzu jian shi*) Writing Group

1985 *Mengguzu jian shi* (A concise history of the Mongolian *minzu*). Hohhot: Nei Menggu Renmin Chubanshe.

Moerman, Michael

1965 "Ethnic Identification in a Complex Civilization: Who Are the Lue?" *American Anthropologist* 67 (5), part 1: 1215–30.

1967 "A Minority and Its Government: The Thai-Lue of Northern Thailand." In Peter Kunstadter, ed., *Southeast Asian Tribes, Minorities, and Nations,* 401–24. Princeton: Princeton University Press.

1968 "Being Lue: Uses and Abuses of Ethnic Identification." In June Helm, ed., *Essays on the Problem of Tribe,* 153–69. Seattle: University of Washington Press.

Morgan, Lewis Henry

1985 (1877) *Ancient Society.* Tuscon: University of Arizona Press.

Morrison, George E.

1895 *An Australian in China.* London: Horace Cox.

Moseley, George
  1973   *The Consolidation of the South China Frontier.* Berkeley and Los
         Angeles: University of California Press.
Moses, Larry William
  1977   *The Political Role of Mongol Buddhism.* Indiana University Uralic
         Altaic Series, vol. 133. Bloomington: Indiana University.
Mueller, Herbert
  1913   "Beiträge zur Ethnographie der Lolo." *Bässler Archiv für Ethno-
         graphie* 3: 39–69.
Mungello, D. E.
  1985   *Curious Land: Jesuit Accommodation and the Origins of Sinology.* Ho-
         nolulu: University of Hawaii Press.
MZWYH (Meng-Zang Weiyuanhui [Mongolian-Tibetan Committee])
  1962   *Bianjiang zhengzhi* (Frontier politics). Taipei: Meng-Zang
         Weiyuanhui.
Nagata, Judith
  1974   "What Is Malay?" *American Ethnologist* 1(2): 331–50.
  1981   "In Defense of Ethnic Boundaries: The Changing Myths and Char-
         ters of Malay Identity." In Charles F. Keyes, ed., *Ethnic Change,* 87–
         116. Seattle and London: University of Washington Press.
Nakamura, Mitsuo
  1969   "Political Systems of Sip-Song-Panna: An Attempt at an Ethno-
         historical Exploration into a Lue Kingdom in Yunnan, China."
         Paper presented at the annual meeting of the American Society for
         Ethnohistory, Cornell University.
Nash, Manning
  1989   *The Cauldron of Ethnicity in the Modern World.* Chicago and Lon-
         don: University of Chicago Press.
Nassen-Bayer and Kevin Stuart
  1989   "I Am Anguished to Have Been a Mongol: Lubsangchuiden, Re-
         corder of Mongol Customs." Unpublished manuscript.
Nisbet, R. A.
  1969   *Social Change and History: Aspects of the Western Theory of Develop-
         ment.* New York: Oxford University Press.
NMDXRB (*Nei Menggu Daxue ribao* [Inner Mongolia University daily])
  1982   "Women shi caoyuan de ernu: Chengjisi Han de zisun" (We are the
         sons and daughters of the steppes: Children and grandchildren of
         Chinggis Khan), c. Spring 1982.
NMJCB (Nei Menggu Jiaoyu congshu bianweihui [Editorial Committee of
Inner Mongolian education series]), comp.

1987 *Xiaoshi xuanbian: Putong zhongxue, zhiye zhongxue bufen* (Selected school histories: Regular and vocational secondary schools). Tongliao: Nei Menggu Jiaoyu Chubanshe.

NMQEP (National Minorities Questions Editorial Panel)

1985 *Questions and Answers About China's National Minorities.* Beijing: New World Press.

NMQW (Nei Menggu Qu Wei [Inner Mongolia Party Committee])

1984 *Lü Meng shang Da Shengkui* (Da Shengkui: A traveling merchant in Mongolia). Hohhot: Nei Menggu Lishi Wenhua Shuju.

NMZG (*Nei Menggu Zizhiqu Gaikuang*) Writing Group

1983 *Nei Menggu Zizhiqu Gaikuang* (Inner Mongolia Autonomous Region: A general survey). Hohhot: Nei Menggu Renmin Chubanshe.

NMZJJ (Nei Menggu Zizhiqu Jiaoyu Ju [Education Bureau of Inner Mongolian Autonomous Region]), comp.

1979a *Nei Menggu Zizhiqu minzu jiaoyu wenjiao huibian* (Selected documents on ethnic education in IMAR), vol. 1–3. Hohhot: Nei Menggu Zizhiqu Jiaoyu Ju.

NMZJT (Nei Menggu Zizhiqu Jiaoyu Ting [Education Bureau of the Inner Mongolian Autonomous Region]), comp.

1981 *Quanguo disanci minzu jiaoyu gongzuo huiyi ziliao* (Documents on the third national ethnic education conference). Hohhot: Nei Menggu Zizhiqu Jiaoyu Ting.

Number One Historical Archives of China, Center for Qing History Research at the People's University of China, and Guizhou Provincial Archives, eds.

1987 "Qingdai qianqi Miaomin qiyi dangan shiliao" (Archival material of Miao insurrections in the early Qing). Vol. 1–3. Beijing: Guangming Ribao.

NYT (*New York Times*)

1990a "A Mongolian Rock Group Fosters Democracy." March 26.

1990b "For Reawakened Mongolia, It's Genghis the Great." March 22.

1990c "Where Genghis Khan Is In." *New York Times Magazine,* May 27.

Onon, Urgunge

1976 *Mongolian Heroes of the Twentieth Century.* New York: AMS Press.

Oxnam, Robert B.

1975 *Ruling from Horseback: Manchu Politics in the Oboi Regency 1661–1669.* Chicago: University of Chicago Press.

PAC (*Population Atlas of China*)

1987 Oxford: Oxford University Press.

Peirce, Charles S.
1960 *Collected Papers.* Vols. 1–8. Charles Hartshorne and Paul Weiss, eds. New York: Columbia University Press.

Pollard, Samuel
1919 *Tight Corner in China.* London: Henry Hooks.
1921 *In Unknown China: A Record of the Observations, Adventures, and Experiences of a Pioneer Missionary During a Prolonged Sojourn Amongst the Wild and Unknown Nosu Tribe of Western China.* London: Seeley, Service, and Company.
1928 *The Story of the Miao.* London: Henry Hooks.

Prakash, Gyan
1992 "Science Gone Native in Colonial India." *Representations* 40 (Fall): 153–78.

Pratt, Richard Henry
1964 *Battlefield as Classroom: Four Decades with the American Indian, 1867–1904.* New Haven: Yale University Press.

Prunner, G.
1969 "The Kinship System of the Nakhi (SW-China) as Seen in Their Pictographic Script." *Ethnos* 34: 100–106.

QGMZX (Qian Guo'erluosi Mengguzu Zizhi Xian) Writing Group, ed.
1985 *Qian Guo'erluosi Mengguzu Zizhi Xian gaikuang* (A General survey of the Front Gorlos Mongolian Autonomous Banner). Yanbian: Yanbian Renmin Chubanshe.

Qi Qingfu
1987 "Nanzhao wangshi zushu kaobian" (Investigation and analysis of the ethnic identity of the Nanzhao royal house). In *Xinan minzu yanjiu: Yizu zhuanji* (Southwestern *minzu* research: Yi special collection), 136–51. Kunming: Yunnan Minzu Chubanshe.

Qiu Jifeng
1982 "Dianqian bianjing Miaobao jiaoyu zhi yanjiu" (Research on education among the Miao of the Yunnan-Guizhou border region). In Zhang Yongguo et al., eds., *Minguo nianjian Miaozu lunwenji* (Collected essays on the Miao in the Republican period). Guiyang: Guizhou Minzu Yanjiusuo.

Rabinow, Paul
1983 "Facts Are a Word of God." In George Stocking, ed., *Observers Observed: History of Anthropology,* vol. 1, 196–207. Madison: University of Wisconsin Press.

Rasidondug, S.

1975   *Petitions of Grievances Submitted by the People (18th–Beginning of 20th Century)*. Wiesbaden: Otto Harrassowitz.

Rea, George Bronson

1935   *The Case for Manchukuo*. New York: D. Appleton-Century Company.

Rock, Joseph F.

1947   *The Ancient Na-khi Kingdom of Southwest China*. 2 vols. Cambridge, Mass.: Harvard University Press.

1948   "The Muan Bpo Ceremony: Or the Sacrifice to Heaven as Practiced by the Na-khi." *Monumenta Serica* 13: 1–160.

1963a *A Na-khi-English Encyclopedic Dictionary, Part One*. Serie Orientale Roma, vol. 28. Rome: Instituto Italiano per il Medio ed Estremo Oriente.

1963b *The Life and Culture of the Na-khi Tribe of the China-Tibet Borderland*. Wiesbaden: Franz Steiner Verlag.

Rossi, A. S., ed.

1985   *Sociology and Anthropology in the People's Republic of China: Report of a Delegation Visit, February–March 1984*. Washington: National Academy Press.

Roth, Gertraude

1979   "The Manchu-Chinese Relationship, 1618–1636." In Jonathan D. Spence and John E. Willis, eds., *From Ming to Ch'ing*, 1–38. New Haven: Yale University Press.

Ruey, Yi-fu

1972   *China: The Nation and Some Aspects of Its Cultures: A Collection of Selected Essays with Anthropological Approaches* (bilingual volume). Taipei: Yee Wen.

1972   (1951) "Nan Zhao shi" (The history of Nan Zhao). In Ruey 1972, 331–52.

1973a *Eighty-two Aboriginal Peoples of Kweichow Province in Pictures*. (Texts and notes of the *Miao luan tu ce* [Collected pictures of the Miao]). Taipei: Academia Sinica.

1973b *Sixteen Aboriginal Peoples of Kweichow Province in Pictures*. (Texts and notes on the *Fan Miao hua ce* [Portraits of the barbarian Miao]). Taipei: Academia Sinica.

Rupen, Robert Arthur

1963   "Mongolia in the Sino-Soviet Dispute." *China Quarterly* 16: 75–85.

1964   *Mongols of the Twentieth Century*. Bloomington: Indiana University Press.

Said, Edward
1979 *Orientalism.* New York: Vintage.

Sanders, A. J. K.
1968 *The People's Republic of Mongolia.* London and New York: Oxford University Press.

Sandjorj, M.
1980 *Manchu Chinese Colonial Rule in Northern Mongolia.* New York: St. Martin's Press.

Sang Xiuyun
1979 "Luoluo wei Dizu shizheng" (An attempt to show that the Lolo are the Di). *Dalu zazhi* (Mainland magazine) 59 (4): 4–16.

Sangren, P. Steven
1988 "History and the Rhetoric of Legitimacy: The Ma Tsu Cult in Taiwan." *Comparative Studies in Society and History* 30 (4): 674–97.

Saunders, J. J.
1970 "Genghis Khan and the Communists." *History Today* 20 (6): 390–96.
1971 *The History of the Mongol Conquest.* New York: Barnes and Noble.

Schafer, Edward H.
1967 *The Vermilion Bird: T'ang Images of the South.* Berkeley and Los Angeles: University of California Press.

Schein, Louisa
1989 "The Dynamics of Cultural Revival among the Miao in Guizhou." In Chien Chiao and Nicholas Tapp, eds., *Ethnicity and Ethnic Groups in China,* 199–212. Hong Kong: New Asia College.

Schmidt, Wilhelm
1939 *The Cultural Historical Method of Ethnology: The Scientific Approach.* New York: Fortuny's.

Schwartz, Benjamin
1954 "A Marxist Controversy in China." *Far Eastern Quarterly* 13: 143–53.
1959 "Some Polarities in Confucian Thought." In David S. Nivison and Arthur Wright, eds., *Confucianism in Action,* 50–63. Stanford: Stanford University Press.

Schwarz, Henry G.
1979 "Ethnic Minorities and Ethnic Policies in China." In William Petersen, ed., *The Background to Ethnic Conflict,* 137–50. Leiden: E. J. Brill.
1984 "Some Notes on the Mongols of Yunnan." *Central Asiatic Journal* 28 (1–2): 101–118.

The Secret History of the Mongols
1982 (13th cent.) Translated by F. W. Cleaves. Cambridge, Mass.: Harvard University Press.

Sekaquaptewa, Helen, and Louise Udall
1969 *Me and Mine: The Life Story of Helen Sekaquaptewa.* Tuscon: University of Arizona Press.

Shanin, Teodor
1989 "Ethnicity in the Soviet Union: Analytical Perceptions and Political Strategies." *Comparative Studies in Society and History* 31 (3): 409–424.

She I-tse
1947 *Zhongguo tusi zhidu* (China's *tusi* system). Shanghai.

Shepherd, John R.
1988 "Plains Aborigines and Missionaries in South Taiwan." Unpublished paper.

Shepperson, George
1962 "The Comparative Study of Millenarian Movements." In Sylvia L. Thrupp, ed., *Millennial Dreams in Action: Essays in Comparative Study,* 44–52. The Hague: Mouton.

Shi Qigui
1986 *Xiangxi Miaozu shidi diaocha baogao* (Report of field research on the Miao in western Hunan). Changsha: Hunan Renmin Chubanshe.

Shih, Chuan-kang
1985 "A Challenge to the Concept of Universal Male Authority: The Moso Case and Comparative Studies." Ph.D. qualifying paper, Stanford University.

1993 "The Moso: Sexual Union, Household Organization, Ethnicity and Gender in a Matrilineal Duolocal Society in Southwest China." Ph.D. diss., Stanford University.

Shirokogoroff, S. M.
1924 *Social Organization of the Manchus.* Shanghai: Royal Asiatic Society.

Siguret, J.
1937 *Territoires et populations de donfin du Yunnan.* Beiping: Editions Henry Vetch.

Smith, Arthur H.
1970 (1899) *Village Life in China.* New York: Little, Brown.

Song Enchang
1986 "Xishuangbanna Daizu fengjian tudi zhidu" (The feudal land system of the Dai of Xishuangbanna). In *Yunnan shaoshu minzu yanjiu wenti* (Research questions on minorities of Yunnan), 273–81. Kunming: Yunnan Renmin Chubanshe.

Spencer, Herbert
1860 "The Social Organism." *Westminster Review* 17: 90–121.

Spicer, Edward H.
1971 "Persistent Cultural Systems: A Comparative Study of Identity Systems That Can Adapt to Contrasting Environments." *Science* 174: 795–800.
1988 *People of Pascua.* Tuscon: University of Arizona Press.
SR (*Shijie Ribao* [World Daily News]).
1990 "Chongxin kending Chengjisi Han" (Rehabilitating Chinggis Khan). April 7.
Stalin, Joseph
1935 (1913) *Marxism and the National and Colonial Question.* Moscow: Cooperative Publishing Society of Foreign Workers in the USSR.
1950 *The National Question and Leninism.* Moscow: Foreign Languages Publishing House.
Swain, Margaret Byrne
1989 "Developing Ethnic Tourism in Yunnan, China: Shilin Sani." *Tourism Recreation Research* 14 (1): 33–39.
1990a "Commoditizing Ethnicity in Southwest China." *Cultural Survival* 14 (1): 26–32.
1991 "Being Ashima: Living a Commoditized Legend of Resistance." Paper presented at the American Ethnological Association's Invited Session "Defining Women," annual meeting of the American Anthropological Association, Chicago.
forthcoming "Chez L'Indigene la Mere Porte Vraiment le Sceptre de L'Education: A Missionary Response to Sani Gender Construction and Social Reproduction." In Laurel Bossen, ed., *New Perspectives on Ethnicity in Southwest China.*
Tanabe, Shigeharu
1988 "Spirits and Ideological Discourse: The Tai Lu Guardian Cults in Yunnan." *SOJOURN* 3 (1): 1–25.
Tao Jing-shen
1970 "The Influence of Jurchen Rule on Chinese Political Institutions." *Journal of Asian Studies* 30 (1): 121–30.
1977 *The Jurchen in Twelfth-Century China: A Study of Sinicization.* Seattle: University of Washington Press.
Tapp, Nicholas
1989 "The Impact of Missionary Christianity upon Marginalized Ethnic Minorities: The Case of the Hmong." *Journal of Southeast Asian Studies* 20 (1): 70–95.

Togan, Isenbike
1990   "The Impact of the Mongolian Empire on Inner Asia: The Case of 'Monghulistan.' " Paper presented at the China Colloquium, Jackson School of International Studies, University of Washington, May 30.

Tong Enzheng
1988   "Moergen de moshi yu Makesi zhuyi" (Morgan's model and Marxism). *Shehui kexue yanjiu* (Social science research) 12 (2): 177–96.
1989   "Morgan's model and the study of ancient Chinese society." (Translation of Tong 1988). *Social Sciences in China* 10 (2): 182–205.

Torrence, Thomas
1920   *The History, Customs, and Religion of the Ch'iang*. Shanghai.

Trevor-Roper, Hugh
1983   "The Invention of Tradition: The Highland Tradition of Scotland." In Eric Hobsbawm and Terence Ranger, eds., *The Invention of Tradition*, 15–42. Cambridge: Cambridge University Press.

Tsai, Sheng-luen
1983   "Chinese Settlement of Mongolian Lands: Manchu Policy in Inner Mongolia/A Case Study of Chinese Migration in Jerim League." Ph.D. diss., Brigham Young University.

Tylor, Edward B.
1871   *Primitive Culture*. London: J. Murray

Ulanfu
1979   "Cong shaoshu minzu diqu de shiji chufa zhengque zhixing dang de luxian he zhengce" (Implementing the party's policies in response to realistic situations in minority areas). In Wu Shalu, ed., *Minzu zhengce wenxuan* (Selected documents on nationalities policy), 329–42. Urumchi: Xinjiang Renmin Chubanshe, 1985.

Underdown, Michael
1980   "Banditry and Revolutionary Movements in Late 19th Century and Early 20th Century Mongolia." *Mongolian Studies* 6: 109–116.
1989   "De Wang's Independent Mongolian Republic." *Papers on Far Eastern History* (Canberra) 40: 121–32.

University of Washington, Far Eastern and Russian Institute
1956   *A Regional Handbook of Northeast China*. New Haven: Human Relations Area Files.

Vial, Paul
1888   "Yun-nan (Chine), un tournoi chez les sauvages Lolos" (Yunnan, China: A tournament among the wild Lolos). *Les Missions Catholiques* 20 (1007): 445–48.

1890 *De la lanque et de l'écriture indigènes au Yû-nân* (On native language and writing in Yunnan). Paris: Ernest Leroux.

1893 "Les Gni ou Gni-p'a: Tribu Lolotte du Yun-nan" (The Gni or Gni-p'a: A Lolo tribe of Yunnan). *Les Missions Catholiques* 25 (1244): 160–61; (1245): 178–80; (1246): 189–90; (1247): 200–202; (1248): 208–209; (1249): 222–25; (1250): 236–38; (1251): 244–46; (1252): 258–260; (1253): 268–70; (1254): 281–83; (1255): 293–94; (1256): 308–10.

1894 "Les Gni ou Gni-p'a: Tribu Lolotte du Yun-nan," part 2. *Les Missions Catholiques* 26 (1307): 300–302; (1308): 308–310.

1898 *Les Lolos—Histoire, religion, moeurs, langue, écriture* (The Lolos: History, religion, customs, language, writing). *Études Sino-Orientales* (Sino-Oriental Studies), part A. Shanghai: Imprimerie de la Mission Catholique.

1900 "Deux mois chez les Miaotse" (Two months among the Miao). *Les Missions Catholiques* 32 (1632): 434–35; (1633): 443, 447–49; (1634): 455, 464–66; (1635): 472–75; (1636): 485–86; (1639): 524–25; (1640): 529, 533–36; (1643): 571–73; (1645): 594–96.

1902 "Les Joies du retour" (The joys of return). *Les Missions Catholiques* 34 (1707): 85, 89–90; (1708): 105–106; (1709): 111–15; (1710): 121; (1711): 139–42; (1712): 147–49; (1713): 159–61; (1714): 169, 173–77.

1909 *Dictionnaire Français-Lolo, dialecte Gni: Tribu située dans les sous-prefectures de Lou Nan Tcheou, Lou Lean Tcheou, Gouang-si Tcheou, Province du Yunnan* (French-Lolo dictionary, Gni dialect: A tribe situated in the subprefectures of Lunan Zhou, Luliang Zhou, Guangxi Zhou, Yunnan Province). Hong Kong: Imprimerie de la Société des Missions Étrangères.

1917 "A travers la Chine inconnue: Chez les Lolos" (Traveling across unknown China: Among the Lolos). *Les Missions Catholiques* 49 (2527): 537–38; (2528): 254–57.

Wakeman, Frederic, Jr.

1979 "The Shun Interregnum of 1644." In Jonathan D. Spence and John E. Willis, eds., *From Ming to Ch'ing,* 41–87. New Haven: Yale University Press.

1985 *The Great Enterprise.* Berkeley: University of California Press.

Wallerstein, Immanuel

1974 *The Modern World System.* New York: Academic Press.

Wang Daoming and Li Chaoyang

1986 "Jidujiao chuanru Weining, Hezhang Yimiaozu diqu de jingguo" (The process of the spread of Christianity into the Weining and Hezhang Yi and Miao areas). *Guizhou wenshi ziliao xuan-ji* (Selected literary and historical materials on Guizhou) 22: 206–224.

Wang Fushi

1985 *Miaoyu jianzhi* (Concise account of the Miao language). Beijing: Renmin Chubanshe.

Wang Jianming

1982 "Xianzai Xinan Miaozu zuigao wenhua qu: Shimenkan de jieshao" (The area of highest cultural development among Miao in the contemporary Southwest: An introduction to Shimenkan." In Zhang Yongguo et al., eds., *Minguo nianjian Miaozu lunwenji* (Collected essays on the Miao in the Republican period). Guiyang: Guizhou Minzu Yanjiusuo

Wang Jun

1982 "Shi lun Xishuangbanna Meng Nai zhengquan (On the regime of Meeng Nai in Sipsong Panna). Paper submitted to the Second Conference of Chinese Ethnology, June 1982, Kunming, Yunnan.

Wang Tingdong, ed.

1985 *Menguzu jianshi* (A concise history of the Mongolian nationality). Hohhot: Nei Menggu Renmin Chubanshe.

Watson, James

1991 "The Renegotiation of Chinese Cultural Identity in the Post-Mao Era." In Jeffrey N. Wasserstrom and Elizabeth J. Perry, eds., *Popular Protest and Political Culture in Modern China,* 67–84. Boulder: Westview Press.

Wei Huilin

1947 "Lun jianshe Liangshan Yiqu zhi zhongyaoxing" (Discussion of the importance of construction in the Liangshan Yi Area"). *Bianjiang tongxun* (Border bulletin) 4 (8–9): 1–3.

Wei Yuan

1842 *Sheng wu ji* (A record of imperial military activities). In *Jindai Zhongguo shiliao congkan* (Collections of historical materials of contemporary China). *Taipei: Taibei Wenhua Chubanshe.*

Weller, Robert P.

1987 "Historians and Consciousness: The Modern Politics of the Taiping Heavenly Kingdom." *Social Research* 54 (4): 731–75.

Wiens, Herold J.

1967 (1954) *Han Chinese Expansion in South China.* Hamden, Conn.: Shoe String Press.

Wiens, Mi Chu
1969   "Anti-Manchu Thought During the Early Ch'ing." *Papers on China* 22A: 1–24.
Williams, Brackette
1989   "A Class Act: Anthropology and the Race to Nation across Ethnic Terrain." *Annual Review of Anthropology* 18: 401–444.
Wong, How Man
1989   *Exploring the Yangtze, China's Longest River.* San Francisco: China Books and Periodicals.
Worsley, Peter
1968   *The Trumpet Shall Sound: A Study of Cargo Cults in Melanesia.* New York: Schocken.
Wright, Mary Clabaugh
1957   *The Last Stand of Chinese Conservatism.* Stanford: Stanford University Press.
Wu, David Y. H.
1989   "Culture Change and Ethnic Identity among Minorities in China." In Nicholas Tapp and Chien Chiao, eds., *Ethnicity and Ethnic Groups in China*, 11–22. Hong Kong: Chinese University Press.
1990   "Chinese Minority Policy and the Meaning of Minority Cultures: The Example of Bai in Yünnan, China." *Human Organization* 49 (1): 1–13.
Wu Lüe
1984   *Shan lin lian* (Love of mountains and forests). Guiyang: Guizhou Renmin Chubanshe.
Wu, Silas H. L.
1979   *Passage to Power: K'ang-hsi and His Heir Apparent.* Cambridge, Mass.: Harvard University Press.
Wynne, Waller Jr.
1958   *The Population of Manchuria.* Washington: U.S. Bureau of the Census.
Xu Cheng
1985   *Nei Menggu fengwu zhi* (Inner Mongolia: Customs and topics of general interest). Hohhot: Nei Menggu Renmin Chubanshe.
Xu Hong
1988   "Ming chu de renkou yixi zhengce" (The policy of population diaspora of the early Ming). *Hanxue yanjiu* (Sinological research) 6 (2): 179–87.
Xu Jiewu and Deng Wentong
1985   "Cong Yaozu zhixi wenti tanqi" (Discussion arising from the question of Yao subgroups). In *Yaozu yenjiu lunwenji* (Collected papers on Yao research), 49–72. Nanning: Guangxi Minzu Chubanshe.

Yan Ruxian

1982 "A Living Fossil of the Family: A Study of the Family Structure of the Naxi Nationality in the Lugu Lake Region." *Social Sciences in China* 3 (4): 60–83.

——— and Song Zhaolin

1983 *Yongning Naxizu de muxi zhi* (The matrilineal system of the Naxi of Yongning). Kunming: Yunnan Renmin Chubanshe.

Yang Hanxian

1981 "Jidujiao Xundao gonghui zai Weining Miaozu diqu chuanjiao shimo" (History of the Methodist mission in the Miao areas of Weining). *Guizhou wenshi ziliao xuanji* (Selected literary and historical materials on Guizhou) 7: 96–114.

1982 "Jidujiao zai Dian, Qian, Chuan jiaojing yidai Miaozu diqu shilue" (Outline history of Christianity in the Miao area around the borders between Yunnan, Guizhou, and Sichuan). *Minzu cankao ziliao* (Reference materials on nationalities), vol. 14: 1–34. Guiyang: Guizhou Minzu Yanjiu Suo.

Yang, Lien-sheng

1968 "Historical Notes on the Chinese World Order." In J. K. Fairbank, ed., *The Chinese World Order.* Cambridge, Mass.: Harvard University Press.

Yang, Mayfair Mei-Hui

1989 "The Gift Economy and State Power in China." *Comparative Studies in Society and History* 31 (1): 25–54.

Yang Yongsheng

1986 *Dehong Daizu Jingpozu Zizhi Zhou gaikuang* (A general introduction to the Dehong Dai and Jingpuo autonomous prefecture). Luxi, Yunnan: Minzu Chubanshe.

Yao, Esther

1989 "Is China the End of Hermeneutics? Or, Political and Cultural Usage of Non-Han Women in Mainland Chinese Films." *Discourse* 11 (2): 115–36.

Yaozu jianshi

1983 *Yaozu jianshi* (A concise history of the Yao). Nanning: Guangxi Nationality Publishing House.

Yi-Han Dictionary

1984 *Yi-Han jianming cidian* (Concise Yi[Sani]-Han dictionary). Kunming: Yunnan Minzu Chubanshe.

Yi Jing (The book of changes)

1991 Translated by Wu Lingnuan. Washington, D.C.: Taoist Center; Honolulu, Hawaii: University of Hawaii Press.

You Zhong

1985   *Zhongguo Xinan minzu shi* (History of the peoples of Southwest China). *Kunming: Yunnan Renmin Chubanshe.*

1987   "Yuan, Ming, Qing shiqi Yizu shehui de fazhan yanbian" (Change and development in Yi society during the Yuan, Ming, and Qing periods). In *Xinan minzu yanjiu, Yizu zhuanji* (Southwest nationalities research, special collection on the Yi), 186–200. Kunming: Yunnan Renmin Chubanshe.

Young, Robert

1990   *White Mythologies: Writing History and the West*. New York and London: Routledge.

Yu Dong

1986   "Saishang miaopu: Temut xuexiao" (Frontier nursery: The Temut School). *Minzu jiaoyu* (Ethnic education) 3: 49.

Zeng Chaolun

1945   *Liangshan Yiqu gaikuang* (The general situation in the Yi areas of Liangshan). In *Liangshan Yiqu diaocha ji* (Record of investigations in the Yi areas of Liangshan). Chongqing. Translated by Josette M. Yen as *The Lolo District in Liangshan* (New Haven: HRAF Press).

Zhan Chengxu

1982   "Matriarchal/Patriarchal Families of the Naxi Nationality in Yongning, Yunnan Province." *Social Sciences in China* 3 (1): 140–55.

Zhan Chengxu, Wang Chengquan, Li Jinchun, and Liu Longchu

1980   *Yongning Naxizu de azhu hunyin he muxi jiating* (The *azhu* marriage and matrilineal household among the Naxi of Yongning). Shanghai: Shanghai Renmin Chubanshe.

Zhang Gongjin

1980   "Zhengshi shiyong he fazhan shaoshu minzu de yuyan wenzi" (Paying great attention to application and development of minority languages). In *MWYMZ* editorial group, ed., *Minzu wenti yu minzu zhengce* (Ethnic issues and ethnic policies), 41–49. Chengdu: Sichuan Minzu Chubanshe.

Zhang Kaiyuan

1984   "The Slogan 'Expel the Manchus' and the Nationalist Movement in Modern Chinese History." In Eto Shinkichi and Harold Z. Schiffrin, eds., *The 1911 Revolution in China*, 33–48. Tokyo: University of Tokyo Press.

Zhang Quanchang

1984   (1980) "Shehui zhuyi shiqi de minzu guanxi" (Ethnic relationships in the period of socialism). In *Shehui zhuyi minzu guanxi wenxian lunwenji* (Collected documents on socialist ethnic relationships), 330–37. Kunming: Yunnan Minzu Chubanshe.

Zhang Tingyu

1739 *Ming shi* (The history of the Ming dynasty).

Zhang Wenchang (Père Laurent Zhang)

1987 *Deng Mingde Shenfu xiaozhuan* (A short biography of Father Deng Mingde [Paul Vial]). Kunming: Privately printed.

Zhang Yongguo et al.

1982 *Minguo nianjian Miaozu lunwenji* (Collected essays on the Miao in the Republican period). Guiyang: Guizhou Minzu Yanjiu Suo.

Zhao Hongci

1976 *Zhonggong zhengquan shaoshu minzu zhengce* (Chinese Communist policies towards minorities). Taipei: Zhongguo Wenhua Xueyuan Da Lu Wenti Yanjiusuo.

Zhao Jie

1988 "Lun Man-Han minzu de jiechu yu ronghe" (On the relationship and integration between the Manchu and the Han). *Minzu yanjiu* (Nationalities research) 1: 45–51.

Zhao Yuchi et. al., ed.

1985 *Clothing and Ornaments of China's Miao People*. Beijing: Nationalities Press.

Zheng Kangmin

1950 "Luoluo chuanshuo de chuangshi ji" (A traditional Lolo account of the creation of the world). *Dalu zazhi* (Mainland magazine) 22 (2): 5–13.

Zheng Peng and Ai Feng

1986 *Xishuangbanna Daizu Zizhi Zhou gaikuang* (The general situation of the Xishuangbanna Dai Nationality Autonomous Prefecture). Kunming: Yunnan Minzu Chubanshe.

Zhou Chunyuan et al.

1982 *Guizhou gudai shi* (Ancient history of Guizhou). Guiyang: Guizhou Renmin Chubanshe.

Zhu Depu

1987 "*Lue shi* jiao bu" (Complementary notes on *The history of the state of Lue*). In *Daizu shehui lishi diaocha* (Social and historical investigations of the Dai), vol. 10: 127–229. Kunming: Yunnan Minzu Chubanshe.

Contributors

WURLIG BORCHIGUD received her Ph.D. from the anthropology department at the University of Washington and is a postdoctoral fellow at the East-West Center. She has conducted research on ethnic education in Inner Mongolia and on comparative studies of Alaskan Natives and Ewenky tribes in Northeast China.

SIU-WOO CHEUNG received his Ph.D. from the Department of Anthropology at the University of Washington and is now assistant professor of anthropology at Hong Kong University of Science and Technology. He studies ethnicity and nationalism in China, focusing on the interaction between the state and minorities in the Southwest. His dissertation concerns the politics of representation and the construction and contestation of ethnic identities in the interaction between ethnic classification and the development of ethnic tourism in Guizhou.

NORMA DIAMOND is professor of anthropology and an associate of the Center for Chinese Studies at the University of Michigan. She is the editor of the *China* volume of the *Encyclopaedia of World Cultures* and author of a number of articles dealing with China's peasantry, gender issues, and the minorities of Southwest China. Her future publications include a study of Christian missions among the Hua Miao and an analysis of Hua Miao oral literature.

STEVAN HARRELL is professor and chair of the Department of Anthropology at the University of Washington. He has recently edited a spate of volumes, including *Chinese Families in the Post-Mao Era* (with Deborah Davis), *Cultural Change in Postwar Taiwan* (with Huang Chun-chieh), and *Chinese Historical Micro-Demography*. He is now working on a book about ethnic relations in the Liangshan area of southern Sichuan.

SHIH-CHUNG HSIEH is associate professor of anthropology at National Taiwan University. His interests include ethnicity, Fourth

367

World studies, the anthropology of tourism, and the anthropology of Mainland Southeast Asia and Southwest China. He is now working on studies of tourism in aboriginal regions of Taiwan and on ethnic change among Tai-speaking residents of Taiwan.

ALMAZ KHAN is a Ph.D. candidate in Department of Anthropology at the University of Washington. He is writing a dissertation on local history and ethnic relations in an agricultural area of Inner Mongolia.

RALPH A. LITZINGER received his Ph.D. in anthropology from the University of Washington and is now assistant professor of anthropology at Duke University. His research with the Yao has focused on tradition, modernity, and the politics of representation. He conducted research in 1991 and 1992 in Beijing and in Jinxiu County, Guangxi.

CHARLES F. MCKHANN is assistant professor of anthropology at Whitman College in Walla Walla, Washington. His doctoral thesis, "Fleshing Out the Bones: Kinship and Cosmology in Naxi Religion," (University of Chicago, 1992), is a historical study of Naxi ritual and social theory based on several years of field research in Lijiang, Yunnan.

SHELLEY RIGGER is the Brown Assistant Professor of East Asian Politics at Davidson College in Davidson, North Carolina. She received a Ph.D. in government from Harvard University in 1993. Her current research interests include electoral politics in Taiwan and the People's Republic of China.

MARGARET BYRNE SWAIN teaches anthropology at the University of California, Davis. She received her Ph.D. from the University of Washington in 1978, for research on the impact of tourism on the Kuna Indians of Panama. She is the author of several articles on tourism in Panama and China, and has recently completed a year's research in Yunnan on the impact of tourism on gender and social roles among the Sani.

Index